THE INTERPERSONAL COMMUNICATION BOOK

THE INTERPERSONAL COMMUNICATION BOOK

THIRD EDITION

JOSEPH A. DEVITO Queens College, City University of New York

with illustrations by John Langmaack

HARPER & ROW, PUBLISHERS, New York
Cambridge, Philadelphia, San Francisco,
London, Mexico City, São Paulo, Sydney

1817

Sponsoring Editor: George A. Middendorf
Project Editor: Karla Billups Philip
Designer: Gayle Jaeger
Production: Marion Palen/Delia Tedoff
Compositor: University Graphics, Inc.
Printer and Binder: R. R. Donnelley & Sons Company
Art Studio: J&R Art Services, Inc.
Cover Design: Bill Hartman

THE INTERPERSONAL COMMUNICATION BOOK, Third Edition
Copyright © 1983 by Joseph A. DeVito

Library of Congress Cataloging in Publication Data

DeVito, Joseph A., 1938–
    The interpersonal communication book.

    Includes bibliographies and index.
    1. Interpersonal communication.   I. Title.
BF637.C45D49   1983   158'.2   83-54
ISBN 0-06-041651-3

CONTENTS IN BRIEF

CONTENTS IN DETAIL

PREFACE

I would like to explain the point of view that underlies the topics included and their treatment; the purposes, content, and format of the text; as well as some of the major additions and revisions to this third edition of *The Interpersonal Communication Book.*

POINT OF VIEW

The field of interpersonal communication has no one unifying theme; no one school of thought is yet so strong that all others may be reasonably eliminated in an introductory text. This, however, should present no problem. Psychology has no one theme; basic psychology books are not devoted exclusively to Gestalt theory or conditioning theory or cognitive theory, for example. Rather, the better introductory texts attempt to present the insights of each system. The same is true for sociology and economics and the same is true for communication. Each approach—each theoretical position in communication—has made some contribution. These contributions, these advancements, these insights are presented here and are closely integrated with each other. Thus, there are insights provided by rhetorical theory, information theory, systems theory, behavior theory, transactional theory, and numerous others. The standard used for inclusion or exclusion is always the worth of the idea, never the tradition from which it comes.

Because of the absence of a single theory of interpersonal communication, it should not be assumed that there is no point of view or philosophical position taken here—quite the contrary. The viewpoint or philosophical basis is the notion of choice, which is not a theory of interpersonal communication but rather an approach to systematizing and presenting its theories, data, and insights. This notion of choice in communication is not new. Marie Nichols, in *A History and Criticism of American Public Address* and again in *Rhetoric and Criticism*, refers to rhetoric (or what we might call communication) as the art of making choices, and to the study of public address as an attempt to study people at their moments of choice. Karl Wallace, in his *Understanding Discourse*, makes choice a central element in his view of rhetorical action. Sissela Bok, in her insightful *Lying: Moral Choice in Public and Private Life*, makes choice the defining concept in evaluating the morality of an action—a view that is explained in depth in our study of ethics. Richard Bandler and John Grinder, in their *Frogs into Princes: Neuro-Linguistic Programming*, make the notion of choice the defining feature of their therapeutic approach. Therapy, in

this view, functions to equip the client with an increased response repertoire
from which he or she may make appropriate choices.

Choice figures into interpersonal communication in a number of central ways. The communicator (speaker-listener) and the communication analyst are confronted with choice points at all stages in the interpersonal communication process—choices between saying something and remaining silent, between saying one thing and another, between structuring the content in this way or that way, between attempting to alter the deterioration of a relationship and terminating it as fast as possible, between assuming the right to make a choice for someone else and not assuming this right, between making interpersonal contact with this method or that method, and a host of other choices that are considered in the pages that follow. Consequently, my introduction to interpersonal communication focuses on enabling the student to make more effective choices.

PURPOSES, CONTENT, AND FORMAT

In accordance with this point of view, my primary purpose is to provide the student with the information, the insight, and the knowledge concerning the choices that are available in interpersonal communication. In this text I provide the student with the theory, research, and evidence bearing on the various choices. Research clearly demonstrates the efficiency of certain choices over others and this evidence is presented as clearly and as directly as possible. In other situations, we do not have "evidence" as such; instead, we have only reasoned arguments concerning which choice should be preferred. These arguments, sometimes concerning effectiveness and sometimes concerning values and ethics, are also presented. And, unlike most texts, I provide the student with the opportunity and the specific means for learning and internalizing, for actually experiencing, the relevant concepts. This, in turn, provides the student with the opportunity to try out the various choices. This function is served by the Experiential Vehicles at the end of each unit. Some instructors will prefer to devote considerable class time to the Experiential Vehicles and have students do the reading independently. Other instructors will prefer to devote some time to the vehicles and some to an explanation or elaboration of textual material. In either case, the Experiential Vehicles will make the concepts more interesting and enjoyable to learn and the material learned will be more meaningful and personal.

The last Experiential Vehicle in each of the six parts of the book—subtitled "Review Quiz"—is a kind of review or summary exercise in which some of the major terms or principles are presented in the form of a quiz. These quizzes are not designed to test the student's knowledge so much as to provide an interesting means for the student to call to memory some of the major concepts covered in the units contained in each part.

The topics chosen and the information included are those that seem most relevant to the choices that students will be making in their own interpersonal interactions—choices concerning friendships, conflict, love, and relational development, for example.

The text consists of 27 short units rather than the traditional long chapters. This format should make the text easier and more enjoyable to read. Since most studying is done in relatively short periods of time, this short-unit approach should enable these short time periods to be used efficiently by providing complete units that can be read and mastered in their entirety during any typical study period. At the same time, the units are sufficiently developed to enable the reader to gain a sense of having mastered some significant whole. The result should be both efficient and enjoyable learning.

The 27 units are grouped into six major parts. Each of these six parts begins with a unit on universals which details the essential propositions for the topics covered in that part. Part One focuses on "Interpersonal Communication Preliminaries" and covers (1) the essential concepts and processes, (2) some axioms or general propositions of interpersonal communication, (3) the characteristics of effective interpersonal communication, and (4) ethics, the right and wrong dimension of interpersonal communication. These units are designed to provide insight into the structures and functions of communication and the principles by which interpersonal communication is made effective.

Part Two covers the role of "The Self in Interpersonal Communication." Without an adequate understanding of the self, it is impossible to understand the structures or functions of interpersonal communication or the processes by which one person interacts with another. The reason for this is simple: we can only predict and control our behaviors to the extent that we know ourselves. In Part Two, then, such issues as self-awareness, self-disclosure, assertiveness, and shyness are covered.

In Part Three we consider "Verbal Messages"—the concepts of sublanguages, meaning, and barriers to effective verbal communication.

Part Four focuses on "Nonverbal Messages"—messages from the body, from spatial relationships, and from silence and paralinguistic phenomena (the vocal but nonverbal dimension). The more we understand about messages, the more effectively we will be able to deal with both verbal and nonverbal messages—as senders, as receivers, and as analysts.

In Part Five, "Message Reception," we consider perception, listening, communication effects, and feedback—some of the most significant processes in the complex transaction of message reception. Part Six, "Interpersonal Relationships," explores relational development, interpersonal attraction, conflict, friendship, love, family communication, and relational deterioration—the ways in which relationships break down and some of the ways in which they might be managed.

SOME MAJOR ADDITIONS AND REVISIONS

This third edition improves on and clarifies a number of important issues and contains some important additions. Among the most significant additions and revisions are the following.

1. There is an increased emphasis on interpersonal relationships (for example, friendship, love, and the development and deterioration of relationships).

2. A new unit on family communication has been written for this edition. Family communication is rapidly becoming one of the most important new areas within interpersonal communication and certainly one of the most relevant and exciting.

3. The units have been given a clearer and more meaningful organizational pattern; new headings and subheadings have been added to more effectively focus the students' attention on the key issues.

4. New material has been added to many of the units to reflect new insights and emphases. Especially revised and updated are the units on Effectiveness in Interpersonal Communication; Self-Awareness (integrated with material from transactional analysis); Self-Disclosure; Language, Sublanguage, and Culture; Body Communication (especially the area of touching behavior); Silence, Paralanguage, and Temporal Communication; Perception; Attraction; Conflict; Friendship; and Love. In addition, I have integrated insights from pertinent theories such as social penetration, attribution, and gain-loss and from relevant research in self-monitoring and numerous other areas.

5. Seventeen new Experiential Vehicles (including three extensive dialogues designed to illustrate effectiveness in interpersonal communication, relationship development and its analysis, and family communication) have been developed for this edition. Other new experiences focus on sex differences in language usage and nonverbal communication, message reception, causal attribution, conflict, friendship, and primary relationships.

6. A preview list of questions, "Getting Acquainted with Interpersonal Communication," has been prefaced to the book to provide students with a brief overview of what to expect throughout the book. In one sense, these questions (and their answers) are the "payoffs" that the students can expect to receive from reading the text. I also hope that these questions will make the student enthusiastic about reading the text and about taking the course in interpersonal communication.

Additional changes include a more clearly refined and focused view of the nature and scope of interpersonal communication, an expanded Glossary, and new behavioral Objectives and Sources.

In this third edition I have retained a number of features from the first two editions that proved popular and helpful to student learning, particularly the short-unit approach, the emphasis on experiential learning, the informality of style, and the development of the book as a complete learning package. The basic organizational pattern of the second edition—particularly the six-part format with each part opening with a unit on universals—has been retained.

ACKNOWLEDGMENTS

It is a pleasure to record my indebtedness to those who helped me in conceptualizing, writing, and producing this book. As with my other books, my major debt is to "Boo" who contributed to my development as a teacher, as a writer, and, most important, as a thinking-feeling individual. From the beginning, Maggie provided me with the support and encouragement so essential in this type of endeavor, and the students in my interpersonal communication classes helped me to clarify my ideas and provided numerous insights of their own. I especially appreciate the comments from the students of Professors Bernard Brommel of Northeastern Illinois University; Hal Dalrymple of Kent State, Ashtabula Campus; Ken Leibowitz of Philadelphia College of Pharmacy and Science; and Kathy Wenell of Wartburg College. This type of feedback was most helpful and most reinforcing; it made the task of writing this edition a positive learning experience for me.

I am most grateful to those persons who reviewed the first two editions and the manuscript for this edition and who made many valuable suggestions that I tried to incorporate here; many of these people went far beyond the normal responsibilities of reviewers. Needless to say, they are neither responsible for any deficiencies that may remain nor are they necessarily in agreement with what appears here. For their time, their energy, and their willingness to share their expertise and insights, I am most thankful to: Ronald Bassett, University of Texas; Charles Berger, Northwestern University; Bernard Brommel, Northeastern Illinois University; Matt Campbell, Johnson County Community College; Sumitra Chakrapani, Queens College; James Chesebro, Queens College; Ronald Coleman, Edinboro State College; Paul Feingold, University of New Mexico; Mary Anne Fitzpatrick, University of Wisconsin; James E. Hasenauer, California State University; Michael Hecht, University of Southern California; Catherine Konsky, Illinois State University; Larry Miller, Indiana University; Charles Rossiter, Hood College; Alan L. Sillars, Ohio State University; Dennis Smith, Temple University; and Paul Westbrook, Ithaca College.

The people at Harper & Row, as always, all contributed significantly to the final product. I am especially grateful to Karla Billups Philip who, for the sixth time, has supervised the editorial and production processes on my books. With good humor and good sense, she made book production an enjoyable and rewarding experience. To many others I am also most thankful: to editors George A. Middendorf and Neale Sweet for their help at various stages of development, to Gayle Jaeger for this most attractive and functional design, and to John Langmaack for the original cartoons that appear throughout the text. To all of these and others I am most appreciative of their labors and their willingness to put up with a most difficult author.

Joseph A. DeVito

GETTING ACQUAINTED WITH INTERPERSONAL COMMUNICATION: A PREVIEW FOR THE READER

As a kind of preview, here are just a few of the questions and issues that will be considered in the pages that follow. The questions are designed to provide you with a quick overview of what interpersonal communication is all about. In addition, these questions should enable you to see at a glance some of the information and skills that a course in interpersonal communication attempts to provide. The question numbers correspond to the units in the text.

PRELIMINARIES

1. When is communication interpersonal? How does it differ from impersonal communication? What purposes does interpersonal communication serve?
2. When in an interactional situation, can you not communicate? How would you go about not communicating? What is double-binding? How is it created? What effects does it have?
3. What makes interpersonal communication effective? How effective are you in an interpersonal interaction? What qualities of effectiveness do you feel you lack? How might your interpersonal effectiveness be improved? How effective are you in controlling the image you wish to communicate?
4. When is interpersonal communication unethical or immoral? Is it ethical/unethical to lie, to use fear and emotional appeals, to prevent others from engaging in certain interpersonal interactions? Why or why not?

THE SELF

5. Of what does the self consist? What are the important dimensions of the self that influence what we say and what we do? What is present-moment living? Why should we live in the present?
6. How can we achieve greater self-awareness? How will increased self-awareness improve our interpersonal interactions? How does our self-concept influence our interpersonal interactions?
7. What is self-disclosure? Why do we resist disclosing ourselves to others? What are the benefits of self-disclosing? What are the dangers? Are men and women similar (or different) in their self-disclosing behaviors? What do we self-disclose? To whom? When? Why? What guidelines should we use in deciding what, when, to whom, and whether we should self-disclose?
8. How does shyness develop? How can we become more assertive and less shy in our interpersonal interactions?

VERBAL MESSAGES

9. What characterizes human language systems? How does human language differ from the "language" of animals? How does language operate in interpersonal interaction?

10. What is the social role of language? How do different subcultures communicate? Do men and women speak the same language? Is language racist? Sexist? What is taboo? Euphemism? Slang? Jargon? How do these language uses influence interpersonal communication?

11. What is meaning? Why can't two people ever have the same meaning? Can we measure meaning? How do first names influence our perceptions of people?

12. What are some of the barriers to verbal interaction? How might we deal with these to eliminate or lessen their effects on our interpersonal interactions? Does our language influence our thoughts and behaviors?

NONVERBAL MESSAGES

13. What is nonverbal communication? Can we determine what people are thinking by watching their body language? What features do all nonverbal communications share? Why is nonverbal communication highly believable?

14. How do we communicate with our bodies? Our facial expressions? Our eyes? Does the type of body we have influence our perceptions of others? What does touch communicate? Who touches whom where? Do all cultures touch in the same way? Do fathers and mothers touch their children in the same way?

15. How does space communicate? What can we learn about people from their use of space? Are there cultural differences? How is the concept of territoriality— the ownershiplike behavior of an animal for a particular territory— applicable to us in our daily interpersonal interactions? Do colors have different meanings? Do our color preferences reveal our personality characteristics?

16. How does silence communicate? How do we communicate with our vocal rate or volume? How are our perceptions of a person influenced by speech patterns? Is the fast talker a more effective persuader than the slow talker? How does time communicate? In what ways do different cultures treat time (and its meanings) differently?

MESSAGE RECEPTION

17. How are messages received? Why can two people never receive the same message? Why is every message unique?

18. On what basis do we form impressions of other people? What makes for accuracy in our judgments of people? Why do we expect a person we like to like us in return and to also like our friends but to dislike our enemies? Why do we believe some people and disbelieve others? What influences us more: what comes first or what comes last?

19. How important is listening? What are some of the obstacles to effective listening? How might we learn to become more effective listeners? What is feedback? How can feedback help us to improve our interpersonal behaviors? How can we improve our feedback-giving skills? Our feedback-receiving skills? What is feedforward?

INTERPERSONAL RELATIONSHIPS

20. What are interpersonal relationships? What stages do we go through in establishing and in dissolving a relationship? In what ways are all relationships similar?

21. Why do we seek to develop and maintain interpersonal relationships? What are some of the ways we can establish contact (verbally and nonverbally) with another person? How do you establish contact? How might your effectiveness be improved? What are some of the obstacles to the development of interpersonal relationships? What causes difficulties in your present relationships? How can we overcome these difficulties?

22. What makes us attracted to some people and not to others? Why are some people attracted to us while others are not? What qualities are judged most important in a partner? Do men and women look for the same qualities in a partner?

23. What are the advantages of interpersonal conflict? Disadvantages? How might we go about resolving interpersonal conflicts? How (and why) do people fight unfairly? Do women and men fight in the same way? What fight strategies are most effective? Least effective?

24. When is someone a "friend"? What qualities make for friendship? What functions does a friendship serve? How do friendships develop? What does a friend do that a nonfriend does not do? What kind of a friend are you?

25. What is love? What is infatuation? Are love and infatuation different? What is jealousy? Why do people become jealous? What are the types of love? How do men and women differ in their approach to love and loving? Can you make someone love you? Can you make someone fall out of love with you? How do we communicate our love for someone? How do we communicate when we are in love?

26. How does communication operate within the family? What keeps families together? What causes family conflicts? What strategies do people use to resolve conflicts in the family? Is the communication in your family satisfactory? Unsatisfactory? How can family communication be improved?

27. At what point would you go about ending a close interpersonal relationship? How would you do it? What causes some relationships to deteriorate? What role does commitment play in relational deterioration? How do people communicate in a deteriorating relationship? How can we best manage relationship deterioration?

INTERPERSONAL COMMUNICATION PRELIMINARIES
PART ONE

UNIVERSALS OF INTERPERSONAL COMMUNICATION

OBJECTIVES

Upon completion of this unit, you should be able to:

1. cite examples of interpersonal communication from your own observations and experiences
2. define *interpersonal communication*
3. distinguish between a componential and a developmental definition of interpersonal communication
4. discuss the nature of the universals of interpersonal communication
5. define the following terms: *source-receiver, encoding-decoding, competence and performance, message, noise, feedback, context, field of experience, effect,* and *ethics*
6. explain the transactional nature of interpersonal communication
7. diagram the model of communication presented in this unit and label all of its parts
8. explain Lasswell's or Gerbner's model of communication
9. construct an original model of communication that incorporates the following: context, source-receiver, message, encoding-decoding, noise, feedback, and field of experience
10. distinguish intrapersonal from interpersonal communication

You enter your interpersonal communication class and spot a person you would like to date. You get the person's phone number from a mutual friend and call that evening. A previous engagement prevents this person from saying yes, and you decide to call next week. At the same time, you wonder if this "previous engagement" was merely another way of saying no.

You are sitting on a bus reading a book when a person who smells of cigar smoke sits next to you. The odor is so strong that you change your seat.

You are on a basketball team and are discussing strategy for the next quarter with the other members. The captain wants to do certain things, while other members want to do something else. The members argue and fight.

You are having dinner with your family and the conversation covers a variety of topics—what each person did during the day, the accident that happened down the street, the plans for tomorrow, and so on.

3

These and thousands of similar examples are considered interpersonal communication situations. We all know basically what interpersonal communication is, and, for most purposes, this intuitive understanding is adequate. For our in-depth study of interpersonal communication, however, we need something a bit more specific. One of the best ways to approach the definition of interpersonal communication is to attempt to identify and describe its *universals*—those characteristics (elements and processes, for example) that are integral to any and all interpersonal communication encounters; for example, source-receiver, message, context, noise, effect, and ethics. With these characteristics of universals in mind, we can explore the nature of interpersonal communication from the perspectives afforded by both a componential and a developmental definition.

A COMPONENTIAL DEFINITION OF INTERPERSONAL COMMUNICATION

In attempting to construct a componential definition—that is, one that identifies the components or elements of the interpersonal communication pro-

Who
Says what
In what channel
To whom
With what effect

Source: Based on Harold D. Lasswell, "The Structure and Function of Communication in Society," in Lyman Bryson, ed., *The Communication of Ideas* (New York: Harper & Row, 1948), p. 37.

TABLE 1.1
Lasswell's Model of Communication

Someone
Perceives an event
And reacts
In a situation
Through some means
To make available materials
In some form
And context
Conveying content
Of some consequence

Source: Based on George Gerbner, "Toward a General Model of Communication," *Audio-Visual Communication Review* 4 (1956): 173.

TABLE 1.2
Gerbner's Model of Communication

cess—there are many time-honored sources on which we might draw. On[ ] the most popular was presented by political scientist Harold Lasswell. Lassw[ ] viewed communication as being concerned with five basic questions, as pr[ ] sented in Table 1.1. In a similar vein, George Gerbner identified ten compo[ ] nents (presented in Table 1.2), all of which need to be studied in a complete[ ] analysis of the communication act.

Both of these "models," it should be noted, are relatively linear; they seem to imply that communication begins at one end and moves through various discrete steps to the other end. Notice that by studying Lasswell's or Gerbner's models of communication, you can easily visualize a message being traced through space from left to right. These linear views of communication are much too limiting since they fail to emphasize the circular nature of communication and they fail to take into consideration the fact that each participant in the communication act both sends and receives messages. These aspects of communication need to be reflected in any visual or verbal description of communication. For our purposes, then, the model presented in Figure 1.1 should prove more helpful. It is a bit more complex, but it seems to be a more accurate reflection of what interpersonal communication is—namely, the process of sending

FIGURE 1.1
A Model of Some Universals of Interpersonal Communication.

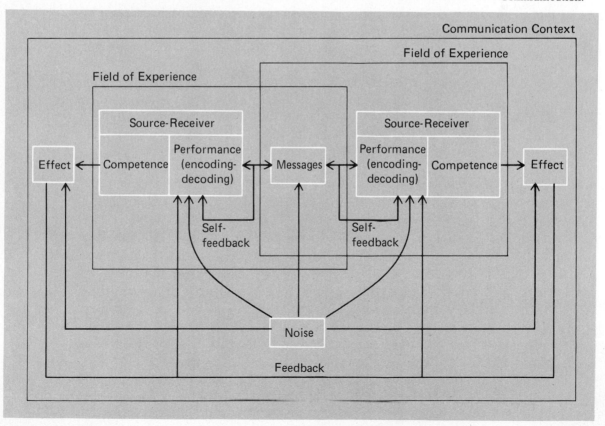

. eiving messages between two persons, or among a small group of per-
. s, with some effect and some immediate feedback.

Source-Receiver

Interpersonal communication involves at least two persons. Each of these
persons formulates and sends messages (source functions) and also perceives
and comprehends messages (receiver functions). The hyphenated term *source-
receiver* is used to emphasize that these source and receiver functions are performed by each individual engaging in interpersonal communication. Interpersonal communication may, however, involve a small group of persons. But
regardless of whether there are two, three, or four persons, each person per-
forms both source and receiver functions.

A number of additional and related issues require explanation. First,
interpersonal communication cannot occur with oneself. Communication with
oneself is termed *intra*personal communication. It is essential to understand
intrapersonal communication if we are to fully understand interpersonal communication. Yet it is best to keep these two forms of communication separate.
Second, interpersonal communication deals with people—human beings. Communication by or with animals, machines, plants, pictures, and the like are not
interpersonal communication experiences. Third, interpersonal communication occurs between two people or among a small group of people. It excludes
mass communication and public speaking situations, in which there is a large
audience and the messages go essentially in one direction—from speaker to
audience but not from audience to speaker.

Who people are, what they know, what they believe in, what they value,
what they want, what they have been told, how intelligent they are, what their
attitudes are, and so on, all influence what they say and how they say it, what
messages they receive, and how they receive them. Each person is unique; each
person's communications are unique.

Encoding-Decoding

In communication theory the processes of speaking or writing and understanding or comprehending are referred to as *encoding* and *decoding*, respec-
tively. The act of producing messages—for example, speaking or writing—is
termed *encoding*. By putting our ideas into sound waves, we are putting these
ideas into a code, hence encoding. By translating sound waves into ideas, we
are taking them out of the code they are in, hence decoding. Thus we may refer
to speakers and writers as encoders and to listeners and readers as decoders.
Since encoding and decoding activities are combined in each participant, the
hyphenated form *encoding-decoding* is used to designate and emphasize this
important and inevitable dual function.

If further discrimination among the various communicative components
is necessary, the idea-generating aspect (that is, the brain) and the message-
producing aspect (such as the vocal mechanism) may be distinguished. The

idea-generating component would be referred to as the *source*, while the signal- or message-producing aspect would be referred to as the *encoder*. Or, if one were talking on a telephone, the source would be the speaker and the vocal mechanism (and the telephone mouthpiece) would be the encoder. Conversely, in listening, the brain would be the receiver, while the auditory mechanism would be the decoder. The listener in a telephone conversation would be the receiver, while the auditory mechanism (and the earpiece of the telephone) would be the decoder.

In order for interpersonal communication to occur, messages must be encoded and decoded. The situation in which a parent talks to a child who has his or her eyes closed and is wearing stereo headphones is not an interpersonal communication situation simply because the messages, verbal and nonverbal, are not being received.

Competence and Performance

Each of us has a certain amount of competence, essential to all forms of communication. When we speak of *language competence,* we are generally referring to the knowledge that a speaker has of his or her own language. A speaker's language competence would consist of knowing the sound system of the language and how the individual sounds are combined to form words, knowing the meanings of words and how certain words are made plural or past tense, and knowing how various words may be strung together to form questions or statements which in turn are used to form more compound and complex sentence structures. *Communication competence,* on the other hand, uses language competence as a base but goes beyond it to include a knowledge of the rules for communication interaction. These would include, for example, rules pertaining to the ways in which we address each other, the role that status plays in determining how we address the president of the college, and how we address another student. It includes the knowledge of how to adjust our communications on the basis of the context in which we are interacting, the person with whom we are interacting, and a host of other variables that will be discussed throughout this text. Communication competence also includes a knowledge of the nonverbal rules of interaction—when to speak and when to remain silent, when silence is uncomfortable and when it is welcomed, the appropriateness of touching, of vocal volume, and of physical closeness.

Performance, however, refers to the actual sending and receiving of both verbal and nonverbal signals. That is, whereas competence is concerned with a knowledge of the elements and rules that go into language and communication, performance is concerned with the application of these elements and rules in the actual sending and receiving of the message.

A few implications of this distinction should be pointed out here. First, competence is essential if performance is to be consistently effective. If we are to perform effectively in communication, then it is essential that we have the relevant knowledge or competence. Second, competence is not translated automatically or directly into performance. On a language level this can be illustrated by noting that although we know the rules of language, we nevertheless make errors: we make false starts, use double negatives, speak in ungrammatical sentences, and the like. Performance is actually a combination of our competence and various other factors—our attention level, our level of fatigue, our anxiety, our interest, and so on. Similarly, in communication we may know what should be done—we may know the rules for effectively meeting another person and asking for a date and sometimes we can almost see ourselves doing it in our heads—yet, our performance often falls short of this idealized competence. This is because in communication, as in language, there are a great number of factors that influence performance. For example, our shyness or our nervousness may prevent us from asking for the date or asking the boss for a raise. Third, we continue to acquire communication competence throughout our lives. Although we learn the basic rules early, say by the time we are 10 or 12, we are forever refining and improving these basic rules as we learn more and more about communication. Fourth, and perhaps most important, is that if we are to improve our performance, if we are to function more effectively in communication, we must do so in at least two steps. The first is to acquire the appropriate competence, the knowledge of how communication should operate. This will be covered in the following units and can be acquired by learning the relevant theories and research in communication. This competence is identified specifically in the behavioral objectives that preface each of the units in the text. The second step is to put this knowledge into practice, to experience applying the various rules to different situations. Opportunities for applying competence to performance are provided by the Experiential Vehicles following each unit as well as by our everyday experiences. Because we are social creatures who cannot exist without communication, we are forever engaging in communication performance. The key is to put these experiences to good use by practicing effective communication patterns.

Messages

In order for interpersonal communication to exist messages—signals that serve as stimuli for a receiver—must be sent and received. These messages may be auditory, visual, tactile, olfactory, gustatory, or any combination of these. Interpersonal communication does not have to be oral; we can communicate by gestures, touch, smell, or taste, as well as by sounds.

For example, the clothes we wear communicate something to other people and, in fact, probably communicate to us as well. The way we walk communicates, as does the way we shake hands or the way we cock our heads or the way we comb our hair or the way we sit or the way we smile or frown. In fact, everything about us communicates. All of these signals constitute our interpersonal communication message.

Interpersonal communication does not have to occur face-to-face. It can occur over the telephone, through prison cell walls, or through videophone hookups. Note, too, that messages need not be sent intentionally. Through slips of the tongue, a lingering body odor, or a nervous twitch we also communicate.

Noise

Noise may enter into any communication system, however well designed or technically proficient. Noise is anything that distorts or interferes with the message and is present in a communication system to the extent that the message sent differs from the message received. The screeching of passing cars, the hum of an air conditioner, the lisp of a speaker, and the sunglasses a person wears may all be regarded as noise since they interfere with the effective and efficient transmission of messages from one person to another. Noise is also present in written communication and would include blurred type, the print that shows through from the back of the page, creases in the paper, and anything that prevents a reader from getting the message sent by the writer. The concept of noise might also refer to psychological interference and would include biases and prejudices in senders and receivers that lead to distortions in processing information, and closed-mindedness, which is perhaps the classic example of psychological noise preventing information from being received.

Feedback

Another type of message is feedback. When we send a message, say, in speaking to another person, we also hear ourselves. We get feedback from our

Feedback comes in many forms.

own messages—we hear what we say, we feel the way we move, we see what we write, and so on. On the basis of this information we may correct ourselves, rephrase something, or perhaps smile at a clever turn of phrase. This is self-feedback. Also significant is the feedback we get from others. In speaking with another individual, not only are we constantly sending messages, but we are also constantly receiving messages. Both parties are sending and receiving messages at the same time. The messages that are sent in response to other messages are termed *feedback*. This feedback, like other messages, can be in many forms—auditory, tactile, or visual, for example. A frown or a smile, a yea or a nay, a pat on the back or a punch in the mouth are all feedback.

Effectiveness in interpersonal communication seems largely due to the ability of the communicator to respond appropriately to feedback. Teaching effectiveness may be seen in the same way. Effective teachers seem to be those who can read the responses of their students accurately and adjust their messages accordingly. Ineffective teachers seem oblivious to how students are responding and just carry on as usual. In interpersonal communication there must be some relatively immediate feedback. In a face-to-face situation the feedback comes in words and sentences, eye movements, smiles and frowns, nodding and shaking the head, and so on. In a telephone situation the feedback is exclusively vocal. If there is no opportunity for immediate feedback, the situation does not involve interpersonal communication. In television, public speaking, newspapers, magazines, and the like, there is little opportunity for immediate feedback. On this basis, such communication forms are excluded from what we would call interpersonal communication.

Context

Communication always takes place within a context. At times this context is not obvious or intrusive; it seems to be so natural that it is ignored, like background music. At other times the context stands out, and the ways in which it restricts or stimulates our communications are obvious. Compare, for example, the differences in communicating in a funeral home, in a football stadium, in a quiet restaurant, and at a rock concert.

The context of communication has at least three dimensions: physical, social-psychological, and temporal. The room or hallway or park in which communication takes place—that is, the tangible or concrete environment—is the *physical dimension*. This physical dimension, whatever it is, exerts some influence on the content as well as the form of our messages. The *social-psychological dimension* includes, for example, the status relationships among the participants, the roles and the games that people play, the norms and cultural mores of the society in which they are communicating, the friendliness or unfriendliness of the situation, the formality or informality, and the seriousness or humorousness of the interaction. The *temporal dimension* includes the time of day as well as the time in history in which the communication act takes place. For many people the morning is not a time for communication; for others the morning is ideal. Some interpersonal communication behaviors seem to many to be more appropriate at night than in the morning or afternoon. Time in history is particularly important for the communication analyst since the messages—their appropriateness, their importance, and their insightfulness—depend in great part on the times in which they are uttered. Consider how difficult it would be to evaluate messages on religious or political attitudes and values if we did not know the time in which these messages were communicated.

These three dimensions of context interact with each other; each influences and is influenced by the other. If, for example, the temperature in a room becomes extremely hot (a physical change), it would probably lead to changes in the social-psychological dimension as well. General discomfort seems to make people more talkative, as many have witnessed when a subway train or bus gets stuck. A change in the context, then, may be brought about from outside influences, for example, a train failure; from a change in one of the basic dimensions, for example, time change or temperature change; or, from the interaction among the dimensions, for example, talkativeness increasing as a result of a train breakdown.

Field of Experience

The squares that overlap in Figure 1.1 refer to what is called the *field of experience*. The assumption here is that effective communication takes place to the extent that the participants share the same experiences. Communication is ineffective to the extent that the participants do not share the same experiences. Parents have difficulty communicating with their children, in this view, because the children cannot share the parental experience and because the parents have forgotten what it is like to be children. When management forgets what it is like to be labor and labor does not share any of management's experiences, communication becomes extremely difficult, if not impossible. Differences among people serve to make communication more and more difficult; the larger the differences, the more difficult communication becomes. Although many differences cannot be eliminated, communication is still not hopeless. While we cannot always share the experiences of others, we can learn to empathize with people different from ourselves—to feel what they are feeling—and thus extend the overlap in our respective fields of experience.

Effect

Communication always has some effect. For every communication act there is some consequence, and the effect may be on one person or on both. When communication affects the environment or context, it is done through people. The effects of communication, then, occur first on people and are always personal. Even when we cannot observe an effect (which is perhaps most of the time), we assume that for every interpersonal communication act there is an effect, somewhat like "for every action there is a reaction." As students of communication, part of our task is to determine what these effects are.

Ethics

To the degree that interpersonal communication has an effect, it also has an ethical dimension. Because communication has consequences, there is a rightness-wrongness aspect to any communication act. Unlike principles of effective communication, however, principles of ethical communication are difficult if not impossible to formulate. We can often observe the effect of communication and on the basis of these observations formulate principles of effective communication. But we cannot observe the rightness or wrongness of a communication act. The ethical dimension of communication is further complicated by the fact that it is so interwoven with one's personal philosophy of life that it is difficult to propose universal guidelines. Given these difficulties, we nevertheless include ethical considerations as being integral to any communication act. The choices that we make concerning communication must be guided by considerations of ethics as well as effectiveness, satisfaction, or whatever other effects may seem desirable.

A DEVELOPMENTAL DEFINITION OF INTERPERSONAL COMMUNICATION

In addition to distinguishing interpersonal communication from, say, mass or intrapersonal communication on the basis of its components, as we do in a componential definition, we might also distinguish it from impersonal communication. Not only is interpersonal communication a special form of communication in terms of its components, it is also special in that it is personal rather than impersonal. To distinguish interpersonal or personal from impersonal communication we need what has been called a *developmental approach*. I here follow Gerald Miller's (1978) excellent analysis.

In the developmental approach communications are viewed as existing on a continuum ranging from impersonal at one end to increasingly interpersonal or intimate at the other end. Interpersonal communication is characterized by, and distinguished from, impersonal communication on the basis of at least three factors. First, interpersonal interactions are characterized by the participants' basing their predictions about each other on psychological data—that is, the ways in which this person differs from the members of his or her group. In impersonal encounters we respond to each other according to the class or group to which we belong, for example, initially we respond to a particular college professor in the way we respond to college professors in general. Similarly, the college professor responds to a particular student in the way professors respond to students generally. As the relationship becomes more and more personal, however, both the professor and the student begin to respond to each other not as members of their groups but as individuals; each begins to respond to the other on the basis of the individual's uniqueness. Another way of putting this would be to say that in impersonal encounters the social or cultural role of the person tells us how to interact, while in personal or interpersonal encounters the psychological role of the person tells us how to interact.

Second, interpersonal interactions are based on an explanatory knowledge of each other. When we know a particular person, we can better predict how that person will react in a variety of situations. In interpersonal situations we cannot only predict how a person will act but we can also advance explanations for the behaviors of the person. The college professor may in an impersonal relationship know that Pat will be 5 minutes late to class each Friday. That is, the professor is able to predict Pat's behavior. In an interpersonal situation, however, the professor can not only predict Pat's behavior but can also offer generally valid explanations for the behavior—in this case, give reasons why Pat is late.

Third, in impersonal situations the rules of behavioral interaction are set down by social norms. Students and professors behave toward each other—at least in impersonal situations—according to the social norms that have been established by the culture or subculture in which they are operating. However, as the relationship between a student and a professor becomes interpersonal, the rules established by the social norms are no longer the important ones and no longer totally regulate their interaction; the individuals establish rules of their own. To the extent that the individuals establish their own rules for interacting, the situation is interpersonal.

These three characteristics vary in degree. We respond to each other on the basis of psychological data *to some degree;* we base our predictions of another's behavior *to some degree* on the basis of our explanatory knowledge; and we interact on the basis of mutually established rules rather than on socially established norms *to some degree.* As already noted, a developmental approach to communication implies a continuum ranging from highly impersonal to highly intimate. "Interpersonal communication" occupies a broad area of this continuum, although each person might draw its boundaries a bit differently. Therefore, although this developmental view does not enable us to make universally agreed-upon decisions concerning what is or what is not interpersonal, the three characteristics noted should give us some added insight into interpersonal communication and how it might be distinguished from formal or impersonal communication.

One frequent misconception about interpersonal communication (and particularly about its developmental definition) is that an interpersonal relationship is one characterized by liking or loving. This is not the case. We may have an interpersonal relationship and engage in interpersonal communication with people we dislike intensely as well as people we love. Our interactions may be interpersonal in conflict as well as in love, in competition as well as in cooperation, in relationships that are getting stronger as well as in relationships that are deteriorating.

These two definitions of interpersonal communication are not actually as separate and as distinct as they may at first appear. Both are useful in explaining what interpersonal communication is, with each giving a somewhat different perspective to this important form of human behavior. The developmental definition serves to emphasize those types of interactions that are most significant to people—the kinds of relationships that make a substantial difference in our lives. The developmental definition clearly defines the more intimate types of interpersonal interaction. The componential definition serves to emphasize the numerous elements and processes that have to be taken into consideration before an adequate understanding of interpersonal communication can be achieved. The componential definition enables us to recognize the nature of each part of the interpersonal communication process.

Note that by the componential definition, all four of the situations cited at the beginning of the unit are interpersonal; by the developmental definition only the fourth (and possibly the third) is interpersonal.

SOME PURPOSES OF INTERPERSONAL COMMUNICATION

Four general purposes of interpersonal communication can be distinguished: (1) to discover oneself, (2) to discover the external world, (3) to establish and maintain meaningful relationships, and (4) to change attitudes and behaviors. These purposes need not be conscious at the time of the interpersonal encounter, nor do they need to be the intended purpose of the encounter; purposes may be conscious or subconscious, intentional or unintentional.

To Discover Oneself

One of the major purposes of interpersonal communication is personal discovery. When we engage in an interpersonal encounter with another person, we learn a great deal about ourselves as well as about the other person. In fact, our self-perceptions are in large part a result of what we have learned about ourselves from others during interpersonal encounters.

Interpersonal communication provides an opportunity for us to talk about our favorite subject—ourselves. Nothing seems as interesting, as exciting, or as worthy of discussion as our own feelings, thoughts, and behaviors. By talking about ourselves with another individual we are provided with an excellent source of feedback on our feelings, thoughts, and behaviors. From this type of encounter we learn, for example, that our feelings about ourselves, others, and the world are not so different from someone else's feelings. And the same is true about our behaviors, our fears, our hopes, and our desires. This positive reinforcement helps to make us feel "normal." Through these communications we also learn how we appear to others, what our strengths and weaknesses are, who likes us and who dislikes us and why. We usually choose our interpersonal partners carefully so that most of what we hear is positive or at least more supportive than not. This helps us to build a stronger self-image.

To Discover the External World

Just as interpersonal communication enables us to better understand ourselves and the other person with whom we are communicating, it also enables us to better understand the external world—the world of objects, events, and other people. Much of the information we now have comes from interpersonal interactions. While it is true that a great deal of information comes to us from the mass media, it is often discussed and ultimately "learned" or internalized through interpersonal interactions. In fact, our beliefs, attitudes, and values have probably been influenced more by interpersonal encounters than by the media, or even by formal education.

To Establish and Maintain Meaningful Relationships

One of the greatest desires (some would say "needs") people have is establishing and maintaining close relationships with other people. We want to feel loved and liked, and in turn we want to love and like others. Much of the time we spend in interpersonal communication is devoted to establishing and maintaining social relationships with others. Recall the times you spotted a friend on campus and felt good about it; you were concerned not with the topic that would be discussed but rather simply with the idea that a relationship exists. The importance of this is probably best seen in our lack of concern for the subject matter of discussion when we are with someone we care for a great deal. It does not matter whether we talk about a movie, about philosophy, about cars, or about people. What does matter is that we are together and that we are relating to each other.

To Change Attitudes and Behaviors

Many times we attempt to change the attitudes and behaviors of others in our interpersonal encounters. We may wish them to vote a particular way, try a new diet, buy a particular item, listen to a record, see a movie, read a book, enter a particular field, take a specific course, think in a particular way, believe that something is true or false, value some idea, or marry us—the list is endless. We spend a good deal of our time engaged in interpersonal persuasion.

It is interesting to note that studies that have been done on the effectiveness of the mass media versus interpersonal situations in changing attitudes and behaviors seem to point to the conclusion that we are more often persuaded through interpersonal than through mass media communication.

We may also look at these four purposes of interpersonal communication from two other perspectives. First, these purposes may be seen as motivating factors or as reasons why we engage in interpersonal communication. Second, these purposes may be viewed as outcomes or as general effects of interpersonal encounters. It should be clear, of course, that interpersonal communication usually is motivated by a combination of factors and has not one but a combination of outcomes or effects. Any given interpersonal interaction, then, seems to serve a unique combination of purposes, seems motivated by a unique combination of factors, and seems to produce a unique combination of outcomes or effects.

SOURCES

The nature of interpersonal communication is surveyed in a number of excellent sources. See, for example, Gerald Miller and Mark Steinberg, *Between People* (Chicago: Science Research Associates, 1975); Murray S. Davis, *Intimate Relations* (New York: Free Press, 1973); Kurt Danziger, *Interpersonal Communication* (Elmsford, N.Y.: Pergamon Press, 1976); Michael D. Scott and William G. Powers, *Interpersonal Communication: A Question of Needs* (Boston: Houghton Mifflin, 1978); and Mark L. Knapp, *Social Intercourse: From Greeting to Goodbye* (Boston: Allyn & Bacon, 1978). An interesting eclectic view of interpersonal communication is presented by George L. Shapiro, Jerie M. Pratt, and Maryan Schall, "The Eclectic Perspective on Interpersonal Communication: An Explanation and a Description," *Communication Education* 30 (April 1981):133–145. Communication concepts are considered in most of the available texts on communication. One starting place would be my reader, *Communication: Concepts and Processes*, 3d ed. (Englewood Cliffs, N.J.: Prentice-Hall, 1981). An excellent introduction to communication terminology is provided by Wilbur Schramm and William E. Porter, *Men, Women, Messages, and Media: Understanding Human Communication*, 2d ed. (New York: Harper & Row, 1982). A useful collection of articles on communication in the future is *Communications Tomorrow: The Coming of the Information Society*, Edward Cornish, ed. (Bethesda, Md.: World Future Society, 1982). A definitional paper is James H. McBath and Robert C. Jeffrey, "Defining Speech Communication," *Communication Education* 27 (September 1978): 181–188. On communicative competence, see John M. Wiemann, "Explication and Test of a Model of Communicative Competence," *Human Communication Research* 3 (Spring 1977): 195–213. For an excellent discussion of communication competence and performance see James C. McCroskey, "Communication Competence and Performance: A Research and Pedagogical Perspective," *Communication Education* 31 (January 1982):1–7.

Two excellent but somewhat advanced articles that influenced this discussion are Gerald R. Miller, "The Current Status of Theory and Research in Interpersonal Communication," *Human Communication Research* 4 (Winter 1978): 164–178, and Art Bochner, "On Taking Ourselves Seriously: An Analysis of Some Persistent Problems and Promising Directions in Interpersonal Research," *Human Communication Research* 4 (Winter 1978): 179–191. The Winter 1977 issue of *Communication Quarterly* (vol. 25, no. 1) contains a series of articles on the different theoretical approaches to communication, specifically the covering law perspective, the systems perspective, and the rules perspective. Analyses and critiques of these positions are also presented.

For intrapersonal communication, see Genelle Austin-Lett and Jan Sprague, *Talk to Yourself: Experiencing Intrapersonal Communication* (Boston: Houghton Mifflin, 1976), Carolyn M. Del Polito, *Intrapersonal Communication* (Menlo Park, Calif.: Cummings, 1977), and Blaine Goss, *Processing Communication: Information Processing in Intrapersonal Communication* (Belmont, Calif.: Wadsworth, 1982).

On different approaches to teaching interpersonal communication, see W. Barnett Pearce, "Teaching Interpersonal Communication as a Humane Science: A Comparative Analysis," *Communication Education* 26 (March 1977): 104–112.

1.1 MODELING SOME UNIVERSALS OF INTERPERSONAL COMMUNICATION

The following concepts are generally considered to be essential ingredients in even the most basic model of interpersonal communication. Read over the terms and their definitions (in this unit and/or in the Glossary) and construct an original visual representation of the process of interpersonal communication that includes (as a minimum) the concepts noted below.

source-receiver	context
messages	noise
encoding-decoding	feedback
competence	effect
performance	field of experience

When each student has completed the model, groups of five or six should be formed so that members may pool their insights in order to construct one improved model of communication. After this is completed, all models should be shared with the entire class.

You may wish to consider some or all of the following issues:

1. Why is it important to speak of a source-receiver rather than of a source and a receiver? Why is it important to speak of encoding-decoding rather than encoding and decoding?

2. Most models of communication do not include the concepts of competence and performance. Do these concepts help to clarify the nature of interpersonal communication? If so, in what ways?

3. Some theorists have argued that it is not necessary to consider feedback as a separate and distinct element. They argue that feedback is just another message and does not differ in any essential way from "regular" messages. Do you think that the concept of feedback helps in understanding the nature of interpersonal communication? If so, in what ways?

4. Could your model also serve as a model of intrapersonal communication? Explain it as a description of the intrapersonal communication process.

5. What elements or concepts other than those noted above might be added to the model? Why would they help us to better understand interpersonal communication?

AXIOMS OF INTERPERSONAL COMMUNICATION

Upon completion of this unit, you should be able to:

1. explain the transactional nature of interpersonal communication
2. explain why one cannot not communicate
3. identify the alternatives available when one does not wish to communicate but another person does
4. distinguish between the content and the relationship dimensions of interpersonal communication
5. explain the concept of punctuation in interpersonal communication
6. distinguish between symmetrical and complementary interactions

Interpersonal communication is a very special process. It is nothing like running a race, drinking a soda, or working out a math problem. Nor is it like writing an essay, delivering a public speech, or designing an advertising campaign. In this unit, this very special nature of interpersonal communication is explained in two ways. First, the nature of interpersonal communication as a transactional process is examined. We will identify some of the assumptions concerning interpersonal communication and some of the implications entailed in making these assumptions. Second, we will examine four transactional axioms or postulates of interpersonal communication. Taken together, these two approaches should clarify what interpersonal communication is and especially how it operates in the real world of person-to-person communication.

INTERPERSONAL COMMUNICATION AS A TRANSACTIONAL PROCESS

When we say that interpersonal communication is transactional, we mean that (1) interpersonal communication is a process, (2) whose components are interdependent, and (3) whose participants act and react as whole beings.

Interpersonal Communication Is a Process

Interpersonal communication is a process; it is an act, an event, an activity. It is not something static and at rest; it is an ongoing process. Everything involved in interpersonal communication is in a state of change: we are constantly changing, the people we are communicating with are changing, and our **18** environment is changing. Sometimes these changes go unnoticed, sometimes they intrude in obvious ways, but always the changes are occurring.

The interpersonal communication process is best described as a circular and continuous one. When we consider communication as the transmitting of messages from speaker to listener, we imply that the process begins with the speaker and ends with the listener. This is a linear view. In reality interpersonal communication is a circular process with each person serving both functions—each is simultaneously a speaker and a listener, an actor and a reactor.

The interpersonal communication process is continuous. It has no clear-cut beginning and no clear-cut end; it is perpetual. Although we may, for convenience, appear to stop the process and talk about when a particular communication act began, in reality the process has not stopped and a beginning may never be clearly distinguished.

Consider a "simple" interpersonal act: you meet and talk with another person. Because it is convenient, we may say that this interaction began when you started to speak or when you first saw each other. But that is too simplistic because what each of you say and how each of you respond during the interaction is greatly dependent upon factors having their beginnings at some unidentifiable point in time, for example, your self-confidence, your previous experience, your fears, your communicative competencies, your expectations, your needs, and hundreds of other factors.

Interdependent Components

The elements in interpersonal communication are integrally related to each other; they are interdependent (never independent). Each element—each part of interpersonal communication—exists in relation to the other parts and to the whole. For example, there can be no source without a receiver; there can be no message without a source; there can be no feedback without a receiver. Each aspect of the interpersonal communication process is intimately connected with all other aspects, and because of this interdependency, a change in any one element leads to changes in the others. For example, you are talking with a group of fellow students about the course or a recent examination and the teacher enters the group. This change in participants will lead to other changes—perhaps in the content of what is said, perhaps in the manner in which it is expressed. But regardless of what change is introduced, other changes will occur as a result of the initial change.

Because of this interdependency and change, no action or reaction is exactly repeatable. No person ever does the same thing in exactly the same way. The major reason for this is that no human being is the same from one moment to the next. Changes have occurred. More formally, we might say that interpersonal communication possesses the feature of *unrepeatability* so that all interpersonal interactions are novel experiences.

Interpersonal communication is *irreversible*—partly because of interdependence and unrepeatability and partly because of the way in which the brain works. The process of only some systems can be reversed. For example, water may be turned into ice and the ice may be turned back into water again—a reversible process. Other systems, however, are irreversible; the process can only unfold in one direction. Interpersonal communication is such a process. We can never undo what has already been done. What has been communicated remains communicated, however much we may attempt to quantify or negate it.

Action and Reaction of Participants as Whole Beings

In a transactional process each person acts and reacts as a whole. We are designed to act as whole persons. One cannot react, for example, solely on an intellectual level or solely on an emotional level; we are not so compartmentalized. Rather, we respond intellectually and emotionally, with body and mind. Our reactions in interpersonal communication, then, are not based solely on what is said or on body gestures, but on our entire beings—on our previous experiences, our present emotions, our knowledge, our physical well-being or ill health, and a multitude of other factors.

SOME TRANSACTIONAL POSTULATES

In *Pragmatics of Human Communication: A Study of Interactional Patterns, Pathologies, and Paradoxes*, Paul Watzlawick, Janet Beavin, and Don Jackson present an analysis of the behavioral effects of communication derived from the study of behavior disorders. Perhaps the most essential part of their analysis of human communication is their postulates of communication—propositions that are essential to an understanding of interpersonal communication. Four of these postulates are considered here.

We Cannot Not Communicate

Often we think of communication as being intentional, purposeful, and consciously motivated. In many instances it is. But in other instances we are communicating even though we might not think we are or might not even want to communicate. Take, for example, the student sitting in the back of the room with an "expressionless" face, perhaps staring at the front of the room, perhaps staring out the window. Although the student might say that she or he is not communicating with the teacher or with the other students, that student is obviously communicating a great deal—perhaps disinterest, perhaps boredom, perhaps a concern for something else, perhaps a desire for the class to be over as soon as possible. In any event, the student is communicating whether she or he wishes to or not; we cannot not communicate. Further, when we are in an interactional situation with this person, we must respond in some way. Even if we do not actively or overtly respond, that lack of response is itself a response and communicates. Like the student's silence, our silence in response also communicates.

Watzlawick, Beavin, and Jackson give the example of two strangers on a plane; one wishes to communicate, while the other does not. When we do not wish to communicate we have four general ways of dealing with the situation.

1. We may simply and explicitly state the desire not to communicate. We may do this nonverbally, which is perhaps the less socially offensive way, or we may do this verbally. Despite the fact that the person next to us is a complete bore and that we might want just to daydream, we are under social pressure not to ignore anyone. Yet the option to indicate that we do not wish to communicate is still open to us.

2. We may simply give in and communicate. This, it seems, is what many people do, and it seems to be the road of least effort. In fact, it may take more psychic energy to tell the person that we do not wish to communicate than to communicate. And we can still hope that the person will soon tire and go away.

3. We may disqualify our communications in various ways. For example, we may contradict ourselves, speak in incomplete sentences, or change the subject without any apparent motivation. In all of these cases the intent is to get the other person bored or confused so that he or she will then go away. Of course, it often happens that the person becomes all the more interested in figuring us out and consequently seems to stay with us for what seems like forever.

4. Perhaps the most ingenious way is to pretend to want to talk but to also pretend that something is preventing us from doing so. For example, we might say that we would like to talk but we are just so sleepy that we cannot keep our eyes open, and then doze off. Or perhaps we feign a toothache, which makes speaking difficult. Or we might pretend to be drunk or sick or deaf. At times, of course, the other person is aware that we are pretending. Yet this is a more socially acceptable manner of getting out of talking than honestly stating that we do not want to communicate.

Notice that regardless of what we do or do not do we are still communicating. All behavior is communication; all behavior has message value.

All Communications Have a Content and a Relationship Dimension

Communications, to a certain extent at least, refer to the real world, to something external to both speaker and listener. At the same time, however, communications also refer to the relationship between the parties. For example, a teacher may say to a student, "See me after class." This simple message has a content aspect that refers to the behavioral responses expected—namely, that the student see the teacher after class—and a relationship aspect that tells us how the communication is to be dealt with. Even the use of the simple command states that there is a status difference between the two parties that allows the teacher to command the student. This is perhaps seen most clearly when we visualize this command being made by the student to the teacher. It appears awkward and out of place simply because it violates the normal relationship between teacher and student.

In any communication the content dimension may be the same but the relationship aspect different, or the relationship aspect may be the same and the content dimension different. For example, the teacher could say to the student, "You had better see me after class" or "May I please see you after class?" In each case the content is essentially the same; that is, the message being communicated about the behavioral responses expected is the same in both cases. But the relationship dimension is very different. In the first it signifies a very definite superior-inferior relationship and even a put-down of the student, but in the second a more equal relationship is signaled and a respect for the student is shown. Similarly, at times the content may be different but the relationship essentially the same. For example, a son might say to his parents, "May I go away this weekend?" or "May I use the car tonight?" The content is clearly very different in each case, and yet the relationship dimension is essentially the same. It is clearly a superior-inferior relationship in which permission to do certain things must be secured.

Many problems between people are caused by the failure to recognize the distinction between the content and the relationship levels of communication. For example, consider the engaged couple arguing over the fact that the woman made plans to study during the weekend with her friends without first asking her fiancé if that would be all right. Probably both would have agreed that to study over the weekend was the right choice to make; thus the argument is not primarily concerned with the content level. The argument centers on the relationship level; the man expected to be consulted about plans for the weekend; the woman, in not doing this, rejected this definition of their relationship. Similar situations exist among married couples when one person will buy something or make dinner plans or invite a guest to dinner, without asking the other person first. Even though the other person would have agreed with the decision made, the couple argue because of the message communicated on the relationship level.

This is not to say that the relationship level is often discussed or even that it should be explicitly discussed by both parties. In fact, Watzlawick, Beavin, and Jackson argue the contrary: "It seems that the more spontaneous and 'healthy' a relationship, the more the relationship aspect of communication recedes into the background. Conversely, 'sick' relationships are characterized by a constant struggle about the nature of the relationship, with the content aspect of communication becoming less and less important."

We might also note that arguments over the content dimension are relatively easy to resolve. Generally, we may look something up in a book or ask someone what actually took place or perhaps see the movie again. It is relatively easy to verify facts that are disputed. Arguments on the relationship level, however, are much more difficult to resolve, in part because we seldom recognize that the argument is in fact a relationship one. One of the clearest examples of the confusion between the content and the relationship aspects was reported in a letter to Ann Landers. A woman and her husband were playing bridge with her sister and her husband. The writer notes that her husband had a habit of overbidding his hand and on this particular evening made a "reckless bid of six spades." The writer reports that all she said was "either you are crazy or I'm blind." The husband then said, "Why don't you just keep your mouth shut and play the hand." "The dumb remark of yours," he later continued, "cost us the game. I don't want to play cards with you ever again." On one level this argument concerns content—the bridge game, proper bidding, winning strategies, and the like. On another level, however, the argument concerns the relationship between the husband and wife. We might venture to postulate that the relationship level involved such issues as the husband's feeling that his wife should be supportive regardless of what he does, the appropriateness of the wife's public criticism of her husband and of the husband's criticism of his wife, who was really the offended party, and probably many more. As long as the husband and wife assume that their conflict is totally content oriented, they are probably never going to resolve it. A resolution can only come about, it seems, if the relational aspect is understood and confronted.

"It all started when his mother came to live with us. Then everything changed."

"The trouble really began when she got that promotion at the office."

A Relationship Is Defined, in Part, by the Punctuation of Communication Sequences

Communication events are continuous transactions. They are broken up into short sequences only for purposes of convenience. What is stimulus and what is response is not very easy to determine when we, as analysts of communication, enter after the communication transaction is under way.

Consider, for example, the following incident. A couple is at a party. The husband is flirting with the other women and the wife is drinking; both are scowling at each other and are obviously in a deep nonverbal argument with each other. In explaining the situation the husband might recall the events by observing that the wife drank and so he flirted with the sober women. The more she drank the more he flirted. The only reason for his behavior was his anger over her drinking. Notice that he sees his behavior as the response to her behavior; her behavior came first and was the cause of his behavior.

In recalling the "same" incident the wife might say that she drank when he started flirting. The more he flirted, the more she drank. She had no intention of drinking until he started flirting. To her, his behavior was the stimulus and her's was the response; he caused her behavior. Thus he sees the behavior as going from drinking to flirting, and she sees it as going from flirting to drinking. This example is depicted visually in Figure 2.1.

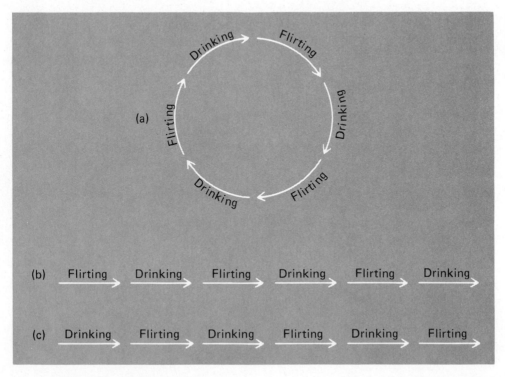

FIGURE 2.1
Punctuation and the Sequence of Events.

In Figure 2.1(a) we see what we assume to be the actual sequence of events. We see this as a continuous series of events with no absolute beginning and no absolute end. Each action (drinking and flirting) stimulates another action, but there can be no initial cause identified. In Figure 2.1(b) we see the same sequence of events, but this time it is punctuated by the wife. She sees the sequence as beginning with the husband's flirting. She sees her drinking behavior as a response to her husband's stimulus (flirting). In Figure 2.1(c) the same sequence of events is portrayed, but this time from the husband's point of view. He sees the sequence beginning with the wife's drinking. He sees his flirting as a response to his wife's stimulus (drinking).

This continuous nature of communication has also been visualized as a spiral, as presented in Figure 2.2. The spiral emphasizes the fact that communication has no clear observable beginning and no clear observable end; the spiral continues indefinitely. No communication transaction may be said to have fixed boundaries. Each transaction is, in part, a function of previous communications, and each transaction in turn influences future communications.

This tendency to divide up the various communication transactions into sequences of stimuli and responses is referred to by Watzlawick, Beavin, and Jackson as the punctuation of the sequences of events. They do not argue that punctuation is wrong; obviously, it is a very useful technique in providing some organization for thinking about and talking about communication transactions. At the same time, because we each see things differently, we each punctuate

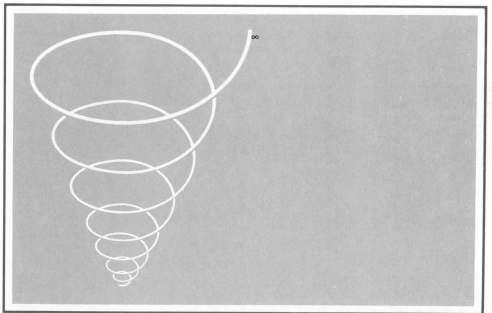

FIGURE 2.2
Helical Spiral.
Source: Frank E.
X. Dance,
"Toward a Theory
of Human Com-
munication," in
*Human Communi-
cation Theory:
Original Essays,*
Frank E. X. Dance,
ed. (New York:
Holt, Rinehart and
Winston, 1957), p.
296.

events differently. To the extent that these differences are significant, the possibility for a communication breakdown exists.

All Communication Interactions May Be Viewed as Either Symmetrical or Complementary

Some 40 years ago anthropologist Gregory Bateson formulated the concepts of symmetrical and complementary relationships while studying the interactions between the Sepik and the Fly River people of New Guinea. Bateson and others soon realized that the concepts were applicable to all forms of interpersonal relationships.

In a symmetrical relationship the two individuals mirror each other's behavior, with the behavior of one reflected in the behavior of the other. If one member nags, the other member responds in kind. If one member expresses jealousy, the other member expresses jealousy. If one member is passive, the other member is passive. The relationship is one of equality with the emphasis on minimizing the differences between the two individuals.

In a complementary relationship the two individuals engage in different behaviors, with the behavior of one serving as the stimulus for the complementary behavior of the other. In complementary relationships the differences between the parties are maximized. It is necessary in a complementary relationship for both parties to occupy different positions, one being the superior and one being the inferior, one being passive and one being active, one being strong and one being weak. At times such relationships are established by the culture, as, for example, the complementary relationship existing between teacher and student or between employer and employee.

Problems may arise in both symmetrical and complementary relationships. In the symmetrical relationship it is easy to appreciate that two individuals who mirror each other's jealousy will find very little security. The jealous behavior is likely to escalate to the point where one or both parties will quit from exhaustion. As Watzlawick, Beavin, and Jackson put it, "In marital conflict, for instance, it is easy to observe how the spouses go through an escalation pattern of frustration until they eventually stop from sheer physical or emotional exhaustion and maintain an uneasy truce until they have recovered enough for the next round."

A problem created in complementary relationships, familiar to many college students, is that of *rigid complementarity*. Whereas the complementary relationship between mother and child was at one time vital and essential to the life of the child, that same relationship when the child is older becomes a handicap to further development, when essential change is not allowed to occur.

The problem of progressive differentiation may result from either type of relationship—a condition Bateson called *schismogenesis*. Consider this development first in the complementary relationship. Let us say that we have two brothers and that the older brother overprotects the younger. This overprotection fosters increased dependency from the younger brother. As the younger brother becomes more and more dependent, the older brother becomes more and more protective. The result is often a breakdown in the relationship, with each coming to resent the behavior of the other and perhaps coming to dislike or even hate the other.

Progressive differentiation may also occur in a symmetrical relationship. Consider the situation of a husband and wife, both of whom are very aggressive. The aggressiveness of the husband fosters aggressiveness in the wife; the aggressiveness of the wife fosters aggressiveness in the husband. As this escalates, the aggressiveness can no longer be contained, and the relationship blows up.

These four axioms as set forth by Watzlawick, Beavin, and Jackson seem essential to any introductory or advanced analysis of interpersonal communication. They provide us with insight into the nature and function of human communication as well as into the intricacies of human interpersonal relationships and interactions.

SOURCES

For the axioms I relied on Paul Watzlawick, Janet Helmick Beavin, and Don D. Jackson, *Pragmatics of Human Communication: A Study of Interactional Patterns, Pathologies, and Paradoxes* (New York: Norton, 1967). Another useful work in this area is Jurgen Ruesch and Gregory Bateson, *Communication: The Social Matrix of Psychiatry* (New York: Norton, 1951). Many of the ideas set forth in *Pragmatics* may be found in the work of Bateson. For a useful collection of Bateson's writings, see *Steps to an Ecology of Mind* (New York: Ballantine Books, 1972). An interesting interview with Paul Watzlawick that elaborates on some of the topics presented here may be found in *Journal of Communication* 28 (Autumn 1978): 35–45. Popular accounts of these principles may be found in Paul Watzlawick, *How Real Is Real? Confusion, Disinformation, Communication* (New York: Random House [Vintage Books], 1976) and in his *The Language of Change: Elements of Therapeutic Communication* (New York: Basic Books, 1978). A useful review article is Carol Wilder, "The Palo Alto Group: Difficulties and Directions of the Interactional View for Human Communication Research," *Human Communication Research* 5 (Winter 1979): 171–186. For the discussion of the nature of the transactional view of interpersonal communication, I utilized the insights of Dean C. Barnlund, "A Transactional Model of Communication," *Language Behavior: A Book of Readings in Communication,* comp. J. Akin, A. Goldberg, G. Myers, and J. Stewart (The Hague: Mouton, 1970), and William W. Wilmot, *Dyadic Communication,* 2d ed. (Reading, Mass.: Addison-Wesley, 1979). The spiral model comes from Frank E. X. Dance, "Toward a Theory of Human Communication" in *Human Communication Theory: Original Essays,* Frank E. X. Dance, ed. (New York: Holt, Rinehart and Winston, 1957).

2.1 ANALYZING A TRANSACTION

The axioms of human communication proposed by Watzlawick, Beavin, and Jackson and discussed in this unit should prove useful in analyzing any interpersonal transaction. To better understand these axioms and to obtain some practice in applying them to an actual interaction, a summary of Tennessee Williams' *Cat on a Hot Tin Roof* is presented. Ideally, all students would read the entire play or see the movie and then apply the four axioms to the interpersonal interactions that take place. This brief summary is presented, then, more in the nature of a "mental refresher." (Note that the original play, as it has been published, differs from the film, particularly in the last act. The film version of the play is somewhat more positive. The summary presented here is from the original stage play, the version Williams prefers.)

> *Big Daddy and Big Mama Pollitt, owners of a huge estate, have two sons: Brick (married to Maggie, the cat), an ex-football player who has now turned to drink, and Gooper (married to Mae), a lawyer and the father of five children, with one more on the way. All are gathered together to celebrate Big Daddy's sixty-fifth birthday. The occasion is marred by news that Big Daddy may have cancer, for which there is no hope of a cure. A false report is given to Big Mama and Big Daddy stating that the test proved negative and that all that is wrong is a spastic colon—a sometimes painful but not fatal illness. It appears to Maggie, and perhaps to others as well, that Gooper and Mae are really here to claim their share of the inheritance.*
>
> *The desire to assume control of Big Daddy's fortune (estimated at some $10 million and 28,000 acres "of the richest land this side of the valley Nile") has created considerable conflict between Gooper and Mae, on the one hand, and Maggie, on the other. Brick, it appears, does not care about his possible inheritance.*
>
> *Throughout the play there is conflict between Brick and Maggie. Brick refuses to go to bed with Maggie although Maggie desperately wants him. This fact is known by everyone, since Mae and Gooper have the adjoining room and hear everything that goes on between Brick and Maggie. The cause of this conflict between Brick and Maggie goes back to Brick's relations with Skipper, his best friend. Brick and Skipper were football players on the same team and did just about everything together. So close were they that rumors about their love for each other began to spread. While Brick is in the hospital with a football injury, Maggie confronts Skipper and begs that he either stop loving Brick or tell him of his love. In an attempt to prove Maggie wrong, Skipper goes to bed with her but fails and as a result takes to drink and drugs. Maggie repeatedly attempts to*

thrash this out with Brick, but he refuses to talk about it or even to listen to Maggie. All he wants to do is drink—waiting for the little click in his head that tells him he can stop.

In a confrontation with Big Daddy, Brick talks of his disgust with lying and his using liquor to forget all the lies around him. Under pressure from Big Daddy, Brick admits that Skipper called to make a drunken confession after his attempted relationship with Maggie but that Brick hung up and refused to listen. It was then that Skipper committed suicide. And this, it appears, is what Brick uses alcohol to forget. In his anger Brick tells Big Daddy that he is dying of cancer.

Gooper and Mae confront Big Mama with the news that Big Daddy has cancer and attempt to get Big Mama to sign some papers concerning the disposition of the property now that Big Daddy has not much longer to live. Perhaps Gooper and Mae's major argument is that they are responsible (as shown by their five children), while Brick and Maggie are not responsible (as shown by Brick's drinking and by his refusal to sleep with Maggie and have a child, something Big Daddy wants very much). At this point Maggie announces that she is pregnant. Big Mama is overjoyed and seems to be the only one who believes her. This, Big Mama reasons, will solve all the problems, even the problem of Brick's drinking. Brick of course knows that Maggie is lying but says nothing to betray her.

In the final scene Maggie locks up all the liquor and pressures Brick into going to bed with her in order to make her lie become truth. Afterward she promises to unlock the liquor so that they may both get drunk. She sobs that she really loves Brick, while Brick thinks if only that were true.

After reading the play or viewing the film, identify instances and explain the importance of the following:

1. the impossibility of not communicating
   a. What alternatives does Brick use in attempting to avoid communicating with Maggie?
   b. What alternatives does Brick use in attempting to avoid communicating with Big Daddy?
2. the content and relationship dimensions of specific messages
   a. How does Brick deal with the self-definitions of Maggie and Big Daddy?
   b. How does Big Daddy deal with Big Mama's definition of herself?
   c. Are any problems caused by the failure to recognize the distinction between the content and the relationship levels of communication?
3. the different punctuation of the sequences of events
   a. How do Maggie and Brick differ in their punctuation of the events?
   b. Why do they punctuate the sequences differently?
4. the symmetrical and complementary relationships
   a. What type of relationship exists between Brick and Maggie; Gooper and Mae; Big Daddy and Big Mama; Big Daddy and Brick; Big Daddy and Gooper; Maggie and Mae?

As an alternative to analyzing *Cat on a Hot Tin Roof,* the entire class may watch a situation comedy show, television drama, or film and explore these four communication postulates in these presentations. The questions used in this exercise should prove useful in formulating parallel questions for the television program or film. Another way of approaching this topic is to have all students watch the same television programs for an entire evening and have groups of students focus on the operation of different postulates. Thus, one group would focus on examples and illustrations of the impossibility of not communicating, one group on the content and relationship dimensions of messages, and so on. Each group can then report back their findings and insights to the entire class.

EFFECTIVENESS IN INTERPERSONAL COMMUNICATION

OBJECTIVES

Upon completion of this unit, you should be able to:
1. explain the concept of effectiveness in interpersonal communication
2. define *openness* and identify the three aspects of interpersonal communication to which it refers
3. define *empathy* and distinguish it from sympathy
4. define *supportiveness*
5. define *positiveness* and explain the three aspects of interpersonal communication to which it refers
6. explain the concept of stroking
7. define *equality* as it relates to interpersonal communication
8. identify the presence of these qualities (openness, empathy, supportiveness, positiveness, and equality) in interpersonal interactions

Interpersonal communication, like any form of behavior, can vary from being extremely effective to extremely ineffective. No interpersonal encounter is a total success or a total failure; each could have been better, but each could have been worse. We will review the characteristics of effective interpersonal communication while emphasizing that each communicative act is different and that any principles or rules must be applied judiciously with a full recognition of the uniqueness of each communication event.

Generally, we may view effectiveness as consisting of two basic dimensions. First, there is the pragmatic dimension in which effectiveness concerns the achievement of the aim or goal of the communicator. This dimension of effectiveness may be further defined and measured by, for example, the time necessary to achieve the goals, the number of errors made in the interpersonal process, and the number of messages to be communicated. Second, there is the personal satisfaction dimension, and here effectiveness is defined in terms of the enjoyment derived from the interpersonal encounter. If the participants enjoy the interaction, it is judged effective according to a satisfaction standard.

These dimensions of effectiveness are not always separate and distinct. Often one's satisfaction is determined by whether the goals of the interaction have been accomplished; alternatively, the achievement of one's goals is often **31** dependent upon the level of satisfaction derived from the interaction. At times an interpersonal encounter may be effective by the pragmatic standard and ineffective by the satisfaction standard, or ineffective pragmatically but extremely satisfying.

CHARACTERISTICS OF EFFECTIVENESS

The principal objective of this unit is to offer insight into interpersonal communication effectiveness. To this end, five characteristics of effectiveness—conceived in terms of pragmatics or in terms of satisfaction—are discussed. These characteristics are openness, empathy, supportiveness, positiveness, and equality (Figure 3.1). These are not the only qualities that promote effectiveness; rather, they seem to be some of the most important ingredients. The presence of these five characteristics does not guarantee effectiveness, nor does their absence always result in ineffectiveness. But generally, they can be expected to contribute significantly to effective communication. These characteristics, however, must be internalized and integrated with your own personality and customary behavior patterns if they are to be truly meaningful.

Openness

The quality of *openness* refers to at least three aspects of interpersonal communication. First, and perhaps most obvious, is that effective interpersonal communicators must be open to the people with whom they are interacting. This does not mean that one should immediately pour out one's entire life history. Interesting as that may be, it is not usually very helpful to the communication or interesting to the other individuals. Rather, there should be a willing-

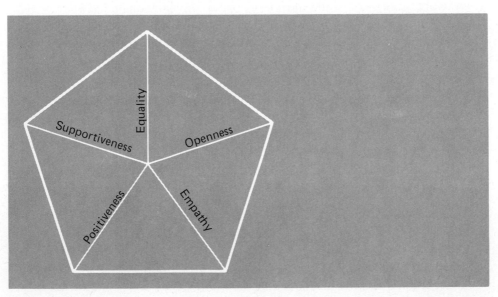

FIGURE 3.1
Effective Interpersonal Communication.

ness to "self-disclose," to reveal information about oneself that might normally be kept hidden but that is relevant to the interpersonal encounter. With openness we act in accordance with our feelings rather than according to some prescribed role that may be socially acceptable.

A second aspect of openness refers to the willingness of a communicator to react honestly to incoming stimuli. Silent, uncritical, and immovable psychiatrists may be of some help in a clinical situation, but they are generally boring conversationalists. We want people to react openly to what we say and have a right to expect it. Nothing seems worse than indifference; even disagreement seems more welcome. Of course there are extremes here, too. We demonstrate openness by responding spontaneously and without subterfuge to the communications and the feedback of others.

A third aspect of openness concerns the owning of feelings and thoughts. To be open in this sense is to acknowledge that the feelings and thoughts we express are ours and that we bear the responsibility for them; we do not attempt to shift the responsibility for our feelings to others. Arthur Bochner and Clifford Kelly put it this way: "The person who owns his feelings or ideas makes it clear that he takes responsibility for his own feelings and actions. Owning shows a willingness to accept responsibility for oneself and commitment to others. It is the antithesis of blaming others for the way one feels." Bochner and Kelly advise us not to say, "Isn't this group supposed to listen to people?" but rather, "I feel ignored. I don't think people in this group listen to me." This difference is interesting from another point of view as well. When we own our feelings and thoughts we say in effect, "This is how *I* feel," "This is how *I* see the situation," "This is what *I* think," with the *I* always paramount. And so instead of saying, "This discussion is useless," one would say something like, "*I'm* bored by this discussion," or "*I* want to talk more about myself," or any other such statement that includes reference to the fact that *I* am making an evaluation and not describing objective reality. By including in such statements what the general semanticists call "to me-ness," we make explicit the fact that our feelings are the result of the interaction between the outside reality and our own preconceptions, attitudes, prejudices, and the like.

Self-Monitoring

Integrally related to interpersonal effectiveness and openness—almost its opposite—is self-monitoring. Self-monitoring may be viewed as the manipulation of the image that we present to others in our interpersonal interactions. High self-monitors, for example, will carefully adjust their behaviors on the basis of feedback from others so that they may produce the most desirable effect. Their interpersonal interactions are manipulated in an attempt to give the best and most effective interpersonal impression. Low self-monitors, on the other hand, are not concerned with the image they present to others. Rather, their interactions are characterized by an extreme openness in which they communicate their thoughts and feelings with no attempt to manipulate the impres-

SELF-MONITORING TEST*

These statements concern personal reactions to a number of different situations. No two statements are exactly alike, so consider each statement carefully before answering. If a statement is true, or mostly true, as applied to you, circle the T. If a statement is false, or not usually true, as applied to you, circle the F.

1. I find it hard to imitate the behavior of other people.   (T)   F
2. I guess I do put on a show to impress or entertain people.   T   (F)
3. I would probably make a good actor.   T   (F)
4. I sometimes appear to others to be experiencing deeper emotions than I actually am.   T   (F)
5. In a group of people, I am rarely the center of attention.   (T)   F
6. In different situations and with different people, I often act like very different persons.   T   (F)
7. I can only argue for ideas I already believe.   (T)   F
8. In order to get along and be liked, I tend to be what people expect me to be rather than who I really am.   T   (F)
9. I may deceive people by being friendly when I really dislike them.   T   (F)
10. I am not always the person I appear to be.   T   (F)

Scoring

Give yourself one point for each of questions 1, 5, and 7 that you answered F. Give yourself one point for each of the remaining questions that you answered T. Add up your points. If you are a good judge of yourself and scored 7 or above, you are probably a high self-monitoring individual; 3 or below, you are probably a low self-monitoring individual.

*Source: This self-monitoring test appeared in Mark Snyder, "The Many Me's of the Self-Monitor," *Psychology Today* 13 (March 1980), p. 34, and is reprinted here by permission of Mark Snyder.

sions they create. Somewhere between the high and the low self-monitors lie most of us. You may wish, at this point, to take the brief self-monitoring test on page 34.

When high and low self-monitors are compared, a number of interesting differences are noted. For example, high self-monitors are more apt to take charge of a situation, are more sensitive to the deceptive techniques of others, and are better able to detect self-monitoring or impression management techniques when used by others. High self-monitors prefer to interact with low self-monitors. They seem to prefer to live in a relatively stable world with people who will not be able to detect their self-monitoring techniques. By interacting with low self-monitors, the high self-monitors are more likely to be able to assume positions of influence and power. High self-monitors also seem better able to present their true selves than are low self-monitors. For example, if an innocent person is charged with a crime, to use the example cited by Mark Snyder (on whose research this discussion is based), the high self-monitor would be able to present his or her innocence more effectively than would a low self-monitor.

Although there seem to be two relatively clear-cut types of persons—high and low self-monitors—we all engage in selective self-monitoring depending on the situation. If we go for a job interview, we are likely to monitor our behaviors very carefully. On the other hand, if we are interacting with a group of friends we are less likely to monitor our performance; we are more apt to express our feelings and thoughts openly and without any great attempt at impression management.

A careful reading of the research and theory on self-monitoring, on openness, and on self-disclosure (a topic reviewed in detail in Unit 7) supports the conclusion that our effectiveness will normally be increased if we are selectively self-disclosing, selectively open, and engage in selective self-monitoring. To be totally open, to self-disclose everything to everyone, to ignore the feedback of others, and to refuse to engage in any self-monitoring seems absurd. The opposite extreme of the closed, never disclosing individual who monitors each and every utterance is equally absurd and should likewise be avoided.

There are no easy and simple answers to such questions as, "To what degree should we be open?," "How much and to whom should we self-disclose?," and "To what extent should we attempt to self-monitor our communication behaviors?" Fortunately, however, there are competencies that we can develop that will guide us and enable us to function more effectively interpersonally. It is to the development of these competencies that a course and a text on interpersonal communication are directed.

Empathy

Perhaps the most difficult of all the communication qualities to achieve is the ability to experience *empathy* for another individual. *Empathy* comes from the German word *Einfühling*, meaning "to feel with." To empathize with someone is to feel as that person does. As Henry Backrack puts it, empathy refers to "the ability of one person to experientially 'know' what another is experiencing at any given moment, from the latter's frame of reference, through the latter's eyes." To sympathize, on the other hand, is to feel *for* the individual—to be sorry for the person, for example. To empathize is to feel *as* the individual feels, to be in the same shoes, to feel the same feelings in the same way.

If we are able to empathize with people, we are in a better position to understand, for example, their motivations and past experiences, their present feelings and attitudes, their hopes and expectations for the future. "One cannot grasp subtle and complicated feelings of people," notes R. Greenson, "except by this emotional knowing, the experiencing of another's feeling that is meant by the term *empathy*. It is a very special model of perceiving." Empathy, then, enables one to understand (emotionally and intellectually) what the other person is experiencing. This empathic understanding in turn enables the individual to better adjust his or her communications—what is said, how it is said, what is to be avoided, if and when silence is to be preferred, if self-disclosures should be made, and so on. In fact, C. Truax includes one's communication ability as part of the definition of empathy. "Accurate empathy," says Truax, writing from the point of view of the psychotherapist, "involves both the sensitivity to current feelings and the verbal facility to communicate this understanding in a language attuned to the client's own feelings."

More difficult than defining *empathy* is describing or advancing ways to increase our empathic abilities. Perhaps the first step is to avoid evaluating the other person's behaviors. If we evaluate them as right or wrong, good or bad, we will see these behaviors through these labels and will fail to see a great deal that might not be consistent with these labels. Therefore, resist the temptation to evaluate, to judge, to interpret, to criticize. It is not that these responses are "wrong," but merely that they often get in the way of understanding. First, focus on understanding. Second, the more we know about a person—her or his desires, experiences, abilities, fears, and so on—the more we will be able to see what that person sees and feel as that person feels. We need to try to understand the reasons and the motivations that contribute to making the person feel as she or he does. Even if these reasons and motivations may appear illogical or self-destructive to you, they need to be understood if you are to achieve a meaningful degree of empathy with the other person. Third, we should try to experience what the other person is feeling from his or her point of view. Playing the role of the other person in our minds (or even out loud) should help us to see the world a little more as he or she does.

Supportiveness

An effective interpersonal relationship is one in which there is supportiveness, a concept that owes much of its formulation to the work of Jack Gibb. Open and empathic communication cannot survive in an unsupportive atmosphere. Supportiveness is demonstrated and fostered by our being (1) descriptive rather than evaluative, (2) spontaneous rather than strategic, and (3) provisional rather than certain.

Descriptive

An atmosphere that is descriptive rather than evaluative leads to supportiveness. When we perceive a communication as being a request for information or a description of some event, we generally do not perceive it as threatening. We are not being challenged and have no need to defend ourselves. On the other hand, a communication that is judgmental or evaluative often leads us to become defensive, to back off, and to otherwise erect some kind of barrier between ourselves and the evaluator. This is not to imply that all evaluative communications will elicit a defensive response. Positive evaluations are often responded to without defensiveness and in fact with all sorts of positive reactions. Even here, however, it must be recalled that the very fact that someone has the power or the knowledge or the "right" to evaluate us in any way (even if positively) may lead us to feel uneasy and perhaps defensive. Perhaps we anticipate that the next evaluation may not be so positive. In a similar way, negative evaluations do not always elicit a defensive response. The would-be

Supportiveness may be expressed in many ways.

actor who wants to improve and perfect technique often welcomes negative evaluations. Similarly, many students welcome negative evaluations when they feel they are constructive and lead to substantial improvement in their ability to communicate, to calculate appropriate statistical tests, or to construct valid and reliable experimental designs.

Generally, however, an evaluative atmosphere leads people to become more defensive than would a descriptive atmosphere. Maybe we feel that whatever we do or say is going to be evaluated, and so we shy away from expressing ourselves freely, perhaps fearing that we will be criticized. Despite the usefulness of some criticism, it is still threatening, and it can be difficult to express ourselves openly when there is a strong possibility of evaluation.

Spontaneous

A spontaneous as opposed to a strategic style also helps create supportiveness. Individuals who are spontaneous in their communications, individuals who are straightforward and open about what they think, generally receive the same response—straightforwardness and openness. But in many situations we feel that certain people are hiding their true feelings—that they have some hidden plan that they are attempting to implement for some unrevealed purpose. This strategy approach leads us to become defensive and to resist any such attempts at manipulation.

Most people employ some kind of strategy in their communications. For example, you may preface your remarks in such a way as to get the listener into a more receptive mood, or you may say over and over again that you are doing something for the good of someone else and are not concerned with the benefits you yourself might receive. That is, you might do things to gain the favor of the individuals with whom you interact. This is a rather common approach in communicating. Often, of course, it is clear to the listener that you are in fact employing some kind of strategy. You clearly recognize it in the salesperson who tells you that you look just great in this new jacket. What we all forget is that our own strategies are often just as apparent and are just as often met with by resistance and resentment.

Provisional

Provisionalism—the state of being provisional—refers to an attitude of tentativeness, of open-mindedness, of a willingness to hear opposing points of view and to change one's own position if warranted. It is provisionalism, rather than unwavering certainty, that further assists in creating a supportive atmosphere.

We resist people who "know" everything and who always have a definite answer to any question. Such people are set in their ways and will tolerate no differences. They have arguments ready for any possible alternative attitude or belief. After a very short time we become defensive with such people, and we hold back our own attitudes rather than subjecting them to attack. But we open up with people who take a more provisional position, who are willing to change their minds should reasonable arguments be presented. With such people we feel equal.

Closed-minded people are heavily dependent upon being reinforced for their reactions to information. They will evaluate information on the basis of the rewards and the punishments they receive. We all do this to some extent; the closed-minded person, however, does this to a greater degree than do most people. The open-minded person is better able to resist the reinforcements of other people and outside situations.

In terms of interpersonal relationships, "certain," or closed-minded, people will evaluate others according to the similarity-dissimilarity of others' belief systems with their own. They evaluate positively those people who have similar belief systems and negatively those people who have dissimilar belief systems. "Provisional," or open-minded, individuals do not use similarity of belief systems or homophily as the measure of interpersonal relationships. The "certain" and the "provisional" individuals are extreme types. Few people are completely closed or completely open. The vast majority exist somewhere in between these two extremes. What is most important to understand is that to the extent that we act "certain" and closed-minded, we encourage defensive behavior in the listener. To the extent that we act in a provisional manner, with an open mind, with a full recognition that we might be wrong, and with a willingness to revise our attitudes and opinions, we encourage supportiveness.

Positiveness

We may consider positiveness in interpersonal communication in at least two ways. First we may look at positiveness in terms of the attitudes that a person may hold that can influence interpersonal effectiveness. Second, we may look at positiveness in terms of the concept of stroking behavior.

Attitudes

Attitudinal positiveness in interpersonal communication refers to at least three different aspects or elements. First, interpersonal communication is fostered if there is a certain positive regard for the self. People who feel negative about themselves will invariably communicate these feelings to others, who in turn will probably develop similar negative feelings. On the other hand, people who feel positive about themselves will convey this feeling about themselves to others, who in turn are likely to return the positive regard.

Second, interpersonal communication will be fostered if a positive feeling for the other person is communicated. One will, for example, be more likely to self-disclose.

Third, a positive feeling for the general communication situation is important for effective interaction. Nothing is more unpleasant than communicating with someone who does not enjoy the exchange or does not respond favorably to the situation or context. A negative response to the situation makes one feel almost as if one is intruding, and communication seems sure to quickly break down.

Stroking

Positiveness may be further explained by reference to the concept of stroking. *Stroking* is a term that is creeping into the general vocabulary, no doubt because of its central importance in transactional analysis and in human interaction generally. Stroking behavior acknowledges the existence, and in fact the importance, of the other person; it is the antithesis of indifference. When we stroke someone, whether positively or negatively, we are acknowledging her or him as a person, as a significant human being.

Stroking may be verbal, as in "I like you," "I enjoy being with you," "You're a pig," or nonverbal, such as a smile, a wink, a pat on the back, a hug, or a punch in the mouth. As these examples illustrate, stroking may be positive or negative. Positive stroking generally takes the form of compliments or rewards and consists of those behaviors we would normally look forward to, enjoy, and take pride in. They would bolster our self-image and make us feel a little bit better than we did before we received them. Negative strokes, on the other hand, are punishing; they are aversive. Sometimes, like cruel remarks, they hurt us emotionally or psychologically; sometimes, like a punch in the mouth, they hurt us physically.

Transactional analysts argue that people *need* to be stroked; otherwise, they will shrivel up and die. And, of course, it is positive stroking that most people are after. But if they cannot secure positive stroking, they will settle for negative stroking. The assumption here is that indifference is the worst fate anyone could suffer and that anything short of that is welcomed. If positive stroking cannot be had, and if the only alternatives are negative stroking or indifference, the individual will choose the negative stroking. I should add that other theorists, most notably the rational emotive theorists such as Albert Ellis, would argue that people may *want* to be stroked but they do not *need* it; they can and do function without stroking. Personal difficulties arise, Ellis argues, when people assume that they *need* to be stroked and then are not. If, on the other hand, they recognize that they may *want* to be stroked but do not *need* it, they can be quite productive and happy even when they are not stroked. I agree with Ellis, but you may wish to explore the issue in more detail yourselves in Ellis's *A New Guide to Rational Living* and in any of the transactional analysis works cited at the end of this unit. Despite this interesting and important difference between the two theories, all theorists seem to agree that stroking is significant and that it has a great effect on interpersonal interactions of all types.

It is important to recognize that many interpersonal encounters are structured by one or even both participants almost solely to get stroked. People may buy new clothes to get stroked, may compliment associates so that they stroke back, may do favors for people in order to get stroked in return, may associate with certain people because they are generous with their strokes, and so on. Marriages and other primary relationships are often entered into because they hold the promise of frequent stroking. Similarly, it is important to recognize our own needs (or wants) in regard to stroking. We also do these things and for the same basic reason—to receive strokes, to be acknowledged as people, to ward off any possibility of indifference. Stroking leads to more effective interpersonal communication when it helps to reinforce productive and satisfying behavior patterns or, alternatively, when it functions to decrease unproductive and unsatisfying patterns.

Equality

Equality is a peculiar characteristic. In any situation there is probably going to be some inequality. One person will be smarter, richer, better looking, or more athletic. Never are two people absolutely equal in all respects. Even identical twins would be unequal in some ways. Despite this inequality, interpersonal communication is generally more effective when the atmosphere is one of equality. This does not mean that unequals cannot communicate. Certainly they can. Yet their communication, if it is to be effective, should recognize the equality of personalities. By this is meant that there should be a tacit recognition that both parties are valuable and worthwhile human beings and that each has something important to contribute.

Equality should also characterize interpersonal communication in terms of speaking versus listening. If one participant speaks all the time while the other listens all the time, effective interpersonal communication becomes difficult if not impossible. There should be an attempt at achieving an equality of sending versus receiving. Depending on the situation, one person will normally speak more than the other person, but this should be a function of the situation and not of the fact that one person is a "talker" and another person is a "listener."

In an interpersonal relationship characterized by equality, disagreement and conflict, for example, are seen as attempts to understand inevitable differences rather than as opportunities to put the other person down. Disagreements are viewed as ways of solving problems rather than of winning points, getting one's way, or somehow proving oneself superior to the other. "Equality" does not require that we accept and approve of all the verbal and nonverbal behaviors of the other person. Some behaviors are self-destructive or have negative consequences for others and should be challenged—not out of a desire to win an argument or prove a point, but out of concern for the other person and for the interpersonal relationship. Equality means acceptance and approval of the person or, to use Carl Rogers's terms, equality asks that we give the other person "unconditional positive regard."

A NOTE ON HOMOPHILY–HETEROPHILY

These five characteristics of effective interpersonal communication are qualities that can be learned, and so it seemed important that they be singled out for discussion. We should, lastly, make note here of the concepts of homophily and heterophily which, although not learned behaviors, greatly influence interpersonal communication effectiveness. *Homophily* refers to the degree of similarity between the parties engaged in interpersonal communication, and *heterophily* refers to the degree of difference between the parties. The similarity and difference may refer to just about any characteristic—age, religion, political leaning, financial status, educational level, and so forth.

Generally, research has shown that interpersonal communication is more effective when the parties are homophilous. James McCroskey, Carl Larson, and Mark Knapp, for example, state: "More effective communication occurs when source and receiver are homophilous. The more nearly alike the people in a communication transaction, the more likely they will share meanings." We will, according to this principle, communicate best with people who are most like ourselves. Butchers will communicate best with butchers, conservatives will communicate best with conservatives, and college students will communicate best with college students.

The more homophilous the individuals, the more open they will be with each other. This seems quite valid since we do seem to be most comfortable with those who are like us. Consequently, we are more apt to reveal ourselves and to self-disclose to people like ourselves. We feel perhaps that they would, in turn, reveal themselves and disclose to us. And so by being open we do not risk as much as we would in a heterophilous situation.

Empathy is greatest when people are homophilous and least when people are heterophilous. We can more easily feel as other people do (which is the essence of empathy) when we are like them to begin with. There is little distance to travel in order to empathize when we are similar to the individuals but much distance when they are not like us. Consider the difficulty a poor person would have empathizing with the disappointment of a rich one because she or he must give up the second car, or the difficulty a rich person would have in empathizing with a poor person's hunger.

It seems that we all want to support people who are like us more than people who are very different from us. By supporting homophilous people we are in effect supporting ourselves. People like us, we may feel, will be supportive to us, and so we respond in kind and support them. We can be silent with people who are like us and not be uncomfortable. We do not feel we have to impress them with our knowledge or intelligence.

Perhaps the most obvious relationship that exists with homophilous people is that of equality. By definition, homophilous people are equal to us, neither inferior nor superior. Hence there is more likely to be an atmosphere of equality, a free give-and-take of ideas, and an awareness that both participants have something to contribute.

Although communication is most effective when the individuals are homophilous, we should note that change is often brought about when the parties involved are "optimally heterophilous" in regard to the subject under discussion. According to McCroskey, Larson, and Knapp, if two people are homophilous in regard to the subject matter, then neither will be competent enough to change the attitudes, beliefs, or behaviors of the other. Also, when the individuals are too far apart in their competence on a subject, the more competent one will obviously not be changed by the less competent one, and the less competent one will probably have difficulty in understanding the more competent one. Consequently, no change will take place here, either. But when one party is optimally heterophilous, optimally more competent than the other, she or he will be better able to effect change in the other.

SOURCES

For this unit I relied (sometimes consciously and at other times subconsciously) on the work of Jack Gibb, particularly his insightful "Defensive Communication," *Journal of Communication* 11 (1961):141–148. This article has been reprinted in a number of different places, for example, in the reader by DeVito cited in the "Sources" for Unit 1. For an experimental investigation of defensiveness and supportiveness see William F. Eadie, "Defensive Communication Revisited: A Critical Examination of Gibb's Theory," *Southern Speech Communication Journal* 47 (Winter 1982):163–177.

For empathy, see R. Greenson, "Empathy and Its Vicissitudes," *International Journal of Psychoanalysis* 41 (1960):418–424, and C. Truax, "A Scale for the Measurement of Accurate Empathy," Wisconsin Psychiatric Institute Discussion Paper no. 20 (Madison, 1961). These and various other contributions to the study of empathy are discussed by Henry M. Backrach, "Empathy," *Archives of General Psychiatry* 33 (1976):35–38. William S. Howell, in his *The Empathic Communicator* (Belmont, Calif.: Wadsworth, 1982), has built his entire introduction to communication around the concept of empathy.

For an overview of homophily and heterophily, see James C. McCroskey, Carl E. Larson, and Mark L. Knapp, *An Introduction to Interpersonal Communication* (Englewood Cliffs, N.J.: Prentice-Hall, 1971). For a more extensive treatment, see E. M. Rogers and F. F. Shoemaker, *Communication of Innovations* (New York: Free Press, 1971). See Mark I. Alpert and W. Thomas Anderson, Jr., "Optimal Heterophily and Communication Effectiveness: Some Empirical Findings," *Journal of Communication* 23 (September 1973):328–343 for a review of relevant findings and an example of an experimental study of this question. A book that provides an excellent transition between the characteristics of effective interpersonal communication and the self is Edmond G. Addeo and Robert E. Burger, *Egospeak: Why No One Listens to You* (New York: Bantam Books, 1973). The concept of owning thoughts was taken from Arthur P. Bochner and Clifford W. Kelly, "Interpersonal Competence: Rationale, Philosophy, and Implementation of a Conceptual Framework," *Communication Education* 23 (November 1974):279–301. Also, see Arthur P. Bochner and Janet Yerby, "Factors Affecting Instruction in Interpersonal Competence," *Communication Education* 26(March 1977):91–103.

On satisfaction, see Michael L. Hecht, "The Conceptualization and Measurement of Interpersonal Communication Satisfaction," *Human Communication Research* 4 (Spring 1978):253–264, and "Toward a Conceptualization of Communication Satisfaction," *Quarterly Journal of Speech* 64 (February 1978):47–62.

3.1 PETER AND BARBARA

Presented here is a dialogue between two college students: Peter and Barbara. Carefully read the dialogue, noting especially their use or misuse of the principles of effective interpersonal interaction discussed in this unit. Read the dialogue at least twice.

This exercise is designed to enable you to see more clearly how the principles of effective interpersonal interaction operate in actual practice. The exercise consists of two parts. First, analyze the brief interaction in terms of the five principles of effective interpersonal interaction. Identify specific verbal behaviors that violate the principles of effectiveness or that demonstrate their effective application. Second, write a continuation of the dialogue. Assume that Peter and Barbara meet a week later and that neither has seen or spoken to the other throughout the week. These continuations should illustrate the ways in which both Peter and Barbara might correctly apply the principles for effective interpersonal interaction. These continuation dialogues may be written independently or in small groups of four or five.

After this dialogue has been analyzed and completed, discuss in small groups or with the class as a whole, the principles of effective interpersonal interaction and how they may operate to facilitate mutual understanding or to hinder it, to aid in the development of an interpersonal relationship or to contribute to its dissolution.

[*Peter and Barbara have been dating for the past 2 years and are now in their senior year of college. The scene takes place in Peter's apartment near campus.*]

Barbara: *I really think we should sit down and talk about it. About us. I feel something is wrong but you just won't talk about it.*
Peter: *Nothing's wrong. I just don't have anything to say. You always want to talk about it. Well, what do you want to say?*
Barbara: *I just want to know what is going to happen with us. We're going to graduate in June—five months from now. What's going to happen then?*
Peter: *Nothing. I mean the same as now.*
Barbara: *Do you want to talk about plans for after graduation? You want to talk about marriage?*
Peter: *No. I don't see any reason to talk about that now. We always seem*

44

to have arguments when we do that. Can't we just continue going along like we have been?

Barbara: *It's Nancy, isn't it?*

Peter: *Nancy? What are you talking about? Nancy was 6 months ago.*

Barbara: *Well, you lied about her then, so how do I know you're not lying now?*

Peter: *I'm not. Take my word for it. I'm not.*

Barbara: *What good is your word? You lied before and you'll lie again. And anyway, Nancy is still after you.*

Peter: *She's not after me.*

Barbara: *Then you're after her.*

Peter: *Neither of us is after the other. We're just friends. Can't I have a friend? Must I be with you 24 hours a day? I have my own life you know. Or rather I had my own life 2 years ago.*

Barbara: *Then you don't care for me. We might as well break up.*

Peter: *Well, if that's what you want then, fine.*

Barbara: *But, I don't want that. You know I don't. I want us to be together.*

Peter: *So, we're together. What more do you want?*

Barbara: *I want to know you care for me.*

Peter: *I care.*

Barbara: *I want to know more than that.*

Peter: *I care. I care. I care. What else do you want me to say?*

Barbara: *Even Carol and Donald say we should talk about the relationship. Even my mother said we should. I should know where we stand.*

Peter: *I'm not going out with Carol and Donald and I'm certainly not going out with your mother. She's a real pain.*

Barbara: *You always say that. You never did like my mother.*

Peter: *Correct. I never did. And I don't now.*

Barbara: *And your mother is so great? Always calling up to find out if we're living together? Always calling to see if you need anything? She treats you like a real baby. Maybe that's why you're the way you are— never wanting to make a decision or a commitment. Maybe you're afraid of leaving the womb, of leaving mother.*

Peter: *I'm not afraid of leaving my mother. I'm afraid of you becoming my mother. I've had enough of my mother. I don't want to marry my mother.*

Barbara: *Oh, so that's it. You don't want to marry me.*

Peter: *I didn't say that.*

Barbara: *But that's what you meant. Well, if that's the case then I might as well leave.*

Peter: *Fine. If that's the way you feel.*

Barbara: *Maybe that is better. Maybe I'll find someone who doesn't always have a headache.*

Peter: *What is that supposed to mean?*

Barbara: *It means that you never seem to want to do anything.*

Peter: *I would if you gave me a chance. I'm supposed to be the one to* make the first moves, not you. I'm the man, remember. And I wasn't as experienced as you were.

Barbara: *Sometimes I'm not so sure you're the man. Sometimes I really wonder. [After an extended pause.] Don't I have needs too? Why can't I make the first move?*

Peter: *I don't know. But I'm supposed to be the aggressor.*

Barbara: *Then why don't you?*

Peter: *I would if you gave me a chance. Anyway, if that's all you want, then maybe you should find somebody else. Who cares?*

Barbara: *I guess nobody.*

[Barbara walks out in anger while Peter turns up the stereo and falls onto the couch.]

ETHICS IN INTERPERSONAL COMMUNICATION

Upon completion of this unit, you should be able to:
1. explain Karl Wallace's ethical basis of communication
2. explain Paul Keller's and Charles Brown's interpersonal ethic for communication
3. explain the concept of choice as it relates to ethics in interpersonal communication
4. formulate your own tentative theory of ethics in interpersonal communication

All interpersonal communication interactions have an ethical dimension. All interpersonal interactions, therefore, must be considered not only in terms of effectiveness-ineffectiveness or satisfaction-dissatisfaction, for example, but also in terms of right-wrong, justified-unjustified, moral-immoral. Ethical considerations are an essential and integral component of all interpersonal interactions.

This unit outlines three systems of ethics—three positions on the ethics of interpersonal interaction—and attempts to raise a number of questions concerning this right-wrong dimension of communication by focusing on three communication situations that raise ethical issues. This discussion is intended to stimulate you to develop and to crystalize your own position concerning the ethics of interpersonal communication rather than to persuade you to accept any of the positions explained here.

POSITION ONE: AN ETHICAL BASIS OF COMMUNICATION

Karl Wallace, in "An Ethical Basis of Communication," postulates certain principles, or guidelines, for ethical communication. These guidelines, contends Wallace, are not external to communication; rather, "communication carries its ethics within itself. Communication of any kind is inseparable from the values which permeate a free and democratic community."

Wallace's ethic is based on the essential values of a free and democratic society. According to Wallace, these values include the dignity and worth of the **47** individual, equality of opportunity, freedom, and the opportunity of an individual to grow and develop to the limits of his or her capacity. On the basis of these four democratic values, Wallace suggests four "moralities," four principles that he feels should govern speech communication behavior.

1. "A communicator in a free society must recognize that during the moments of his utterance he is the sole source of argument and information." This calls for communicators having a thorough knowledge of their topic, an ability to answer any relevant questions, and an awareness of the significant facts and opinions.

2. "The communicator who respects the democratic way of life must select and present fact and opinion fairly." The communicator must, in Wallace's words, "preserve a kind of equality of opportunity among ideas." This principle calls upon the communicator to provide the hearer with an opportunity to make fair judgments.

3. "The communicator who believes in the ultimate values of democracy will invariably reveal the sources of his information and opinion." The communicator must assist the audience in evaluating any prejudices and biases that might be inherent in the sources by revealing them to the audience.

4. "A communicator in a democratic society will acknowledge and will respect diversity of argument and opinion." The ethical communicator should be able to admit the weight of the opposing argument and evidence if he or she intends to ethically defend an opposing position. This principle calls for a "tolerance of dissent."

There are a number of difficulties in putting this system into operation. What constitute a "thorough knowledge of the topic" and "an ability to answer relevant questions" are not easy to determine. Similarly, what constitute a fair presentation of facts and opinions, a full presentation of (all) sources of information, and a respect for diversity of argument and opinion are equally difficult to determine. Yet the four principles provide some guidance in this most difficult area.

POSITION TWO: AN INTERPERSONAL ETHIC
FOR COMMUNICATION

For the most part, traditional approaches to ethics have focused on the message. They have concerned themselves with, for example, falsification of evidence, lying, distortion of facts and figures, and extreme emotional appeals. To Paul Keller and Charles Brown, these message aspects, although important, are not the only factors to consider in developing an ethic for communication.

Keller and Brown propose an interpersonal ethic for communication—an ethical perspective that focuses on the speaker and the hearer and their attitudinal and behavioral responses to each other. In this system communication is ethical (or, perhaps more correctly, communicators are ethical) when there is acceptance of the responses of others. Assume, for example, that a hearer does not agree with something for which you have argued. Although you have presented what to you is incontrovertible evidence and argument, the hearer remains adamant in his or her contradictory belief. Your communications, according to this position, are ethical to the extent that they are accepting of this hearer's freedom of choice to agree or not to agree.

This point of view is based on the democratic value that "conditions be created and maintained in which the potential of the individual is best realized." The assumption, based on this value, which leads to the formulation of the ethical perspective of Keller and Brown, is that people will best be able to realize their potential when they are psychologically free; when they are not afraid to disagree; when their beliefs, opinions, and values are accepted rather than rejected.

The crucial questions to consider in this system, then, are, "How does the speaker respond to the listener's responses?" and "How does the listener respond to the speaker's responses?" Speakers communicate ethically if they react to enhance the self-determination of others. Speakers communicate unethically if they react to inhibit the self-determination of others.

Keller and Brown's system is particularly interesting because it lends an ethical dimension to matters not normally considered questions of ethics. For example, the instructor who will tolerate no disagreement and will belittle students who disagree is, according to this system, unethical. Group members who sulk and withdraw whenever they do not get their way are likewise unethical in their communications. The instructor and the group members are guilty of unethical behavior since they are acting in a manner that inhibits rather than enhances the self-determination of others.

This system also raises the problem of operationalizing the processes by which an individual's self-determination is enhanced. To what extent does disagreement (verbal or nonverbal) restrict an individual's freedom? How does one behave so that an individual feels free, unafraid to disagree, and accepted? How do we disagree with someone and still conform to the principles set forth in this system of interpersonal ethics?

POSITION THREE: AN ETHICAL BASIS
FOR CHOICE

Although the first two positions have much to recommend them, I find the following approach more satisfying, more complete, and applicable to a greater number of situations. In this system, the major determinant of whether communications are ethical or unethical is to be found in the notion of choice. It is assumed that individuals have a right to make their own choices. Interpersonal communications are ethical to the extent that they facilitate the individual's freedom of choice by presenting the other person with accurate bases for choice. Communications are unethical to the extent that they interfere with the individual's freedom of choice by preventing the other person from securing information relevant to the choices she or he will make. Unethical communications, therefore, would be those that force the individual (1) to make choices she or he would not normally make and/or (2) to decline to make choices she or he would normally make.

An interpersonal ethic based on choice, an ethic which is based on the belief that each person has a right to make her or his own choices, assumes a view of interpersonal communication as dialogue rather than as monologue. The distinction between these two forms of communication should further clarify this ethical position. *Monologue* refers to a form of communication in which one person speaks and the others listen; there is no interaction among participants. The focus is clearly and solely on the one person doing the speaking. The term *monologic communication* or "communication as monologue" is a kind of extension of this basic definition and refers to communication in which there is no genuine interaction, in which one speaks without any real concern for the other person's feelings or attitudes, in which one is concerned only with his or her own goals and is interested in the other person only insofar as he or she can benefit the speaker.

"Of course it needs a little touching up. What house doesn't?"

In *dialogue* there is a two-way interaction; each person is both speaker and listener, both sender and receiver. In *dialogic communication* or "communication as dialogue" there is deep concern for the other person and for the relationship formed between the two individuals. The objective of dialogic communication is mutual understanding and empathy. There is a respect for the other person not because of what this person can do for you, but simply because this person is a human being and therefore deserves to be treated with honesty, with caring, and with sincerity.

In a monologic interaction one communicates to the other that which will advance one's own goals, that which will prove most persuasive, that which will benefit oneself. In a dialogic interaction, the individual respects the other person enough to allow that person the right to make his or her own choices without coercion, without the threat of punishment, without fear or social pressure. A dialogic communicator respects other people enough to believe that they can make decisions that are right for them and will implicitly or explicitly let them know that whatever choices they make, they will still be respected as people. In Carl Rogers's terms, the dialogic communicator gives unconditional positive regard to others. This is true regardless of whether one agrees or disagrees with their choices. When we feel that the choices another makes are illogical or unproductive, we may attempt to persuade them to do otherwise, but we do not withdraw (or threaten to withdraw) our positive regard for them as human beings who, because they are human beings and for no other reason, have the right to make their own choices (and mistakes).

The ethical communicator, then, provides others with the kind of information that is helpful in making their own choices. In this ethic based on choice, however, there are a few qualifications that may restrict one's freedom of choice. It is assumed that these individuals are of the age and mental condition to allow free choice to be reasonably executed and that they are in situations in which their free choice does not prevent the free choice of others. A child of 5 or 6 is not ready to make certain choices, and so someone else must make them instead. Similarly, some mentally incompetent individuals need others to make certain decisions for them. The circumstances under which one is living also can restrict free choice; for example, persons in the military will at times have to give up free choice and eat hamburger rather than steak, wear uniforms rather than jeans, and march rather than stay in bed. By entering the armed forces, the right to make one's own choices has been given up, at least partially.

The free choices we make must not prevent others from making their free choices. We cannot permit a thief to have freedom of choice to steal, because in the granting of that freedom we are in effect preventing the victims from exercising their free choice. These, then, are some of the qualifications that must be considered in any theory of choice as an ethical guide. Admittedly, it is not always easy to determine when people possess the mental ability to make their own decisions or when the choice of one person actually prevents the choices of another from being exercised. Yet these are the vagaries we must contend with in any theory concerned with the morality of human behavior.

With these qualifications recognized, some of the applications of this position to relatively specific situations may be pointed out. It is generally easier to proceed in this type of situation from the negative, and so I will attempt to explain those situations in which interpersonal communications are unethical.

Lying

Lying or otherwise hiding the truth is unethical because it prevents another person from learning about possible alternative choices. Consider the situation in which a patient is given 6 months to live. Is it ethical for the doctor or for family members to tell the patient that he or she is doing fine and that the tests were all negative? Utilizing our notion of choice, we would have to conclude that this is unethical. In not telling the patient the truth, we are making choices for him or her; we are, in effect, preventing the individual from living these last 6 months or so as he or she might want to, given the knowledge of imminent death. Similarly, the parents who keep the truth about their child's adoption secret (after the child has become "of age") are eliminating the child's right to make a number of choices she or he might wish to make. Such choices might, for example, concern the finding of her or his biological parents or the recognition of a different ethnic or religious heritage.

To lie about one's infidelity (whether or not we see infidelity itself as unethical) would be unethical because it prevents the other person from making choices that might be made if this information were available. Knowing that a partner was unfaithful may lead the individual to make choices that would not be made under the assumption or belief of complete fidelity. To falsely say "I love you," to misrepresent your abilities in a job interview, or to lie about the cleaning power of a soap are all examples of preventing people from making certain choices that they might make if they knew our actual romantic feelings, our true abilities, or the real power of the soap.

It must be assumed that each person has the right to make his or her own choices; thus, if we misrepresent or hide certain facts, then we prevent that person from making choices he or she has a right to make. If we take the position that the truth is manipulated for the person's own good, then we are in effect saying that we—and not the individual—have the right to make the choice. I like to think that we each have the right to hear those messages that bear our names.

Individuals may, of course, give up their right to such information. The patient may have made it known that she or he does not want to know when death will occur. Marital partners may make an agreement not to reveal their affairs. When this is the case, there is no lying, no deceit, and hence no unethical behavior in not revealing this information.

Another issue involved here is that of the request for an honest opinion versus the request for positive stroking (praise, compliments, and the like). Consider the person who arrives in a new outfit, looking pretty awful. The person asks you what you think of the new look. There seem to be a number of options. First, you can say something to the effect that it sure is different—unique, even—something quite unlike anything you have ever seen before. Second, you might, in a burst of total honesty, say that it is the worst outfit you have ever seen: "It makes you look fat, old, and sickly." Third, you might say that the outfit is really becoming—attractive, even—and suits your personality and body structure really well.

The first response, although technically and literally evasive and noncommittal, is actually leading the other person to conclude the opposite of what you mean, and this seems to me to be lying. The second response is truthful but insensitive and cruel. And the third is dishonest, although at the time you make the comment it may seem kind. But on future occasions—when, for example, the person shows up for an important job interview or date dressed in this way—it may turn out to be the cruelest of all responses.

If our primary concern is for the person asking us the question, then we must consider what that person is really seeking. If the question really asks us to evaluate the new outfit, then we should focus on this and give our honest opinion in as kind and responsive (but truthful) a manner as possible. Thus, instead of saying, "It makes you look fat, old, and sickly," we can more appropriately say, "I think you would look much better in something different, something more colorful, something with vertical rather than horizontal stripes." If, on the other hand, the question asks us to say something nice about the person (and the question about the outfit is just an excuse to get some positive stroking), then we should address that question and say something that will provide the positive strokes the person is seeking. Here is one of the many instances in which specific content is not important; it is the psychological need of the person that must be our concern.

Fear and Emotional Appeals

One of the most widely discussed ethical issues in communication is the legitimacy of fear and emotional appeals. Although this topic is frequently focused on public and mass communication situations, it is even more applicable to interpersonal encounters.

Consider the mother and father who are afraid that their child will be molested by some stranger. They warn the child to stay away from strangers, not to take candy or money from people the child does not know, and to stay out of cars, hallways, and dark alleys where strangers might loiter. They attempt to gain compliance by instilling fear in the child. To the child's natural question, "Why?" they build elaborate stories about what strangers do to little boys and girls. Depending upon their originality, such stories could range from the imposition of slavery to starvation, beating, and death. The real reason, that they might be sexually molested, is probably never mentioned.

In this type of situation many would side with the mother and father. The young child, it would be argued, is not knowledgeable enough to understand about sexual molestation, and yet some means is needed to persuade the child to keep his or her distance from strangers. The use of fear, then, serves the parents well and protects the child from various dangers.

This same type of appeal is used frequently in interpersonal situations. Take, for example, the mother who does not want her teenage son or daughter of 18 or 19 to move out of the house. Again, depending upon her creativity, her method might focus on instilling fear in the teenager for his or her own well-being ("Who'll care for you? You won't eat right. You'll get sick.") or, more frequently, for the mother's well-being. The caricature of a mother having a heart attack at the first sign of the child's leaving is probably played every day, in various forms, throughout the world. But whether a heart attack is used or some other gross difficulty that is sure to result should the teenager leave home, fear is nevertheless relied on. Obviously, no child wants to be the cause of his or her mother's suffering. It is interesting to note that in our culture the father is

At least in our stereotypes (and perhaps in experience), this is the classical unethical communicator.

not permitted to use his own suffering as an argument. Rather, his task is to show the children how much their leaving home will hurt their mother. Together, parents can make a most effective team.

Parents are actually quite adept at using fear appeals and will use them to discourage anything from smoking (tobacco or grass) to premarital sex to interracial dating. The list—as any young person knows, or, indeed, as any person who has ever been young knows—is endless. Similar issues are raised when we consider the use of emotional appeal in attempting to change attitudes, beliefs, and behaviors. The case of the real estate broker appealing to our desire for status, the friend who wants a favor appealing to our desire for social approval, and the salesperson appealing to our desire for sexual rewards are all familiar examples. The question they all raise is simply, "Is this type of appeal justified?"

There are many arguments that can be adduced for both sides of the issue. The "everyone is doing it" argument is perhaps the most familiar but does not really answer the question of whether or not such appeals are justified. We are a combination of logic and emotion; consequently, we are persuaded by both types of appeals. To be effective, one would thus have to utilize both types of appeals. Again, however, this does not answer the question of whether or not such emotional appeals are ethical; it merely states that they are effective. (But we knew that already.)

At times we consider the extent of the appeals and their effect on the individuals. One argument says that emotional appeals are justified as long as individuals retain their powers of reasoning. Emotional appeals become unjustified when they short-circuit the reasoning processes. Exactly when people are in possession of such "powers" or when their reasoning is "short-circuited" is, unfortunately, not made clear.

The question of fear and emotional appeals is not as easy to fit into the issue of freedom of choice as is lying. The reason is that it is difficult to determine at what point the use of fear or emotion prevents certain choices from being selected. Furthermore, we must recognize that both parties have the right to free choice. Some might argue that the parents of the teenager who wishes to leave home are unethical when they force the teenager to choose between leaving home and hurting them, on the one hand, and staying home and pleasing them, on the other. To many this would not be *free* choice. Similarly, a group of individuals who withdraw social support from an individual unless he or she does as they wish may be charged by some with unethically limiting the individual's freedom of choice. Although it is true that the teenager and the deviant group member are physically free to do as they wish, they may be emotionally pressured to the point where they may not be free in any meaningful sense of the term.

On the other hand, it might be argued that the parents of the teenager also have rights and that they have the specific right to display their emotional hurt should the child wish to leave home. Similarly, it might be argued that the group members have the right to withdraw their social support from an individual if they so wish.

Clearly this is a difficult situation to resolve. To preserve the freedom of choice for both sides of a conflict and at the same time not allow the freedoms of one side to unduly restrict the freedoms of the other side is not easy. Part of the difficulty, I think, is due to the fact that we are on the outside looking in rather than being actual participants in the conflict. My own feeling is that the parents, for example, have the right to display their hurt if this is their honest emotional response to the child's leaving home. However, if it is a technique designed to develop guilt in the child and to prevent the child from exercising certain options, then their behaviors must be judged unethical. Similarly, the group members who withdraw their support from the individual have a right to do so if they decide that because of these deviant behaviors they do not wish to associate or interact with this individual any longer. However, if they are using the withdrawal of social support to "force" the individual to conform and consequently to limit the individual's freedom of choice to select certain options rather than others, then the group members, I think, are behaving unethically. In these situations, it is only the participants (the parents and the group members, in these examples) who can decide if they are acting fairly or unfairly, ethically or unethically.

The Prevention of Interaction

Among the most obvious instances where interactions are prevented are those concerning interracial marriage and homosexual relations. These prohibitions prevent certain groups of persons from interacting in the manner in which they wish. If an interracial couple wish to get married, the places in which such a marriage is performed and where they settle must be chosen carefully. Interracial couples will run into difficulty in finding housing, employment, and, most significantly, acceptance into a community. Likewise, homosexuals will have difficulty in much the same way, and consequently many of them are forced to live "straight" lives—at least on the surface.

If you run a business, for example, should you have the right to refuse a job to a person because that person is married to an individual of another race or because that person has an affectional orientation different from yours? And if you do have the right to choose your employees on the basis of such preferences, do you still retain the rights to protection of the law which the society as a whole has granted to everyone?

Homosexuals are currently prevented from holding jobs as teachers, police officers, firefighters, and so forth in most states. These discriminatory laws are not terribly effective, but this is not the issue. The relative ineffectiveness of such prohibitions should not blind us to the social realities that these laws incorporate. What should be considered is that the homosexual cannot work as a homosexual but only as a heterosexual. We do not ask that a black act white—although society once did demand this in often subtle ways. We do not ask a Jew to act like a Christian or a Christian to act like a Jew if he or she wants a job—although, again, some persons do. Yet we do ask homosexuals that they not reveal their true identities. These persons are only accepted if they act like the majority. But are we being ethical when we require such concealment of identity?

Human Communication Research 7 (Summer 1981):325–339.

For communication as dialogue and its ethical implications, see, for example, Richard L. Johannesen, "The Emerging Concept of Communication as Dialogue," *Quarterly Journal of Speech* 57 (1971):373–382, and Charles T. Brown and Paul W. Keller, *Monologue to Dialogue: An Exploration of Interpersonal Communication,* 2d ed. (Englewood Cliffs, N.J.: Prentice-Hall, 1979), pp. 294–310. The concept of dialogue, of course, was most insightfully explained by Martin Buber, *I and Thou,* 2d ed. (New York: Scribner's, 1958), and *Between Man and Man,* Ronald Gregor Smith, trans. (New York: Macmillan, 1972). The dialogic approach to interpersonal communication is perhaps best outlined by T. Dean Thomlison, *Toward Interpersonal Dialogue* (New York: Longman, 1982).

EXPERIENTIAL VEHICLES

4.1 SOME ETHICAL ISSUES

This exercise is designed to raise only a few of the many questions that could be raised concerning the ethics of interpersonal communication and to encourage you to think in concrete terms about some of the relevant issues. The purpose is not to persuade you to a particular point of view but rather to encourage you to formulate your own point of view.

The exercise consists of a series of cases, each raising somewhat different ethical questions. This exercise will probably work best if you respond to each of the cases individually and then discuss your decisions and their implications in groups of five or six. In these small groups simply discuss those cases that you found most interesting. The most interesting cases for small group discussion will probably be those that were the most difficult for you to respond to, that is, those that involved the most internal conflict. A general discussion in which the various groups share their decisions and insights may conclude the session.

Guidelines

1. Carefully read each of the following cases and write down your responses. By writing your decisions, many issues that may be unclear will come to the surface and may then be used as a basis for discussion.
2. Your responses will not be made public, your papers will not be collected, and your decisions will be revealed only if you wish to do so. If individuals wish not to reveal their decisions, do not attempt to apply any social pressure to get them to make these decisions public.
3. Do not attempt to avoid the issues presented in the various cases by saying, for example, "I'd try other means." For purposes of these exercises, other means are ruled out.
4. Focus some attention in the small group discussions on the origin of the various values implicit in your decisions. You might, as a starting point, consider how your parents would respond to these cases. Would their decisions be similar or different from yours?
5. Devote some attention to the concept of change. Would you have responded in similar fashion 5 years ago? If not, what has led to the change? Would you predict similar responses 5 or 10 years from now? Why? Why not? This concept of change is also significant in another

respect. Focus attention on the changes or possible changes that might occur as a result of your acting in accordance with any of the decisions. That is, is the student who sells drugs the same individual he or she was before doing this? Can this student ever be the same individual again? How is this student different? If we accept the notion, even in part, that how we act or behave influences what we are, how does this relate to the decisions we make on these issues?

6. Consider the concept of acceptance. How willing is each group member to accept the decisions of others? Are you accepting of your own decisions? Why? Why not? Would you be pleased if your children would respond in the same way you did?

7. Note that there are three questions posed after each case. The first two focus on what you *should* do and what you *would* do. The distinction between these two questions is crucial and is particularly significant when your answers for the two questions are different. When answers for the *should* and the *would* questions differ, try to analyze the intrapersonal dynamics. How do you account for the difference? Is there intrapersonal conflict? Are these differences the result of changes you are going through? How pleased/displeased are you with the differences in answers? The third question asks you to consider the implications of your choices on the *should* and *would* questions. That is, what do your answers to the first two questions mean in a more general sense?

Imminent Death

You have a very close friend or relative who has a fatal illness that is sure to result in the person's death within the next 6 months. The person knows that the illness is a progressive one but does not know that death is imminent. Assume here that there is no possibility of an error having been made in the diagnosis or prognosis; the person is sure to die within the next 6 months. Since you are the closest friend (or relative), the doctors have left the decision as to whether or not this person should be informed up to you.

1. What should you do?
2. What would you do?
3. What are the implications of your choices?

Self-Disclosure

You are currently dating a wonderful person whom you eventually hope to marry, perhaps in the next year or so. You get along in every way. You have similar interests and values, you are supportive of each other—in short, you just enjoy being with each other. There seems to be only one problem: you were married for a short time and then quietly divorced. You have a 3-year-old child who lives with your ex-spouse and whom you have not seen for over 2 years. You fear that if your previous marriage,

*child, and divorce were made known, the relationship might break up.
You do not want to keep this information secret, and yet you do not want to
endanger the relationship.*

1. What should you do?
2. What would you do?
3. What are the implications of your choices?

Children's Hospital

*You have been put in charge of raising money for your town's new
children's hospital—a hospital that is badly needed. There are a number
of crippled children who are now wearing heavy braces and who must
walk with crutches. These children, you reason, would be very effective in
influencing people to give to the hospital fund. As a conclusion to a
program of speeches by local officials and entertainment, you consider
having these children walk through the audience and tell the people how
desperately they need this hospital. An appeal by these children, you feel,
would encourage many of the people to make donations, which they
would not make if a more reasoned and logical appeal was presented. You
know from past experience that other available means of persuasion will
not be effective.*

1. What should you do?
2. What would you do?
3. What are the implications of your choices?

The Interview and the Self-Monitor

*You are in the middle of a job interview. The interviewer has left the room
for a few minutes and you are now reflecting on the previous few minutes
and on your chances of getting the job. During these first few minutes you
have been able to tell what the interviewer is looking for. You can easily
modify and monitor your behaviors so that you make the best impression
possible—you have done so frequently in the past. This often amounts to a
pretense of being someone you are not. Recently, you've begun to wonder
if this type of behavior—if this impression management or self-monitoring
that you are so adept at—is really ethical. You wonder if it is morally
justified to appear to be someone you are not. You hear the interviewer
returning and your dilemma becomes clearly focused. It comes down to
this: You will stand a better chance of getting the job if you carefully
monitor your behavior and present an image of yourself that is not your
"real" self. You stand to make a less favorable impression if you convey
what you really think and feel. You want the job and yet you also want to
present your real self.*

1. What should you do?
2. What would you do?
3. What are the implications of your choices?

The Honest Versus the Effective Resumé

You are currently a college teacher. You have worked actively for numerous women's liberation groups and have written extensively on the issues involved in women's liberation. You are firmly committed to the philosophy of women's liberation and number it among your most important identifications. Unfortunately, you recently received notice that you are not to be rehired next semester. You have decided to enter the business world and you have your eyes set on one particular position. Regrettably, they are not in favor of women's liberation. In fact, you know that they would view your work negatively, which may lead them to select another candidate for the job. You are now preparing your resumé and are considering what to include and what not to include. You honestly feel that your work in the area has been good and you are proud of it. Yet, you know that this will work against you in getting the position you want.

1. What should you do?
2. What would you do?
3. What are the implications of your choices?

The Right to Privacy

You are a counselor at a local high school and for the past 3 years have been counseling students in academic and personal-social matters. Although your job is to counsel students in all areas, a great deal of your time is taken up with counseling them in the area of sex education and especially in the area of birth control. You have given the students information of all sorts—about the various types of birth control devices, where to obtain them, how to use them, and so on. You have also, on occasion, given the students the birth control devices. The Parents Association now wants you to inform the parents as soon as a student requests birth control information. The Parents Association argues that it is the parents' right to give or to refuse to give their children such information. Teenagers living at home and supported by their parents do not, their parents argue, have the right to privacy that has often been mentioned in situations like these. On the one hand, you do not want to assume the role of the parent but you know that the students come to you because you do respect their privacy. They come to you because they will not or cannot go to their parents. Your job is not in jeopardy; you may do whatever you think is right without suffering any sort of harm. Your problem is to decide what is the right thing to do.

1. What should you do?
2. What would you do?
3. What are the implications of your choices?

Buying a Paper

You are now taking an elective course in anthropology. You need an A in this course in order to maintain the average you think you will need to graduate. *Although you have done the required work, you are running only a B— at best. The instructor has told you that you will get an A in the course if you write an extra paper and get an A on it. You want to write this paper but are too pressed for time; you need to put what time you do have available into your other courses. You hear about one of those "paper mills" that, for approximately $100, will provide you with a paper that should get you the A in the course. You can easily afford the $100 fee.*

1. What should you do?
2. What would you do?
3. What are the implications of your choices?

4.2 A TENTATIVE THEORY OF INTERPERSONAL ETHICS

Formulate here what might be called, "My Tentative Theory of Interpersonal Ethics." Formulate a theory that you feel is reasonable, justified, internally consistent, and consonant with your own system of values. Construct your theory so that it incorporates, at a minimum, all of the situations presented in the previous exercise. That is, given this statement of ethical principles, another individual should be able to accurately predict how you would behave in each of the situations presented in the cases in Experiential Vehicle 4.1.

4.3 TERMINOLOGICAL MAZE: REVIEW QUIZ I

Fifteen terms used in the study of interpersonal communication are hidden in the following "Terminological Maze." The terms may be read forward, backward, up, down, or diagonally but are always in a straight line. The terms may overlap, and individual letters may be used more than once. The terms are those used in the first four units; their definitions and some identifying clues follow.

1. a relationship in which one person's behavior is the stimulus for similar behavior from the other person
2. effective communication is
3. the moral dimension of communication
4. feeling what another person feels
5. has physical, temporal, and social-psychological dimensions
6. is always present in a communication interaction and interferes with one's receiving the message sent
7. all communications have this, but it is often difficult to locate and measure
8. a type of message that provides the source with information as to the effect he or she is having; may be positive or negative

9. a basis for ethics
10. this may be either verbal or nonverbal
11. language is one example
12. postulate or commonly accepted truism
13. most prefer the positive type but seem to prefer even a negative one to none at all
14. the geometric figure that seems to best describe communication
15. when there is great overlap there is a greater likelihood of effective communication; field of . . .

TERMINOLOGICAL MAZE

L	A	C	I	R	T	E	M	M	Y	S
A	X	I	Y	O	Q	T	Y	L	E	T
B	I	R	A	U	E	H	E	D	E	R
C	O	C	A	F	T	I	O	K	L	O
M	M	L	U	A	U	C	I	Z	O	K
P	W	E	P	M	E	S	S	A	G	E
T	N	M	O	T	X	E	T	N	O	C
C	E	S	I	O	N	P	I	D	E	I
E	A	E	I	U	Y	Q	C	V	I	O
F	B	I	P	U	W	M	P	S	L	H
F	E	E	D	B	A	C	K	A	B	C
E	X	P	E	R	I	E	N	C	E	E

THE SELF IN INTERPERSONAL COMMUNICATION
PART TWO

UNIVERSALS OF THE SELF

Upon completion of this unit, you should be able to:
1. diagram and explain the model of the semantic transactor
2. distinguish among and give examples of electrochemical, self-moving, feeling, and thinking activities
3. state three corollaries of the semantic transactor model
4. discuss critically Bois's semantic transactor model
5. explain the relevance of Bois's model to your own intrapersonal and interpersonal interactions
6. prepare an original model of the self

The self—its nature, its parts, and its functions—is perhaps the most complex of all interpersonal communication components, and our knowledge of this area is admittedly far from complete. Yet if we are to arrive at a reasonably complete understanding of interpersonal communication, then we need to explore the self, however complex it is and however incomplete our knowledge might be. The reason for this is simple: an understanding of the self is a prerequisite to an understanding of interpersonal communication.

This is true for a number of reasons. First, if we are to understand any process, we need to understand its parts, and the self is a part—perhaps the most important part—of the interpersonal communication process. Second, the messages generated and received are in large part a function of the self, and to understand the messages, we need to understand the self. Third, the effectiveness of our interpersonal communications is related to the effectiveness of the self generally, and if we are to understand effective communication, we must understand the effective self.

The self is best approached through a general model of its essential components and relationships. Although there are numerous models to choose from, the one proposed by J. S. Bois seems to be the most useful and the most insightful for interpersonal communication. The self, in this view, is referred to as a *semantic transactor*. "We call this complex transaction of the whole organism a *semantic* transaction," says Bois; "that is, a transaction that is determined by what the actual situation—the outside event, the word that is spoken, the thought that occurs, the hope that emerges—means to the individual at the moment."

A MODEL OF THE SELF

Bois's model of the semantic transactor is presented in Figure 5.1. Focus first on the four activities in the center of the model.

The Activities of the Self

Electrochemical Activities

Electrochemical activities refer to the bodily functions that begin with the operation of DNA and RNA in the genes and include neuronal activity and bodily reactions to drugs—the effects of LSD, of birth control pills, of marijuana, of caffeine, of diet pills, and the like. Such bodily activities are revealed through laboratory analyses of blood and tissue, and through electrocardiograms and electroencephalograms.

Self-Moving Activities

Self-moving activities include the autonomic movements of the various bodily organs, such as the heart, lungs, and intestines, as well as the consciously controlled movements of body parts such as the hands, legs, and head. The activities labeled "self-moving" would include anything from the beating of the heart to the skilled movements of the surgeon or artist. Also included here would be the movements involved in such activities as marching, singing, flag waving, playing basketball, and boxing.

Feeling Activities

Feeling activities include the operation of needs and drives, wants and fears, hopes and ambitions. This group of activities, more uniquely human than the first two groups, would include love and hate, commitment and indifference, trust and distrust, happiness and sorrow, contentment and frustration.

Thinking Activities

Thinking activities include all those functions that involve symbolic processes, such as the mathematical operations of adding and subtracting, conceptualizing and abstracting, speaking and writing, listening and reading, asking and answering questions, decision making, and strategy formulation. Thinking activities may vary from writing a short note to conceptualizing the plans for building a skyscraper.

The Self as a Whole in Transaction

The way in which these four activities are represented in Figure 5.1 attempts to emphasize that each activity is related to each of the other activities. No activity is separate or distinct from any other activity; rather, all are closely related and mutually dependent. They are all aspects or dimensions of the self as a whole—of the self as a semantic transactor. For example, if we attempt to

solve a very difficult mathematical problem, this activity is not limited solely to
the thinking aspect of the self. It also influences and is influenced by our feeling
activities; witness how angry we become when we fail to solve a problem and
how difficult it is to think clearly when emotionally upset. In this problem-solv-
ing experience our self-moving and electrochemical activities are likewise
involved. Our heart rate might increase and the energizer we took to stay awake
would further influence our responses. On the other hand, if you participate in
a ceremony of some sort—for example, a religious ceremony—you will probably emerge with a more sympathetic attitude than if you had not participated.
Demagogues have long known that one of the best ways to persuade people is
to elicit an overt expression of agreement. When this happens (on the surface,
a purely self-moving activity not involving any original conceptualization), the
individual's attitude almost always moves in the direction of the verbal advo-
cacy. This seems to be true even if the person is aware that he or she is only
participating in an experiment or exercise.

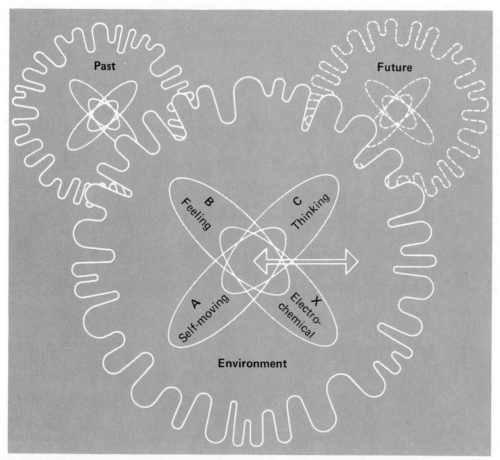

FIGURE 5.1
*Individuals as
Semantic
Transactors.
Source:* J. Samuel
Bois, *The Art of
Awareness,* 3d ed.
(Dubuque, Iowa:
Brown, 1978), p.
29.

The Self in a Context

The environment is indicated in the model as uneven and indefinite. This is to illustrate that at times the environment presses close to the individual and greatly limits the range of possible behaviors, while at other times it stretches far and does not exert significant influence. Nevertheless, the environment is always present and always exerts some influence. The self is never alone; it always operates within a context. This context influences the self and the behaviors in which the self engages. Similarly, however, the self also influences the context or environment. The environment that we were born into is not the same environment that exists now. People have changed it. And, of course, the environment that we leave when we die will be different still, in part because of what we have done to change it.

The environment, or context, as viewed here should be seen as consisting of a number of different aspects or dimensions. It has a physical dimension (the specific place we are in, such as a room or building), a social dimension (the type of function we are attending, whether a funeral or a wedding or a union meeting), a psychological dimension (the atmosphere of the context, whether friendly or hostile), and a cultural dimension (the prevailing value systems or the unwritten codes of acceptable and unacceptable behaviors). These four dimensions are not the only ones that could be singled out. Yet they seem to be four of the most important aspects. The self's interaction with the environment is signified in the model by the double arrow connecting the center of the interrelated ellipses with the environment.

The Self in Time

The self also functions in relation to time. The self lives not only in space but also in a world defined by time. The self operates in the present but always with some reference to the past and to the future. Present actions of the self are greatly influenced by its past experience and by the future it envisions. That the past influences the self is obvious; this seems to have been acknowledged since the beginning of recorded history—almost universally since Freud. We do or do not do things in part because of some past experience, insight, reward, or punishment. How much we are influenced by past experiences cannot be stated. Some theorists would argue that we are influenced by the past very little, while others would claim that the past influences us completely. The way we envision the future, the way we plan for it, and the way in which we see ourselves 10 or 20 years from now also influence what we do or think or feel in the present. You are now, for example, in college. This is the present. Yet you are here largely because of the future. Perhaps you anticipate getting a better job with a college degree, or you anticipate financial or social rewards. Or you may be in school because of some past situation, such as a promise to a parent or an unspoken expectation that you would go to college.

This, then, is the self—though not the whole self or the complete explanation. It represents some of the significant dimensions of the self that are especially pertinent to interpersonal communication. This model or point of view would define a human being, to use Bois's terms, as a "thinking, feeling, self-moving, electrochemical organism in continuous transaction with a space-time environment."

PRINCIPLES OF THE MODEL

Bois has suggested a number of corollaries that might be derived from his model. Here we look at a few of those that are especially relevant to understanding our specific selves and ourselves as interpersonal communicators.

Living in the Present

The larger frame—that of the present—is the center of the diagram and its center of gravity. If the future or the past becomes too large, it will physically unbalance the model, pulling it to the right or to the left. Psychologically, the same principle seems to operate when we place too much emphasis on the past or on the future. The model becomes unbalanced and the self becomes disoriented; it has difficulty functioning effectively and efficiently in the present. And the present is, of course, the only reality the self ever really knows.

We are probably all familiar with people who live their entire lives in the past; they recall the good old days when beer was a nickle a glass and when a satisfying dinner cost less than a dollar. They remember when there was clean air, no traffic jams, and low taxes. Remembering such details poses no real problem. A problem is caused, however, when all one does is remember the past. We are living in the present, and our primary attention must be to it. If we force ourselves to live in the past, we unbalance the self. People also live in the past when they carry attitudes and values from the past and attempt to apply them uncritically to the present. "Women belong in the home," is a classic example.

Then there is the individual who lives entirely for the future. This person refuses to enjoy anything now, refuses to spend a penny, and never engages in an activity that will not bring rewards in the future. This person's problem is that the future never comes. To such an individual the future is always tomorrow. He or she saves for the future but never sets a date for actually spending what is saved and so throughout life does nothing but save, eventually to die wealthy.

The effective self seems to live in the present with a recognition of (though not a reverence for) the past and the future. Present experiences are enjoyed as experiences and not merely as steps to some future goal. Put more concretely, one does not sit in college classes merely to obtain the bachelor's degree because of the desire to be an accountant, because of the desire to earn a lot of money, because one's brother went to college, because one wants to own one's own house, because of being promised a new car, because one wants to buy a boat, and so on. Rather, one should sit in a college class because the class is in itself an experience from which one can benefit, now and in the future. This concern for living in the present, for "present-moment living," has been defined by Richard Ruch as "the active realization that the past is over and final, the future does not exist, and the present is our only chance to have integrity." Put differently, we need to recognize intellectually as well as instinctively—in our thoughts as well as in our behaviors—that the present is the only reality we can ever know, that the past is gone and only exists in our memories, and that the future never really comes.

If we do not view the present as the most important period, we run the risk of spending too much time worrying about the future and feeling guilty about the past. Because we may worry too much about the future, we will often waste a great deal of our present time in worried planning for a future that

To live in the past or in the future prevents us from enjoying the present and from benefiting fully from the present experience.

never comes. By concentrating too heavily on the past, we risk spending a great deal of our present time feeling guilty about having done something wrong or having made a mistake some time ago.

Just as damaging as overemphasizing the past or the future is totally neglecting them. We are in part a product of our past and a product of our imagined and planned-for future. Consequently, we cannot ignore these aspects of the self. They are part of the self and exert influence on what the self is, what it does, and what it becomes. Persons who roll along without any consideration for the future are soon going to have problems, as rainy days do come. Similarly, individuals who think they can get along without any regard for yesterday soon find that the past has helped to make them what they are and that their past mistakes as well as successes are still a part of them and a part of other people's perceptions of them.

Balancing the Four Activities

Just as there is a tendency for the model to balance itself in terms of time, it also tends to balance itself in terms of the various dimensions of the self. The four activities have a tendency to stay in balance, and if there is excessive emphasis on one to the total or near exclusion of the others, the model will become unbalanced. This again has its realistic counterpart in the individual who attempts to be solely intellectual—to be devoid of feelings and emotions and to maintain full control. This excessive emphasis on the thinking activities will surely unbalance the model. Excessive emphasis on the feeling or emotional activities likewise creates problems. Excessive emphasis on drugs (on electrochemical activities) or on self-moving activities (caricatured in the superjock) likewise leads to unbalancing.

This is not to say that these four activities are evenly distributed at all times of our lives. Certainly they are not. At times the thinking activities are emphasized, at time the feeling activities, and so on. This is natural and productive. The problem seems to arise when one aspect is neglected to the point where it is never emphasized or when it is emphasized to the point that it becomes the central and only focus.

Our transactions, whether with people or objects or events or ideas, are always transactions of the organism as a whole and are never totally logical or totally emotional or totally self-moving or totally electrochemical. Whether we are conscious of it or not, we react as a whole and not in parts, with our logical part responding to a math problem and our feeling part responding to a naked body. Feeling is involved in the math problem and logic in our response to the naked body. Consequently, solving a mathematical problem, which may be primarily logical, may be aided or hindered by changes in the feeling, self-moving, or electrochemical aspects of the self. Our ability to solve a difficult problem will be greatly influenced by liquor, by a previous fight with a friend, by financial worries, by a sprained back, and so on.

Appreciating the Uniqueness of Semantic Transactions

The semantic transactor is always in process; it is forever moving, changing, and transforming. Its seven aspects are interacting with each other and are all in part formed from unique experiences and expectations. Because of the complex and dynamic qualities of the self, it is impossible for any two semantic transactions to be identical. One implication of this is that no two people can ever perceive the same event in the same way or react to the same person in the same way. We are each unique individuals (our semantic transactor dimensions are never the same as any one else's); each sees the world and each reacts to the world in a different way.

Much as no two people can have the same semantic transactions, no one person can have the same semantic transaction on two different occasions. This must be true since the model is in a constant state of change and one's semantic transactor model of today must be different from one's semantic transactor model of tomorrow and even of 10 minutes from now. No transaction, therefore, can ever be repeated. No two perceptions, no two evaluations, no two conceptualizations can ever be exactly the same.

The implication here is that contrary to much of what we have been taught, we should not assume that we should be extremely consistent in our behavior and in our evaluations. We are changing human beings, and we should not hold ourselves responsible tomorrow for an evaluation we make today. All our transactions are made, or should be made, on the best evidence we can assemble at the time. We should not assume that other evidence will not arise tomorrow. We should have an open mind and not lock ourselves into responding in a fixed way just to maintain some semblance of the consistency that someone, somewhere told us was a good thing and something to admire.

Exchanging Semantic Transactions

In this view we look at communication not as a transfer of some abstract idea from one head to another or of some words from one person's mouth to another person's ear, but rather as an exchange of semantic transactions. For the most meaningful communication—communication in its idealized form— we would have an interchange of semantic transactions. If you were to fully understand what I am trying to say right now, you would not only be participating in my thoughts but would be feeling what I am feeling emotionally and physically and electrochemically. You would experience my past and my anticipated future as I do, so that you would know more completely what my present semantic transactions are. Obviously, most people do not even come close to this kind of communication; most people seem content to hear the words and respond with other more-or-less appropriate words, which in turn are responded to with another group of more-or-less appropriate words, and so on. Rarely are attempts made to empathize with another, to feel what the other person is feeling, to exchange semantic transactions.

Bois's model does not explain completely how and why the self operates as it does. Yet it does explain some of the important dimensions and some of the important relationships of the self. In considering the various approaches to the self that follow, we should recognize a self such as the one presented here. For example, when we consider self-disclosure—revealing ourselves to others—it should be clear that this interaction is an electrochemical, self-moving, feeling, and thinking activity—that our past and envisioned future as well as our space-time environment influences and is influenced by self-disclosure. Whenever we talk of the self, we should visualize a semantic transactor.

SOURCES

The model and related insights presented in this unit are based on J. S. Bois, *The Art of Awareness: A Textbook on General Semantics and Epistemics,* 3d ed. (Dubuque, Iowa: Brown, 1978). A book from a totally different perspective but that deals with many of the same concepts is Albert Ellis and Robert A. Harper, *A New Guide to Rational Living* (Hollywood, Calif.: Wilshire, 1973). A readable and insightful discussion of the self and its functions may be found in Jess Lair, *I Ain't Much, Baby—But I'm All I've Got* (Garden City, N.Y.: Doubleday, 1972). An interesting study of the self-concept of students is Carolyn B. Smith and Larry R. Judd, "A Study of Variables Influencing Self-Concept and Ideal Self-Concept Among Students in the Basic Speech Course," *Speech Teacher* 23 (1974). For an extended discussion of the logic and importance of living in the present, see Richard S. Ruch, "Present-Moment Living," *Humanist* 39 (January–February 1979):32–35.

5.1 SELF-CONCEPT: PART I

Every experience we engage in should change us in some way, it is hoped for the better but sometimes for the worse. In order to determine whether this course and everything else that happens between the beginning and the end of the semester has any effect on the way in which we view ourselves, complete the following series of bipolar scales according to the way you see yourself now. Ideally, the responses should be dated, placed in a sealed envelope, and deposited with the instructor. At the end of the course you should fill out an identical set of scales and examine the differences (Unit 27).

A number of the exercises in this text make use of semantic differential scales such as these. The instructions given here should be followed whenever semantic differential scales are used.

Instructions for Completing Semantic Differential Scales

Rating a concept on the kind-cruel scale as an example, the seven positions should be interpreted as follows.

If you feel that the concept being rated is extremely kind or extremely cruel, mark the end positions as shown here:

Kind X ———————————————————— Cruel

or

Kind ————————————————— X Cruel

If you feel that the concept is *quite* kind or *quite* cruel, mark the scale as follows:

Kind ——— X ———————————— Cruel

or

Kind ————————————— X ——— Cruel

If you feel that the concept is *slightly* kind or *slightly* cruel, mark the scale as follows:

Kind ————————— X ————————— Cruel

or

Kind ————————————— X ——— Cruel

If you feel that the concept is neutral in regard to kindness or cruelty mark the center of the scale as follows:

Kind ——————— X ——————— Cruel

Note: Mark each scale in order, do not omit any scales; mark each scale only once; mark each scale on one of the seven scale positions; do not put a mark between positions.

ME

Happy							Sad
Positive							Negative
Healthy							Sick
Strong							Weak
Beautiful							Ugly
Honest							Dishonest
Good							Bad
Self-confident							Not self-confident
Active							Passive
Interesting							Boring
Graceful							Awkward
Pleasant							Unpleasant
Powerful							Powerless
Fast							Slow
Successful							Unsuccessful
Sociable							Unsociable
Realistic							Unrealistic
Optimistic							Pessimistic
Brave							Cowardly
Organized							Disorganized

5.2 VALUES AND COMMUNICATION

Divide the class into groups of approximately five or six. Each group is charged with the same basic task, but each discharges its task from a different perspective.

The general task is to select those objects that best reflect American values.

By "values" we mean those objects or ideas that people regard as positive or negative, beautiful or ugly, clean or dirty, pleasant or unpleasant, valuable or worthless, moral or immoral, just or unjust, true or false, and so forth, and those objects or ideas that influence the judgments and decisions that people make.

The only limitations or restrictions are that (1) five objects be selected—no more and no less (size, weight, and cost are of no consequence and should not influence your decisions), and that (2) the objects be in existence at the present time in the same form they will be in when chosen; that is, you may not construct objects specifically for selection or combine several objects and count them as one.

Each group is to select objects representing American values as seen from the point of view of one of the following groups:

1.	the previous generation	11.	college students
2.	the current generation	12.	professors
3.	the next generation	13.	blacks
4.	males	14.	whites
5.	females	15.	American Indians
6.	the poor	16.	Hispanics
7	the rich	17.	college-educated adults
8	the middle class	18.	high school-educated adults
9.	homosexuals	19.	scientists
10.	heterosexuals	20.	artists

Each group is then to report to the entire class the selections made and the specific values each selection represents. Discussion may then focus on any number of communication-related issues, such as:

1. the accuracy with which each group represented the values of the group it was assigned
2. the difficulty of communication across generations, sex, economic class, race, and so forth
3. the degrees of stereotyping evidenced by the objects and values selected
4. the degree to which the members' own values influenced their selections of values for the group assigned
5. the role of values in influencing interpersonal communication generally and of divergent values in hindering communication
6. the ways in which interpersonal communication might be facilitated when basic values differ

SELF-AWARENESS IN
INTERPERSONAL COMMUNICATION

OBJECTIVES

Upon completion of this unit, you should be able to:

1. explain the structure and general function of the Johari window
2. define the open, blind, hidden, and unknown selves
3. provide examples of information that might be contained in each of the four selves
4. define the concept of *congruence*
5. explain the concept of life positions or "scripts"
6. identify and explain the ways in which people in the four different life positions see themselves and others
7. explain at least three specific suggestions for increasing self-awareness

If we had to list some of the qualities we would like to possess, that of self-awareness would surely rank high. Most of us wish to know ourselves better. The reason is logical enough: we are in control of our thoughts and our behaviors only to the extent that we understand ourselves, that we are aware of our strengths and our weaknesses, our wants and our needs. Likewise, self-improvement is dependent on self-awareness; we need first to know where we are and who we are if we are to effectively improve our abilities and competencies, to effectively chart our futures.

The concept of self-awareness is central to an understanding of interpersonal communication and seems best explained by reference to two insightful theoretical models. The first is a model of the Johari window, which explains the four different selves of which we are each composed. The second is the model of transactional analysis, particularly that portion dealing with the four major life positions, those four attitudes that we maintain about ourselves and about others. With these as a foundation, we will then examine some of the ways we might increase our own self-awareness.

THE FOUR SELVES

This concept of self-awareness, basic to an understanding of both intrapersonal and interpersonal communication, is explained by the model of the four selves, the Johari window, presented in Figure 6.1. The model is broken **79** up into four basic areas, or quadrants, each of which contans a somewhat different self.

The Open Self

The open self represents all the information, behaviors, attitudes, feelings, desires, motivations, ideas, and so on that are known to the self and also known to others. The type of information included here might vary from one's name, skin color, and sex to one's age, political and religious affiliations, and batting average. Each individual's open self will vary in size depending upon the time and upon the individuals he or she is dealing with. At some times we are more likely to open ourselves up than at other times. If, for example, we opened ourselves and got hurt because of it, we might then close up a bit more than usual. Similarly, some people make us feel comfortable and support us; to them, we open ourselves wide, but to others we prefer to leave most of ourselves closed.

"The smaller the first quadrant," says Joseph Luft, "the poorer the communication." Communication is dependent upon the degree to which we open ourselves to others and to ourself. If we do not allow others to know us (that is, if we keep the open self small), communication between them and us becomes extremely difficult, if not impossible. We can communicate meaningfully only to the extent that we know each other and know ourselves. To improve communication, we have to work first on enlarging the open self.

We should also note that a change in the open area—or in any of the quadrants—will bring about a change in the other quadrants. We might visualize the entire model as being of constant size but each section as being variable, sometimes small, sometimes large. As one section becomes smaller, one or more of the others must become larger. Similarly, as one section becomes larger, one or

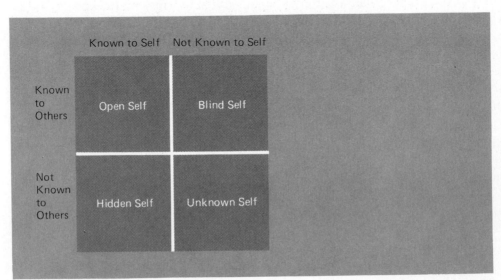

FIGURE 6.1
The Johari Window. The name Johari was derived from the first names of the two persons who developed the model: Joseph Luft and Harry Ingham.
Source: Joseph Luft, Group Processes: An Introduction to Group Dynamics (Palo Alto, Ca.: National Press Books, 1970), p. 11.

more of the others must become smaller. For example, if we enlarge the open self, this will shrink the hidden self. Further, this revelation or disclosure in turn will function to lead others to decrease the size of our blind selves by revealing to us what they know and we do not know.

Note that both the Johari window model and the semantic transactor model (considered in Unit 5) emphasize that the several aspects or dimensions of the self are not separate and distinct pieces but are parts of a whole that interact with each other; each part is intimately dependent upon each other part.

In Figure 6.2 two models of the self are presented to illustrate the different sizes of the four selves, depending upon the particular interpersonal situation. In Figure 6.2A let us assume that we are with a friend to whom we have opened up a great deal. Consequently, our open self is large and our hidden self is small. In Figure 6.2B let us assume that we are with a new employer who we do not know very well and with whom we are still a bit uncomfortable. Thus our open self is relatively small and our hidden self is large.

The Blind Self

The blind self represents all those things about ourselves that others know but of which we are ignorant. This may vary from the relatively insignificant habit of saying "you know" or rubbing your nose when you get angry or having a peculiar body odor to something as significant as defense mechanisms or fight strategies or repressed past experiences.

Some people have a very large blind self and seem to be totally oblivious to their own faults and sometimes (though not as often) their own virtues. Others seem overly concerned with having a small blind self. They seek therapy at

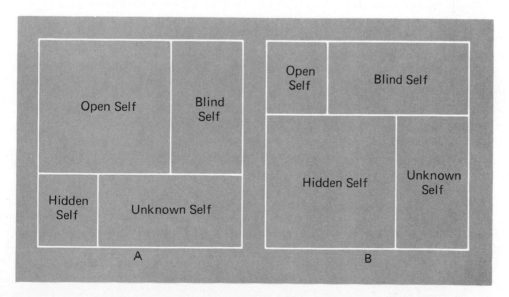

FIGURE 6.2
Two Models of the
Four Selves.

every turn and join every encounter group. Some are even convinced that they know everything there is to know about themselves, that they have reduced the blind self to zero. Still others only pretend to want to reduce the size of the blind self. Verbally they profess a total willingness to hear all about themselves, but when confronted with the first negative feature the defenses and denials go up with amazing speed. In between these extremes lie most of us.

Interpersonal communication depends in great part on both parties sharing the same basic information about each other. To the extent that blind areas exist, communication will be made difficult. Yet blind areas will always exist for each of us. Although we may be able to shrink our blind areas, we can never totally eliminate them. If, however, we recognize that we do in fact have blind areas, that we can never know everything that others know about us, this recognition will help greatly in dealing with this most difficult and elusive self and with other selves as well.

The only way to decrease the size of the blind self is to seek out information that others have and that we do not have. In everyday interactions, we influence how much of the blind area will be made open by others. This need not be done directly, although at times it is, as when we ask someone's honest opinion about our appearance or our speech or our home. Most often, however, it is done indirectly; in fact, it is a consequence of everything we do. In any interaction with another person we invariably reveal how much of ourselves we want to know about, how much we prefer not to know, which aspects we want to know about, and which aspects we prefer to leave hidden. We also reveal in these interactions how we will react to such revelations. In some contexts we would react defensively, in other contexts openly. Throughout our interactions we give cues as to how we will react in future situations, and we in effect enable others to accurately predict our future behaviors. Generally, if we are open about ourselves and reveal our inner selves to others, others in turn will reveal what is contained in the blind area more readily than they would if we did not engage in any self-disclosure.

Although communication and interpersonal relations are generally enhanced as the blind area becomes smaller, it should not be assumed that people should therefore be forced to see themselves as we see them. Forcing people to see what we see may cause serious trauma. Such a revelation might cause a breakdown in defenses; it might force people to see their own masochism or jealousy or prejudice when they are not psychologically ready to deal with such information. It is important to recognize that such revelations, since they may cause problems, might best be dealt with in the company of trained personnel.

The Hidden Self

The hidden self contains all that you know of yourself and of others but that you keep to yourself. This area includes all your successfully kept secrets about yourself and others. In any interaction this area includes all that is relevant or irrelevant to the conversation but that you do not want to reveal.

At the extremes we have the overdisclosers and the underdisclosers. The overdisclosers tell all. They keep nothing hidden about themselves or others. They will tell you their family history, their sexual problems, their marital difficulties, their children's problems, their financial status, their strategies for rising to the top, their goals, their failures and successes, and just about everything else. For them this area is very small, and had they sufficient time and others sufficient patience, it would be reduced to near zero. The problem with these overdisclosers is that they do not discriminate. They do not distinguish between those to whom such information should be disclosed and those to whom it should not be disclosed. Nor do they distinguish among the various types of information that should be disclosed and that should not be disclosed.

The underdisclosers tell nothing. They will talk about you but not about themselves. Depending upon one's relationship with these underdisclosers, we might feel that they are afraid to tell anyone anything for fear of being laughed at or rejected. Or we may feel somewhat rejected for their refusal to trust us. To never reveal anything about yourself comments on what you think of the people with whom you are interacting. On one level, at least, it is saying, "I don't trust you enough to reveal myself to you."

The vast majority of us are somewhat between these two extremes. We keep certain things hidden and we disclose certain things. We disclose to some people and we do not disclose to others. We are, in effect, selective disclosers.

When dealing with our feelings, especially our present feelings, self-disclosure is especially useful, helpful, and conducive to meaningful dialogue. A few years ago, for example, on the first day of an interpersonal communication course I was teaching I became extremely nervous. I was not sure of the reason, but I was nervous. At that point I had three basic choices open to me. One was to withdraw from the situation by saying that I was not feeling well or that I had forgotten something and to just walk out. Second, I could have attempted to hide the nervousness, hoping that it would subside as the class progressed. The third choice, and the one I chose (although I did not go through these options consciously at the time), was simply to tell the class that I was nervous and did not understand why. The class was most supportive, telling me I had nothing to be nervous about and that I should not worry. They revealed that they were the ones who felt anxious; for many, this was their first college class. Others were anxious because it was a communication course and they did not know what to expect. I in turn assured them that they should not be nervous. After this very simple exchange, all of which happened without any conscious planning or strategy, as an expression of what our feelings were at the time, we worked together closely and warmly for the rest of the semester. This incident was not in itself responsible for the success of the course, yet it helped greatly to set the tone for an open and supportive atmosphere.

The Unknown Self

The unknown self represents those truths that exist but that neither we nor others know about. One could legitimately argue that if neither we nor anyone else knows what is in this area, we cannot know that it exists at all. Actually, we do not *know* that it exists but rather we *infer* that it exists.

We infer its existence from a number of different sources. Sometimes this area is revealed to us through temporary changes brought about by drug experiences or through special experimental conditions such as hypnosis or sensory deprivation. Sometimes this area is revealed by various projective tests or dreams. There seem to be sufficient instances of such revelations to justify our including this unknown area as part of the self.

Although we cannot easily manipulate this area, we should recognize that it does exist and that there are things about ourselves and about others that we simply do not and will not know.

THE FOUR LIFE POSITIONS

One of the basic tenets of transactional analysis is that we live our lives largely according to "scripts." These scripts are very similar to dramatic scripts, complete with a list of characters and roles, stage directions, dialogue, and plot.

Our culture provides us with one kind of script. This cultural script provides us with guides to proper dress; rules for sexual conduct; roles for men and women; a value system pertaining to marriage, children, money, and education; the concepts of success and failure; and so on. Families provide another kind of script. Family scripts contain more specific instructions for each of the family members—the boys should go into politics, the girls should get involved in social work; this family will always have its own business; this family may not earn much money but will always have adequate insurance; the oldest son takes over the father's business; the oldest daughter gets married first; and so on.

From all of our early experiences, particularly from the messages received from our parents (both verbal and nonverbal), we develop a psychological script for ourselves and, for the most part, follow this throughout our lives. Individual scripts are generally "written" by the age of three; they provide us with specific directions for functioning within the larger cultural script. Should we play the victim or the persecutor, the slave or the master, the clown or the intellectual?

Some children, for example, are told that they will be successes. Nonverbally, they are given love and affection; verbally, they are reinforced for numerous actions. Other children have been told that they will never succeed. Statements such as, "No matter what you do, you'll be a success" as well as statements such as, "You'll never amount to anything" are extremely important in determining the script the child will assume in later life. Generally, people follow the scripts their parents have written for them. But such scripts can be broken—we do not *have* to follow the script written for us by our parents. One of the major purposes of transactional analysis is to break the negative and unproductive scripts and to substitute positive and productive scripts in their places. Transactional analysis is used to prevent destructive messages from getting written into the script.

These scripts, which we all have, are the bases on which we develop what are called "life positions." In transactional analysis there are four basic life positions.

I'm Not O.K., You're O.K.

This person sees others as being well-adjusted and generally effective (you're O.K.) but sees himself or herself as maladjusted and ineffective (I'm not O.K.). This is, according to Thomas A. Harris, the first position we develop as very young children. This is the position of the child who sees himself or herself as helpless and dirty and sees the adult as all-powerful and all-knowing. This person feels helpless and powerless in comparison to others and withdraws from confrontations rather than competing. This kind of life position leads one to live off others, to make others pay for their being O.K. (and for oneself's being not O.K.). Such people are frequently depressed; at times they isolate themselves, lamenting, "If only . . ." or "I should have been . . ."

I'm Not O.K., You're Not O.K.

People in this category think badly of themselves (I'm not O.K.) as well as of other people (you're not O.K.). They have no real acceptance of either themselves or others. They give themselves no support (because they are not O.K.), and they accept no support from others (because others are not O.K.). These people have given up. To them, nothing seems worthwhile, and so they withdraw. Interpersonal communication is extremely difficult since they put down both themselves and others, and intrapersonal communication does not seem particularly satisfying either. Attempts to give such people help are generally met with refusals since the would-be helpers are seen as being not O.K.

Such people seem to have lost interest in themselves, in others, and in the world generally. Living seems a drag. In the extreme they are the suicides and homicides, the autistics and pathologicals.

I'm O.K., You're Not O.K.

Persons in this position view themselves as generally effective (I'm O.K.) but see others as ineffective (you're not O.K.); "I am good, you are bad." These people have little or no respect for others and easily and frequently find fault with both friends and enemies. They are supportive of themselves but do not accept support from others. They are independent and seem to derive some satisfaction from *intrapersonal* communication but reject *interpersonal* interaction and involvement. Literally and figuratively they need space, elbow room; they resent being crowded by those "not O.K." Criminals are drawn with disproportional frequency from this class, as are the paranoids who feel persecuted and who blame others for their problems.

I'm O.K., You're O.K.

This is the adult, normal, healthy position. This, says Eric Berne in *What Do You Say After You Say Hello?*, is "the position of genuine heroes and princes, and heroines and princesses." These people approach and solve problems constructively. They have valid expectations about themselves and others and accept themselves and others as basically good, worthy, and significant human beings. These people feel free to develop and progress as individuals. They enter freely into meaningful relationships with other people and do not fear involvements. They feel neither inferior nor superior to others. Rather, they are worthy and others are worthy. This is the position of winners.

It is impossible to say how many people are in each class. Many pass through the "I'm not O.K., you're O.K." position. Few arrive at the "I'm O.K., you're O.K." position; few people are winners in this sense. Very probably the vast majority of people are in the "I'm not O.K., you're O.K." and "I'm O.K., you're not O.K." positions. It should be clear, of course, that these are general classes and that human beings resist each classification. Thus these four positions should be looked at as areas on a continuum, none of which have clear-cut boundaries and yet all of which are different.

INCREASING SELF-AWARENESS

Throughout this unit, the role of self-awareness in interpersonal communication has been discussed, and imbedded in that discussion were suggestions on how to increase our own self-awareness. I should now like to make some of these suggestions explicit.

Actively Seek Information about the Self

We have to actively seek out information that might reduce our blind selves. People will not reveal what they know about us if they are not encouraged to do so—at least most sensitive people will not. Active information seeking is necessary. To want such information to be revealed but to do nothing about securing it—and many people do not—is simply ineffective; it does not work. We need not be so blatant as to say, "Tell me about myself" or "What do you think of me?" But we can utilize some of the situations that arise every day to gain self-information. It would be perfectly legitimate to say to a friend, for example, "Do you think I came down too hard on the instructor today?" or "Do you think I was assertive enough when asking for the raise?" or "Do you think I'll be thought too forward or pushy if I invite myself over to their house for dinner?" I am not implying that we should seek this information constantly; our friends would then surely and quickly find others with whom to interact. And yet, we can make use of some situations—perhaps those in which we are particularly unsure of what to do or of how we appear—to increase self-awareness.

In our interactions with others we monitor or regulate what kind of information and how much information we want others to reveal about ourselves to us. If, for example, someone tells us about some negative trait he or she feels we possess, and if we in turn become defensive or hurt or respond by cataloguing that person's negative traits, we are in effect saying that we do not want our blind selves revealed and we effectively cut off one of the best avenues for increasing self-awareness. This, I admit, is a difficult suggestion to follow, and yet it is essential that we learn to respond openly and nondefensively so that we will be given the information we need to increase self-awareness.

In every interpersonal communication interaction others are constantly giving us feedback; they are always commenting on us in some way—on what we do, on what we say, on how we look, and so on. These comments are most often only implicit; often they are "hidden" in the way in which others look at us, in what they talk about, in their interest in what we say, and so on. We need

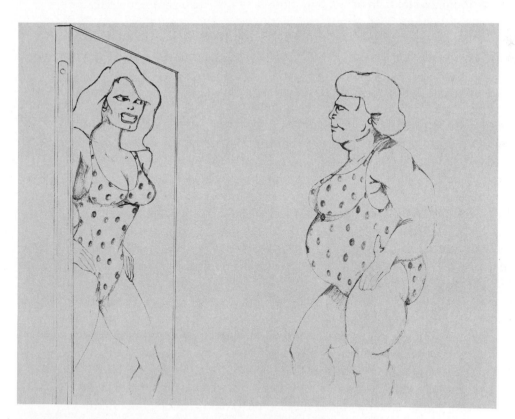

It is difficult to see ourselves as others do. Often we have to seek out the views of others if we want to get a clearer picture of who we are.

to pay close attention to this kind of information and to utilize it to increase our own self-awareness.

Increase the Open Self

The extent to which we reveal ourselves to others—the degree to which we increase our open self—will influence at least three dimensions of self-awareness. First, when we reveal ourselves to others, we reveal ourselves to ourselves at the same time. At the very least we bring into consciousness or into clearer focus what we may have buried within us. As we discuss ourselves we may see connections that we had previously missed, and with the aid of feedback from others we may gain still more insight. All this helps us to increase our self-awareness. Second, by increasing the open self we increase the likelihood that a meaningful and intimate relationship will develop, and it is through these interactions that we best get to know ourselves. Third, we get to know ourselves, in part, through the perceptions, responses, and reactions of others. If we keep a great deal hidden, we prevent ourselves from securing this feedback and from learning more about ourselves.

It should not be thought, however, that there are only rewards and no risks involved in revealing one's hidden self; clearly there are risks, and there are a number of cautions to be observed. Some of these have already been noted and they will be explored in more detail in Unit 7.

Be Conscious of Your Life Position

We need to be able to recognize when we are functioning with an inappropriate and self-destructive script, to understand that a negative self-image (the "I'm not O.K." position) may have been internalized when we were very young and may be a totally inadequate reflection of what we are now. Further, we need to see that a negative self-image will almost invariably impair our general effectiveness; it often makes us frightened to take risks, to see our accomplishments as less important than they really are, to see in many situations failure when it would be just as easy to see success. It is essential to realize that these scripts can be changed; the scripts can be rewritten. We need to substitute the productive "I'm O.K." position script for the unproductive, self-destructive "I'm not O.K." script.

Similarly we need to realize that other people, too, are "O.K." and have a great deal to contribute to society in general and to each of us in particular. There is strength in unity, and we will profit a great deal from utilizing the insights and talents of others. Others, for example, see in us a great deal that we cannot see, and we profit to the extent that we can utilize these insights of others to increase our own self-awareness. For example, we would probably only admit that an "O.K." person would be in a position to reduce our blind self—a self that can and should be reduced by the insights of others.

Perhaps the most general observation that could be made about the insights to be derived from an understanding of the four life positions is that the "I'm O.K., You're O.K." position frees us to think positively about ourselves and about others, to open ourselves to new experiences, and to interact openly with other people. When we do this, self-awareness is sure to follow.

These few suggestions are certainly not the *only* means for increasing self-awareness, but they seem to be some of the most important implications that can be derived from the models presented here. Additional suggestions are contained throughout the text.

SOURCES

The model of the four selves is based on the Johari window, which is thoroughly discussed in the works of Joseph Luft, particularly *Group Processes: An Introduction to Group Dynamics*, 2d ed. (Palo Alto, Calif.: Mayfield Publishing Company, 1970) and *Of Human Interaction* (Palo Alto, Calif.: Mayfield Publishing Company, 1969). Ronald B. Levy's books cover this area but in a more elementary fashion: *Self-Revelation Through Relationships* (Englewood Cliffs, N.J.: Prentice-Hall, 1972) and *I Can Only Touch You Now* (Englewood Cliffs, N.J.: Prentice-Hall, 1973). John Powell's *Why Am I Afraid to Tell You Who I Am?* (Niles, Ill.: Argus Communications, 1969), *Why Am I Afraid to Love?* (Niles, Ill.: Argus Communications, 1972), and *The Secret of Staying in Love* (Niles, Ill.: Argus Communications, 1974) are three of the most interesting and perceptive works in this area. They are deceptively simple, so do not dismiss them if they appear too elementary. Nathaniel Branden's *The Psychology of Self-Esteem* (New York: Bantam Books, 1969) and *The Disowned Self* (New York: Bantam Books, 1971), and Henry Clay Lindgren's *How to Live with Yourself and Like It* (New York: Fawcett, 1953) are useful for understanding ourselves. Patricia Niles Middlebrook, in *Social Psychology and Modern Life* (New York: Knopf, 1974), provides a thorough overview of the social-psychological dimensions of the self. On congruence, see Thomas C. Oden, *Game Free: The Meaning of Intimacy* (New York: Dell [Delta Books], 1974).

The discussion of the life positions is based on the work of the transactional analysts. When you read this, new books on transactional analysis will probably be on the best-seller list. Most of the popular works on transactional analysis cover essentially the same basics but apply them to different areas. In writing this section I made most use of Thomas A. Harris, *I'm O.K., You're O.K.* (New York: Harper & Row, 1969), which I wholeheartedly recommend to any college student. Also useful are Muriel James and Dorothy Jongeward, *Born to Win: Transactional Analysis with Gestalt Experiments* (Reading, Mass.: Addison-Wesley, 1971), and Eric Berne, *Games People Play* (New York: Grove Press, 1964). A more simplified account of transactional analysis is Jut Meininger, *Success Through Transactional Analysis* (New York: New American Library, 1973). An excellent overview may be found in Gerald M. Goldhaber and Marylynn B. Goldhaber, *Transactional Analysis: Principles and Applications* (Boston: Allyn & Bacon, 1976).

George Weinberg, in his *Self-Creation* (New York: St. Martin's Press, 1978), provides numerous insights into the self that relate directly to many of the issues raised in the discussions of relationships (Units 20–27). A useful compendium of techniques for increasing self-awareness and for dealing with various psychological problems is provided by Salvatore V. Didato, *Psychotechniques* (New York: Playboy Paperbacks, 1980).

EXPERIENTIAL VEHICLES

6.1 I'D PREFER TO BE

This exercise should enable members of the class to get to know each other better and at the same time get to know themselves better. The questions asked here should encourage each individual to think about and increase awareness of some facet(s) of his or her thoughts or behaviors.

Rules of the Game

The "I'd Prefer To Be" game is played in a group of four to six people. The general procedure is as follows:

1. Each member individually ranks each of the three traits in the 20 groupings listed below, using 1 for the most-preferred and 3 for the least-preferred choice.
2. Then the group considers each of the 20 categories, with each member giving his or her rank order.
3. Members may refuse to reveal their rankings for any category by saying "I pass." The group is not permitted to question the reasons for any member's passing.
4. When a member has revealed his or her rankings for a category, the group members may ask questions relevant to that category. These questions may be asked after any individual member's account or may be reserved until all members have given their rankings for a particular category.
5. In addition to this general procedure, the group may establish any additional rules it wishes, for example, appointing a leader or chairperson or establishing time limits.

"I'D PREFER TO BE"

1. ——— intelligent
   ——— wealthy
   ——— physically attractive

2. ——— a movie star
   ——— a senator
   ——— a successful businessperson

3. _____ blind
   _____ deaf
   _____ mute

4. _____ on a date
   _____ reading a good book
   _____ watching television

5. _____ loved
   _____ feared
   _____ respected

6. _____ bisexual
   _____ heterosexual
   _____ homosexual

7. _____ applying for a job by letter
   _____ applying for a job by face-to-face interview
   _____ applying for a job by telephone interview

8. _____ adventurous
   _____ scholarly
   _____ creative

9. _____ successful in social life
   _____ successful in family life
   _____ successful in business life

10. _____ traitor to one's friend
    _____ traitor to one's country
    _____ traitor to oneself

11. _____ a professional athlete
    _____ a professional chess player
    _____ a professional actor or actress

12. _____ angry
    _____ guilty
    _____ fearful

13. _____ introverted
    _____ extroverted
    _____ ambiverted

14. _____ traveling in uncharted areas
    _____ traveling in Europe
    _____ traveling in the United States

15. _____ the loved
    _____ the lover
    _____ the good friend

16. _____ a lion
    _____ an eagle
    _____ a dolphin

17. _____ a tree
    _____ a rock
    _____ a flower

18. _____ the sun
    _____ the wind
    _____ the waters

19. _____ a leader
    _____ a follower
    _____ a loner

20. _____ married
    _____ single
    _____ living with someone but unmarried

Areas for Discussion

Some of the areas for discussion that might prove of value are:

1. What are the reasons for the individual choices? Note that the reasons for the least-preferred choice may often be as important, or even more important, than the reasons for the most-preferred choice.

2. What do the choices reveal about the individual? Can persons be differentiated on the basis of their choices of these and similar alternatives?

3. What is the homogeneity/heterogeneity of the group as a whole? Do the members evidence relatively similar choices or wide differences? What does this mean in terms of the members' ability to communicate with each other?

4. Do the members accept/reject the choices of other members? Are some members disturbed by the choices other members made? If so, why? Are some apathetic? Why? Did hearing the choices of one or more members make you want to get to know them better?

5. Did any of the choices make you aware of preferences you were not aware of before?

6. Are members reluctant to share their preferences with the group? Why?

6.2 COMMUNICATIONS OF DIFFERENT LIFE POSITIONS

How would you respond to each of the following situations? Write down what you think your initial response would be.

1. being offered a promotion to a position of responsibility
2. being fired from a job held for the past 5 years
3. being asked out on a date
4. being robbed
5. being designated leader in a small group situation
6. being complimented for something you made
7. being criticized for something you did
8. being asked a favor that will take about an hour of your time
9. being assigned an unpleasant job that will last about a month
10. being given the opportunity to vote for or against the promotion of your interpersonal communication instructor

Respond again to the 10 situations, but this time identify how each of the four life positions would respond in the same situation. Try not to refer back or even to think about your initial responses.

Analyze your own responses in terms of the four life positions. Do you see any patterns in your responses? How would these responses influence your day-to-day experiences?

As an alternative, this exercise may be conducted by having the sheets of paper on which each person has indicated how he or she would respond collected (without names). The instructor or some member of the class would read the responses aloud and the class would attempt to classify these into the four life positions. More important than classification would be a discussion of what these responses mean in terms of our views of ourselves and of others.

SELF-DISCLOSURE IN INTERPERSONAL COMMUNICATION

Upon completion of this unit, you should be able to:

1. define *self-disclosure*
2. identify and define at least four dimensions of self-disclosure
3. explain at least five factors influencing self-disclosure
4. explain at least three sources of resistance to self-disclosure
5. explain at least three rewards of self-disclosure
6. explain the dangers of self-disclosure
7. identify at least four guidelines for use in self-disclosing

Probably the most important form of interpersonal communication is that of self-disclosure. This entire unit is devoted to this topic and we consider the nature of self-disclosure, some of the factors influencing self-disclosure, the sources of resistance to self-disclosure, the rewards to be derived from self-disclosing, the dangers of self-disclosing, and, last, we suggest some guidelines that may prove useful in your decisions concerning your own self-disclosures.

THE NATURE OF SELF-DISCLOSURE

A Definition of Self-Disclosure

Self-disclosure is a type of communication in which information about the self that is normally kept hidden is communicated to another person. Special note should be taken of several aspects of this elementary definition. Because self-disclosure is a type of communication, overt statements pertaining to the self as well as slips of the tongue, unconscious nonverbal movements, written confessions, and public confessions would all be classified as self-disclosing communications. Only new knowledge is useful. To tell someone something he or she already knows would not be self-disclosure; in order to be self-disclosure some new knowledge would have to be communicated. Further, to be self-disclosure the information must be such that it is normally kept hidden. To tell someone your age, religion, or political leanings would only be self-disclosure if you normally keep these data secret or hidden from most people.

94

Self-disclosure involves at least one other individual. In order to self-disclose, the communication act must involve at least two persons; it cannot be an *intrapersonal* communication act. Nor can we, as some people attempt to, "disclose" in a manner that makes it impossible for another person to understand. This is not a disclosure at all. Nor can we write in diaries that no one reads and call this self-disclosure. To be self-disclosure, the information must be received and understood by another individual.

Gerard Egan, in *Encounter*, makes another distinction that may prove useful. He distinguishes between *history*, which he calls "the mode of noninvolvement," and *story*, which he calls "the mode of involvement." History is a manner of revealing the self that is only pseudo–self-disclosure. It is an approach that details some facts of the individual's life but does not really invite involvement from listeners. From a person's history we may learn what the individual did or what happened to him or her throughout that person's life, but somehow we really do not get to know the person. Story, on the other hand, is authentic self-disclosure. In story individuals communicate their inner selves to others and look for some human response rather than just simple feedback. The speaker takes a risk, puts himself or herself on the line, and reveals something significant about who he or she is and not merely what he or she has done.

Dimensions of Self-Disclosure

Self-disclosures may differ from one another in terms of five basic dimensions or qualities. Perhaps the most obvious is the *amount* of self-disclosure that takes place. The amount of self-disclosure may be gauged by examining the frequency with which one self-discloses and the duration of the self-disclosing messages, that is, the time taken up with self-disclosing statements. A second factor is the *valence* of the self-disclosure, that is, the positiveness or negativeness of the self-disclosure. We can self-disclose favorable and flattering things about ourselves as well as unfavorable and unflattering things, and, as can easily be appreciated, the resultant self-disclosures will be drastically different in their effect on the self-discloser as well as on the listener. As explained in the next section, this valence factor will also influence the nature and extent of our self-disclosures. A third factor is the *accuracy* and *honesty* with which one self-discloses. The accuracy of our self-disclosures will be limited by the extent to which we know ourselves; some of us know ourselves quite thoroughly and therefore may make extremely accurate self-disclosures. Others of us seem totally out of touch with what is going on inside our skins, and there would be little chance of these persons' self-disclosures being accurate. Further, our self-disclosures may vary in terms of honesty. We may be totally honest or we may exaggerate, omit crucial details, or simply lie. The fourth factor is *intention* to self-disclose; that is, the extent to which we disclose what we intend to disclose, the extent to which we are in conscious control of the self-disclosures we make. Some people reveal a great deal but rarely intend to be so revealing; others may wish to reveal a great deal but, for one reason or another, their self-reference statements are difficult to "read" or to interpret. Fifth, self-disclosures may vary in terms of *intimacy*. We can disclose the most intimate details of our lives (or at least those details that we regard as the most intimate), we may disclose items that we regard as relatively peripheral or impersonal, or we may disclose items that lie anywhere in between these extremes.

FACTORS INFLUENCING SELF-DISCLOSURE

As a particular form of communication, self-disclosure occurs more readily under certain circumstances than under others. Generally, self-disclosure is reciprocal. In any interaction self-disclosure by one person is more likely to take place if another person engages in self-disclosure than if this other person does not. This seems quite obvious and predictable, yet its consequences are interesting. It implies that a kind of spiral effect operates here, with each person's self-disclosure serving as the stimulus for additional self-disclosure by the other person, which in turn serves as the stimulus for self-disclosure by the other person, and on and on.

Audience Size

Self-disclosure, perhaps because of the numerous fears we have about revealing ourselves, is more likely to occur in small groups than in large groups. Dyads are perhaps the most frequent situations in which self-disclosure takes place. This seems true for any number of reasons. A dyad seems more suitable because it is easier for the self-discloser to deal with one person's reactions and responses than with the reactions of a group of three or four or five. The self-discloser can attend to the responses quite carefully and, on the basis of the support or lack of support, monitor the disclosures, continuing if the situation is supportive and stopping if it is not supportive. With more than one listener such monitoring is impossible since the responses are sure to vary among the listeners. Another possible reason is that when the group is larger than two, the self-disclosure takes on aspects of exhibitionism and public exposure. It is no longer a confidential matter; now it is one about which many people know. From a more practical point of view, it is often difficult to assemble in one place at one time only those people to whom we would want to self-disclose.

Topic

There are differences in the amount and type of self-disclosures people make, depending upon the topics being discussed, the persons doing the disclosing, and the audience or persons to whom the disclosures are being made. Certain areas of the self are more likely to be self-disclosed than are others. Intuitively we can appreciate that one would be more likely to self-disclose information about one's job or hobbies, for example, than about one's sex life or financial situation. In studying this issue, Sidney M. Jourard found that self-disclosures about money (for example, the amount of money one owes), personality (for example, the things about which one experiences guilt), and body (for example, one's feelings of sexual adequacy) were less frequent than disclosures about tastes and interests, attitudes and opinions, and work. Clearly, the first three topics are more closely related to one's self-concept, and disclosures about these are therefore potentially more threatening than are disclosures about one's tastes in clothing, one's views on religion, or one's pressures at work.

Valence

The valence, or positive or negative quality, of the self-disclosure is also a significant factor here. Positive self-disclosures are more likely to be engaged in than negative self-disclosures and may be made to nonintimates as well as to intimates. Negative self-disclosures, on the other hand, take place most often with close intimates and usually after considerable time has elapsed in a relationship. This finding is consistent with the evidence that shows that self-disclosure and trust are positively related. Trust, of course, is a relationship between two persons that develops after they get to know each other fairly well and after they have spent considerable time with each other.

Research indicates that we develop greater attraction for those who engage in positive self-disclosure than for those who engage in negative self-disclosure. This is particularly significant in the early stages of a relationship. Negative self-disclosures to a stranger or even a casual acquaintance are perceived as inappropriate, no doubt because such self-disclosures violate our culture's norms for such communications. This may suggest a warning: If your aim is to be perceived as attractive, you should consider curtailing negative self-disclosures at least in the early stages of your relationships.

Sex

Certain people are more likely to self-disclose than others. For example, it has been found that males disclose less than do females. Recent research, however, would have this general observation qualified by noting that females are more likely to disclose positive statements. Commenting on the male reluctance to self-disclose that most researchers have found, Middlebrook notes that "part of the male role in our society may involve not discussing the self, which, in turn, may add to the level of stress experienced by males and to their early death." Although we may not wish to accept so extreme a relationship as Middlebrook suggests, it does seem that the need or pressure to not self-disclose creates stress and discomfort for males.

It is interesting to note that men and women give different reasons for avoiding self-disclosure. The main reason for avoiding self-disclosure, how-

ever, is common to both men and women and it is: "If I disclose, I might project
an image I do not want to project." In a society where one's image is so important—where one's image is often the basis for success or failure—this reason
for avoiding self-disclosure is expected. Other reasons for avoiding self-disclo-

sure, however, are unique for men and women. For men the reasons reported
are: "If I self-disclose, I might give information that makes me appear inconsistent," "If I self-disclose, I might lose control over the other person," and
"Self-disclosure might threaten relationships I have with people other than
close acquaintances." Lawrence Rosenfeld sums up the male reasons for self-
disclosure avoidance as: "If I disclose to you, I might project an image I do not
want to project, which could make me look bad and cause me to lose control
over you. This might go so far as to affect relationships I have with people other
than you." The principal objective of men is to avoid self-disclosure so that
control can be maintained.

In addition to fearing the projection of an unfavorable image, women
avoid self-disclosure for the following reasons: "Self-disclosure would give the
other person information which he or she might use against me at some time,"
"Self-disclosure is a sign of some emotional disturbance," and "Self-disclosure
might hurt our relationship." The general reason, then, that women avoid self-
disclosure, says Rosenfeld, is: "If I disclose to you I might project an image I
do not want to project, such as my being emotionally ill, which you might use
against me and which might hurt our relationship." The principal objective for
avoiding self-disclosure for women is "to avoid personal hurt and problems
with the relationship."

Rosenfeld summarizes the results of his investigation by observing: "The
stereotyped male role—independent, competitive, and unsympathetic—and
the stereotyped female role—dependent, nonaggressive, and interpersonally
oriented—were evident in the reasons indicated for avoiding self-disclosure.
Seeking different rewards from their interpersonal relationships, many males
and females go about the business of self-disclosing, and *not* self-disclosing,
differently." You might wish to test some of these findings yourself by talking
with your peers about the reasons they avoid self-disclosure and about the reasons for their reasons. That is, why do men and women have different reasons
for avoiding self-disclosure? What is there in the learning histories of the two
sexes that might account for such differences?

Race, Nationality, and Age

There are racial and national differences in self-disclosure as well. Black
students disclose significantly less than do white students, and students in the
United States were found to disclose more than similar groups in Puerto Rico,
Germany, Great Britain, and the Middle East. There are even differences in the
amount of self-disclosure in different age groups. Self-disclosure to a spouse or
to an opposite-sex friend increases from the age of about 17 to about 50 and
then drops off.

Receiver Relationship

The person to whom the disclosures are made is also a significant factor in determining the frequency of or likelihood of self-disclosure. Research, however, has not been able to identify fully the specific characteristics of the person with whom self-disclosure is most likely to take place. There seems to be a great deal of individual variation here. Some studies have found that we disclose more often to those people who are close to us, for example, our spouses, our family, our close friends. Other studies claim that we disclose to persons we like and do not disclose to persons we dislike regardless of how close they are to us. Thus an individual may disclose to a well-liked teacher even though they are not particularly close and yet not disclose to a brother or sister with whom he or she is close but who is not liked very much. Other studies claim that a lasting relationship between people increases the likelihood of self-disclosure, while still others claim that self-disclosure is more likely to occur in temporary relationships, for example, between prostitutes and clients or even between strangers on a train. It has been found, for example, that male college students are more likely to disclose to a close friend than to either of their parents. But college females will disclose about equally to their mothers and to their best friends but will not disclose very much to their fathers or to their boyfriends. As might be expected, most husbands and wives self-disclose to each other more than they do to any other person or group of persons, although there is some evidence to suggest that wives from the lower social class disclose most not to their husbands but to their women friends. "This confirms the view," says Jourard in *The Transparent Self,* "that marriage is the 'closest' relationship one can enter, and it may help us the better to understand why some people avoid it like the plague. Anyone who is reluctant to be known by another person and to know another person—sexually and cognitively—will find the prospective intimacy of marriage somewhat terrifying."

When the receiver is positive and reinforcing, there is naturally a greater tendency to self-disclose than there is when the receiver is negative and punishing. Generally, it has been found that people tend to like others who disclose about the same amount as they do. If you disclose much more or much less than do the people to whom you are disclosing, you may be in line for a negative evaluation.

SOURCES OF RESISTANCE TO SELF-DISCLOSURE

For all its advantages and importance, self-disclosure is a form of communication that is often fiercely resisted. Some of the possible reasons for its resistance should be examined so that we may better understand our own reluctance to enter into this type of communication experience.

Perhaps the most obvious—and some would argue the only—reason for our reluctance to self-disclose, according to Gerard Egan, is that there is a societal bias against it, and we have internalized this bias. We have been conditioned against self-disclosure by the society in which we live. The hero in American folklore is strong but silent; he bears responsibilities, burdens, and problems without letting others even be aware of them. He is self-reliant and does not need the assistance of anyone. Males have internalized this folk hero, it seems, at least to some extent. Women are a bit more fortunate in this respect than men. They are allowed the luxury of some self-disclosure; they are allowed to tell their troubles to someone, to pour out their feelings, to talk about themselves. Women are allowed great freedom in expressing emotions, in verbalizing love and affection; men are more restricted, they are somehow conditioned to avoid such expressions. These, men have been taught, are signs of weakness rather than strength. This societal bias is reflected even in our evaluations of self-disclosing men and women. For example, women who disclose a great deal are generally evaluated positively but men who disclose a great deal, regardless of the subjects they disclose, are evaluated negatively.

Although it is difficult to admit, many people resist self-disclosing because of a fear of punishment, generally in the form of rejection. We may vividly picture other people laughing at us or whispering about us or condemning us if we self-disclose. These mental pictures help to convince us that self-disclosure is not the most expedient course of action.

We may also fear punishment in the form of tangible or concrete manifestations, such as the loss of a job or of friends. At times this does happen. The ex-convict who self-discloses his or her past record may find himself or herself without a job or out of a political office. Generally, however, these fears are overblown. These fears are often in the nature of excuses that allow us to rest contentedly without self-disclosing.

Gerard Egan, in *Encounter*, points out that this fear of rejection operates like a reverse halo effect. *Halo effect* refers to the generalizing of virtue from one area to another. For example, your communication teacher may know a great deal about communication and may be perceived as highly credible in that field. The halo effect operates to generalize that perceived credibility to other fields as well, and so when he or she talks about politics or economics or psychology we are more apt to see him or her as credible and knowledgeable in these areas, too. The reverse halo effect operates in a similar manner. We assume that if we tell others something negative about ourselves, their negative responses will generalize to other aspects of our behavior and they will see us as generally negative, much as we may see the teacher of one field as competent in other fields.

Another possible reason why we resist self-disclosure is what Egan calls fear of self-knowledge. We may have built up a beautiful, rationalized picture of ourselves—emphasizing the positive and eliminating or minimizing the negative. Self-disclosure often forces us to see through the rationalizations. We see the positive aspects for what they are, and we see the negative aspects that were previously hidden.

THE REWARDS OF SELF-DISCLOSURE

The obvious question when the topic of self-disclosure arises is, "Why?" Why should anyone self-disclose to anyone else? What is it about this type of communication that merits its being singled out and discussed at length? There is no clear-cut answer to these very legitimate questions. There is no great body of statistical research findings that attests to the usefulness or importance of self-disclosure. Yet there is evidence in the form of testimony, observational reports, and the like that have led a number of researchers and theorists to argue that self-disclosure is perhaps the most important form of communication in which anyone could engage. This is not to imply that there are no risks involved; there are dangers in self-disclosing, and we will consider some of these later. Here, however, we focus on the rewards or advantages of this form of interpersonal communication.

One argument in favor of self-disclosure is that we cannot know ourselves as fully as possible if we do not self-disclose to at least one other individual. It is assumed that by self-disclosing to another we gain a new perspective on ourselves, a deeper understanding of our own behavior. In therapy, for example, very often the insight does not come directly from the therapist; while the individual is self-disclosing, he or she recognizes some facet of behavior or some relationship that was not known before. Through self-disclosure, then, we may come to understand ourselves more thoroughly. Sidney M. Jourard, in *The Transparent Self,* notes that self-disclosure is an important factor in counseling and psychotherapy and argues that people may need such help because they have not disclosed significantly to other people. This relationship between self-disclosure and mental health is frequently discussed, and not everyone would agree with Jourard's rather strong claim. A more reasoned hypothesis, I think, is offered by Paul Cozby, who after a thorough review of the self-disclosure and mental-adjustment literature concluded that "persons with positive mental health . . . are characterized by high disclosure to a few significant others and medium disclosure to others in the social environment. Individuals who are poorly adjusted . . . are characterized by either high or low self-disclosure to virtually everyone in the social environment." It is selective self-disclosure, or self-disclosure in moderation, then, that seems to characterize the well-adjusted personality.

Closely related is the argument that we will be better able to deal with our problems, especially our guilt, through self-disclosure. One of the great fears that many people have is that they will not be accepted because of some deep, dark secret, because of something they have done, or because of some feeling or attitude they might have. Because we feel these things as a basis for rejection, we develop guilt. If, for example, you do not love—or even hate—one of your parents, you might fear being rejected if you were to self-disclose such a feeling; thus a sense of guilt develops over this. By self-disclosing such a feeling and being supported rather than rejected, we are better prepared to deal with the guilt and perhaps reduce or even eliminate it. Even self-acceptance is difficult without self-disclosure. We accept ourselves largely through the eyes of others. If we feel that others will reject us, we are apt to reject ourselves as well. Through self-disclosure and subsequent support, we are in a better position to see the positive responses to us and are more likely to respond by developing a positive self-concept.

Keeping our secrets to ourselves and not revealing who we are to others takes a great deal of energy and leaves us with that much less energy for other things. We must be constantly on guard, for example, lest someone see in our behavior what we consider to be a deviant orientation, attitude, or behavior pattern. We might avoid certain people for fear that they will tell this awful thing about us, or avoid situations or places because if we are seen there, others will know how terrible we really are. By self-disclosing we rid ourselves of the false masks that otherwise must be worn. Jourard puts this most clearly:

> Every maladjusted person is a person who has not made himself known to another human being and in consequence does not know himself. Nor can he be himself. More than that, he struggles actively to avoid becoming known by another human being. He works at it ceaselessly, twenty-four hours daily, and it is work! In the effort to avoid becoming known, a person provides for himself a cancerous kind of stress which is subtle and unrecognized, but none the less effective in producing not only the assorted patterns of unhealthy personality which psychiatry talks about, but also the wide array of physical ills that have come to be recognized as the province of psychosomatic medicine.

Self-disclosure is also helpful in improving communication efficiency. Since we understand the messages of others largely to the extent that we understand the other individuals, we can better understand what an individual means if we know the individual well. We can tell what certain nuances mean, when the person is serious and when he or she is joking, when the person is being sarcastic out of fear and when out of resentment, and so on. Self-disclosure is an essential condition for getting to know another individual. You might study a person's behavior or even live with a person for years, but if that person never self-discloses, you are far from understanding that individual as a complete person.

Perhaps the main reason why self-disclosure is important is that it is necessary if a meaningful relationship is to be established between two people. Without self-disclosure meaningful relationships seem impossible to develop. There are, it is true, relationships that have lasted for 10, 20, 30, and 40 years without self-disclosure. Many married couples would fall into this category, as would colleagues working in the same office or factory or people living in the same neighborhood or apartment house. Without self-disclosure, however, these relationships are probably not terribly meaningful, or at least they are not as meaningful as they might be. By self-disclosing we are in effect saying to other individuals that we trust them, that we respect them, that we care enough about them and about our relationship to reveal ourselves to them. This leads the other individual to self-disclose in return. This is at least the start of a meaningful relationship, a relationship that is honest and open and goes beyond surface trivialities.

DANGERS OF SELF-DISCLOSURE

Undoubtedly there are numerous advantages to be gained from self-disclosure. Yet these should not blind us to the fact that self-disclosure often involves very real risks. An investment analogy may prove useful: when the payoffs or potential gains are great, so are the risks. When the payoffs are small, so are the risks. The same seems true of self-disclosure. When the potential rewards of self-disclosure are great so are the risks. These potential rewards and risks need to be weighed carefully before engaging in significant self-disclosure. The risks may be of various types—risks to one's job, to one's professional advancement, to one's social and family life, and to just about any and every aspect of one's life. Politicians who disclose that they have been seeing a psychiatrist may later find their own political party no longer supporting their candidacy and voters unwilling to risk having someone who needed analysis in a position of power. Men and women in law enforcement agencies, such as city or state police officers or FBI agents, who disclose that they are homosexuals or lesbians may soon find themselves confined to desk jobs at some isolated precinct, prevented from further advancement, or charged with criminal behavior and fired. Teachers who disclose their former or present drug behavior or that they are living with one of their students may find themselves denied tenure, teaching the undesirable courses at the undesirable hours, and eventually being victims of "budget cuts." And the teachers or students who find a supportive atmosphere in their interpersonal communication course and who disclose about their sex lives, their financial conditions, or their self-doubts, anxieties, or fantasies may find that some of the less sympathetic listeners may later use that information to the self-discloser's detriment.

All communication revolves around questions of choice, an observation I have made repeatedly. With self-disclosure, the choices are particularly difficult to make, largely because the advantages and the disadvantages are so significant and cannot be easily predicted. To one person, self-disclosures may bring only rewards; to another, the same self-disclosures may bring only punishments. One may receive a promotion for demonstrated self-confidence; the other may be fired for unbecoming behavior.

In attempting to make your choice between disclosing and not disclosing, it is important to keep in mind—in addition to the advantages and dangers already noted—the irreversible nature of communication that was noted in Unit 2. Regardless of how many times we may attempt to qualify something, "take it back," or deny it, once something is said, it cannot be withdrawn. We cannot erase the conclusions and inferences listeners have made on the basis of our disclosures. I am not advocating that you therefore refrain from self-disclosing, but only reminding you to consider the irreversible nature of communication as one additional factor involved in your choices.

GUIDELINES IN SELF-DISCLOSING

Because self-disclosure involves both potential rewards and dangers, its predicted consequences should be carefully examined before deciding whether or not to self-disclose. In attempting to make this decision, it may prove helpful to consider some or all of the following guidelines.

1. *Consider the motivation for the self-disclosure.* Self-disclosure should be motivated out of a concern for the relationship, for the others involved, and for oneself. Some people self-disclose out of a desire to hurt the listener. Persons who tell their parents that they never did love them, or that they hindered rather than helped their emotional development, may be disclosing out of a desire to hurt and perhaps to punish rather than out of a desire to improve the

"I wanted to be a psychiatrist ever since I can remember. My father wanted me to be a football player, but what did he know? I never listened to him; never cared much for him. But my mother—now there was a woman! She had charm, beauty, . . ."

relationship. Nor, of course, should the self-disclosure function be used primarily to punish oneself (perhaps because of some guilt feeling or unresolved conflict). Self-disclosure should not be an exercise in exhibitionism, an opportunity to parade one's sexual fantasies, past indiscretions, or psychological problems. Self-disclosure should serve a useful and productive function for all persons involved.

2. *Consider the appropriateness of the self-disclosure.* Self-disclosure should be appropriate to the context and to the relationship between speaker and listener. Before making any significant self-disclosure we should ask if this is the right time and place. Could a better time and place be arranged? Is this self-disclosure appropriate to the relationship? Is it important that this particular listener hear this particular self-disclosure? Is this self-disclosure something that will help the relationship grow and prosper? Will the listener be better able to understand us as a result of this specific self-disclosure?

3. *Consider the opportunity available for open and honest responses.* Self-disclosure should occur in an atmosphere where open and honest responses can be made. Don't hit and run. Self-disclosure is best avoided when the people involved are under pressures of time or when they are in a situation that will not allow them to respond as they might wish. Ask yourself, then, if there is sufficient time and if the atmosphere is such that the individual can respond at length to your self-disclosures if she or he wishes. If the answer is no, you should wait, if possible, for another time and perhaps another place.

4. *Consider the clarity and directness with which the self-disclosure will be made.* The goal of self-disclosure is to inform—not to confuse—the other person. Often, however, we may self-disclose only partially or may self-disclose in such an oblique and roundabout way that the listener walks away more confused than before the disclosure. If you are going to self-disclose, consider the extent of the disclosure and be prepared to disclose enough to ensure the necessary understanding, or perhaps reconsider whether you should self-disclose at all. This does not mean that you have to disclose everything you have hidden concerning the matter, but only that you need to consider whether the omitted information is going to prevent the achievement of the understanding you seek. One of the ill effects that too sketchy a disclosure often has is that the other person will fill in the omitted portions incorrectly with the result that you are more misunderstood now than before. Surely this defeats the very purpose of self-disclosure.

5. *Consider the possible burdens self-disclosure might entail.* Any potential self-discloser should carefully weigh the potential problems that may be incurred as a result of a disclosure. Can you afford to lose your job should you disclose your previous prison record? Are you willing to risk failing the course should you confess to having plagiarized your term paper?

You should also ask yourself whether you are making unreasonable demands on the listener. For example, consider the person who swears his or her mother-in-law to secrecy and then self-discloses to having an ongoing affair with a neighbor. This type of situation, it seems, places an unfair burden on the mother-in-law who is now in a bind to either break her promise of secrecy or allow her son or daughter to believe a lie. Parents often place unreasonable burdens on their children by self-disclosing marital problems or infidelities or self-doubts without realizing that the children may be too young or too emotionally involved to deal effectively with this information. Often such disclosures do not make the relationship a better one but instead add tension and friction, something we can all do easily without. Often such disclosures are made to ease one's own guilt without considering the burden this places on the other person.

These guidelines are certainly not the only ones that may be used in deciding whether or not to self-disclose. They are, however, suggestive of the types of guidelines that may be used in making your self-disclosing decisions.

SOURCES

On self-disclosure, see Sidney M. Jourard, *Disclosing Man to Himself* (New York: Van Nostrand Reinhold, 1968) and *The Transparent Self*, rev. ed. (New York: Van Nostrand Reinhold, 1971). In writing this unit I relied heavily on the insights of Gerard Egan; see especially his *Encounter: Group Processes for Interpersonal Growth* (Belmont, Calif.: Brooks/Cole, 1970), or, if you prefer a shorter version, *Face to Face: The Small-Group Experience and Interpersonal Growth* (Belmont, Calif.: Brooks/Cole, 1973). An overview of self-disclosure in communication is provided by W. Barnett Pearce and Stewart M. Sharp, "Self-Disclosing Communication," *Journal of Communication* 23 (December 1973): 409–425. This article also provides an excellent review of the research on self-disclosure and communication. Another excellent review is by Paul Cozby, "Self-Disclosure: A Literature Review," *Psychological Bulletin* 79 (1973): 73–91.

Sam Keen and Anne Valley Fox, *Telling Your Story: A Guide to Who You Are and Who You Can Be* (New York: New American Library, 1973) provides some interesting insights on self-disclosure.

A great deal of research is currently being conducted on self-disclosure. For example, for the five dimensions of self-disclosure, see Lawrence R. Wheeless and Janis Grotz, "Conceptualization and Measurement of Reported Self-Disclosure," *Human Communication Research* 2 (Summer 1976): 338–346. On sex differences, see Shirley J. Gilbert and Gale G. Whiteneck, "Toward a Multidimensional Approach to the Study of Self-Disclosure," *Human Communication Research* 2 (Summer 1976): 347–355. On valence, see Shirley J. Gilbert and David Horenstein, "The Communication of Self-Disclosure: Level Versus Valence," *Human Communication Research* 1 (Summer 1975): 316–322. On the relationship between trust and self-disclosure, see Lawrence R. Wheeless and Janis Grotz, "The Measurement of Trust and Its Relationship to Self-Disclosure," *Human Communication Research* 3 (Spring 1977): 250–257. For the study on self-disclosure avoidance, see Lawrence Rosenfeld, "Self-Disclosure Avoidance: Why I Am Afraid to Tell You Who I Am," *Communication Monographs* 46 (March 1979): 63–74.

7.1 DISCLOSING THE HIDDEN SELF*

On an index card write a statement of information that is currently in the hidden self. Do not put your names on these cards; the statements are to be dealt with anonymously. These cards will be collected and read aloud to the entire group.

Discussion of Statement and Model

1. Classify the statements into categories, for example, sexual problems, attitudes toward family, self-doubts, and so forth.
2. Why do you suppose this type of information is kept in the hidden self? What advantages might hiding this information have? What disadvantages?
3. How would you react to people who disclosed such statements to you? For example, what difference, if any, would it make in your interpersonal relationship?
4. What type of person is likely to have a large hidden self and a small open self? A large open self and a small hidden self?
5. In relation to the other group members, would your open self be larger? Smaller? The same size? Would your hidden self be larger? Smaller? The same size?

7.2 SELF-DISCLOSURE QUESTIONNAIRE

Complete the following questionnaire by indicating in the appropriate spaces your willingness-unwillingness to self-disclose these matters to members of a group of students chosen at random from those in this class.

In a group of five or six persons discuss the questionnaires, self-disclosing what you wish to self-disclose and not disclosing what you do not wish to disclose. Consider at least the following:

1. Are there any discrepancies between what you indicated you would self-disclose and what you were actually willing to self-disclose?

*The general idea for this exercise comes from Gerard Egan, *Encounter* (Belmont, Calif.: Brooks/Cole, 1970).

	Would Definitely Self-disclose	Would Probably Self-disclose	Don't Know	Would Probably Not Self-disclose	Would Definitely Not Self-disclose
1. My religious beliefs					
2. My attitudes toward other religions					
3. My attitudes toward different nationalities and races					
4. My political beliefs					
5. My economic status					
6. My views on abortion					
7. My views on pornography					
8. My views on premarital relations					
9. My major pastime					
10. My parents' attitudes toward other religions					
11. My parents' attitudes toward different nationalities and races					
12. My parents' political beliefs					
13. My parents' economic status					
14. My relationship with my parents					
15. My sexual fantasies					
16. My past sexual experiences					
17. My perceived sexual attractiveness					
18. My desired physical attractiveness					
19. My most negative physical attribute					
20. My physical condition or health					
21. My ideal mate					
22. My drinking behavior					
23. My drug behavior					
24. My gambling behavior					
25. My personal goals					
26. My most embarrassing moment					
27. My unfulfilled desires					
28. My major weaknesses					
29. My major worries					
30. My major strengths					
31. My present happiness or unhappiness					
32. My major mistakes					
33. My general attractiveness					
34. My general self-concept					
35. My general adequacy					

2. What areas were people most unwilling to self-disclose? Why?

3. After the group got going and a number of people self-disclosed, did you feel more willing to self-disclose? Explain your feelings.

4. Were negative qualities (or perceived negative qualities) more likely to remain undisclosed? Why?

5. How would the results of your questionnaire have differed if this information was to be disclosed to your parents, a stranger you would never see again, a counselor, and a best friend? Would the results differ depending on the sex of the individual to whom the disclosures were to be made? Explain the reasons why.

ASSERTIVENESS AND SHYNESS IN INTERPERSONAL COMMUNICATION

OBJECTIVES

Upon completion of this unit, you should be able to:

1. identify the differences and the similarities between assertiveness and shyness as communication concepts
2. define and give examples of assertive behavior
3. distinguish among assertiveness, nonassertiveness, and aggressiveness
4. identify at least two types of situations in which one may choose not to be assertive
5. identify some of the types of shy people and some of the types of situations in which people experience shyness
6. identify a few of the symptoms of shyness
7. explain the three positions identified in this unit concerning the origins of nonassertivenss and shyness
8. state and explain the five principles for increasing assertiveness and decreasing shyness
9. create a hierarchy for a specific desired assertive or nonshy behavior
10. explain why feedback is particularly important in increasing assertiveness or decreasing shyness
11. identify the cautions that should be observed in adopting new assertive behaviors

Recently there have been a number of best sellers devoted to what generally has been called assertiveness training. *Your Perfect Right: A Guide to Assertive Behavior; Stand up, Speak Out, Talk Back: The Key to Self-Assertive Behavior; Don't Say Yes When You Want to Say No; Winning Through Intimidation; When I Say No, I Feel Guilty; The Assertive Woman,* and numerous other books have done much to popularize the principles and techniques of assertiveness. The general assumption made by assertiveness theorists is that most of us are not assertive; most of us allow our rights to be trampled on; most of us are afraid to demand what is justly ours. As Herbert Fensterheim and Jean Baer put it in *Don't Say Yes When You Want to Say No,* "Parents, teachers, clergymen, and businessmen have unwittingly conspired to produce a nation of timid souls." Other popular books have focused on shyness. Philip Zimbardo's *Shyness: What It Is, What to Do About It,* originally published as a college textbook, became a best seller. *The Shy Person's Book, Shy?,* and various other books have also enjoyed considerable popularity.

Some researchers view nonassertiveness and shyness as essentially the same. While in many cases the behaviors are similar, and in some cases identical, there are distinctions between the two that are useful to make. Shyness is generally anxiety provoking, whereas nonassertiveness is not necessarily so. Anxiety may be provoked when, for example, an individual is determined to act assertively and fears that it may not come off as expected or as hoped for. Shyness is something of which we are painfully aware. Every time the shy person is pointed to, asked a question, or somehow put on the spot, she or he becomes aware of the problem of shyness. Nonassertiveness, on the other hand, often functions below our level of consciousness. Numerous nonassertive individuals are totally unaware that their behaviors are not assertive; it is only when this is pointed out to them that they become aware that there are alternative ways of behaving that may be more effective. The shy person prefers to remain anonymous; nothing seems more frightening to the shy person than being made the center of attention. The nonassertive person, on the other hand, may not stand up for his or her rights but may very much enjoy the role of attention-getter. Shyness is not sex-related; nonassertiveness is. In our culture shyness or antishyness learning occurs without regard to sex. It is drastically different with assertiveness; in our culture, men are taught to be assertive and women are taught to be nonassertive. This is not always true for all people in all situations, and it is less true today than it was 5 or 10 years ago, but it nevertheless seems generally true.

These, then, are some of the differences between these two types of behaviors. Despite these differences, however, shyness and nonassertiveness are in other respects quite similar. Both are essentially responses to interpersonal communication situations. Both may hinder, and in many cases prevent, effective and meaningful interpersonal communication from taking place. The origins of both shyness and nonassertiveness have been explained with the same general theoretical approaches. Perhaps most important, the same general principles may be used for increasing assertiveness and for decreasing shyness. That the shy person is usually and frequently nonassertive adds additional logic to our considering them in the same unit.

Because assertiveness and shyness are different in some respects and similar in others, I will focus first on each concept individually and then bring the concepts together in considering their origins and the principles that may be used to increase assertiveness and to decrease shyness.

ASSERTIVENESS

Thomas Moriarty has conducted a number of interesting experiments to illustrate just how passive we have learned to become. For example, in one experiment subjects taking a psychological test were placed near a confederate of the experimenter who played loud rock-and-roll music during the test. Of the 20 subjects, 16 made no comment at all. Even when the students were told that they would receive mild electric shocks for wrong answers, 16 of the 20 subjects still said nothing to the music player. Similar experiments were repeated in natural settings like the library and the movies, both with loud talking. Rarely did anyone object.

In perhaps the most clever variation, subjects approached people after they had left a phone booth, saying that they had lost a ring and would the person mind emptying his or her pockets to see if he or she had perhaps picked up the ring. Of the 20 adult males who were approached, 16 emptied their pockets (80 percent). When the experiment was repeated using graduate students, 20 of the 24 men (83 percent) emptied their pockets. "I believe," concludes Moriarty, "that many of us have accepted the idea that few things are worth getting into a hassle about, especially with strangers. And I believe this is particularly true of younger people."

The aims of assertiveness training are to convince us that we would be happier if we were more assertive and to show us how we might increase our own assertive behaviors.

Assertiveness is, as I see it, largely an interpersonal communication characteristic. It is mainly in interpersonal situations (though also in small groups and at times in large group situations) that the occasion and the need to assert ourselves arises. Our own assertiveness, or lack of it, will greatly influence our interpersonal interactions—a premise that will be demonstrated in this unit and in the Experiential Vehicles that follow it.

It is also interesting to note that the qualities that assertiveness theorists consider characteristic of the assertive individual are also the qualities that communicologists consider characteristic of the effective interpersonal communicator. The relevance of assertiveness to interpersonal communication in particular and to communication in general will be even more apparent as we explain the distinctions among assertiveness, nonassertiveness, and aggressiveness; the characteristics of the assertive person; and the principles for increasing assertiveness.

NONASSERTIVENESS, AGGRESSIVENESS, AND ASSERTIVENESS

There are two kinds of nonassertiveness. First, there is *situational nonassertiveness*. This is the nonassertiveness that is only displayed in certain situations, for example, situations that create a great deal of anxiety—perhaps because of the person one is interacting with or because of the topic being considered.

Generalized nonassertiveness is, as the term implies, behavior that is normally or typically nonassertive. People who exhibit these behaviors are timid and reserved, and regardless of the specifics of the situation, they are unable to assert their rights. These people do what others tell them to do—parents, employers, and the like—without questioning and without concern for what is best for them. When these persons' rights are infringed upon, they do nothing about it and even at times accuse themselves of being nonaccepting. Generalized nonassertive persons often ask permission from others to do what is their perfect right. Social situations create anxiety for these individuals, and they more often than not find that their self-esteem is generally low. In the extreme, a generalized nonassertive person would be characterized as inhibited and emotionally unresponsive with feelings of personal inadequacy.

Aggressiveness may also be considered as being of two types: situational and generalized. Situationally aggressive people are aggressive only under cer-

Sometimes it's difficult to be assertive, especially when there are large status differences.

tain conditions or in certain situations. For example, they may become aggressive after being taken advantage of over a long period of time or after being taken advantage of by someone for whom they have done a great deal. Or perhaps these people would be aggressive in dealing with teachers or fellow classmates or parents or older people. The important characteristic is that these people are usually not aggressive; only in certain situations do they behave aggressively.

Generally aggressive people, on the other hand, meet all or at least most situations with aggressive behavior. These persons seem in charge of almost all situations; regardless of what is going on, they take over. These individuals appear to think little of the opinions, values, or beliefs of others and yet are extremely sensitive to others' criticisms of their own behavior. Consequently, they frequently get into arguments with others and find that they have few friends. They think little of others, and others think little of them.

Assertive behavior is the desired alternative and has been characterized in various ways by various writers. Basically, assertive individuals are willing to assert their own rights, but unlike their aggressive counterparts they do not hurt others in the process. Assertive individuals speak their minds and welcome others doing likewise. Robert Alberti and Michael Emmons in *Your Perfect Right,* the first book on assertiveness training, note that "behavior which enables a person to act in his own best interest, to stand up for himself without undue anxiety, to express his honest feelings comfortably, or to exercise his own rights without denying the rights of others we call *assertive behavior.*" Furthermore, "the assertive individual is fully in charge of himself in interpersonal relationships, feels confident and capable without cockiness or hostility, is basically spontaneous in the expression of feelings and emotions, and is generally looked up to and admired by others." Surely this is the picture of a most effective individual.

In an exploration of assertiveness as a communication variable, Robert Norton and Barbara Warnick found that four characteristics may be identified as describing and defining assertiveness in interpersonal communication. Assertive individuals are, first, *open* persons. They engage in frank and open expression of their feelings to people in general as well as to those for whom there may be some sexual interest. Second, assertive individuals are *not anxious;* they readily volunteer opinions and beliefs, deal directly with interpersonal communication situations that may be stressful, and question others without fear. Their communications are dominant, frequent, and of high intensity. They have a positive view of their own communication performance and this view seems to be shared by those with whom they communicate. Third, assertive interpersonal communicators are *contentious;* they stand up and argue for their rights, even if this entails a certain degree of unpleasantness with relatives or close friends. Fourth, assertive persons are *not intimidated* and are not easily persuaded.

It should be emphasized that assertive people are assertive when they want to be but can be nonassertive if the situation seems to call for it. For example, we might wish to be nonassertive in a situation in which our assertiveness might emotionally hurt the other person. Let us say that an older relative wishes us to do something for him or her. We could assert our rights and say no, but in doing so we would probably hurt this person, and so it might be better to simply do as was asked. But, of course, there are limits that should be observed. The individual should be careful, in such a situation, that he or she is not hurt instead. For example, the parents who wish their child to remain living at home until marriage may be hurt by the child's assertive behavior, and yet the alternative is for the son or daughter to hurt himself or herself. So here assertive behavior seems the better choice, even though someone may be hurt in the process.

SHYNESS

The *Random House Dictionary* defines *shy* as "bashful, retiring, easily frightened away, timid, suspicious, distrustful, reluctant, wary." *Roget's Thesaurus* groups *shy* with such terms as *cowardly, fearful, spiritless, soft, fainthearted, unobtrusive, unassuming, modest, diffident, retiring, humble, sheepish,* and *blushing.* Contemporary researchers have wisely avoided a specific definition of the term and have chosen instead to characterize the behaviors of shyness—an approach that seems a great deal more enlightening.

Shyness may vary from extremely mild to extremely severe. Some people are shy only to the point of being a bit uncomfortable in certain situations or with certain people, while others are so shy that they are totally debilitated and cannot function interpersonally at all. Most shy people exist somewhere in between these extremes.

An individual might be shy with certain people, in certain situations, or with certain people in certain situations. Some people become shy when dealing with specific types or classes of people. Philip Zimbardo notes that of the students who indicated that they were shy with certain people, 70 percent specified that they were especially shy with strangers, while 64 percent said "opposite sex persons," 55 percent said "authorities by virtue of their knowledge," 40 percent said "authorities by virtue of their role," and 21 percent said "relatives."

Of the contexts that generate shyness, being the focus of attention in a large group, as in giving a speech, was noted by 73 percent of the shy students, while 68 percent noted that they were shy in large groups generally. Other contexts noted for inducing shyness were general social situations, new social situations, situations calling for assertiveness, situations in which the person is being evaluated, situations in which the individual needs help, and small task-oriented groups.

Most people experience shyness at some time in their lives; shyness seems nearly universal but varies in terms of degree. Shyness seems not to be restricted to any specific age group or to either sex, although it does appear to be somewhat more prevalent among children of school age than among adults. And so there seems to be some evidence that some people may grow out of their shyness. Contrary to some popular conceptions shyness is not necessarily more prevalent in women, although nonassertiveness is.

The symptoms of shyness vary greatly from one person to another and from one situation to another. Perhaps the most commonly experienced symptom of shyness is an increased heart rate, when one can almost hear the heart pounding. Perspiration increases, sometimes to the point at which beads of perspiration stream down the face. We may blush and when we become conscious of it, we may become even more self-conscious so that the blush deepens. When others call it to our attention, we may experience a further increase in both self-consciousness and blushing—but also a release because we no longer have to try to hide it. We may experience "knots" or "butterflies" in the stomach accompanied by rumblings and a tenseness. In extreme cases we may experience shaking and trembling—a sight that is quite common among novice public speakers. The audience gets the feeling that the speaker's legs are never going to hold out and that sooner or later he or she will collapse.

When in an interactional situation some shy people avoid direct eye contact and bodily directness, finding it difficult, for example, to stand parallel with others. Instead they stand at an angle, almost as if they will be better able to run away in that position. Shy people may experience breaks in fluency, they may stammer or stutter, make frequent word and sentence corrections and changes, and use numerous and prolonged periods of pause. Some of these pauses are filled with vocalizations such as *ur, ah,* and the like, while others are totally silent.

Shy people may also experience feelings of inadequacy because they cannot function effectively in such situations; sometimes the harder they try, the more difficult it becomes. Feelings of self-consciousness increase and make matters even worse.

All that has been said about shyness should be tempered with the rather obvious observation that some people may be quite content to be shy; they may find their shyness comfortable and productive for their purposes. Not every shy person wants to or should change.

ORIGINS OF NONASSERTIVENESS AND SHYNESS

There are numerous explanations about the origins of nonassertiveness and shyness. One position is that people are simply born that way and that there is an innate factor that determines whether a person will be assertive or nonassertive, shy or not shy. If, as it seems, people are born with different sensitivities to sound or pain, for example, then it seems not too great a leap to argue that people are also born with different sensitivities to strangers or to new situations or to interpersonal encounters that call for the assertion of one's individual rights.

A second set of explanations may be found in the approach of clinical psychology and psychiatry. Here it is argued that one's shyness or lack of assertiveness is a symptom of personal inadequacy, of some problem or conflict the individual might have. This symptom may be the result of some early traumatic experience or rejection by one's mother, for example, or of some later problem, for example, repeated failure in athletic activities or rejection by peers. In a more Freudian interpretation, shyness would be seen as a symptom of unfulfilled desires, primarily sexual. There are probably hundreds of variations on this same basic theme, but all seem to agree that both nonassertive and shy behaviors are symptoms of some problem or inadequacy. All such approaches also agree that the remedy for nonassertive and shy behavior is to be found in these early experiences and in the problems and inadequacies that they generated. According to this position, to reduce shyness or increase assertiveness, one would need intensive therapy.

A more satisfying explanation, I feel, would be that nonassertiveness and assertiveness, shyness and nonshyness are learned behaviors and that somewhere in our personal history we have learned to act as we do. Some people, because of their unique set of experiences, learned assertive behaviors, while others, because of their unique set of experiences, learned nonassertive behaviors. But we all learned the behaviors, whatever they are, in essentially the same way. Here, too, there are a number of explanations concerning how the specific learning took place. A reinforcement or conditioning position would argue that we learned those behaviors, whether assertive or shy, that were followed by reinforcement (the presentation of a rewarding stimulus or the removal of an aversive or painful stimulus) and failed to learn (or, if already learned, unlearned) those behaviors that were followed by punishment. Thus, if our attempts at being assertive were rewarded, we learned to repeat assertive behaviors on further occasions. If, on the other hand, our assertive behaviors were punished, socially or physically, we learned not to engage in such behaviors in other situations; that is, we learned nonassertive behaviors.

Another type of learning position, often referred to as "semantogenic," argues that we learned shyness because we were labeled "shy" and we conformed to the label that people placed on us. The awkward person, for example, can often trace the awkwardness back to being called "awkward" by family and friends. Stutterers, according to some theories, were developed or "created" from normal speakers who experienced normal speech hesitations but who were labeled "stutterer" by their parents. They then attempted not to hesitate (which is impossible at certain early ages) and as a result hesitated all the more. These increased hesitations are the essence of what we consider stuttering.

Whether it is by reinforcement or by labeling or by some other learning process, the evidence clearly favors the notion that such behaviors are learned rather than inborn or symptoms of some psychological trauma or conflict. The important implication of this learning position is that if the behaviors were learned, then they can be unlearned. We can, for example, rearrange the reinforcement contingencies and thus alter our behavior, or we can focus attention on the labels and substitute more appropriate ones. All this is not to say that such change will therefore be easily effected but only that such change is possible without rearranging our innate structure (even if that were possible) or solving all one's early psychological problems (even if that were possible).

PRINCIPLES FOR INCREASING
ASSERTIVENESS AND DECREASING SHYNESS

The general assumption made by most assertiveness and shyness trainers is that the majority of people are situationally nonassertive or shy. Most people are able to modify their behavior, with a resultant increase in general interpersonal effectiveness and in self-esteem.

Those who are generally nonassertive or extremely shy, however, probably need extensive training with a therapist. Those who are only moderately nonassertive or shy and who wish to understand their assertiveness and shyness—and perhaps to behave differently in certain situations—should find the following principles of value. The rationale and the specific principles derive from the behavior modification techniques of B. F. Skinner and the systematic desensitization techniques of Joseph Wolpe and others. In formulating these five principles, the techniques of these theorists, as well as the specific assertiveness and shyness training manuals noted in the introduction to this unit, were most helpful.

It should be said at the outset that this training or retraining deals with behavior and not with abstract or repressed needs and desires. The emphasis is on behavior, and it is assumed that if one behaves in assertive or nonshy ways, one will in fact become more assertive and less shy. Further, it is assumed that these behaviors will reflect on the way in which these people think of themselves. For example, if we act assertively, we will soon think of ourselves as assertive individuals, and, more importantly, our self-concepts in general will be improved.

1. Analyze the Assertive and
Nonshy Behavior of Others

The first step in increasing our assertiveness or reducing our shyness is to understand the nature of these behaviors. On an intellectual level this understanding should already have been achieved. What is necessary and more important than an intellectual understanding, however, is to understand actual assertive and nonshy behavior, and the best way to start is to observe and analyze the behaviors of others. We should become able to distinguish the differences among assertive, aggressive, and nonassertive behaviors and between shy and nonshy behaviors. Focus on what makes one behavior assertive and another behavior shy, or aggressive, or nonassertive. Listen to what is said and how it is said. Recall the nonverbal behaviors and try to categorize nonverbal behaviors as assertive, aggressive, nonassertive, shy, or nonshy.

2. Analyze Your Own Behaviors

It is generally easier to analyze the behaviors of others than our own. We find it difficult to be objective with ourselves. After we have acquired some skills in observing the behaviors of others, we can turn our analysis to ourselves. We should be able to analyze those situations in which we are normally assertive, nonassertive, aggressive, shy, and nonshy. What characterizes these situations? What do the situations in which you are normally aggressive have in common? How do these situations differ from the situations in which you are normally nonassertive? What do the situations in which you are normally shy have in common?

We should also be able to analyze our nonverbal behaviors. How do we stand when we are assertive? Aggressive? Nonassertive? Shy? Nonshy? What tone of voice do we use? What kind of eye contact do we maintain? What do we do with our hands? All our nonverbal behaviors are probably different for each of these types of behaviors.

3. Record Your Behaviors

It is essential in any training program that you record your behaviors as accurately as possible. The advantages of this practice are many. First, it will force you to pay special attention to all your behaviors and will force you to question whether they are assertive or shy. Second, it will enable you to see if improvements have been made, and, assuming they have been, this will provide reinforcement and will encourage you to continue your efforts. Third, this record will spotlight where improvement is particularly needed and will then serve as a guide for future behaviors.

A simple three-part form with space for recording assertive, aggressive, and nonaggressive behaviors and a two-part form for recording shy and nonshy behaviors will suffice. Be as specific as possible in recording your behaviors, and give as many details of the actual situation as seem reasonable.

4. Rehearse Assertive and Nonshy Behaviors

A number of different systems have been proposed for effective rehearsal of assertive and nonshy behaviors. One of the most popular is to select a situation in which you are normally nonassertive or shy and build a hierarchy that begins with a relatively nonthreatening behavior and ends with the desired behavior. For example, let us say that you have difficulty speaking in class and that the desired behavior is to speak your mind in class. You might construct a hierarchy of situations that lead up to speaking in class. Such a hierarchy might begin with something like simply visualizing yourself sitting in class. You might then visualize yourself sitting in class while you are in a state of relaxation. Once you have mastered this visualization you may proceed to the next step—visualizing the instructor asking a question. Once you are able to visualize this situation and remain relaxed throughout, visualize the instructor asking you the question. Visualize this situation until you can do so while relaxed. Then try visualizing yourself answering the question. Again, do this until you can do it while fully relaxed. Next you might rehearse visualizing your volunteering your opinion in class—the desired behavior. Do this until you can do it while totally relaxed.

This is the mental rehearsal. You might add an actual vocal dimension to this by actually answering the question you imagine the teacher asking you and vocalizing your opinion. Again, do this until you have no difficulty. Next, try doing this in front of a supportive friend or group of friends. After this rehearsal you are probably ready for the next step.

5. Do It

This step is naturally the most difficult but obviously the most important. You can only increase assertiveness and decrease shyness when you act out these behaviors; you cannot become assertive by acting nonassertively, nor can you significantly reduce shyness by acting shy.

Again, do this in small steps. Staying with the previous example, attempt to answer a question that you are sure of before attempting to volunteer an opinion or argue with the position of the instructor. Once you have done this, it is essential and most pleasant to *reward yourself* in some way. Give yourself something you want—an ice cream cone, a record, a new jacket. The desired behavior will be more easily and permanently learned if you reward yourself immediately after engaging in the behavior. Try not to delay the reward too long: rewards work best when they are immediate.

After performing the behavior, attempt to get some feedback from others. Start with people who are generally supportive. They should provide you with the social reinforcement so helpful in learning new behavior patterns. This feedback is particularly important because your intention and the perception of your behavior by a receiver may be totally different. (This distinction between the intention of the source and the perception of the receiver is referred to repeatedly in this book; see especially Unit 18.) While you may behave in certain ways with the intention of communicating confidence or determination, the receiver may perceive them as arrogance or stubbornness. Consequently, another person's perception of your behavior can often help a great deal in allowing you to see yourself from the outside instead of only from the inside.

In all behaviors, but especially with new behaviors, we should recognize that we may initially fail in what we are attempting to do. We might attempt to assert ourselves only to find that we have been unsuccessful. You might, for example, try to answer the teacher's question and find that not only do you have the wrong answer, but you did not even understand the question. Or you might raise your hand and find yourself lost for words when you are recognized. These incidents should not discourage us; we should recognize that in all attempts to change behaviors we will experience both failure and success. Naturally, we should try to develop these behaviors in situations that are likely to result in success, but any failures should not discourage us. They are only momentary setbacks and not insurmountable problems.

A note of caution should be added to this discussion, especially as it pertains to assertiveness. It is easy to visualize a situation in which people are talking behind us in a movie and, with our newfound enthusiasm for assertiveness, we tell these people to be quiet. It is also easy to visualize our getting smashed in the teeth as a result. Equally easy to visualize is asserting ourselves with someone we care for only to find that as a result this person bursts into tears, totally unable to handle our new behavior.

In applying these principles, be careful that you do not go beyond what you can handle—physically and emotionally. Do not, for example, assert yourself out of a job. It is best to be careful in changing any behavior but especially, it seems, with assertiveness.

SOURCES

I found the following works especially valuable in conceptualizing and in writing this unit. Robert E. Alberti and Michael L. Emmons' two books are perhaps the best starting places: *Your Perfect Right: A Guide to Assertive Behavior* (San Luis Obispo, Calif.: Impact, 1970) and *Stand Up, Speak Out, Talk Back: The Key to Self-Assertive Behavior* (New York: Pocket Books, 1970). Herbert Fensterheim and Jean Baer's *Don't Say Yes When You Want to Say No* (New York: Dell, 1975) and Manuel J. Smith's *When I Say No, I Feel Guilty* (New York: Bantam Books, 1975) are similar in many respects; both provide useful insights from assertiveness trainers. Robert J. Ringer's *Winning Through Intimidation* (New York: Fawcett, 1973) presents many ideas from the point of view of the real estate salesperson, but they are applicable to everyone. S. Phelps and N. Austin's *The Assertive Woman* (San Luis Obispo, Calif.: Impact, 1975) addresses assertive behavior in relation to the particular problems women face. The experiments of Thomas Moriarty are reported in his "A Nation of Willing Victims," *Psychology Today* 8 (April 1975): 43–50. Perhaps the most thorough discussion of assertiveness as communication is Ronald B. Adler's *Confidence in Communication: A Guide to Assertive and Social Skills* (New York: Holt, Rinehart and Winston, 1977). This book contains numerous exercises that may be used individually or in groups. The relationship between assertiveness and communication is examined in Robert Norton and Barbara Warnick, "Assertiveness as a Communication Construct," *Human Communication Research* 3 (Fall 1976): 62–66.

On shyness, see Michel Girodo, *Shy?* (New York: Pocket Books, 1978) and C. Rayner, *The Shy Person's Book* (New York: McKay, 1973). Gerald M. Phillips and Nancy J. Metzger's *Intimate Communication* (Boston: Allyn & Bacon, 1976) discusses many of the issues related to shyness from a communication point of view. Two excellent sources from both academic and popular points of view are Philip G. Zimbardo's *Shyness: What It Is, What to Do About It* (Reading, Mass.: Addison-Wesley, 1977), and Gerald M. Phillips, *Help for Shy People or Anyone Else Who Ever Felt Ill at Ease on Entering a Room Full of Strangers* (Englewood Cliffs, N.J.: Prentice-Hall [Spectrum], 1981).

For an analysis of the varied forms of "shyness," see Lynne Kelly, "A Rose by Any Other Name is Still a Rose: A Comparative Analysis of Reticence, Communication Apprehension, Unwillingness to Communicate, and Shyness," *Human Communication Research* 8 (Winter 1982):99–113. For an up-to-date report on treatment for apprehension, see Susan R. Glaser, "Oral Communication Apprehension and Avoidance: The Current Status of Treatment Research," *Communication Education* 30 (October 1981):321–341.

EXPERIENTIAL VEHICLES

8.1 ASSERTIVENESS QUESTIONNAIRE

Indicate how you would respond to each of the 20 situations presented below. Use the following keys:

AS   Assertively
AG   Aggressively
NO   Nonassertively

Respond instinctively rather than in the way you feel you should respond.

After each person has responded individually, discuss these situations and the responses in groups of five or six in any way you feel is meaningful.

1. _____ A fellow student borrowed a book and has not returned it in two weeks.
2. _____ The people behind you in a movie are talking loudly.
3. _____ Your neighbor is playing a stereo so loud you have difficulty studying.
4. _____ You are shortchanged by 25¢ at a supermarket.
5. _____ Your meal in a restaurant arrives cold instead of hot.
6. _____ A neighbor's dog repeatedly defecates in front of your house.
7. _____ A neighbor's dog barks constantly during the day when the owner is out.
8. _____ A friend borrows $5 but does not show any interest in returning it.
9. _____ A neighbor repeatedly drops by for coffee without being invited.
10. _____ A fellow student does not work on a group project for which each member will receive the same grade.
11. _____ A teacher gives you a grade that you feel is unfair.
12. _____ You are attracted to someone in class and want to ask the person for a date.
13. _____ Your business partner does not do half of the work.
14. _____ A friend is constantly late for appointments.
15. _____ A group of fellow students is unfairly speaking against someone you know.
16. _____ A persistent salesperson keeps showing you merchandise you do not want to buy.
17. _____ Your friend wants to borrow your expensive watch and you are afraid he or she will lose it.

18. _____ Your boss takes advantage of you by asking you to take on all sorts of extra responsibilities.
19. _____ You are at a party where you know no one but the host.
20. _____ Someone asks you for a date but you do not want to go.

8.2 ROLE PLAYING ASSERTIVENESS

In groups of five or six, role play each of the following four situations so that each situation is played by an assertive, an aggressive, and a nonassertive behavior type. The roles should be rotated so that each person in the group gets an opportunity to demonstrate each of the three behavior patterns. The role of the initiator or stimulator should also be rotated.

Discussion should center on the following:

1. What nonverbal behaviors accompany each of the three behavior patterns?
2. What types of verbal statements are used to demonstrate the three behavior patterns?
3. Do some people have difficulty playing certain roles? Explain.
4. What kind of feelings accompany the playing of the various behavior types? Explain as specifically as possible.
5. Does assertiveness seem to come easier as the role playing progresses? Would this hold in the "real world"?
6. How might a hierarchy (as explained in the fourth principle for increasing assertiveness and reducing shyness) be created for any one of the situations?

"Cheating" on an Examination

You and another student turn in examination papers that are too similar to be the result of mere coincidence. The instructor accuses you of cheating by allowing the student behind you to copy your answers. You were not aware that anyone saw your paper.

Decorating Your Apartment

You have just redecorated your apartment and have gone through considerable time and money in making it exactly as you want it. A good friend of yours brings you a house gift—the ugliest poster you have ever seen. Your friend insists that you hang it over your fireplace, the focal point of your living room.

Borrowing Money

A friend borrows $30 and promises to pay you back tomorrow. But tomorrow passes, as do 20 other tomorrows, and yet there is no sign of the

*money. You know that the person has not forgotten about it and you also
know that the person has more than enough money to pay you back.*

Neighbor Intrusions

*A neighbor has been keeping a stereo at an extremely high volume late
into the evening. This makes it difficult for you to sleep.*

8.3 SHYNESS IN COMMUNICATION

Visualize the following communication situations and respond to each
according to this five-point scale:

a.   I have great difficulty with this situation.
b.   I have considerable difficulty with this situation.
c.   I have some difficulty with this situation.
d.   I have no difficulty with this situation.
e.   I enjoy this situation.

1.   _____ You are called on in class when you know the answer.
2.   _____ You are in a group of friends and there is silence.
3.   _____ You are criticized by friends.
4.   _____ You are complimented by friends.
5.   _____ You are called on the phone for a date.
6.   _____ You are shown to be incorrect by friends.
7.   _____ You are approached by a stranger requesting information.
8.   _____ You are speaking before a large audience.
9.   _____ You are in a group and are ignored.
10. _____ You are being interviewed for a job.
11. _____ You are talking with someone who stands very close to you.
12. _____ You are talking with someone who repeatedly touches you.
13. _____ You are called on in class when you do not know the answer.
14. _____ You burst out crying in front of friends.
15. _____ You are told of unfavorable (but true) gossip about yourself.

1.   Create a hierarchy (as explained in the fourth principle for increasing
     assertiveness and reducing shyness) for one of the behaviors you
     responded to with an *a* (indicating "great difficulty") or *b* (indicating
     "considerable difficulty").
2.   What characterizes those situations you have difficulty with? What
     characterizes those situations you have no difficulty with or those you
     enjoy? What are the essential differences?
3.   Role play in your mind how you would act as the initiator of these various
     communications; for example, you criticize a friend, you compliment a
     friend, you call someone for a date, and so on. Does visualizing these

situations contribute anything to your understanding of your own shyness in communication? Explain.

8.4 SOME DEFINITIONS: REVIEW QUIZ II

Here are some of the significant concepts introduced in Part Two (Units 5, 6, 7, and 8). Identify the concept defined in each of the following statements.

1. "A transaction that is determined by what the actual situation—the outside event, the word that is spoken, the thought that occurs, the hope that emerges—means to the individual at the moment."
2. "The active realization that the past is over and final, the future does not exist, and the present is our only chance to have integrity."
3. The self that represents all of those things about ourselves that others know but of which we are ignorant.
4. From out of all our early experiences, particularly from the messages—both verbal and nonverbal—received from our parents, we develop these, and for the most part follow them throughout our lives.
5. "The position of genuine heroes and princes, and heroines and princesses."
6. A type of communication in which information about the self that is normally kept hidden is revealed to another person.
7. A manner of revealing the self that is only pseudo–self-disclosure; an approach that details some facts of the individual's life but does not really invite involvement from listeners. From this type of disclosure, we learn what the individual did or what happened to him or her throughout that person's life, but somehow we really do not get to know the person.
8. The generalizing of virtue from one area to another; a process whereby we perceive a person as credible or knowledgeable in several areas because of that person's credibility or knowledge in one area.
9. An inability or unwillingness to stand up for one's rights in certain situations; for example, in situations that create a great deal of anxiety—perhaps because of the person one is interacting with or because of the topic being considered.
10. "Behavior which enables a person to act in his own best interest, to stand up for himself without undue anxiety, to express his honest feelings comfortably, or to exercise his own rights without denying the rights of others."

VERBAL MESSAGES
PART THREE

UNIVERSALS OF VERBAL MESSAGES

Upon completion of this unit, you should be able to:

1. define the following terms: *specialization, productivity, displacement, rapid fading, arbitrariness,* and *cultural transmission*
2. identify those features that make human language superior to animal communication systems
3. distinguish between immanent reference and displacement
4. define and explain the principle of determinism
5. define *recurrence* in verbal interaction
6. explain the relativity of signal and noise
7. explain reinforcement/packaging
8. explain the way in which the principle of adjustment operates in interpersonal communication
9. identify the operation of the principles of verbal interaction in the verbal interactions of others
10. identify at least three instances of your own behavior in which these principles were operative
11. identify those characteristics that are present or absent from at least one nonhuman communication system
12. explain some of the reasons why words are created

Perhaps the best way to understand language in general and verbal messages in particular is to focus on those features of language systems that are universal. In this unit I focus on two classes, or types, of universals. First, I consider some *universal characteristics of language,* that is, characteristics that are present in all human language systems and that taken together may be said to define what language is, how it is constructed, and what its potentials and limitations are. Six such universal characteristics are defined. Second, I discuss six *universal principles of verbal interaction,* that is, features that are present in all verbal interactions regardless of their specific purpose, their particular context, or their unique participants.

UNIVERSAL CHARACTERISTICS OF
HUMAN LANGUAGE SYSTEMS

The human language system is a specialized, productive system capable of displacement and composed of rapidly fading, arbitrary, culturally transmitted symbols. Contained in this definition are six universal characteristics of all human language systems: specialization, productivity, displacement, rapid fading, arbitrariness, and cultural transmission.

Specialization

When a human speaks, the speech process serves no biological function; it is, instead, specialized for communication. A specialized communication system, according to Charles Hockett, is one whose "direct energetic consequences are biologically irrelevant." Human language serves only one major purpose—to communicate. It aids no biological function. On the other hand, while a panting dog communicates information about its presence and perhaps about its internal state, the panting serves first and foremost the biological function of temperature regulation. The fact that communication accompanies or results from this behavior is only incidental.

Productivity

Human verbal messages evidence productivity—sometimes referred to as openness or creativity. That is, our verbal messages are novel utterances; each utterance is generated anew. There are exceptions to this general rule, but these seem few and trivial. For example, sentences such as, "How are you?," "What's new?," "Good luck," and similar expressions do not evidence productivity; they are not newly created each time they are uttered. Except for sentences such as these, all other verbal messages are created at the time of utterance. When you speak, you are not repeating memorized sentences but rather creating your own sentences. Similarly, your understanding of verbal messages evidences productivity in that you can understand new utterances as they are uttered. Your ability to comprehend verbal messages is not limited to previously heard and learned utterances.

The rules of grammar have imposed some restrictions on the way in which sentences may be generated, and so complete productivity, in regard to form at least, does not exist. For example, we do not utter such sentences as, "The rock thinks quietly" or "The tulip attacked the poor old turtle." Our language has built-in restrictions that, to stick with these examples, require that a "human" or "animal" noun (rather than an "inanimate" noun such as *rock* or *tulip*) serve as the subject of such verbs as *thinks* or *attacked*. The poet, of course, may and frequently does violate such rules.

Another dimension of productivity is that human message systems allow the introduction of new words. When something is discovered or invented, we can create new words to describe it. When new ideas or new theoretical concepts are developed, we can create words to describe them. And it does not seem to matter whether we create the new word by joining together old words or parts of old words or create it from scratch. What does matter is that the language system is open to expansion—a feature that seems absent from just about all known animal communication systems.

Displacement

Human language can be used to talk about things that are remote in both time and space; one can talk about the past and the future as easily as the present. And one can talk about things that one has never and will never perceive—about mermaids and unicorns, about supernatural beings from other planets, about talking animals. One can talk about the unreal as well as the real, the imaginary as well as the actual. This characteristic is known as displacement and refers to the fact that messages may have effects or consequences that are independent of their context. Thus, for example, statements uttered in one place today may have effects elsewhere tomorrow. That is, both the referents (what is talked about) and the effects of messages may be displaced.

Displacement, together with productivity, also makes possible the ability to lie. Humans are able to lie because they are able to form new utterances (productivity) and because their utterances are not limited to what is in one's immediate environment (displacement). Thus, for example, we may say, "I found a sunken treasure off the coast of Manhattan, and for a mere $27.50 I'll give you a map that will make you a millionaire," without this sentence's ever having been uttered before and without any concern for what is or is not actually present in one's environment.

In other words, there are no linguistic limitations that restrict our utterances to accurate descriptions of reality. Although animal lovers are fond of telling stories about pets trying to fool them, it appears that lying is extremely rare, if not totally absent, in animal communication.

Rapid Fading

Speech sounds fade rapidly; they are evanescent. They must be received immediately after they are emitted or else they will not be received at all. Although mechanical devices now enable sound to be preserved much as writing is preserved, this is not a characteristic of human language. Rather, these are nonlanguage or extralinguistic means of storing information and aiding memory. Of course, all signals fade; written symbols and even symbols carved in rock are not permanent. In relative terms, however, speech signals are probably the least permanent of all communicative media.

Arbitrariness

Language signals are arbitrary; they do not possess any of the physical properties or characteristics of the things for which they stand. The word *wine* is no more tasty than the word *sand*, nor is the latter any less wet.

Opposed to arbitrariness is *iconicity*. Iconic signals do bear a resemblance to their referents. A line drawing of a person is iconic in representing the body parts in proper relation to each other. But it is arbitrary in representing the texture and thickness of the anatomical structures.

Both arbitrariness and iconicity are relative. For example, a line drawing is more arbitrary than a black-and-white photograph, which is more arbitrary than a color photograph. Paralinguistic features (volume, rate, rhythm) are more iconic than the features normally classified as belonging to language. Rate, for example, may vary directly with emotional arousal and hence would be iconic. But the sound of the word *fast* is not actually fast. (See Unit 16 for discussions on paralanguage.)

Cultural Transmission

The form of any particular human language is culturally or traditionally transmitted. The child raised by English speakers learns English as a native speaker, regardless of the language of his or her biological parents. The genetic endowment pertains to human ability to use language in general rather than to any specific human language.

One of the consequences of cultural transmission is that any human language can be learned by any normal human being. All human languages—English, Chinese, Italian, Russian, Bantu, or any of the other approximately 3000 languages—are equally learnable; no one language should present any greater difficulty for a child than any other language. It should be added, however, that this ability to learn any language is true only at particular times in the life of the individual. One generally cannot learn to speak a language as fluently as a native after passing a certain age, usually around puberty.

UNIVERSAL PRINCIPLES OF VERBAL INTERACTION

The six principles that follow are applicable to any and all verbal interactions. Universal principles such as these are significant for two major reasons. First, they provide a convenient summary of essential qualities of verbal interaction. In effect, they define what constitutes a verbal interaction—its nature and its essential aspects. Second, these universals provide a set of principles for analyzing verbal interactions that should prove useful for analyzing any interaction that is primarily or even partially linguistic. These universal principles provide us with a set of questions to ask about any verbal interaction.

The Principle of Adjustment

Communication may take place only to the extent that the parties communicating share the same system of signals. This is obvious when dealing with speakers of two different languages; one will not be able to communicate with the other to the extent that their language systems differ.

This principle takes on particular relevance, however, when we realize that no two persons share identical signal systems. Parents and children, for example, not only have different vocabularies to a very great extent but, even more importantly, have different denotative and especially different connotative meanings for the terms they have in common (see Unit 11). Different cultures and subcultures, even when they share a common language, often have greatly differing nonverbal communication systems. To the extent that these systems differ, communication will not take place.

The Principle of Immanent Reference

Human beings have the ability to use what Leonard Bloomfield calls "displaced speech" and what Charles Hockett labels "displacement"; that is, human language may make reference to the past as well as to the future; humans can talk about what is not here and what is not now. Nevertheless, all verbalization makes some reference to the present, to the specific context, to the speaker, and to the hearer(s). All verbal interactions, in other words, contain immanent references. The person who complains that things at work are not going well may be asking for some kind of immediate reinforcement. The person who talks about how great the old days were may be making an oblique reference to the difficulties being experienced today. The parents who talk about how respectful they were of their parents may be expressing their dis-

"I've called this meeting to investigate this principle of adjustment."

pleasure over the way in which their children treat them and may, in fact, be asking their children for respect.

In attempting to understand verbal interaction, then, it is helpful to ask such questions as, "To what extent does this communication refer to this particular situation?," "To what extent does this communication refer to the speaker?," or "In what ways is the speaker commenting on the hearer(s)?"

The Principle of Determinism

All verbalizations are to some extent determined; all verbalization is to some extent purposeful. Whenever something is said, there is a reason. Similarly, when nothing is said in an interactional situation, there is a reason. Words, of course, communicate, and there are reasons why the words used are used; but silence also communicates, and there are reasons why silence is used. Watzlawick, Jackson, and Beavin, in *Pragmatics of Human Communication*, put it this way: one cannot *not* communicate. Whenever we are in an interactional situation, regardless of what we do or say or don't do or say, we communicate. Words and silence alike have message value; they communicate something to other people who in turn cannot *not* respond and are therefore also communicating.

Consequently, it is always useful in analyzing interactions to ask the reasons for the words as well as the reasons for the silences. Each communicates and each is governed by some reason or reasons; all messages are determined.

The Principle of Recurrence

In our interactions individuals will tell us—not once but many times and not in one way but in many ways—about themselves—who they are, how they preceive themselves, what they like, what they dislike, what they want, what they avoid, and so on.

Whatever is perceived as important or significant to an individual will recur in that person's verbal interactions; he or she will tell us in many different ways and on many different occasions what these things are. Of course, these things will rarely be communicated in an obvious manner. People who find themselves in need of approval do not directly ask others for approval. Rather, they go about obtaining approval responses in more subtle ways, perhaps by asking how others like their new outfit, perhaps by talking about their grades on an examination, perhaps by talking about how they never betray a confidence, and so on.

The Principle of Relativity of Signal and Noise

What constitutes a signal and what constitutes noise in any given communication is relative rather than absolute. If we are interested in hearing a particular story and the speaker, in narrating it, breaks it up by coughing, we might become annoyed because the coughing (noise) is disturbing our reception of the story (signal). But suppose this individual seeks some form of medication and in his or her interactions with the doctor coughs in a similar way. To the doctor this coughing might be the signal; the coughing might communicate an important message to the doctor. Similarly, when listening to a stutterer tell a story, we may focus on the story, which would be the signal. The stuttering would be the noise interfering with our reception of the signal. But to the speech pathologist the stuttering is the signal to which he or she attends, and the story might be the noise.

The point is simply this: What is signal to one person and in one context might be noise to another person in another context.

The Principle of Reinforcement/Packaging

In most interactions messages are transmitted simultaneously through a number of different channels. We utter sounds with our vocal mechanism, but we also utilize our body posture and our spatial relationships at the same time to reinforce our message. We say "no" and at the same time pound our fist on the table. One channel reinforces the other; the message is presented as a "package."

The extent to which simultaneous messages reinforce each other or contradict each other, then, is extremely important in understanding human communication. A verbal message when accompanied by different nonverbal messages is not the same message and cannot be responded to in the same way.

SOURCES

For universal characteristics of language I relied on the work of Charles F. Hockett, particularly "The Problem of Universals in Language," in J. H. Greenberg, ed., Universals of Language (Cambridge, Mass.: M.I.T. Press, 1963), and "The Origin of Speech," Scientific American 203 (1960): 89–96. The concepts of language universals are thoroughly surveyed in Greenberg's Universals of Language. Most of the material, however, presumes a rather thorough knowledge of linguistics.

Portions of the material in this unit were adapted from my The Psychology of Speech and Language: An Introduction to Psycholinguistics (Washington, D.C.: University Press, 1981). On language universals, see also Jean Aitchison, The Articulate Mammal (New York: McGraw-Hill, 1977). The six basic principles of verbal interaction were taken from Robert E. Pittenger, Charles F. Hockett, and John J. Danehy, The First Five Minutes: A Sample of Microscopic Interview Analysis (Ithaca, N.Y.: Paul Martineau, 1960). Also in this area, see Eric H. Lenneberg, "Review of The First Five Minutes," Language 38 (1962): 69–73. For additional material on expressive language, see Robert E. Pittenger and Henry Lee Smith, Jr., "A Basis for Some Contributions of Linguistics to Psychiatry," Psychiatry 20 (1957): 61–78, and Norman A. McQuown, "Linguistic Transcription and Specification of Psychiatric Interview Material," Psychiatry 20 (1957): 79–86.

On these universals and the ways in which human communication differs from animal communication, see A. Akmajian, R. A. Demers, and R. M. Harnish, Linguistics: An Introduction to Language and Communication (Cambridge, Mass.: MIT Press, 1979). For an excellent overview of the psychology of language see Blaine Goss, Processing Communication (Belmont, Calif.: Wadsworth, 1982).

9.1 WORD COINAGE

Although language and culture are closely related, and although the language closely reflects the culture, there often seem to be concepts important to a culture or a subculture for which the language does not provide a convenient one-word label.

Sometimes slang or "substandard" forms fill this void, for example, *youse* or *you all* for "you" (plural) or *screw* for "prison guard." Sometimes words are created because of some social issue, for example, *Ms.* for a form of address for women regardless of marital status.

In order to gain greater insight into the relationship between language and culture/subculture and to become more familiar with the dimensions and functions of words, perform the following exercise in groups of five or six.

1. Create a new word for some concept that is important to the culture or to a particular subculture and for which a single-word label does not exist.
2. Define this word as it would be defined in a dictionary and identify its part(s) of speech.
3. List its various inflectional forms and definitions.
4. Provide two or three sentences in which the word is used.
5. Justify the coinage of this new word, considering, for example, why this word is needed, what void it fills, what it clarifies, what its importance is, what its effects might be should it be used widely, and so forth.

9.2 THE CASE OF **WALDON** *V.* **MARTIN AND COMPANY**

The purpose of this experience is to enable you to better understand the universals of verbal interaction covered in this unit. All students should first carefully read the case presented.

Six people should be selected—preferably from volunteers—to role play the six characters involved in this case. Each person should develop his or her role as he or she feels the person would probably act.

All others should pay close attention to the drama as it unfolds. After about 5 minutes or so, try to jot down examples of the universals of verbal interaction. Write down the phrases or sentences used by the role players that illustrate the various universals of verbal interaction.

136

*A popular national magazine specializing in "the new and the different"
ran an article that asked the reader's help in "conducting a scientific
experiment on visual perception." The article advised the readers to cut
out "the specially treated card" inserted in the magazine, dissolve the
card in methanol (CH_3OH), drink the mixture, and focus on some bright
object such as the sun or a powerful lamp. The readers were assured that
if they did this they would have reactions "never experienced before,"
that they would be able "to see with amazing accuracy and clarity," and
that they would "have insights into themselves and the world at large
impossible to attain in any other way." The reader was then advised to
write down any comments or reactions on a specially prepared form in the
magazine and send it to the author, Professor I. C. Kleerly.*

*One week after the publication of this issue, Mr. and Mrs. William
Waldon brought suit against Martin and Company, publishers of the
magazine. Their son Robert, a high school student of 16 who was
interested in chemistry, had tried the experiment and almost died.
(Methanol, or wood alcohol, is a poisonous liquid formed in the distillation
of wood and now generally made synthetically by the catalytic reaction of
carbon monoxide and hydrogen under pressure. It is used chiefly as a
solvent or in antifreeze.) The Waldons sought to have the magazine
banned and to recover damages.*

*The attorney for the Waldons argued that the publishers, in allowing
this article to be published, clearly demonstrated the lack of a responsible
and ethical editorial policy and thereby posed a threat to society.
Although it was not then known, it was likely that other readers had
attempted or would attempt the experiment with similar results, and any
magazine that encourages its readers to take a poisonous substance
without specifying that it is in fact poison should be prevented from
publishing. Robert Waldon is now in the hospital with severely damaged
intestines and throat burns which can never be healed completely. There
is some question as to whether he will survive. For damages incurred as a
result of this article, the Waldons seek $100 million. They also seek to
have the current issue of the magazine taken off the stands and to prohibit
any publication of the magazine in the future.*

*The attorney for Martin and Company points out that the article was
clearly presented in the nature of a satire on scientific experiments and
that the name of the author alone should have made this clear. No person,
they assumed, would be naive enough to think that this was a valid
scientific study. As of this time, no one else has even written a letter of
complaint. The magazine is clearly addressed to "adults only" (largely
because of the nude pictures). No magazine, they argue, can attempt to
prevent people who should not be reading the magazine in the first place
from harming themselves. The publisher does not, and in fact cannot, pass
judgment on the scientific accuracy of the articles appearing in its
magazines. Furthermore, the magazine has already made commitments for
publishing articles and advertisements for another year. If prevented from
doing so, the result would be financial disaster not only for the publishing*

*company and its stockholders but for its 200 employees as well. Lastly, the
attorney argues that any such attempt to prevent publication of the
magazine would be in violation of the company's right of free speech. The
magazine is totally owned by Martin and Company, which in turn is
totally owned by Terrie Shore and Linda Blass, two sisters.*

Both attorneys feel that this matter can be settled out of court and have
invited the principals to meet for discussion. These include:

Ms. Margaret Waldon, mother of Robert
Mr. Raymond Waldon, father of Robert
Ms. Patricia Realyo, attorney for the Waldons
Ms. Terrie Shore, part-owner of Martin and Company
Ms. Linda Blass, part-owner of Martin and Company
Mr. James Basmanian, attorney for Martin and Company

LANGUAGE, SUBLANGUAGE, AND CULTURE

Upon completion of this unit, you should be able to:
1. explain language as a social institution
2. explain the functions of sublanguages
3. define *sublanguage, subculture, codifiability, cant, argot, jargon, slang, taboo,* and *euphemism*
4. identify the three general origins of taboos and provide at least one example of each
5. explain at least four variables that influence the usage of taboo expressions
6. explain the concept of language racism and sexism
7. identify how sociological variables influence the forms of address used

One of the features shared by all human languages is the existence within the language of *sublanguages*—languages used by subcultures or subgroups for communication among their members. In order to explore the concept of sublanguages in depth, the nature of language as a social institution must first be understood.

LANGUAGE AS A SOCIAL INSTITUTION

Language is a social institution designed, modified, and extended (some purists might even say distorted) to meet the ever-changing needs of the culture or subculture. As such, language differs greatly from one culture to another and, equally important though perhaps less obvious, from one subculture to another.

Subcultures are cultures within a larger culture and may be formed on the basis of religion, geographical area, occupation, sexual orientation, race, nationality, living conditions, interests, needs, and so on. Catholics, Protestants, and Jews; New Yorkers, Californians, and mountain folk; teachers, plumbers, and musicians; homosexuals and lesbians; blacks, Chinese, and American Indians; Germans, Italians, and Mexicans; prisoners, suburbanites, and ghetto dwellers; bibliophiles, drug addicts, and bird watchers; diabetics, the blind,

139

and ex-convicts may all be viewed as subcultures, depending, of course, on the context on which we focus. In New York, for example, New Yorkers would obviously not constitute a subculture, but throughout the rest of the world they would. In the United States as a whole, Protestants would not constitute a subculture (though Catholics and Jews would). In New York City, on the other hand, Protestants would constitute a subculture. Blacks and Chinese would be subcultures only outside of Africa and China. As these examples illustrate, the majority generally constitutes the culture, and the various minorities generally constitute the subcultures. Yet this is not always the case. Women, although the majority in our culture, may be viewed as a subculture primarily because society as a whole is male oriented. Whether a group should be regarded as a subculture or a culture, then, depends upon the context being considered and the orientation of the society of which these groups are a part.

Each individual belongs to several subcultures. At the very least he or she belongs to a national, a religious, and an occupational subculture. The importance of the subcultural affiliation will vary greatly from one individual to another, from one context to another, from one time or circumstance to another. For example, to some people in some contexts an individual's religious affiliation may be inconsequential and his or her membership in this subculture hardly considered. When, on the other hand, the individual wishes to marry into a particular family, this once inconsequential membership may take on vast significance.

Because of the common interests, needs, or conditions of individuals constituting a subculture, sublanguages come into being. Like language in general, sublanguages exist to enable members of the group to communicate with each other. And, again like language in general, there are various regional variations, changes over time, and other variations. There are, however, other functions that sublanguages serve, and these functions constitute their reason for existence. If they did not serve these several functions, they would soon disappear.

FUNCTIONS OF SUBLANGUAGES

Sublanguages serve numerous different functions, depending on the particular subculture, the communication context, and a host of linguistic and non-linguistic variables. Here we identify a few of the more pervasive functions.

To Facilitate Subcultural Communication

One of the most obvious facts about language and its relation to culture is that concepts that are important to a given culture are given a large number of terms. For example, in our culture money is extremely important; consequently, we have numerous terms denoting this concept: *finances, funds, capital, assets, cash, pocket money, spending money, pin money, change, bread, loot, swag,* and various others. Transportation and communication are other concepts for which numerous terms exist in our language. Without knowing anything about a given culture, we could probably make some pretty good guesses as to the important concepts in that culture simply by examining one of its dictionaries or thesauruses. With sublanguages, the same principle holds. Concepts that are of special importance to a particular subculture are given a large number of terms. Thus one function of sublanguages is to provide the subculture with convenient synonyms for those concepts that are of great importance and hence are spoken about frequently. To prisoners, for example, a prison guard—clearly a significant concept and one spoken about a great deal—may be denoted by *screw, roach, hack, slave driver, shield, holligan*, and various other terms. Heroin, in the drug subculture, may be called *H, Harry, smack, Carga, joy powder, skag, stuff*, or *shit*.

A related function of sublanguages is to provide the subculture with convenient distinctions that are important to the subculture but generally not to the culture at large—and thus distinctions that the general language does not make. For example, the general culture has no need for making distinctions among various drugs—all may be conveniently labeled *drugs*. But to members of the drug subculture it is essential to make distinctions that to outsiders may seem unimportant or even trivial.

This function is also clearly seen in the technical jargon of the academic world. Whereas to most persons it is sufficient to distinguish between statements and questions, for example, the linguist and psycholinguist find these distinctions too gross. Consequently, they distinguish for questions between active and passive, tag and nontag, open and yes/no and numerous others. Whereas the term *learning* may be sufficient for the general population, the psychologist needs to distinguish between classical and instrumental learning, incidental and instructed learning, response and stimulus learning, and so on. In the field of communication, instead of the general term *message* we distinguish between digital and analogic messages, verbal and nonverbal messages, content and relational messages, content and metamessages, and so on. These distinctions are all helpful in conceptualizing and communicating the data and theories of a discipline.

Sublanguages serve to increase the codifiability of the general language. *Codifiability* refers to the ease with which certain concepts may be expressed in a language. Short terms are of high codifiability; long expressions are of low codifiability. All languages and sublanguages seem to move in the direction of increasing codifiability. As a concept becomes important in a culture or subculture, the term denoting it is shortened or some other simpler expression is adopted to denote it; thus *television* becomes *TV*, *motion picture* becomes *movie*, and *lysergic acid diethylamide* becomes *LSD* or simply *acid*. The expression *turn on* is the drug subculture's highly codifiable term for the general culture's low-codifiable expression "to take a drug or participate in some experience that alters one's awareness."

To Serve As a Means of Identification

By using a particular sublanguage, speakers identify themselves to hearers as members of that subculture—assuming, of course, that the listeners know the language being used. Individuals belonging to various nationality-based subcultures will frequently drop a foreign word or phrase in the conversation to identify themselves to their audience. Similarly, homosexuals and ex-convicts will at times identify themselves by using the sublanguage of their subculture. When the subcultural membership is one that is normally hidden, as in the case of homosexuals and ex-convicts, these clues to self-identification are subtle. Generally, they are only given after the individuals themselves receive some kind of positive feedback that leads them to suspect that the hearer also belongs to the subculture in question or that the hearer is at least sympathetic. In a similar vein, the use of sublanguages also functions to express to others one's felt identification with that subculture. For example, blacks may address each other as *brother* and *sister* when meeting for the first time. The use of these terms by blacks as well as the frequent use of foreign expressions by members of various national groups communicate to others that the speaker feels a strong identification with the group.

Sublanguages, then, serve to provide the group with a kind of identity and a sense of fraternity. Because ex-convicts all over the country know the same sublanguage, they are, in a sense, bound together. Obviously, the more the subculture has a need to band together, the greater the importance of a specialized language.

To Ensure Communication Privacy

Sublanguages also enable members of the subculture to communicate with one another while in the presence of nonmembers without having their conversation completely understood. A common example of this, which many of us may have heard but been unaware of, occurs in stores that attempt to take unfair advantage of customers. Salespersons will describe arriving customers as *J.L.* (just looking), *skank* (cheap individual), *T.O.* (turn over to an experienced salesperson), or *palooka* (one who is on a buying binge).

In certain situations, of course, the sublanguage may reveal the individual as a member of a particular subculture and so he or she will refrain from using the sublanguage. This is often the case among criminals when in a noncriminal environment. At other times, however, the use of a sublanguage does not lead to an individual's identification as a subculture member, and the sublanguage serves the useful purpose of excluding nonmembers from the class of decoders.

To Impress and Confuse

One of the less noble functions of sublanguages—capitalized on by numerous professionals—is to impress and at times confuse outsiders. The two functions, I think, often go hand in hand; many people are impressed in direct proportion to their confusion. Insurance policies and legal documents are perhaps the best examples. I suspect that in many instances this technical language is used to impress and confuse people. Then, when there is doubt about something, the insurance adjustor and the lawyer begin with an advantage—they understand the language whereas you and I do not. Similarly, in evaluating and eventually in signing such documents, we are unable even to ask the right questions because there is so much we do not understand. Fortunately, as *Time* magazine has reported, "the forces of hereinafter, *res ipsa loquitur* and party of the first part are now clearly on the defensive." Recently the Federal Trade Commission and the Department of Health, Education and Welfare have enlisted the aid of communication experts to rewrite much of their incomprehensible prose.

Physicians and many academicians also need to be put into this class. We are easily impressed by the physician's facile use of technical terms and are more apt to pay for the services of those who—like the witch doctors of primitive societies—know the language. To talk of a *singultus spasm* or *bilateral periorbital hematoma* instead of hiccups or a black eye does little to aid meaningful communication. From an analysis of this "medicalese," sociolinguist Joyce Hertzler notes (and I fully agree): "The conclusion must be that the effort is being made to mystify the public with respect to the highly technical and esoteric nature of their knowledge and performance, and to create an aura about their profession." And often, I fear, academicians' use of the technical language of their particular disciplines functions more to impress and confuse than to illuminate and clarify. In fairness to the professionals who make a real effort to communicate effectively with the layperson, it should be observed that in many instances the confusion that is generated is the result of extreme specialization rather than of any conscious desire to mislead or misinform.

KINDS OF SUBLANGUAGES

Sublanguage has been used here as a general term to denote a variation from the general language that is used by a particular group or subculture existing within the broader, more general culture. But there are different kinds of sublanguages.

Cant is the specialized vocabulary of some disreputable or underworld subcultures. It is the sublanguage of pickpockets, murderers, drug dealers, and prostitutes. Expressions such as *college* (meaning prison), *stretch* (jail sentence), *to mouse* (to escape from prison), and *lifeboat* (a pardon) are examples of cant. In its true form cant is not understood by outsiders. Today, with television and movies so much a part of our lives it is difficult for any group, however specialized and "underground," to hide its specialized language. Consequently, many people know some of these expressions as well as those presented in the Experiential Vehicle following this unit.

Argot designates the specialized vocabulary of any nonprofessional (usually noncriminal) group and would include, for example, the specialized sublanguage of the taxi driver, the truck driver, the CB operator, and the soldier. As is the case with cant, these vocabularies would ideally not be understood by nonmembers were it not for television and film. Expressions such as *dog* (meaning a motor vehicle inspector), *kidney buster* (hard riding truck), and *sweatshop* (bulletproof cab with poor ventilation) are examples of argot.

Jargon is the technical language of a professional class, for example, college professors, writers, medical doctors, and lawyers. Terms such as *perceptual accentuation, inflationary spiral, behavioral objectives,* and others used throughout your college experience are examples of professional academic jargon, as are the technical terms for the proofreading and editing of a writer, for the diseases and medications of a doctor, and for the legal documents and criminal offenses of the lawyer.

Slang is the most general of the terms and designates those vocabulary terms that are derived particularly from cant and argot, that are understood by most persons, but that would not necessarily be used in "polite society" or in formal written communications. Terms such as *skirt* (meaning woman), *skiddoo* (leave fast), *goo goo eyes, hush money, booze, brass* (impudence), and *to knock*

"Here's your trouble: There's no lampwick on the joint connecting the nipple and the union."

off (to quit working) are examples of slang. Slang is usually short-lived. Terms such as *skirt, skiddoo,* and *goo goo eyes* are rarely used today, and when used conjure up an image of an antiquated, out-of-touch-with-reality type of person. There are, of course, exceptions to this short life; some slang terms have been around for decades and remain classified as slang. For example, according to famed lexicographer H. L. Mencken, *booze* dates back to the fourteenth century, *brass* to 1594, and *to knock off* to 1662.

With the passage of time and increased frequency of usage, slang terms enter the general language as socially acceptable expressions. When this happens, new terms are needed and therefore coined by the subcultures. The old terms are then dropped from the sublanguage since they now serve none of the functions for which they were originally developed. This is just one of the ways in which new words enter the language and sublanguages are kept distinct from the general language.

LANGUAGE TABOO AND EUPHEMISM

One of the best ways of examining language in general, and the social dimension of language in particular, is to focus on taboo and euphemism. *Language taboo* refers to verbal behavior that is forbidden by the society for reasons that are not always clear; generally it is for some vague and seemingly irrational reason. When we think of taboo we often think of primitive societies with elaborate precautions against and punishments for uttering particular words and phrases. But language taboo is actually universal; all languages and all societies have language taboos built into their social structure.

Taboo Origins

Stephen Ullmann, in his *Semantics,* notes that there are three general origins of language taboo. The first are taboos rooted in fear. We may fear being punished by God, for example, and so we avoid naming the dead or avoid using the name of God or of the Devil. Similarly, fear perhaps motivates our not taking the name of God in vain. The second is the taboo of delicacy. This taboo centers on an avoidance of unpleasant topics. This is the taboo that leads us to avoid talking of topics relating to death, illness, and disease. A familiar example occurs when referring to someone who has a mental deficiency and avoiding such expressions as *idiot* or *imbecile,* using instead such expressions as *mentally retarded* or *intellectually impaired.* The third is the taboo of propriety. This leads us to avoid certain sexual references, swear words, and naming various parts and functions of the body. And although it is true that we no longer say *limbs* or *benders* instead of *legs,* there are many parts of the body for which we avoid speaking the terms we think, and instead employ some other term that is more socially acceptable.

Taboo Variations

Although taboo is a language universal, its form varies from one language to another and from one culture or subculture to another. Thus, the terms under taboo in our culture may not be under a taboo in other cultures. Even within any culture or subculture, what is and what is not taboo will vary on the basis of a number of factors. Taboo varies greatly with age, for example. Young people are more restricted in their language usage than are adults. Adults are allowed to talk about topics that are forbidden to children and in language that children would be punished for using. Taboo also varies on the basis of sex. Our society and, in fact, most societies allow men greater freedom. That these different taboos still operate is seen when the speech of men and women is analyzed; male speech contains a far greater number of taboo expressions than does female speech.

Taboo also varies with the educational and intellectual level of the individual. Uneducated persons generally demonstrate greater freedom of expression—in part because they do not have alternative expressions. The educated do have these alternatives and, at least when in "polite society," will use these rather than the taboo expressions. The communication context also influences the frequency and strength of taboo expressions. Generally, as the formality of a situation increases so do the linguistic restrictions. There are, for example, greater restrictions in a classroom than there are in the cafeteria. Perhaps the most important variable influencing taboo is the speaker-listener relationship. If the speaker and listener are equals there are usually less restrictions on their speech than if they were of widely differing statuses. There is less restriction between two teachers than between either a student and a teacher or a teacher and a dean. You know from your own experiences that you will monitor your speech when you are talking to persons who are higher than you in status as you will with people you may be trying to impress, for example, a new date or a potential employer. If you are talking with equals, you will be less likely to monitor and censor your expressions.

Taboo Effects

Some people use taboo expressions because this is their natural mode of communication and they do not monitor or censor any of it before speaking—"They calls it as they sees it." To these people, these expressions are natural rather than taboo. Others use taboo expressions because they are not aware of their inappropriateness; they are not sensitive to the communication context or to the differences in speaker-listener status. Often, however, the other person is aware and the focus shifts from the content of the communication to the taboo expression and—for a while at least—real and meaningful communication breaks down. This is seen frequently when people talk about throwing up or some particularly gory accident during dinner or when two people who do not know each other well use expressions that prove offensive, crude, or gross to the other. Some persons use taboo expressions for their shock value. They want to shock other people or to present particular images of themselves that taboo expressions help achieve.

When the language taboo is broken there are various forms of punishment that may be meted out. For the most part, we no longer have legal punishments although taboo expressions uttered in court, for example, will often result in a fine, and the use of taboo expressions in print may in some cases bring similar penalties. But for the most part such penalties have been removed. Nevertheless, there are still some severe punishments that are administered. Persons who make frequent use of taboo expressions will often find themselves laughed with over coffee but then not invited to more sophisticated functions; they may find themselves popular in the mail room while corporate advancement seems to elude them.

Taboo Alternatives: Euphemisms

In all languages there are alternative expressions that are used instead of taboo expressions and these are called *euphemisms*. These are the nice words designed to replace taboo expressions and to sweeten topics that may be unpleasant or less than desirable—and so we say *mortician* instead of *undertaker*; and instead of *toilet* we say *restroom* (though few really rest there) or *bathroom* (though we are not going to bathe) or *little boy's* or *little girl's room* (though we are grown men and women). H. L. Mencken, in his *The American Language*, identifies hundreds of such euphemistic substitutions: *collection correspondent* for *bill collector*; *section manager* for *floor walker*; *superintendent* for *janitor*; and *sanitary officer* for *garbage man*. A friend of mine who works for the Department of Sanitation actually refers to himself as a "garbalogist."

LANGUAGE RACISM AND SEXISM

No discussion of sublanguages would be complete without consideration of the terms and phrases used to denigrate various subcultures. These are not themselves sublanguages but are linguistic devices (terms and phrases) used to refer to the various subcultures, usually negatively.

Racism

Perhaps the most obvious examples are those that refer to a person's race. We all know these terms and listing them here would serve no purpose. In fact, I suspect that part of the reason these terms persist is because academicians and the media use them to illustrate how "liberal" they are and feel that in doing so they are really putting down such prejudice. I think that the use of such terms, for example on "All in the Family," did not work against their increased popular use but rather seemed to make them appear more acceptable and more harmless than they really are. We do not have to tell a racist joke to illustrate how racist jokes foster racial prejudice.

These derogatory terms are used by the principal culture to disparage subcultural members, their customs, or their accomplishments. Every subgroup has such negative terms, whose main function is to separate the majority from the minority group and to create a sociological and linguistic hierarchy, with the majority members on the top and the minority members on the bottom. The social consequences of such hierarchies in terms of employment, education, housing opportunities, and general community acceptance seem well known.

One of the qualifications frequently made in this connection is that it is permissible for members of the subculture to refer to themselves with these negative terms without any problems being created. That is, Italians may use the negative terms referring to Italians, blacks may use the negative terms referring to blacks, and so on. The reasoning seems to be that groups should be able to laugh at themselves. I am not sure we should accept this position. In fact, it seems likely that such personal usage is even more damaging, because the negative connotations of these terms feed back to the individual and may well function to reinforce the negative stereotypes that society has already assigned this group. The use of such terms in effect tells the individual that her or his subcultural affiliation is somehow not as good as that of the majority culture.

This is seen clearly when gay men and lesbians use the negative terms of heterosexual society to refer to themselves. By using these terms they seem to be in effect confirming, at least in part and perhaps subconsciously, the connotations that the heterosexual culture has included in these terms. This is not to imply that the connotations in the minds of the subculture member and the majority member will be the same, but only to suggest that the connotations both persons have may have negative aspects that may not necessarily or always be conscious.

Sexism

Consider some of the language used to refer to women. A woman loses her last name when she marries and in certain instances loses her first name as well. She changes from "Ann Smith" to "Mrs. John Jones." On a recent talk show, Gary Morton, for example, noted that when his wife, Lucille Ball, comes home from work, she becomes "Mrs. Morton."

We say that a woman "marries into" a man's family and that a family "dies out" if there are no male children. We do not speak of a man marrying into a woman's family (unless that family is extremely prestigious or wealthy or members of royalty) and a family can still "die out" even if there are 10 female children. In the marriage ceremony we hear "I now pronounce you man and wife," not "man and woman" or "husband and wife." The man retains his status as man, but the woman changes hers from woman to wife.

Many of the terms used for women are used to define them sexually. Consider, for example, the once parallel terms *master* and *mistress*. These terms at one time designated persons who had power and privilege over others. Now, however, *master* refers not to a man who has power over other people but to a man who has power over things, as in, for example, "He is the master of his fate," "He is a master craftsman," or "He is a master teacher." But note that *mistress* did not develop in a parallel way; the term now denotes a sexual relationship and particularly a sexual relationship in which the woman is possessed by and subordinated to the man, as in "She is the senator's mistress." The term *professional,* when applied to a man, refers to his high status occupation. When applied to a woman, it often has a sexual connotation. The same is true for the phrase "in business" in certain parts of the country.

Another interesting lack of parallelism between the sexes is found in the terms *bachelor* and *spinster. Bachelor* varies from neutral to positive in connotation, but *spinster* is always negative. We would say, "Margaret is dating an eligible bachelor," but would not say, "Joe is dating an eligible spinster." The term *spinster* seems to preclude eligibility. Even when the terms are used metaphorically, this same lack of parallelism can be seen. When we say that "Joe is a regular bachelor," we imply that he is free and is living an exciting and sexually fulfilling life. But when we say, "Margaret is a regular spinster," we imply that she is living an uninteresting and sexually unfulfilling life.

The use of *man* to designate "human being" and the use of the masculine pronoun to refer to any individual regardless of sex further illustrate the extent of linguistic sexism. There seems to me no legitimate reason why the feminine pronoun could not alternate with the masculine pronoun in referring to hypothetical individuals or why such terms as *he and she* or *her and him* could not be used instead of just *he* or *him.*

SOURCES

On sublanguages, see H. L. Mencken, *The American Language* (New York: Knopf, 1971). Mencken's chapter entitled "American Slang" is a classic work and a most interesting one. Much interesting research relevant to sublanguages is reported in the various works on sociolinguistics, for example, Joshua A. Fishman, *The Sociology of Language* (Rowley, Mass.: Newbury House, 1972), and Dell Hymes, *Foundations in Sociolinguistics: An Ethnographic Approach* (Philadelphia: University of Pennsylvania Press, 1974). One of the most insightful essays is Paul Goodman, "Sublanguages," in *Speaking and Language: Defence of Poetry* (New York: Random House, 1971). The theory and research on forms of address are thoroughly covered in Roger Brown, *Social Psychology* (New York: Free Press, 1965). Many of the insights and examples concerning language sexism came from Casey Miller and Kate Swift, *Words and Women: New Language in New Times* (Garden City, N.Y.: Doubleday, 1976), and Robin Lakoff, *Language and Woman's Place* (New York: Harper & Row, 1975). I recommend both of these books highly. In this connection, see also Cheris Kramer, "Women's Speech: Separate but Unequal?" *Quarterly Journal of Speech* 60 (February 1974): 14–24. The broad area of sex differences in communication is surveyed in Barbara Eakins and R. Gene Eakins, *Sex Differences in Communication* (Boston: Houghton Mifflin, 1978). For an examination of the effects of qualifying phrases used by men and women, see Patricia Hayes Bradley, "The Folk-Linguistics of Women's Speech: An Empirical Examination," *Communication Monographs* 48 (March 1981):73–90. Richard W. Brislin, in his *Cross-Cultural Encounters: Face-to-Face Interaction* (New York: Pergamon Press, 1981) discusses much that is of relevance to this discussion of sublanguages.

EXPERIENTIAL VEHICLES

10.1 SOME SUBLANGUAGES

Presented below are a few brief lexicons of several sublanguages. Note how these terms serve the functions discussed in this unit and many of them are in the process of passing into the general language.

Assuming that you might like to test your knowledge of the various sublanguages, these lexicons are presented as matching quizzes. Write the number of the sublanguage term (left column) next to the letter of the corresponding general-language term (right column).

CRIMINAL TALK

1.	maker, designer, scratcher, connection	a.	bank burglar
		b.	false key
2.	paper, scrip, stiff	c.	racket involving violence
3.	jug stiff, cert	d.	forger
4.	beat, sting, come-off	e.	wallet
5.	buttons, shamus, fuzz	f.	a parcel with a trap inside for hiding stolen merchandise
6.	mark, hoosier, chump, yap		
7.	poke, leather, hide	g.	burglar alarm
8.	cold poke, dead skin	h.	iron safe
9.	gun, cannon, whiz	i.	forged check
10.	booster	j.	pickpocket
11.	booster box	k.	dynamite
12.	bug	l.	forged bank check
13.	dinah, noise	m.	shoplifter
14.	double	n.	watchman
15.	gopher	o.	policeman
16.	hack	p.	negotiable security
17.	soup, pete	q.	pickpocket victim
18.	jug heavy	r.	nitroglycerine
19.	stiff	s.	empty wallet
20.	heavy racket	t.	picking a pocket

CB TALK

1.	green stamps	a.	unmarked police car
2.	good buddy	b.	other CB owners/operators
3.	seat covers	c.	state police

150

4. X-ray machine
5. plain wrapper
6. ranch
7. bear cave
8. cut some Z's
9. clean
10. ground clouds
11. boy scouts
12. handle
13. bean store
14. green stamp road
15. keep your nose between the ditches and smokey out of your britches
16. mama bear
17. big daddy
18. invitations
19. haircut palace
20. brush your teeth and comb your hair

d. overnight stop
e. radar unit ahead
f. diner
g. FCC (Federal Communications Commission)
h. fog
i. money
j. toll ahead
k. low overhead
l. get some sleep
m. traffic tickets
n. passengers
o. drive safely; watch for speed traps
p. no police in sight
q. CB transmission
r. police station
s. police radar
t. policewoman

PRISONER TALK

1. fish
2. kite
3. drum
4. to slam off
5. to gut
6. sleeping time
7. college
8. greenhouse
9. Cupid's itch
10. big noise
11. screw, roach, hack, slave driver, shield
12. frocker, goody, psalmer
13. croacker, cutemup, pill punk, salts, iodine
14. scraper, butcher
15. leather, young horse
16. water
17. chalk
18. beagle, dog, balloon
19. pig
20. soup jockey

a. prison waiter
b. prison chaplain
c. prison barber
d. new prisoner
e. to escape from jail
f. prison guard
g. prison doctor
h. roast beef
i. meat
j. letter smuggled out of jail
k. venereal disease
l. prison
m. soup
n. sausage
o. cell
p. to die
q. milk
r. prison morgue
s. short sentence
t. warden

MOUNTAIN TALK

1.	a-fixin'	a.	hard rain
2.	doin's	b.	bag
3.	fetch	c.	look at
4.	put out	d.	getting ready to do something
5.	aim	e.	get rid of
6.	smart	f.	hurt
7.	book read	g.	clean up
8.	lollygag	h.	function or event
9.	crick	i.	loaf or loiter
10.	biggety	j.	nervous
11.	plumb	k.	bring
12.	shed of	l.	stiffness
13.	poke	m.	a great distance
14.	red	n.	angry
15.	skittish	o.	geographical area
16.	gander	p.	intend, plan
17.	parts	q.	exactly, on the dot
18.	smack-dab	r.	completely
19.	fur piece	s.	educated
10.	gully-washer	t.	snobbish, stuck up

COMMUNICATION TALK

1. argot
2. codifiability
3. credibility
4. paralanguage
5. batons
6. immanent reference
7. endomorphy
8. empathy
9. homophily
10. ideographs
11. elementalism
12. intensional orientation
13. Machiavellianism
14. metacommunication
15. phatic communion
16. proxemics
17. redundancy
18. emblems
19. specialization
20. stereotype

a. the characteristic of communication by which it always refers to the immediate situation

b. the degree of similarity among individuals

c. the fatty dimension of a body

d. vocal but nonverbal dimension of communication

e. a kind of sublanguage, generally of a criminal class

f. the process of dividing verbally what cannot be divided nonverbally (in reality)

g. the degree to which a message is predictable

h. techniques by which control is exerted by one person over another

i. a perspective in which primary attention is given to labels

j.   communication that is primarily social; communication that opens the channels of communication

k.   communication about communication

l.   nonverbal behaviors that directly translate words or phrases

m.   bodily movements that sketch the path or direction of a thought

n.   the fixed impression of a group through which one then perceives specific individuals

o.   bodily movements that accent or emphasize a specific word or phrase

p.   the feature of language that refers to the fact that human language serves no purpose other than communication

q.   the study of how space communicates

r.   feeling as another feels

s.   believability

t.   the ease with which certain concepts may be expressed in a given language

10.2 FORMS OF ADDRESS

For each of the following persons indicate the form of address you would use in speaking to them *and* the form of address you would expect them to use in speaking to you.

Use the following shorthand:

TLN—title plus last name
FN—first name
TFN—title plus first name
T—title

	You to Them	*Them to You*
1. Your college professor	_____	_____
2. A fellow student	_____	_____
3. A younger child	_____	_____
4. Your doctor or dentist	_____	_____

5. Your employer   _____   _____
6. Your employee   _____   _____
7. Your high school teacher   _____   _____
8. Your uncle or aunt   _____   _____
9. Your nephew or niece   _____   _____
10. Your grandfather or grandmother   _____   _____
11. Your state senator   _____   _____
12. Your college president   _____   _____
13. Your minister, priest, or rabbi   _____   _____
14. Your parents' friend   _____   _____
15. John Travolta or Brooke Shields   _____   _____
16. A street bum   _____   _____
17. A millionaire   _____   _____

On what bases were your decisions made—that is, what sociological variables influenced your decisions?

10.3 FEMALE AND MALE LANGUAGE USAGE

Here are 10 examples of varied language usage. For each indicate whether this usage is more characteristic of women or of men.

1. *in'* instead of *ing* suffixes on such words as *doing, fishing, going*
2. swear and curse words
3. words such as *charming, sweet, lovely,* and *precious*
4. sentence qualifiers such as "This may not be the place to say this, but. . . ." or "I may be wrong about this, but it seems to me that.. . ."
5. tag questions (questions carrying tags at the ends that ask for the listener's agreement) such as "That's a terrible thing to do, isn't it?" or "This teacher is brilliant, don't you think?"
6. the use of rising intonation to change answers into questions as in saying "Seven?" instead of "Seven" to the question "When will you be ready?"
7. joke telling
8. frequency of speech defects (especially stuttering) among children
9. speech onset and development at an earlier age and more rapid development of language generally
10. talk more in mixed-sex dyads

After responding to all 10 of these language examples:

a. What were your reasons for each response? On what basis did you say that the above usages were characteristic of men or women?
b. What do you feel might be causing these differences?

MEANING IN VERBAL INTERACTION

Upon completion of this unit, you should be able to:
1. explain Wendell Johnson's model of communication and some of the assumptions or implications it has for meaning
2. define *meaning*, *denotation*, and *connotation*
3. reproduce and explain Richards's triangle of meaning
4. explain the basic theory of semantic differentation as a method of measuring meaning

The most important aspect of speech and language is meaning. Were it not for the need to communicate meaning from one person to another, there would be no speech, no language. Here we consider the nature of meaning as a process, some of the aspects of meaning as viewed in I. A. Richards's triangle of meaning, and two types of meaning (connotation and denotation).

MEANING AS A PROCESS

Meaning is an active process created in cooperation between source and receiver, speaker and listener, writer and reader. This is illustrated in the model developed by Wendell Johnson, one of the leading semanticists, and depicted here in Figure 11.1. Although it may seem complex, the model is actually rather simple when compared to the truly complex process of transferring meaning from one person to another. The surrounding rectangle indicates that communication takes place in a context that is external to both speaker and listener and to the communication process as well. The twisted loop indicates that the various stages of communication are actually interrelated and interdependent.

The actual process begins at 1, which represents the occurrence of an event—anything that can be perceived. This event is the stimulus. At stage 2 the observer is stimulated through one or more sensory channels. The opening at 2 is purposely illustrated as being relatively small to emphasize that out of all the possible stimuli in the world, only a small part of these actually stimulate the observer. At stage 3 organismic evaluations occur. Nerve impulses travel from the sense organs to the brain, causing certain bodily changes, for example, in muscular tension. At 4 the feelings aroused at 3 are beginning to be translated into words—a process that takes place in accordance with the individual's unique language habits. At stage 5, from all the possible linguistic symbols, certain ones are selected and arranged into some pattern.

At 1' the words that the speaker utters, by means of sound waves, or the words that are written, by means of light waves, serve as stimulation for the hearer, much as the outside event at 1 served as stimulation for the speaker. At 2' the hearer is stimulated, at 3' there are organismic evaluations, at 4' feelings are beginning to be translated into words, at 5' certain of these symbols are selected and arranged, and at 1" these symbols, in the form of sound and/or light waves, are emitted and serve as stimulation for another hearer. The process is a continuous one.

A few of the implications this model has for meaning should be noted here. First, it should be clear that meaning is a function not only of messages (whether verbal or nonverbal, or both) but of the interaction of these messages and the receiver's own nervous system. We do not "receive" meaning; rather, we create meaning. Words do not mean; people mean.

One of the best examples of the confusion that can result when this relatively simple fact is not taken into consideration is provided by Ronald D. Laing, H. Phillipson, and A. Russell Lee in *Interpersonal Perception* and analyzed with insight by Paul Watzlawick in *How Real is Real?* A couple on the

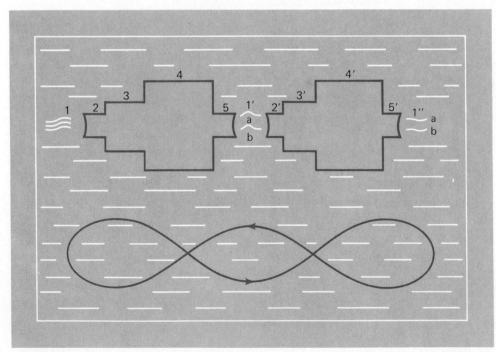

FIGURE 11.1 Johnson's Model of Communication. Source: From Wendell Johnson, "The Spoken Word and the Great Unsaid," Quarterly Journal of Speech 37 (1951): 421.

second night of their honeymoon were sitting at a hotel bar. The woman struck up a conversation with the couple next to her. The husband refused to communicate with the couple and became antagonistic to his wife as well as to the couple. The wife then became angry because he created such an awkward and unpleasant situation. Each became increasingly disturbed, and the evening ended in a bitter conflict in which each was convinced of the other's lack of consideration. Eight years later they analyzed this argument. Apparently "honeymoon" had meant very different things to each of them; to the husband it had meant a "golden opportunity to ignore the rest of the world and simply explore each other." His wife's interaction with the other couple implied to him that there was something lacking in him to make her seek out additional people with whom to interact. To the wife "honeymoon" had meant an opportunity to try out her new role as wife. "I have never had a conversation with another couple as a wife before," she said. "Previous to this I had always been a 'girl friend' or 'fiancée' or 'daughter' or 'sister.'"

The second implication is that although not all communication occurs in reference to some external stimulus, communication makes sense, Johnson argues, only when it does in some way relate to the external world. This quality,

The same word, student, to different people means different things. Meanings are not in words but in people.

it might be added, is often used to distinguish healthy from unhealthy communications and "normal" from "unnormal" persons.

Third, the words selected to communicate are a relatively small sample of all possible words. Consequently, messages created by the same person on different occasions are going to be different as well.

Fourth, the meaning we derive from an event is formed on the basis of only a small sample of stimuli. Out of the infinite number of stimuli that are present in the external world, only a small sample reach the individual. These stimuli will differ from one person to another and for the same person from one time to another. Thus, the meaning we derive from an event is a unique as well as a limited or partial meaning.

THE TRIANGLE OF MEANING

One of the most insightful characterizations of meaning is provided by I. A. Richards, whose "triangle of meaning" provides further insight into the area of meaning in speech and language.

Suppose that you were to ask me what I mean by a "college education." I might answer in any number of ways: (1) I might say that a college education is the accumulation of approximately 125 credits in various subjects with a concentration in one or more of these subjects over a period of approximately 4 years. (2) I might say that a college education can be the most enjoyable and most profitable experience any person could have. (3) Instead of saying anything, I might take you to a college and let you observe the process of a college education, insofar as that is possible.

In each of these instances "meaning" was interpreted differently. In the first, in which I defined a college education in terms of credits, I interpreted "meaning" to refer to the words *college education*. In the second, in which I told you my feelings about a college education, I interpreted "meaning" to refer to my own feelings about college. In the third, in which we observed the process of a college education, I interpreted "meaning" to refer to the actual thing or referent. These three aspects are illustrated in Richard's triangle of meaning, presented in Figure 11.2.

Focus first on the points of the triangle. On the bottom left is the Symbol, a word or phrase or sentence. In this view of meaning the symbol refers objectively to the thing it symbolizes. At the apex is the Thought or Reference. This refers to the thought that the speaker has of the concept, in this case the thoughts about a college education. At the bottom right is the Referent, the actual object or process or event talked about, in this case the process of a college education. The three answers to the question of what I mean by a college education each focused on one of these aspects of meaning. The definition focused on the symbol, the expression of feelings on the reference, and the observation on the referent.

Focus next on the relationships illustrated by the sides of the triangle. Between the symbol and the reference there is a causal relationship in both directions. Using the term *college education* causes various thoughts or references in the mind of the listener which are similar to those in the mind of the symbol user. Also, the thought or reference about a college education will cause the individual to use certain symbols or words.

Between the referent and the reference the causal relationship goes only from the referent to the reference. By observing a particular object (referent), it causes us to have certain thoughts or references about the object. But thinking about an object does not cause it to appear; hence, the arrow does not go from reference to referent.

The relationship between symbol and referent is perhaps the most important of these relationships. Note that between the symbol and the referent, there is no direct causal relationship. The relationship between the symbol and the referent must go through the thought or reference. Put differently, the symbol does not refer directly to the referent; there is nothing inherent in the symbol that will lead us to find a particular referent, nor is there anything in the referent that will lead us to find a particular symbol (assuming, of course, that we had not already learned the words for the thing).

This relationship is also important because it illustrates that meanings are in the thoughts or references that people have and not in the referents themselves. There is nothing four-legged about the word *horse*; there is nothing sweet in the word *sugar*.

Richards's triangle of meaning deals with denotative meaning, that is, with symbols that refer objectively to the events, objects, or persons named. But denotation is only one aspect or type of meaning. The other is connotation. Both of these types of meaning need to be explored in more detail.

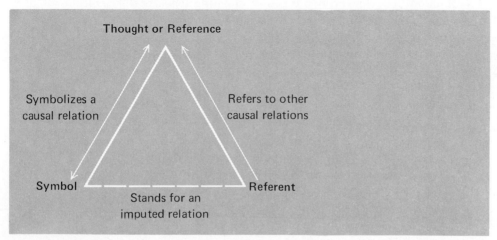

FIGURE 11.2
The Triangle of Meaning.
Source: C. K. Ogden and I. A. Richards, **The Meaning of Meaning** *(New York: Harcourt Brace Jovanovich, 1923),* p. 11.

DENOTATION AND CONNOTATION

To explain denotative and connotative meaning, let us take as an example the word *death*. To a doctor this word might mean, or denote, simply the time when the heart stops beating. Thus to a doctor, this word may be an objective description of a particular event. On the other hand, to a mother whose son has just died, the word means much more. It recalls to her the son's youth, his ambitions, his family, his illness, and so on. To her it is a highly emotional word, a highly subjective word, a highly personal word. These emotional or subjective or personal reactions are the word's connotative meaning. The denotation of a word is its objective definition; the connotation of a word is its subjective or emotional meaning.

Some words are primarily and perhaps even completely denotative. Words like *the, of, a,* and the like are perhaps purely denotative; no one seems to have emotional reactions to such words. Other words are primarily denotative, such as *perpendicular, parallel, cosine, adjacent,* and the like. Of course, even these words might have strong connotative meanings for some people. Words such as *geometry, north* and *south, up* and *down,* and *east* and *west*— words that denote rather specific directions or areas—often produce strong emotional reactions from some people. For example, the student who failed geometry might have a very strong emotional reaction to the word, even though to most people it seems a rather unemotional, objective kind of word. Other words, such as derogatory racial names and curse words, are primarily connotative and often have little denotative meaning. Very simply, words may vary from highly denotative to highly connotative. A good way to determine a word's connotative meaning is to ask where it would fall on a good–bad scale. If "good" and "bad" do not seem to apply to the word, then it has little, if any, connotative meaning for you. If, however, the term can be placed on the good–bad scale with some degree of conviction, then it has connotative meaning for you.

Another distinction between the two types of meaning has already been implied. The denotative meaning of a word is more general or universal, that is, most people agree with the denotative meanings of words and would give similar definitions. Connotative meanings, however, are extremely personal, and few people would agree on the precise connotative meaning of a word. If this does not seem correct, try to get a group of people to agree on the connotative meaning of words such as *religion, God, democracy, wealth,* and *freedom.* Chances are very good that it will be impossible to reach an agreement about such words.

The denotative meaning of a term can be learned from any dictionary. When we consult a dictionary it is the denotative meaning for which we are looking. The dictionary would tell us, for example, that *south* means "a cardinal point of the compass directly opposite to the north, the direction in which this point lies," and so on. Connotative meaning, on the other hand, cannot be found in a dictionary. Instead it must be found in the person's reactions or associations to the word. To some people, for example, *south* might mean poverty; to others it might mean wealth and good land investment; to still others it might recall the Civil War, or perhaps warmth and friendliness. Obviously, no dictionary could be compiled for connotative meanings simply because each person's connotative meaning for a word would be different.

Denotative meaning differs from connotative meaning in yet another way. Denotative meanings are relatively unchanging and static. Although definitions of all words change through time, denotative meanings generally change very slowly. The word *south*, for example, meant denotatively the same thing 1000 years ago that it does now. But connotative meanings change rapidly. A single favorable experience in the South, for example, might change completely one's connotative meaning for the word.

Names and Naming

Very often we are not aware of the connotative meanings of terms and naively assume them to be purely denotative. First names are one of the clearest examples. Through various associations, some recent and some long past, names have acquired strong connotative meanings, which have been the object of considerable research in the past decade. It has been found, for example, that *Michael, James,* and *Wendy* are perceived as active, whereas *Alfreda, Percival,* and *Isadore* are perceived as passive. *Michael* and *James* are are seen as masculine, but not so for *Percival* and *Isadore; Wendy* is perceived as feminine, but not so for *Alfreda.* Common names, such as *James, John, Joseph, Michael,* and *Paul,* are perceived as designating individuals who are better, stronger, and more active than those who have more unusual names, such as *Dale, Edmond, Raymond, Stanley,* and *Lawrence.* (See Table 11.1 for some common popular names.) It has also been shown, for example, that male students with unusual names were more likely to flunk out of Harvard, more likely

1898	1928	1948	1964	1972	1975
Mary	Mary	Linda	Lisa	Jennifer	Jennifer
Catherine	Marie	Mary	Deborah	Michelle	Michelle
Margaret	Annie	Barbara	Mary	Lisa	Christine
Annie	Margaret	Patricia	Susan	Elizabeth	Lisa
Rose	Catherine	Susan	Maria	Christine	Maria
John	John	Robert	Michael	Michael	Michael
William	William	John	John	David	John
Charles	Joseph	James	Robert	Christopher	Robert
George	James	Michael	David	John	David
Joseph	Richard	William	Steven	James	Christopher

TABLE 11.1
The Most Popular Names in New York City

to be neurotic, and had a higher incidence of psychosis than those with common names. Interestingly enough, this relationship did not hold for female names.

In other studies it has been found that teachers rated essays supposedly written by students with unpopular names (for example, *Elmer* and *Bertha*) with lower grades than those supposedly written by students with popular names (for example, *Karen* and *Michael*).

Although this research is in many ways in its infancy, it seems to be demonstrating that few terms, if any, are purely denotative and that the connotative value of names in particular influences a wide variety of perceptions in a wide variety of people.

Semantic Differentiation

Perhaps the most popular and most insightful approach to connotative meaning is that of semantic differentiation—a procedure in which a word is rated on selected bipolar 7-point scales in order to tap an individual's connotative meaning.

The scales are of three types or meaning dimensions. The evaluative dimension uses such scales as good-bad, sad-happy, valuable-worthless, and bitter-sweet. The potency dimension uses such scales as strong-weak and light-heavy. The activity dimension uses such scales as hot-cold, active-passive, and fast-slow. By using such scales, meanings may be indexed for (1) different concepts by the same subject, (2) the same concepts by different subjects, or (3) various concepts by the same subjects at different times (for example, before and after therapy, before and after taking a specific course, or before and after hearing a specific communication).

As an example, take the concept of a "college education" as rated by the typical college graduate. It might look something like Figure 11.3.

If we number the scales, using 7 for the positive end and 1 for the negative end, we can add the various judgments and get summary figures. Taking the

College Education							
Good			X				Bad
Sad			X				Happy
Strong		X					Weak
Light					X		Heavy
Hot				X			Cold
Active	X						Passive
Valuable		X					Worthless
Bitter			X				Sweet
Fast						X	Slow

FIGURE 11.3
An Example of Semantic Differential Scales.

evaluative dimension as an example, we have the scales good-bad, sad-happy, valuable-worthless, and bitter-sweet. On the good-bad scale this subject rated "college education" 5, on the sad-happy scale it was rated 3, on the valuable-worthless scale it was rated 5, and on the bitter-sweet scale it was rated 4 (note that we are considering the positive ends, good and happy, as 7 and the negative ends, bad and sad, as 1). This totals 17 on the evaluative dimension. Note that this score means little if anything unless we compare it to something else. We might, for example, compare it with the ratings of other students or the ratings of students in different colleges or those studying different majors. Or we might test the difference between males and females, or study one's individual changes from freshman to senior year.

IMPLICATIONS FOR INTERPERSONAL INTERACTION

There are a number of implications for interpersonal communication that may be drawn from this journey into meaning. A few of these should be noted here in summary.

1. Meanings differ from one moment to the next and, most importantly, from one person to another. Do not assume that the meaning you attribute is the same as the meaning another person attributes to a word, even though you both may use the exact same words. Before agreeing or disagreeing, check to see if you understand each other's meanings.

2. The words used express only a small part of the meaning an individual has in his or her mind. There is always a great deal more that could be said than what comes out of one's mouth. Try not to draw conclusions too hastily from too few words.

3. Meanings are a combination of—a composite of—thoughts and feelings. The symbols we use do not refer objectively to things but refer to things as interpreted by our feelings and thoughts. Therefore, try not to forget that we always talk about ourselves, and an appropriate response addresses both the things talked about as well as the speaker's feelings that are inevitably reflected in the verbal message.

4. Although there is no inherent or real connection between the word and the thing, as Richards demonstrates in his triangle of meaning, we seem to forget this when it comes to names. Names of people, like names for perfumes or cereals, are arbitrary. Do not allow the name of the person (the symbol) to obscure the person (the referent).

5. By understanding how connotative meanings may be dissected (into, for example, evaluative, potency, and activity dimensions), we will be in a better position to remember that an individual's meaning for a term is multifaceted and that effective communication depends on understanding what the other person means, not on what the word means. Listen, then, not so much to what the person says as to what the person means.

SOURCES

The concept of meaning is covered in the works on semantics and general semantics. The triangle of meaning owes its formulation to the work of I. A. Richards. See C. K. Ogden and I. A. Richards, *The Meaning of Meaning* (New York: Harcourt Brace Jovanovich, 1923). Articles contained in Paul A. Eschholz, Alfred F. Rosa, and Virginia P. Clark, *Language Awareness* (New York: St. Martin's Press, 1974) and my *Language: Concepts and Processes* (Englewood Cliffs, N.J.: Prentice-Hall, 1973) should provide an excellent overview of the area of semantics and meaning.

Numerous examples of meaning confusion as well as insightful analyses may be found in Ronald D. Laing, H. Phillipson, and A. Russell Lee, *Interpersonal Perception* (New York: Springer-Verlag, 1966), and Paul Watzlawick, *How Real is Real? Confusion, Disinformation, Communication* (New York: Random House [Vintage Books], 1977). On names, see Muriel Beadle, "The Game of the Name," *New York Times Magazine* (October 21, 1973): 38ff., and Mary G. Marcus, "The Power of a Name," *Psychology Today 10* (October 1976): 75–76, 108. Both of these articles provide extensive lists of common names. For an interesting discussion of names and our treatment of them as more than just labels, see Myrna Frommer, "Names," *et cetera* 39 (Summer 1982):106–108.

EXPERIENTIAL VEHICLES

11.1 I, YOU, AND HE AND SHE TALK

The way in which we phrase something will often influence the way in which something is perceived. This is especially true when we are dealing with and talking about people. We do not talk about ourselves in the same way that we talk about the people we are with or about the people we know but are not with.

Recognizing this simple language habit, Bertrand Russell, the British philosopher and mathematician, proposed a conjugation of "irregular" verbs. One example he used was:

> I am firm.
> You are obstinate.
> He is a pig-headed fool.

The *New Statesman* and the *Nation* picked up on this and offered prizes for contributions in the style of these irregular verbs. One of the best ones was:

> I am sparkling.
> You are unusually talkative.
> He is drunk.

Ten sentences that are phrased in the first person follow. Using Russell's lead, "conjugate" these irregular verbs.

1. I speak my mind.
2. I believe in what I say.
3. I take an occasional drink.
4. I smoke.
5. I like to talk with people about people.
6. I am frugal.
7. I am concerned with what other people do.
8. I have been known to get upset at times.
9. I am concerned with my appearance.
10. I will put off certain things for a few days.

11.2 MEANINGS IN PEOPLE

Six sets of semantic differential scales, headed by various concepts, are presented. Rate each of these concepts as you see them.

After the ratings are completed, small groups of five or six (or the class as a whole) should discuss the meanings of the words as they are defined in a dictionary (the denotation) and as they are defined by the ratings on these scales (the connotation).

From this experience (the collection of the data and the ensuing discussion) the following should be clear:

1. Disagreement over the meaning of a word usually centers on the connotative meaning rather than on the denotative meaning.
2. Connotative and denotative meanings are very different aspects of a word's total meaning.
3. People are different and hence define words differently.
4. Different people can use the same word but mean very different things by it.
5. Meanings are not in words but in people.

LOVE

Good		Bad
Pleasant		Unpleasant
Ugly		Beautiful
Weak		Strong
Active		Passive
Sharp		Dull
Large		Small
Light		Heavy
Hot		Cold

COLLEGE

Good		Bad
Pleasant		Unpleasant
Ugly		Beautiful
Weak		Strong
Active		Passive
Sharp		Dull
Large		Small
Light		Heavy
Hot		Cold

SEXUAL BEHAVIOR

Good		Bad
Pleasant		Unpleasant
Ugly		Beautiful
Weak		Strong
Active		Passive

Sharp						Dull
Large						Small
Light						Heavy
Hot						Cold

RELIGION

Good						Bad
Pleasant						Unpleasant
Ugly						Beautiful
Weak						Strong
Active						Passive
Sharp						Dull
Large						Small
Light						Heavy
Hot						Cold

WOMEN'S LIBERATION

Good						Bad
Pleasant						Unpleasant
Ugly						Beautiful
Weak						Strong
Active						Passive
Sharp						Dull
Large						Small
Light						Heavy
Hot						Cold

GAY LIBERATION

Good						Bad
Pleasant						Unpleasant
Ugly						Beautiful
Weak						Strong
Active						Passive
Sharp						Dull
Large						Small
Light						Heavy
Hot						Cold

BARRIERS TO VERBAL INTERACTION

Upon completion of this unit, you should be able to:
1. explain the concepts of "barriers" to interpersonal communication
2. define *polarization, intensional orientation, fact-inference confusion, allness, static evaluation,* and *indiscrimination*
3. identify examples of these six barriers in the media
4. identify examples of these six barriers in your own communications

Throughout this book I have stressed the complexity of interpersonal communication. It is also quite fragile—in part because of its complexity and in part because it is a human process, subject to all the failings and problems of fallible people. Chief among these problems are what are generally called *barriers*. In using this term I do not mean to imply that interpersonal communication is a mechanical process, and that somewhere along the communication chain of events, barriers, like roadblocks, are erected that stop or hinder the flow of interpersonal communication messages. The alternative terms *breakdown* and *obstacle* seem to suffer from the same misleading mechanistic connotations.

I use the term *barriers,* then, not to convey the idea that communicators function as machines or that communication is a mechanical process, but rather to convey that effective and meaningful interpersonal communication—the kind that we have been talking about throughout this book—may lose some of its effectiveness and meaningfulness when certain factors are present, or rather when communicators think or behave in certain ways. It must be recognized throughout this discussion that these barriers are of human origin and development; it is the communicators who, for one reason or another, create and maintain these barriers.

All six barriers discussed here—polarization, intensional orientation, fact-inference confusion, allness, static evaluation, and indiscrimination—are ways in which our verbal messages describe the world in illogical, distorted, or unscientific ways. An analogy can be made between verbal messages and geographical maps. Maps that accurately describe the world assist the traveler in getting from one place to another. To the extent that such maps inaccurately describe the world, they hinder the traveler in getting from one place to another. Our verbal messages are like maps. To the extent that they accurately represent reality, they are helpful and aid effective and meaningful interpersonal communication. To the extent that they distort reality, they are hindrances and prevent effective and meaningful interpersonal communication.

An examination of these barriers will enable us to (1) detect distortions when they are present in our own or in others' communications and (2) improve our verbal message-making so that these distortions will be kept to a minimum or even eliminated entirely. Interpersonal communication will be enhanced to the degree that we achieve either or both of these purposes.

POLARIZATION

Polarization refers to the tendency to look at the world and to describe it in terms of extremes—good or bad, positive or negative, healthy or sick, intelligent or stupid, rich or poor, and so on. It is often referred to as the fallacy of

Barriers to verbal interaction.

"either-or" or "black-and-white." Although it is true that magnetic poles may be described as positive or negative and that certain people are extremely rich while others are extremely poor, the vast majority of cases are clearly in the middle, between these two extremes. Most people exist somewhere between the extremes of good and bad, healthy or sick, intelligent or stupid, rich or poor. Yet there seems to be a strong tendency to view only the extremes and to categorize people, objects, and events in terms of these polar opposites.

This tendency may be easily illustrated by attempting to fill in the polar opposites for the following words:

tall → _____
heavy → _____
strong → _____
happy → _____
legal → _____

Filling in these opposites should have been relatively easy and quick. The words should also have been fairly short. Further, if a number of people supplied opposites, we would find a high degree of agreement among them.

Now attempt to fill in the middle positions with words meaning, for example, "midway between tall and short," "midway between heavy and light," and so on. These midway responses (compared to the opposites) were probably more difficult to think of and took more time. The words should also have been fairly long or phrases of two, three, four, or more words. Further, we would probably find rather low agreement among different people completing this same task.

It might be helpful to visualize the familiar bell-shaped curve. Few items exist at either of the two extremes, but as we move closer to the center, more and more items are included. This is true of any random sample. If we selected 100 people at random, we would find that their intelligence, height, weight, income, age, health, and so on would, if plotted, fall into a bell-shaped or "normal" distribution. Yet our tendency seems to be to concentrate on the extremes, on the ends of this curve, and ignore the middle, which contains the vast majority of cases.

It is legitimate to phrase certain statements in terms of two values. For example, this thing that you are holding is either a book or it is not. Clearly the classes of book and not-book include all possibilities. And so there is no problem with this kind of statement. Similarly, we may say that the student will either pass this course or will not pass it, these two categories including all possibilities.

We create problems, however, when we use this basic form in situations in which it is inappropriate; for example, "The politician is either for us or against us." Note that these two possibilities do not include all possibilities; the politician may be for us in some things and against us in other things, or he or she may be neutral. During the Vietnam War there was a tendency to categorize people as either hawk or dove, but clearly there were many people who were neither and many who were probably both—hawks on certain issues and doves on others.

We need to beware of implying and believing that two extreme classes include all possible classes—that an individual must be a hawk or a dove and that there are no other alternatives. "Life is either a daring adventure or nothing," said Helen Keller. But for most people it is neither a daring adventure nor nothing but rather something somewhere in between these two extremes.

INTENSIONAL ORIENTATION

Intensional orientation refers to the tendency to view people, objects, and events in terms of the way in which they are talked about or labeled rather than in terms of the way in which they actually exist and operate. *Extensional orientation,* on the other hand, is the tendency to look first at the actual people, objects, and events and only then to their labels. It is the tendency to be guided by what we see happening rather than by the label used for what is happening.

Intensional orientation is seen when we act as if the words and labels are more important than the things they represent—when we act as if the map were more important than the territory. In its extreme form intensional orientation is seen in the person who is afraid of dogs and begins to sweat when shown a picture of a dog or when hearing people talk about dogs. Here the person is responding to the labels (maps) as if they were the actual thing (territory).

Intensional orientation may be seen clearly in the results of the numerous studies on prestige suggestion. Basically, these studies demonstrate that we are influenced more when we assume that the message comes from a prestigious personality than when it comes from an average individual. Such studies have shown that if given a painting, we will evaluate it highly if we think it was painted by a famous artist, but we will give it a low evaluation if we think it was produced by a little-known artist. Other studies have focused on our agreement with dogmatic statements, our judgments on literary merit, our perceptions of musical ability, and so on. In all of these studies the influencing factor was not the message itself—that is, the painting, the literature, the music—but the name attached to it. Advertisers, of course, have long known the value of this type of appeal and have capitalized on it quite profitably.

One of the most ingenious examples of intensional orientation requires that you role play for a minute and picture yourselves seated with a packet of photographs before you. Each of the photographs is of a person you have never seen. You are asked to scratch out the eyes in each photograph. You are further told that this is simply an experiment and that the individuals whose pictures you have will not be aware of anything that has transpired here. As you are scratching out the eyes you come upon a photograph of your mother. What do you do? Are you able to scratch out the eyes as you have done with the pictures of the strangers, or have you somehow lost your ability to scratch out eyes? If, as with many others, you are unable to scratch out the eyes, you are responding intensionally. You are, in effect, responding to the map (in this case the picture) as if it were the territory (your mother).

In a study conducted not long ago Philip Goldberg claimed that women were prejudiced against women. Specifically, he found that women felt that articles written by men were more authoritative and more valuable than identical articles with feminine by-lines. This result was found for messages in "traditionally masculine fields," such as law and city planning, as well as in "traditionally feminine fields," such as elementary school teaching and dietetics. Again this is a clear example of intensional orientation, of our tendency to look at the label (in this case the by-line) and to evaluate the territory (in this case the actual article) only through the label.

In a letter addressed to Ann Landers a young lady wrote that she was distressed because her parents reacted so negatively to the idea of her fiancé becoming a nurse. Ann Landers offered some comfort but added, "I do feel that they ought to call male nurses something else." This is a classic example of intensional orientation.

An experiment conducted with stutterers further illustrates the notion of intensional orientation. Research has found that stutterers will stutter more when talking with persons in authority than with subordinates. Stutterers will stutter very little when talking with children or when addressing animals, for example, but when it comes to teachers or employers they stutter a great deal. Another finding on stuttering concerns adaptation. This refers to the fact that as a stutterer reads a particular passage he or she will stutter less and less on each successive reading. In this experiment the researcher obtained from the stutterers the names of the persons to whom they had most difficulty speaking. At a later date the researchers had each stutterer read a passage five times. As predicted, the stuttering decreased on each reading to the point where it was almost entirely absent on the fifth reading. Before the sixth reading the experimenter placed in front of the stutterer a photograph of the person the stutterer had named as the most difficult to speak to. On the sixth reading the stuttering increased approximately to the level during the first reading of the passage. Again, the individual was responding to the photograph—the label or the map—as if it were something more—as if it were the actual thing.

Labels are certainly helpful guides, but they are not the things themselves and should not be confused with the things for which they are only symbols.

FACT-INFERENCE CONFUSION

We can make statements about the world that we observe, and we can make statements about what we have not observed. In form or structure these statements are similar and could not be distinguished from each other by any grammatical analysis. For example, we can say, "She is wearing a blue jacket," as well as, "He is harboring an illogical hatred." If we diagramed these sentences, they would yield identical structures, and yet we know quite clearly that they are very different types of statements. In the first one we can observe the jacket and the blue color. But how do we observe "illogical hatred"? Obviously, this is not a descriptive statement but an inferential statement. It is a statement that we make not solely on the basis of what we observe but on the basis of what we observe plus our own conclusions.

There is no problem with making inferential statements; we must make them if we are to talk about much that is meaningful to us. The problem arises when we act as if those inferential statements were factual statements.

Consider, for example, the following anecdote: A woman went for a walk one day and met her friend, whom she had not seen or heard from or heard of in 10 years. After an exchange of greetings, the woman said, "Is this your little boy?" and her friend replied, "Yes, I got married about 6 years ago." The woman then asked the child, "What is your name?" and the little boy replied, "Same as my father's." "Oh," said the woman, "then it must be Peter."

The question, of course, is how did the woman know the boy's father's name if she had not seen or heard from or heard of her friend in the last ten years? The answer, of course, is obvious. But it is obvious only after we recognize that in reading this short passage we have made an inference which, although we are not aware of our having made it, is preventing us from answering a simple question. Specifically, we have made the inference that the woman's friend is a woman. Actually, the friend is a man named Peter.

This is very similar to the example used to illustrate sexism in our language. One version goes like this: A boy and his father are in an accident. The father is killed and the little boy is rushed to the hospital to be operated on. The surgeon is called in, looks at the boy, and says, "I can't operate on this boy; he's my son." The question is, how could the boy be the surgeon's son if his father was killed in the accident? This question should not have caused any problems, but we were sensitized to making inferences on the basis of sex. Of course, the surgeon is the boy's mother. This is a particularly good example for illustrating our expectations in regard to male and female occupations. Because of our prior conditioning, we almost feel compelled to qualify the term *surgeon* if the surgeon is female but not if the surgeon is male. Similarly, we speak of "women lawyers" and "women doctors" but "male nurses."

Perhaps the classic example of this type of fact-inference confusion concerns the case of the "empty" gun that unfortunately proves to be loaded. With amazing frequency we find in the newspapers examples of people being so sure that the guns are empty that they point them at another individual and fire. Many times, of course, they are empty. But, unfortunately, many times they are not. Here one makes an inference (that the gun is empty) but acts on the inference as if it were a fact and fires the gun.

Some of the essential differences between factual and inferential statements are summarized in Table 12.1.

Distinguishing between these two types of statements does not imply that one type is better than the other. We need both types of statements; both are useful, both important. The problem arises when we treat one type of statement as if it were the other. Specifically, the problem arises when we treat an inferential statement as if it were a factual statement.

Inferential statements need to be accompanied by tentativeness. We need to recognize that such statements may prove to be wrong, and we should be aware of that possibility. Inferential statements should leave open the possibility of other alternatives. If, for example, we treat the statement, "The United States should enforce the blockade," as if it were a factual statement, we eliminate the possibility of other alternatives. When making inferential statements we should be psychologically prepared to be proven wrong. This requires a great deal of effort, but it is probably effort well spent. If we are psychologically prepared to be proven wrong, we will be less hurt if and when we are shown to be incorrect.

ALLNESS

The world is infinitely complex, and because of this we can never say all about anything—at least we cannot logically say all about anything. And this is particularly true in dealing with people. We may *think* we know all there is to know about individuals or about why they did what they did, yet clearly we do not know all. We can never know all the reasons we ourselves do something, and yet we often think that we know all the reasons why our parents or our friends or our enemies did something. And because we are so convinced that we know all the reasons, we are quick to judge and evaluate the actions of others with great confidence that what we are doing is justified.

We may, for example, be assigned a textbook to read and because previous texts have been dull and perhaps the first chapter is dull, we infer that

Factual Statements	Inferential Statements
1. may be made only after observation	1. may be made at any time
2. are limited to what has been observed	2. go beyond what has been observed
3. may be made only by the observer	3. may be made by anyone
4. may only be about the past or the present	4. may be about any time— past, present, or future
5. approach certainty	5. involve varying degrees of probability
6. are subject to verifiable standards	6. are not subject to verifiable standards

TABLE 12.1
Differences Between Factual and Inferential Statements

all the rest of the book will likewise be dull. Of course, it often turns out that the rest of the book is even worse than the beginning. Yet it could be that the rest of the book would have proven exciting had it been read with an open mind. The problem here is that we run the risk of defining the entire text (on the basis of previous texts and perhaps the first chapter) in such a way as to preclude any other possibilities. If we tell ourselves that the book is dull, it probably will seem dull. If we say a course will be useless ("all required courses are useless"), it will be extremely difficult for that instructor to make the course anything but what we have defined it to be. Only occasionally do we allow ourselves to be proven wrong; for the most part we resist rather fiercely.

The parable of the six blind men and the elephant is an excellent example of an allness orientation and its attendant problems. You may recall from elementary school the poem by John Saxe that concerns six blind men of Indostan who came to examine an elephant, an animal they had only heard about. The first blind man touched the elephant's side and concluded that the elephant was like a wall. The second felt the tusk and said the elephant must be like a spear. The third held the trunk and concluded that the elephant was much like a snake. The fourth touched the knee and knew the elephant was like a tree. The fifth felt the ear and said the elephant was like a fan. And the sixth grabbed the tail and concluded that the elephant was like a rope. Each of these learned men reached his own conclusion regarding what this marvelous beast, the elephant, was really like. Each argued that he was correct and that the others were wrong. Each, of course, was correct; but at the same time, each was wrong. The point this poem illustrates is that we are all in the position of the six blind men. We never see all of something; we never experience anything fully. We see part of an object, an event, a person—and on that limited basis conclude what the whole is like. This procedure is a relatively universal one; we have to do this, since it is impossible to observe everything. And yet we must recognize that when we make judgments of the whole based only on a part, we are actually making inferences that can later be proven wrong. If we assume that we know all of anything, we fall into the pattern of misevaluation called *allness*.

Students who walk into a class convinced that they cannot learn anything probably will not learn anything. And while it may be that the teacher was not very effective, it may also be that the students have closed their minds to the possibility of learning anything. Disraeli once said that "to be conscious that you are ignorant is a great step toward knowledge." That observation is an excellent example of a nonallness attitude. If we recognize that there is more to learn, more to see, more to hear, we will leave ourselves open to this additional information and will be better prepared to assimilate it into our existing structures.

STATIC EVALUATION

In order to understand the concept of static evaluation, try to write down a statement or two that makes no reference to time—that is, we must not be able to tell whether the statement refers to the past, present, or future. Write this statement down before reading on. Next, attempt to date the following quotation. Approximately when was it written?

> *Those states are likely to be well administered in which the middle class is large, and larger if possible than both the other classes or at any rate than either singly; for the addition of the middle class turns the scale and prevents either of the extremes from being dominant.*

These two brief exercises should illustrate an interesting dimension of the English language. It was probably extremely difficult, if not impossible, for you to produce a sentence that made no reference to time whatsoever. Time, in English, is an obligatory category, which means that all sentences must contain some reference to past, present, or future. Our verb system is constructed in such a way that it is impossible to produce a sentence without including a reference to time in the verb. This is not true in all languages. In dating the quotation, most persons would find themselves missing the actual date by at least a few hundred years. The statement was actually written by Aristotle in his *Politics* approximately 2300 years ago.

Thus while it is impossible to make statements without reference to the past, present, or future, it is almost impossible to tell when statements were produced. These, of course, are obvious facts about language. Yet their consequences are often not so obvious.

Often when we form an abstraction of something or someone—when we formulate a verbal statement about an event or a person—that abstraction, that statement, has a tendency to remain static and unchanging, while the object or person to whom it originally referred may have changed enormously. Alfred Korzybski used an interesting illustration in this connection. In a tank we have a large fish and many small fish that are the natural food for the large fish. Given freedom in the tank, the large fish will eat the small fish. After some time we partition the tank, with the large fish on one side and the small fish on the other, divided only by a clear piece of glass. For a considerable time the large fish will attempt to eat the small fish but will fail each time; each time it will knock into the glass partition. After some time it will "learn" that attempting to eat the small fish means difficulty and will no longer go after them. Now, however, we remove the partition, and the small fish swim all around the big fish. But the big fish does not eat them and in fact will die of starvation while its natural food swims all around. The large fish has learned a pattern of behavior, and even though the actual territory has changed, the map remains static.

While we would probably all agree that everything is in a constant state of flux, the relevant question is whether we act as if we know this. Put differently, do we act in accordance with the notion of change, instead of just accepting it intellectually? Do we realize, for example, that just because we have failed at something once, we need not fail again? Do we realize that if someone does something to hurt us, he or she is also in a constant state of change? Our

evaluations of ourselves and of others must keep pace with the rapidly changing real world; otherwise we will be left with attitudes and beliefs about a
world that no longer exists.

T. S. Eliot, in *The Cocktail Party,* said that "what we know of other people
is only our memory of the moments during which we knew them. And they
have changed since then . . . at every meeting we are meeting a stranger."

INDISCRIMINATION

Nature seems to abhor sameness at least as much as vacuums, for nowhere
in the universe can we find identical entities. Everything is unique, unlike
everything else.

Our language, however, provides us with common nouns, such as teacher,
student, friend, enemy, war, politician, liberal, and the like, which lead us to
focus on similarities. Such nouns lead us to group all teachers together, all students together, all friends together, and perhaps divert attention away from the
uniqueness of each individual, object, and event.

The misevaluation of *indiscrimination,* then, occurs when we focus on
classes of individuals or objects or events and fail to see that each is unique,
each is different, and each needs to be looked at individually.

This misevaluation is at the heart of the common practice of stereotyping
national, racial, and religious groups. A stereotype is a relatively fixed mental
picture of some group that is applied to each individual of the group without
regard to his or her unique qualities. It is important to note that although stereotypes are usually thought of as negative, they may also be positive. We can,
for example, consider certain national groups as lazy or superstitious or mer-
cenary or criminal, but we can also consider them as intelligent, progressive,
honest, hard-working, and so on. Regardless of whether such stereotypes are
positive or negative, however, the problems they create are the same. They provide us with shortcuts that are most often inappropriate. For example, when we
meet an individual, we invariably fail to devote sufficient attention to his or her
unique characteristics.

It should be emphasized that there is nothing wrong with classifying. No
one would argue that classifying is unhealthy or immoral. It is, on the contrary,
an extremely useful method of dealing with any complex matter. Classifying
helps us to deal with complexity; it puts order into our thinking. The problem
arises not from classification in itself but from our classifying, then applying
some evaluative label to that class, and then utilizing that evaluative label as
an "adequate" map for each individual in the group. Put differently, indiscrimination is a denial of another's uniqueness.

SOURCES

The barriers to verbal interaction owe their formulation to the work of the general semanticists. I
would especially recommend for beginners John C. Condon, Jr., *Semantics and Communication,*

2d ed. (New York: Macmillan, 1974), William V. Haney, *Communication and Organizational Behavior: Text and Cases*, 3d ed. (Homewood, Ill.: Irwin, 1973), S. I. Hayakawa, *Language in Thought and Action*, 4th ed. (New York: Harcourt Brace Jovanovich, 1978).

The nature of E-prime is discussed in detail in D. David Bourland, Jr., "A Linguistic Note: Writing in E-Prime," *General Semantics Bulletin*, nos. 32 and 33, 1965–1966.

Much that appears in this unit appears in more detail in my *General Semantics: Guide and Workbook*, rev. ed. (DeLand, Fla.: Everett/Edwards, 1974). Experiential Vehicle 12.2 is taken from this book as well. My cassette tape series *General Semantics: Nine Lectures* (DeLand, Fla.: Everett/Edwards, 1971) also covers this material. Perhaps the most useful introduction to the barriers to verbal interaction is J. Dan Rothwell's *Telling It Like It Isn't* (Englewood Cliffs, N.J.: Prentice-Hall/Spectrum, 1982).

EXPERIENTIAL VEHICLES

12.1 E-PRIME

E-prime (E') is normal English minus the verb *to be.* The term *E* refers to the mathematical equation $E - e = E'$, where E = the English language and e = the verb *to be. E'*, therefore, refers to normal English without the verb *to be.*

D. David Bourland, Jr., suggests that if we wrote and spoke without the verb *to be,* we would more accurately describe events. The verb *to be* often suggests that qualities are in the person or thing rather than in the observer making the statement. We often forget that these statements are evaluative rather than purely descriptive. For example, we say, "Johnny is a failure," and imply that failure is somehow *in* Johnny instead of in someone's evaluation of Johnny. This type of thinking is especially important in making statements about ourselves. We say, for example, "I can't learn mathematics," or, "I'm unpopular," or "I'm lazy," and imply that these qualities (the inability to learn mathematics, the unpopularity, and the laziness) are *in* us. But these are simply evaluations which may be incorrect or, if at least partly accurate, may change. The verb *to be* implies a permanence that simply is not true of the world in which we live.

To further appreciate the difference between statements that use the verb *to be* and those that do not, try to rewrite the following sentences without using the verb *to be* in any of its forms—that is, *is, are, am, was,* or any other tenses.

1. I'm a poor student.
2. They are inconsiderate.
3. What is artistic?
4. Is this valuable?
5. Happiness is a dry nose.
6. Love is a useless abstraction.
7. Is this book meaningful?
8. Was the movie any good?
9. Dick and Jane are no longer children.
10. This class is boring.

12.2 FACTS AND INFERENCES*

Carefully read the following report and the observations based on it. Indicate whether you think the observations are true, false, or doubtful on the basis of

*This experiential vehicle is taken from Joseph A. DeVito, *General Semantics: Guide and Workbook,* rev. ed. (DeLand, Fla.: Everett/Edwards, 1974), p. 55, and is modeled on those developed by William V. Haney.

the information presented in the report. Circle T if the observation is definitely true, F if the observation is definitely false, and ? if the observation may be either true or false. Judge each observation in order. Do not reread the observations after you have indicated your judgment, and do not change any of your answers.

A well-liked college teacher had just completed making up the final examinations and had turned off the lights in the office. Just then a tall, dark, broad figure appeared and demanded the examination. The professor opened the drawer. Everything in the drawer was picked up and the individual ran down the corridor. The Dean was notified immediately.

1.	The thief was tall, dark, and broad.	T	F	?
2.	The professor turned off the lights.	T	F	?
3.	A tall figure demanded the examination.	T	F	?
4.	The examination was picked up by someone.	T	F	?
5.	The examination was picked up by the professor.	T	F	?
6.	A tall, dark figure appeared after the professor turned off the lights in the office.	T	F	?
7.	The man who opened the drawer was the professor.	T	F	?
8.	The professor ran down the corridor.	T	F	?
9.	The drawer was never actually opened.	T	F	?
10.	In this report three persons are referred to.	T	F	?

12.3 MATCHING SOME LANGUAGE JARGON: REVIEW QUIZ III

Match up the definitions with the concepts. The 15 terms included in this brief quiz are all taken from Part Three.(Units 9, 10, 11, and 12).

1. a system whose "direct energetic consequences are biologically irrelevant."

2. openness, creativity

3. the characteristic of language that enables us to communicate about matters remote in time and space

4. the principle of verbal interaction that refers to our messages commenting on the present context, the speaker, and the hearer

a. polarization

b. immanent reference

c. connotation

d. adjustment

e. euphemism

f. specialized system

g. jargon

5. the principle of verbal interaction that refers to the notion that communication may take place only to the extent that the communicators share the same system of signals

6. the specialized vocabulary of a disreputable or underworld subculture

7. the technical language of a professional class, for example, professors, doctors, lawyers

8. verbal behavior that is forbidden by a society or social group

9. "nice" words that are designed to make unpleasant topics seem less unpleasant

10. the emotional, subjective, personal meaning

11. an objective definition; the type of definition found in a dictionary

12. a measurement of connotative meaning that utilizes 7-point bipolar scales and measures the evaluation, potency, and activity dimensions of terms

13. the tendency to view and describe the world in terms of opposite extremes

14. the tendency to view people, objects, and events in terms of their labels rather than in terms of the way they actually exist and operate

15. a misevaluation resulting from a failure to see each individual, object, or event as unique and different

h. indiscrimination

i. taboo

j. productivity

k. denotation

l. semantic differentiation

m. cant

n. intensional orientation

o. displacement

NONVERBAL MESSAGES
PART FOUR

UNIVERSALS OF NONVERBAL MESSAGES

Upon completion of this unit, you should be able to:
1. identify the goals of studying nonverbal communication
2. explain the principle that nonverbal communication occurs in a context
3. explain the reasons why nonverbal behaviors in an interactional situation always communicate
4. explain the rule-governed nature of nonverbal communication
5. explain why nonverbal communication is purposeful
6. explain the packaged nature of nonverbal behaviors
7. define and give examples of double-bind messages
8. identify the reasons for assuming that nonverbal communication is highly believable
9. define *metacommunication*
10. provide at least three examples of the ways in which nonverbal behavior is frequently metacommunicational
11. cite at least three examples of unwritten nonverbal rules of behavior

Today everyone seems interested in nonverbal communication, in what is popularly called "body language." The gimmick used in selling books or articles on this topic is the promise that we will learn to decipher what other people are thinking simply by observing their "body language." The cover of Julius Fast's *Body Language*, for example, shows the picture of a woman sitting in a chair with her arms folded and her legs crossed. Surrounding the woman are such questions as, "Does her body say that she's a loose woman?," "Does your body say that you're hung up?," "Does his body say that he's a manipulator?," and so on. Who could resist learning this kind of information? It would be indispensable at parties and all sorts of social gatherings, and success in one's business and social life would almost be assured.

But, as anyone who has read such works knows, such significant insight is not so easy to attain. Perhaps the primary reason is simply that we do not know enough about nonverbal communication to enable the layperson to make instant and accurate readings of the inner workings of the mind. And yet we **185** have—especially in the last few years—learned a great deal about nonverbal communication.

This unit will identify a few universals pertaining to nonverbal communication that seem valid and useful. The goal of such a discussion is not to provide the means for personality diagnosis or for dating success or for determining when someone is bluffing in a poker game, but rather to enable us to (1) better understand ourselves, (2) better understand others, and (3) communicate more effectively.

NONVERBAL COMMUNICATION OCCURS IN A CONTEXT

Like verbal communication, nonverbal communication exists in a context, and that context helps to determine to a large extent the meanings of any nonverbal behaviors. The same nonverbal behavior may have a totally different meaning when it occurs in another context. A wink of the eye to a beautiful person on a bus means something completely different from a wink of the eye that signifies a put-on or a lie. Similarly, the meaning of a given bit of nonverbal behavior will differ depending on the verbal behavior it accompanies or is close to in time. Pounding the fist on the table during a speech in support of a particular politician means something quite different from that same fist pounding in response to news about a friend's death. When divorced from the context, it is impossible to tell what any given bit of nonverbal behavior may mean. Of course, even if we know the context in detail, we still might not be able to decipher the meaning of the nonverbal behavior. In attempting to understand and analyze nonverbal communication, however, it is essential that full recognition be taken of the context.

NONVERBAL BEHAVIOR IN AN INTERACTIONAL SITUATION ALWAYS COMMUNICATES

The observation that all behavior in an interactional situation is communicative is true of all forms of communication, but it seems particularly important to stress it in regard to nonverbal communication. It is impossible not to behave; consequently, it is impossible not to communicate. Regardless of what one does or does not do, one's nonverbal behavior communicates something to someone (assuming that it occurs in an interactional setting).

Sitting silently in a corner and reading a book communicates to the other people in the room just as surely as would verbalization. Staring out the window during class communicates something to the teacher just as surely as would your saying, "I'm bored." Notice, however, an important difference between the nonverbal and the verbal statements. The student looking out the window, when confronted by the teacher asking, "Why are you bored?" can always claim to have been momentarily distracted by something outside. Saying, "I'm bored," however, prevents the student from backing off and giving a more socially acceptable meaning to the statement. The nonverbal communication, however, is also more convenient from the point of view of the teacher. The teacher, if confronted with the student's, "I'm bored," must act on that in some way. Some of the possibilities include saying, "See me after class," "I'm just as bored as you are," "Who cares?," "Why are you bored?," and so on. All of them, however, are confrontations of a kind. The teacher is in a sense forced to do something even though he or she might prefer to ignore it. The nonverbal staring out the window allows the teacher to ignore it. This does not mean that the teacher is not aware of it or that the staring is not communicating. Rather, nonverbal communication allows the "listener" an opportunity to feign a lack of awareness. And, of course, this is exactly what so many teachers do when confronted by a class of students looking out the window, reading the newspaper, talking among themselves, and so on.

There are, however, exceptions to this general rule. Consider, for example, if the student, instead of looking out the window, gave the teacher some unmistakable nonverbal signal, such as the thumbs-down gesture. This type of nonverbal communication is not so easy to feign ignorance of. Here the teacher

Nonverbal behavior always communicates; even when you don't want to.

must confront this comment just as surely as he or she would have to confront the comment, "I'm bored."

Even the less obvious and less easily observed behaviors communicate. The smaller movements of the eyes, hands, facial muscles, and so on also communicate, just as the gross movements of gesturing, sitting in a corner, or staring out a window do.

These small movements are extremely important in interpersonal relationships. We can often tell, for example, when two people genuinely like each other and when they are merely being polite. If we had to state how we know this, we would probably have considerable difficulty. These inferences, many of which are correct, are based primarily on these small nonverbal behaviors of the participants—the muscles around the eyes, the degree of eye contact, the way in which the individuals face each other, and so on. All nonverbal behavior, however small or transitory, is significant—all of it communicates.

A number of theorists have recently pointed out how we communicate even in our gift-giving. Aside from the obvious messages—remembering one's birthday or celebrating Christmas, for example—gifts often communicate less noble motives. For example, giving candy or chocolates to a diabetic or to someone who wants to lose weight or a bottle of liquor to someone with a drinking problem are examples of destructive gifts. Their selection seems to communicate an underlying hostility. One type of gift has been referred to as the "Pygmalion gift," the gift that is designed to change the person into what the donor wants that person to become. The husband who buys his wife sexy lingerie may be asking his wife to be sexy; the wife who buys her husband a weight-lifting machine or tight-fitting underwear may well be asking the same thing. The parent who repeatedly gives the child books or science equipment may be asking the child to be a scholar. The problem with some of these gifts is that the underlying motives—the underlying displeasures—may never be talked about and hence never resolved. When a parent gives a child a nonplay gift—for example, practical gifts of clothes or books—the parent may be responding to her or his own inability to play, to enjoy spontaneous and seemingly impractical pleasures.

This is not to say that all such gifts are motivated by the more negative aspects of our personalities, but only to suggest that even in gift-giving there are messages communicated that are often overlooked and that often function below the level of conscious awareness. Nevertheless, such messages may have considerable impact on the recipient, the donor, and the relationship itself.

NONVERBAL COMMUNICATION IS RULE-GOVERNED

The characteristic of rule-governed behavior is easily appreciated when applied to verbal communication. In fact, the entire field of linguistics is devoted to explaining the rule-governed nature of language. The formulation of rules governing the sound, meaning, and structural systems of language occupies the bulk of the contemporary linguist's time. These are the rules that native speakers of the language follow in producing and in understanding sentences—rules that they may be unable to state explicitly.

Nonverbal communication is also rule-governed; it is regulated by a system of rules or norms that state what is and what is not appropriate, expected, and permissible in specific social situations. We learned both the ways to communicate nonverbally *and* the rules of appropriateness at the same time from observing the behaviors of the adult community. For example, we learned how to express sympathy along with the rules that our culture has established for appropriately communicating sympathy. We learned that touch is permissible under certain circumstances but not under others, and we learned which type of touching is permissible and which is not. That is, we learned the rules governing touch behavior. We learned that women may touch each other in public; for example, they may hold hands, walk arm in arm, engage in prolonged hugging, and even dance together. Men may not do this, at least not without social criticism. And perhaps most obviously we learned that there are certain parts of the body that may not be touched and certain parts that may. As the relationship changes, so do the rules of touching. Generally, as we become more and more intimate, the rules for touching become less and less restrictive.

Another clear example are the rules governing eye contact. In our culture we are permitted to gaze at a stranger on a train or a bus for only a very short time, and then we are supposed to turn away. If we do not follow this rule, our intentions are questioned. We learned rules for sitting and walking behavior. Boys sit with their legs open and girls sit with the legs closed. Men take big steps when they walk; women take small steps. Men sit with their arms stretched out; women sit with the arms close to their body.

As can readily be appreciated even from these brief illustrations, these rules will vary from one culture to another. Different cultures often have very different rules governing the nonverbal behavior of their members. The very same behavior may be thought polite and considerate in one culture and aggressive and impolite in another. Further, as this short list should also have illustrated, many of the rules are sex-specific. Men and women do not learn the same rules, although they know the appropriate rules for each other and will frequently criticize each other for not following the appropriate rules for their sex. *Sissy* and *tomboy* are two of the milder designations for those who do not follow these rules.

Like the nonverbal behaviors themselves these rules are learned without conscious awareness. We learn them largely from observing others. The rules are only brought to our attention, to conscious awareness, in formal discussions of nonverbal communication, such as this one, and when the rules are violated and the violations are called to our attention—either directly by some tactless snob or indirectly through the examples of others. While linguists are attempting to formulate the rules for verbal messages, nonverbal researchers are attempting to formulate the rules for nonverbal messages—rules that native communicators know and utilize every day but cannot necessarily verbalize. A major function of the following units on nonverbal communication is to bring to consciousness some of these implicit rules and the meanings and implications behind their appropriate and inappropriate usage.

NONVERBAL COMMUNICATION IS DETERMINED

Like verbal messages, nonverbal messages evidence the quality of determinism. All messages (verbal and nonverbal alike) are motivated in some way; all are determined. The smile or frown, the forward or backward glance, the strong or mild hug, the long or short kiss—all are motivated in different ways. Much as the smile and the frown, for example, will communicate different meanings to receivers, they will also be reflections of different meanings in the source. Smiling seems obviously motivated by a different set of factors than does frowning. From this rather weak claim, many will make the further assumption that we can therefore learn a person's motives (or subconscious desires or repressed fears or strengths and weaknesses) by analyzing her or his nonverbal behaviors. As we noted above, such significant insight into a person's personality and motivation does not come so easily. We cannot tell what is going on inside a person's skin by focusing solely on what is going on nonverbally.

This is illustrated in an experiment in which analysts looked for various nonverbal cues in videotapes of happily and unhappily married couples who were experiencing considerable interpersonal conflict. It was found that the happy couples sat closer together, looked more frequently into each other's eyes, and touched each other more than they touched themselves. The unhappy couples, on the other hand, crossed their arms and legs, made less direct eye contact with each other, and touched themselves more than they touched each other. Clearly, then, happy and unhappy couples behave differently nonverbally. But this is not the same as saying that couples who touch themselves more than they touch each other are unhappy or are experiencing interpersonal conflict. Their touching means something, but exactly what it means for the person himself or herself cannot be accurately determined from the nonverbal behavior alone.

Our analysis of nonverbal behaviors and our assumption of purposefulness may assist us in suggesting possible hypotheses about what is going on inside the person. But that is about as far as we can legitimately go with our present level of knowledge of nonverbal communication. One of the reasons for this is simply that people are different; one person's smile may mean "I'm happy," whereas another person's smile may cover up seething hostility. Also, there are contextual factors that influence nonverbal behaviors; a smile with one person in one place may mean something totally different from a smile with someone else in another place. Social and cultural factors also influence what a person means when he or she engages in various nonverbal behaviors; whereas one culture may encourage direct eye contact in interpersonal interaction, another culture may discourage it. These are just a few of the many influencing factors that should caution us against postulating specific meanings for specific nonverbal behaviors.

NONVERBAL BEHAVIORS ARE NORMALLY PACKAGED

Nonverbal behaviors, whether they involve the hands, the eyes, or the muscle tone of the entire body, normally occur in "packages" where the various other nonverbal behaviors reinforce or support each other. All parts of our bodies normally work together to communicate a particular meaning. We do not express fear with our eyes while the rest of our body relaxes as if sleeping. We do not express anger through our posture while our face smiles. Rather, the entire body expresses the emotion. For purposes of analysis we may wish to focus primarily on the eyes or the facial muscles or the hand movements, but we need to recognize that these do not occur apart from other nonverbal behaviors. In fact, it is physically difficult to express an intense emotion with only one part of the body. Try to express an emotion with your face while ignoring the rest of your body. You will probably find that the rest of your body takes on the qualities of that emotion as well.

It is even more difficult to express widely different or contradictory emotions with different parts of your body. For example, when you are afraid of something and your body tenses up, it becomes very difficult to relax your facial muscles and smile. In fact, it has been argued that even our graphic gestures (that is, our handwriting) are correlated with and echo or imitate our habitual body gesture style. For example, the person whose body is normally curled up and closed, who avoids direct eye contact, and who constantly turns away when addressed seems to evidence similar graphic movements in handwriting; the writing will be small and the letters tightly packed together. It also appears, for example, that people who take up more physical space—for example, those who want or need more room between themselves and others than do most people and who literally spread themselves all over—also seem to take up more room with their handwriting. Their signatures, in particular, take up a great deal of space in a manner similar to the signatures of high-status persons, which normally take up more space than those of lower-status persons.

In any form of communication, whether interpersonal, small group, public speaking, or mass media, we generally do not pay much attention to the packaged nature of nonverbal communication—it is so expected that it goes unnoticed. But when there is an incongruity—when the weak handshake belies the smile, when the nervous posture belies the focused stare, when the constant preening belies the relaxed whistling or humming—we take notice. Invariably we are led to question the credibility, the sincerity, the honesty of the individual. And research tells us that our instincts serve us well in this type of situation. When nonverbal behaviors contradict each other, there seems good reason to question the believability of the communicator.

Nonverbal communications also evidence this packaged quality with their accompanying verbal messages. When we express anger verbally, our body and face also express anger by tensing themselves, by scowling, and perhaps by assuming a fighting posture. Again, we often fail to notice this because it seems so natural, so expected. When the nonverbal messages of one's posture or face contradict what one says verbally, we take special notice. For example, a person who says "I'm so glad to see you," but who avoids direct eye contact and who looks around as if to see who else is there is sending contradictory messages. Contradictory messages (also called "mixed messages" by some writers) are seen frequently in couples (whether newly dating or long married) who say they love each other but who seem to go out of their ways to hurt each other nonverbally—for example, by being late for important dates, by dressing in ways the other person dislikes, by flirting with others, by avoiding direct eye contact, or by not touching each other. In the film *The Graduate* there is a particularly interesting example of contradictory messages. Dustin Hoffman (Benjamin Braddock, the graduate) and Anne Bancroft (Mrs. Robinson) are having an affair, which, under normal circumstances, would indicate a fair degree of intimacy. But Benjamin repeatedly and consistently calls his partner "Mrs. Robinson," which seems to indicate that he was uncomfortable with the relationship, that he felt unequal in the partnership (he was still a boy, while Mrs. Robinson was a mature woman), that she was married, and that he felt the relationship would not progress or develop further.

Double-Bind Messages

A particular type of contradictory message that deserves special mention is the *double-bind* message. Consider the following interpersonal interaction:

> **Pat:** *Love me.*
> **Chris:** *(Makes advances of a loving nature.)*
> **Pat:** *(Nonverbal tenseness, failure to maintain eye contact and, in general, nonverbal messages that say, "Don't love me.")*
> **Chris:** *(Withdraws.)*
> **Pat:** *See, you don't love me.*

Notice the elements involved for an interaction to constitute a double-bind.

(1) The two persons interacting must share a relatively intense relationship where the messages and demands of one and the responses of the other are important. Clearly with lovers we have this first element or condition. If the relationship is not intense, then the various demands and counterdemands will

have little effect. Examples of such intense relationships are many and include relationships between various family members, between husband and wife, and in some instances between employer and employee.

(2) There must be two messages that demand different and incompatible responses. That is, the messages must be such that both cannot logically be verbalized. Usually, the positive message is communicated verbally, for example, "love me." The accompanying message, usually communicated nonverbally, contradicts the first message, for example, the withdrawal and general tenseness which communicates "stay away," "don't love me." Both parties in a double-bind relationship are likely to engage in sending such messages, either both in the same conversation, or separately on different occasions.

(3) At least one or both of the individuals in a double-bind situation must be unable to escape from the contradictory messages. The individual or individuals lack the opportunities to meet their needs elsewhere or have been in their roles or positions so long that alternatives no longer seem available. People in double-bind situations feel trapped. Preventing an individual's escape from the contradictory message may be a legal commitment (like a marriage license) or, in the case of lovers, an understood but unwritten agreement that implies that each loves the other and cares about meeting mutual needs. No matter what response is made, the person receiving the message is failing to comply with at least one of the demands. If, for example, Chris makes loving advances, then the nonverbal injunction "Don't love me" is violated. If Chris does not make any loving advances, then the verbal injunction "Love me" is violated.

(4) There must be a threat of punishment of some sort for the failure of the message receiver to comply with the sender's verbal or nonverbal demands. In our example, there is an implied threat of punishment for the failure to make loving advances but also for the failure to comply with the demand not to love. Regardless of how the lover responds—whether making loving advances or not making such advances—some form of punishment will follow. This is one reason why the relationship between the people must be relatively intense; otherwise, the threat of punishment would not be significant.

(5) For double-binding to be a serious communication problem, there must be frequent occurrences of it. Such frequent exposure has the effect of setting up a response pattern in the individual such that he or she comes to anticipate that whatever is done will be incorrect; that there is no escape from these confused and confusing communications; and that punishment will follow noncompliance (and since noncompliance is inevitable, punishment is inevitable).

Double-bind messages are particularly significant to children because they can neither escape from such situations, nor can they communicate about the communications. They cannot talk about the lack of correspondence between the verbal and the nonverbal. They cannot ask their parents why they do not hold them or hug them when they say they love them.

Ernst Beier has argued that these double-bind messages—which he refers to as "discordance"—are the result of the desire of the individual to communicate two different emotions or feelings. For example, we may like a person and want to communicate this positive feeling but we may also dislike this person and want to communicate this negative feeling as well. The result is that we communicate both feelings, one verbally and one nonverbally.

NONVERBAL BEHAVIOR IS HIGHLY BELIEVABLE

For some reasons, not all of which are clear to researchers in nonverbal communication, we are quick to believe nonverbal behaviors even when these behaviors contradict verbal behaviors. Consider, for example, a conversation between a teacher and a student. The student is attempting to get a higher grade for the course and is in the process of telling the teacher how much hard work he or she put into the classes and how much enjoyment he or she derived from them. Throughout the discussion, however, the student betrays his or her real intentions with various small muscle movements, inconsistent smiles, a lack of direct eye contact, and so on. Somehow, the teacher goes away with the feeling, based on the nonverbal behavior, that the student really hated the class. For the most part, research has shown that when the verbal and nonverbal messages differ, we believe the nonverbal. In fact, Albert Mehrabian argues that the total impact of a message is a function of the following formula:

Total impact = .07 verbal + .38 vocal + .55 facial.

This formula leaves very little influence to verbal messages. Only one-third of the impact is vocal (that is, paralanguage elements such as rate, pitch, and rhythm), and over half of the message is communicated by the face. The formula, developed by Mehrabian and his colleagues from their studies on the emotional impact of messages, is not applicable to all messages as is sometimes implied in works on nonverbal communication. Although it is interesting to speculate on what percentage of message impact is due to nonverbal elements, there simply is no valid and reliable answer at this time.

Why we believe the nonverbal over the verbal message is not clear. It may be that we feel verbal messages are easier to fake. Consequently, when there is a conflict, we distrust the verbal and accept the nonverbal. Or it may be that the nonverbal messages are perceived without conscious awareness. We learned them without being aware of any such learning, and we perceive them without conscious awareness. Thus, when such a conflict arises we somehow get this "feeling" from the nonverbal messages. Since we cannot isolate its source, we assume that it is somehow correct.

NONVERBAL BEHAVIOR IS FREQUENTLY METACOMMUNICATIONAL

Metacommunication is communication that refers to other communications; it is communication about communication. All behavior, verbal as well as nonverbal, can be metacommunicational. Any given bit of behavior can make reference to communication. We can say "This statement is false," or, "Do you understand what I am trying to communicate to you?" In each case these statements have made references to communication and are called *metacommunicational statements*.

Nonverbal behavior is very often metacommunicational, functioning to make a statement about some verbal statement. The most obvious example is crossing one's finger behind one's back when telling a lie. We frequently observe someone making a statement and winking; the wink functions as a comment on the statement. These are obvious examples. Consider more subtle instances of metacommunication. Take the first day of class as an example. The teacher walks in and says that he or she is the instructor for the course and might then say how the course will be conducted, what will be required, what the goals of the course will be, and so on. But much metacommunication is also going on. The clothes the teacher wears and how he or she wears them, the length and style of hair, the general physical appearance, the way he or she walks, the tone of voice, and so on, all communicate about the communication—as well as communicating in and of themselves. These nonverbal messages function to comment on the verbal messages the instructor is trying to communicate. On the basis of these cues, students will come to various conclusions. They might conclude that this teacher is going to be easy even though a long reading list was given or that the class is going to be enjoyable or boring or too advanced or irrelevant.

The metacommunicational function of nonverbal communication is not limited to its role as an adjunct to verbal communication; nonverbal communication may also comment on other nonverbal communication. This is actually a very common situation. The individual who when meeting a stranger both smiles and presents a totally lifeless hand for shaking is a good example of how one nonverbal behavior may refer to another nonverbal behavior. Here the lifeless handshake belies the enthusiastic smile.

But most often when nonverbal behavior is metacommunicational, it functions to reinforce (rather than to contradict) other verbal or nonverbal behavior. You may literally roll up your sleeves when talking about cleaning up the room, or smile when greeting someone, or run to meet someone you say you are anxious to see, or arrive early for a party you verbally express pleasure in attending. Or, on the negative (though still consistent) side, you may arrive late for a dental appointment (presumably with a less-than-pleasant facial expression) or grind your teeth when telling off your boss. The point is simply that much nonverbal communication is metacommunicational. This does not mean that nonverbal communication may not refer to people, events, things, relationships, and so on (that is, *object* communication), nor does it mean that verbal communication may not be metacommunication. I merely stress here the role of nonverbal communication as metacommunication because of its frequent use in this role.

SOURCES

General introductions to the area of nonverbal communication are plentiful and make interesting reading. Perhaps the most entertaining is Desmond Morris, *Manwatching* (New York: Abrams, 1977). This work contains numerous photographs that help greatly in explaining the varied aspects of nonverbal behaviors. Two popular works that are also sound from a theoretical point of view are Gerald I. Nierenberg and Henry H. Calero, *How to Read a Person Like a Book* (New York: Pocket Books, 1971), and Flora Davis, *Inside Intuition* (New York: New American Library, 1973). Three excellent works which thoroughly review the research on nonverbal communication are Dale G. Leathers, *Nonverbal Communication Systems* (Boston: Allyn & Bacon, 1976), Mark L. Knapp, *Nonverbal Communication in Human Interaction,* 2d ed. (New York: Holt, Rinehart and Winston, 1978), and Lawrence Rosenfeld and Jean Civikly, *With Words Unspoken* (New York: Holt, Rinehart and Winston, 1976). For Ernst Beier's analysis of discordance, see his "How We Send Emotional Messages," *Psychology Today* 8 (October 1974): 53–56. On handwriting, see Rhoda Riddell, "Writing Personalities," *Human Behavior* 7 (July 1978): 18–23. Some of the issues central to the study of nonverbal communication are considered in a thoughtful essay by Mark L. Knapp, John M. Wiemann, and John A. Daly, "Nonverbal Communication: Issues and Appraisal," *Human Communication Research* 4 (Spring 1978): 271–280. An excellent collection of articles on nonverbal communication is contained in Shirley Weitz, ed., *Nonverbal Communication: Readings with Commentary,* 2d ed. (New York: Oxford University, 1979). For the insights on gift-giving I relied on Georgia Dullea, "Presents: Hidden Messages," *New York Times,* December 14, 1981, p. D12.

13.1 BREAKING NONVERBAL RULES*

The general objective of this exercise is to become better acquainted with some of the rules of nonverbal communication and to analyze some of the effects of breaking such rules.

Much as we learn verbal language (that is, without explicit teaching), we also learn nonverbal language—the rules for interacting nonverbally. Among such "rules" might be some of the following:

1. Upon entering an elevator turn to the door and stare at it or at the numbers indicating where the elevator is until your floor is reached.
2. When sitting next to someone (or in the general area) do not invade his or her private space with your body or your belongings.
3. When strangers are talking do not enter their group.
4. When talking with someone do not stand too close or too far away. You may move closer when talking about intimate topics. Never stand close enough so that you can smell the other person's body odor. This rule may be broken only under certain conditions, for example, when the individuals involved are physically attracted to each other or when one individual is consoling another or when engaged in some game where the rules require this close contact.
5. When talking in an otherwise occupied area lower your voice so that other people are not disturbed by your conversation.

Procedure

Groups of two students should be formed, with one student designated as rule breaker and the other as observer. The task of the rule breaker is simply to enter some campus situation in which one or more rules of nonverbal communication would normally be operative and to break one or more rules. The task of the observer is to record mentally (or in writing if possible) what happens as a result of the rule breaking.

Each group should then return after a specified amount of time and report back to the entire class on what has happened.

Note: No rules should be broken if it means infringing on the rights of others.

---

*This exercise was suggested to me by Professor Jean Civikly.

BODY COMMUNICATION

Upon completion of this unit, you should be able to:

1. define and provide at least two examples of emblems, illustrators, affect displays, regulators, and adaptors
2. identify instances of the five types of movements in the behaviors of others and in your own behaviors
3. identify the types of information communicated by the face
4. identify at least two problems in determining the accuracy of judging facial expressions
5. explain how context and culture influence facial expressions and their decoding
6. explain micromomentary expressions
7. identify at least three functions of eye movements
8. explain the types of information communicated by pupil dilation and constriction
9. define *tactile communication*
10. explain at least three functions frequently served by tactile communication

In this unit *body communication*—the messages that are sent by one's body—will be explored. This includes the messages of gestures, facial expression, and eye movements, and *tactile communication*—the messages communicated by the touching of oneself and others.

BODY MOVEMENTS

In dealing with nonverbal movements of the body, a classification offered by Paul Ekman and Wallace V. Friesen seems the most useful. These researchers distinguish five classes of nonverbal movements based on the origins, functions, and coding of the behavior: emblems, illustrators, affect displays, regulators, and adaptors.

Emblems

Emblems are nonverbal behaviors that translate words or phrases rather directly. Emblems include, for example, the O.K. sign, the peace sign, the come **198** here sign, the hitchhiker's sign, the "up yours" sign, and so on. Emblems are nonverbal substitutes for specific verbal words or phrases and are probably learned in essentially the same way as are specific words and phrases—without conscious awareness or explicit teaching and largely through imitation.

Although emblems seem rather natural to us and almost inherently meaningful, they are as arbitrary as any word in any language. Consequently, our present culture's emblems are not necessarily the same as our culture's emblems of 300 years ago or the same as the emblems of other cultures.

Emblems are often used to supplement the verbal message or as a kind of reinforcement. At times they are used in place of verbalization, for example, when there is a considerable distance between the individuals and shouting would be inappropriate, or when we wish to "say" something behind someone's back.

Illustrators

Illustrators are nonverbal behaviors that accompany and literally illustrate the verbal messages. In saying, "Let's go up," for example, there will be movements of the head and perhaps hands going in an upward direction. In describing a circle or a square you are more than likely to make circular or square movements with your hands.

In using illustrators we are aware of them only part of the time; at times they may have to be brought to our attention and our awareness. Illustrators seem more natural and less arbitrary than emblems. They are partly a function of learning and partly innate. Illustrators are more universal; they are more common throughout the world and throughout time than emblems. Consequently, it is likely that there is some innate component to illustrators, contrary to what many researchers might argue.

Affect Displays

Affect displays are more independent of verbal messages than illustrators and less under conscious control than either emblems or illustrators. Affect displays are the movements of the facial area that convey emotional meaning; these are the facial expressions that show anger and fear, happiness and surprise, eagerness and fatigue. They are the facial expressions that "give us away" when we attempt to present a false image and that lead people to say, "You look angry today, what's wrong?" We can, however, also consciously control affect displays, as actors do whenever they play a role.

Affect displays may be unintentional—as when they give us away— but they may also be intentional. We may want to show anger or love or hate or surprise, and, for the most part, we do a creditable job. Actors are often rated by the public for their ability to accurately portray affect by movements of their facial muscles.

Regulators

Regulators are nonverbal behaviors that "regulate" (monitor, maintain, or control) the speaking of another individual. When we are listening to another we are not passive; rather, we nod our heads, purse our lips, adjust our eye focus, and make various paralinguistic sounds such as "mm-mm" or "tsk." Regulators are clearly culture bound and are not universal.

Regulators in effect tell speakers what we expect or want them to do as they are talking—"Keep going," "What else happened?," "I don't believe that," "Speed up," "Slow down," and any number of other speech directions. Speakers often receive these nonverbal behaviors without being consciously aware of them. Depending on their degree of sensitivity, they modify their speaking behavior in line with the directions supplied by the regulators.

Regulators would also include such gross movements as turning one's head, leaning forward in one's chair, and even walking away.

Adaptors

Adaptors are nonverbal behaviors that serve some kind of need and occur in their entirety when performed in private but are only partially executed

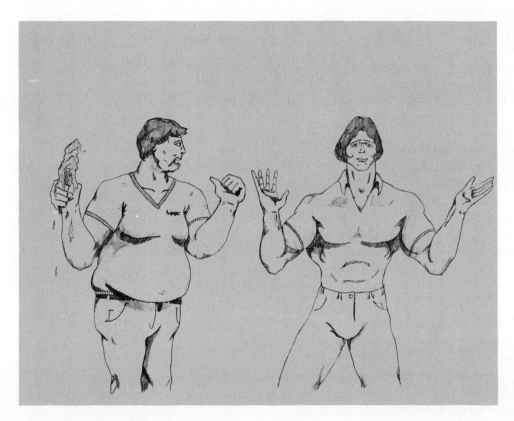

"What's all this fuss about body communication?"

when attempted in public. For example, when you are alone you might scratch your head until the itch is gone, or pick your nose until you are satisfied. In public, when people are watching us, we might perform these actions but only partially. And so you might put your fingers to your head and move them around a bit, but you probably would not scratch enough to totally eliminate the itch. Similarly you might touch your nose but probably would not pursue this simple act to completion.

In observing this kind of nonverbal behavior it is difficult to tell what the partial behavior was intending to accomplish. For example, in observing someone's finger near the nose we cannot be certain that this behavior was intended to pick it, scratch it, or whatever. These adaptors are emitted without conscious awareness.

In many of the popular books on nonverbal behavior it is these adaptors that are given the most attention. The authors talk about people crossing their legs in a certain way, which is supposed to indicate sexual invitation, or in another way, which indicates introversion, or in still another way, to indicate aggressiveness, and so on. The attempt here is to identify nonverbal behaviors that are performed without conscious awareness and that reveal some kind of inner desire or tendencies.

FACIAL AND EYE MOVEMENTS

"The face," Cicero said, "is the image of the soul; and the eyes are its interpreter." Some researchers would claim that the movements of the face and eyes communicate more information than any other verbal or nonverbal system.

Facial Communication

Generally, research has found that facial messages communicate types of emotions as well as selected qualities or dimensions of emotion. Although researchers are not unanimous in their agreement, most agree with Paul Ekman, Wallace V. Friesen, and Phoebe Ellsworth, who claim that facial messages may communicate at least the following eight "emotion categories": happiness, surprise, fear, anger, sadness, disgust, contempt, and interest. Dale Leathers has proposed that in addition to these eight, facial movements may also communicate bewilderment and determination.

The accuracy with which people express emotions facially and the accuracy with which receivers decode the expressions have been the object of considerable research. One problem is that it is difficult to separate the ability of the encoder from the ability of the decoder. Thus, an individual may be quite adept at communicating emotions, but the receiver may prove to be insensitive. On the other hand, the receiver may be quite good at deciphering emotions, but the sender may be inept. And, of course, there are tremendous differences between one person and another as well as with the same person at different times. A second problem is that accuracy seems to vary with the method of the research. In some cases still photographs are used and people are asked to judge the emotions the people pictured are experiencing. Some research uses live models or actors and actresses who have been trained to communicate the different emotions. Still others use more spontaneous methods. For example, an individual judge views a person who is himself or herself viewing and reacting to a film. The judge, without seeing the film, has to decode the emotion the viewer is experiencing. As can be appreciated, each method yields somewhat different results. Accuracy also varies with the emotions themselves. Some emotions are easier to communicate and to decode than others. Ekman, Friesen, and Carlsmith report that happiness is judged with an accuracy ranging from 55 to 100 percent, surprise from 38 to 86 percent, and sadness from 19 to 88 percent. All this is not to say that the results of these studies are of no value; rather, it is merely to inject a note of caution in dealing with "conclusions" drawn from nonverbal research.

Try to communicate surprise using only facial movements. Do this in front of a mirror and attempt to describe in as much detail as possible the specific movements of the face that make up surprise. If you signal surprise like most people, you probably employ raised and curved eyebrows, long horizontal forehead wrinkles, wide-open eyes, a dropped-open mouth, and lips parted with no tension. Even if there were differences—and clearly there would be from one person to another—you could probably recognize the movements listed here as indicative of surprise. Paul Ekman has developed what he calls FAST— the Facial Affect Scoring Technique. With this technique the face is broken up into three main parts: eyebrows and forehead, eyes and eyelids, and the lower face from the bridge of the nose down. Judges then attempt to identify various emotions by observing the different parts of the face and writing descriptions similar to the one for surprise given above for the various emotions.

In Unit 1 we noted that the context greatly influences the other aspects of communication. Communication by facial expression is no exception. It has been found repeatedly that the same facial expressions are perceived differently if people are supplied with different contexts. For example, in a study by M. G. Cline it was found that when a smiling face was presented looking at a glum face, the smiling face was judged to be vicious and taunting, but when the same smiling face was presented looking at a frowning face, it was judged to be peaceful and friendly. This is similar to the experiments done by the Russian filmmaker Kuleshev in the 1920s who "discovered" the technique of "montage" (film editing) by juxtaposing a "reaction shot" of a man's face with various different events. To the viewer, the face seemed to register different emotions depending on what scene it followed.

It appears from cross-cultural research that facial expressions have a somewhat universal nature. For example, people in Borneo and New Guinea who have had little contact with Western cultures were able to match accurately emotions with pictures of facial expressions of Westerners. Further, their own facial expressions, posed to communicate various different emotions, were accurately decoded by Americans. Similarly, studies conducted with children who were born blind and who, therefore, could not see how others facially expressed the various emotions, seem to use the same facial expressions as their sighted peers. Studies such as these point to a universality among facial gestures. The wide variations in facial communication that we do observe in different cultures seem to reflect what is permissible and not permissible to communicate rather than a difference in the way in which emotions are expressed facially. For example, in some cultures it is permissible openly and publicly to show contempt or disgust, but in others people are taught to hide such emotions in public and to display them only in private.

A frequently asked question in this regard concerns whether these emotions can really be hidden or whether they somehow manifest themselves below the level of conscious awareness. Is our contempt encoded facially without our being aware of it or even without observers being aware of it? Although a complete answer to this question is not possible at this time, some indication that we do, in fact, communicate these emotions without awareness comes from research on micromomentary expressions. E. A. Haggard and K. S. Isaacs conducted studies in which they showed films of therapy patients in slow motion. They noted that often the patient's expression would change dramatically. For example, a frown would change to a smile and then quickly back to a frown. If the film was played at normal speed, the change to the smile would go unnoticed. Only when the film was played at slow speed was it apparent that the patient smiled in between frowning. Generally, if a facial expression is of less than two-fifths of a second's duration, the expression goes unnoticed unless it is filmed and then played back at reduced speed. These extremely brief movements are called *micromomentary expressions*, and it has been proposed that these are indicative of an individual's real emotional state and that our conditioning leads us to repress such expressions. A related question would be whether we receive such micromomentary expressions without being aware of it.

Eye Movements

From Ben Jonson's poetic observation, "Drink to me only with thine eyes, and I will pledge with mine," to the scientific observations of contemporary researchers, the eyes are regarded as the most important nonverbal message system. Mark Knapp as well as various other researchers note four major functions of eye communication. One function is to monitor feedback from the other person. In talking with someone we look at her or him intently, as if to say, "Well, what do you think?" or "React to what I've just said." Also, we look at speakers to let them know that we are listening. In studies conducted on gazing behavior and summarized by Knapp, it has been found that listeners gaze at speakers more than speakers gaze at listeners. The percentage of interaction time spent gazing while listening, for example, has been observed in two studies to be 38 percent and 41 percent while the percentage of time spent gazing while talking has been observed to be 62 percent and 75 percent. It is interesting to note that when these percentages are reversed—when a speaker gazes at the listener for longer than "normal" periods or when a listener gazes at the speaker for shorter than "normal" periods, the conversational interaction becomes awkward and uncomfortable. You may wish to try this with a friend; even with mutual awareness, you will note the discomfort caused by this seemingly minor communication change.

A second and related function is to inform the other person that the channel of communication is open and that he or she should now speak. The clearest example of this is seen in the college classroom, where the instructor asks a question and then locks eyes with a student. Without saying anything else it is assumed and presumed that the student should answer the question. Instructors who learn the names of their students do not have to use eye contact to identify student respondents. But whether names or eyes are used, the function is essentially the same; it is a cue to speak.

A third function is to signal the nature of the relationship between two people, for example, one of positive or negative regard. When we attempt to hide our feelings, we avoid eye contact. We may also signal status relationships with our eyes. This is particularly interesting because the same movements of the eyes may signal either subordination or superiority. The superior individual, for example, may stare at the subordinate or may glance away. Similarly, the subordinate may look directly at the superior or perhaps to the floor. Similarly, a direct stare may signal an amorous or a hostile relationship. Because of these contradictory meanings, we generally utilize information from other areas, particularly the face, to decode the message before making any final judgments.

Lastly, eye movements are often used to compensate for increased physical distance. By making eye contact we overcome psychologically the physical distance between us. When we catch someone's eye at a party, for example, we become psychologically close even though we may be separated by a considerable physical distance. Eye contact and other expressions of psychological closeness, such as self-disclosure and degree of intimacy, have been found to vary in proportion to each other.

In addition to eye movements, considerable research has been done on pupil dilation. In the fifteenth and sixteenth centuries in Italy women used to put drops of belladonna (which literally means "beautiful woman") into their eyes to dilate the pupils so that they would look more attractive. Generally contemporary research seems to support the intuitive logic of these women; dilated pupils are in fact judged to be more attractive than constricted pupils. Pupil size is also indicative of one's interest and level of emotional arousal. One's pupils enlarge when one is interested in something or when one is emotionally aroused. When homosexuals and heterosexuals were shown pictures of nude bodies, the homosexuals' pupils dilated more when viewing same-sex bodies, while the heterosexuals' pupils dilated more when viewing opposite-sex bodies. Perhaps we judge dilated pupils as more attractive because we judge the individual's dilated pupils to be indicative of an interest in us.

BODY TOUCHING

Touch is perhaps the most primitive form of communication. In terms of sense development, it is probably the first to be utilized; even in the womb the child is stimulated by touch. Soon after birth the child is fondled, caressed, patted, and stroked by the parents and by any other relative who happens to be around. The whole world wants to touch the new infant. Touch becomes for the child a pleasant pastime, and so he or she begins to touch. Everything is picked up, thoroughly fingered, and put into the mouth in an attempt to touch it as closely as possible. The child's favorite toys seem to be tactile ones—cuddly teddy bears, teething rings, and even pieces of blankets. Much in the same way as children touch objects in the environment, they also touch themselves; children play with toes and fingers, nose and lips, ears and genitals. At some point, children are stopped from picking their noses and playing with their genitals. No reason is given other than the admonition, "Don't do that" or a gentle slap on the hands. As children mature and become sociable, they begin to explore others through touch, though again there are certain parts that are forbidden to touch or to have touched by others. Nonverbal researcher Lawrence Frank has observed that some of the ways in which we dress our bodies—the clothing we wear, the jewelry, and even the make-up and general cosmetics—send out invitations to others to touch us. The way we adorn our bodies indicates our readiness and our willingness to be touched, though often on a subconscious level.

Functions of Touching Behavior

Touching as a form of communication can serve any number of functions. In fact, one would be hard pressed to name a general function of communication that could not be served by tactile communication. Special note, however, should be made of a few major functions normally served by tactile communication.

Perhaps the most obvious is a sexual one. Touch seems to be the primary form of sexual interaction. From fondling one's genitals as a child, to kissing, to fondling another individual, to sexual intercourse, touch plays a primary role. Men shave or grow beards, women shave their legs and underarms, and both use body oils and creams to keep their skin smooth in a conscious or subconscious awareness of the powerful role of touch as a form of communication.

Touch also serves a primary role in consoling another individual. For example, we put our arms around people, hold their head in our hands, hold their hands, or hug them in an attempt to empathize with them more fully. It seems like an attempt to feel what the other person is feeling by becoming one with them—perhaps the ideal in empathic understanding. Try to console some-one, even in role playing, when you are not allowed to touch them, and you will see how unnatural it seems and how difficult it is to say the appropriate words.

In almost all group encounter sessions touch is used as a supportive ges-ture. Generally, we do not touch people we dislike (except in fighting with them). Otherwise, we only touch people we like, and so the very act of touching says, "I like you," "I care about you," "I want to be close to you," and so on. Touching implies a commitment to the other individual; where and how we touch seems to determine the extent of that commitment. To shake someone's hand, for example, involves a very minor commitment. Our culture has, in effect, defined handshaking as a minor social affair. But to caress someone's neck or to kiss someone's mouth implies a commitment of much greater mag-nitude. "Touch is such a powerful signalling system," notes Desmond Morris, "and it's so closely related to emotional feelings we have for one another that in casual encounters it's kept to a minimum. When the relationship develops, the touching follows along with it."

The location, amount, and intensity of tactile communication is culturally determined, at least in part. For example, southern Europeans will touch each other a great deal more than will northern Europeans or Americans.

Touching ourselves, of course, also communicates. We are all familiar with the individual who is constantly fixing his or her hair—to the point where we feel like screaming and perhaps sometimes do. Although we have learned somewhere that these adaptors—these ways of touching oneself—are forbid-den, at least in public, there are still people who pick their noses, scratch their heads, stick their fingers in their ears, or scratch their genitals or buttocks with-out the least concern for those around who might not care to witness this exer-cise in self-gratification.

In her insightful *Body Politics,* Nancy Henley argues that touching behav-ior can be both a sign of affection, which we have already noted, and also a sign of dominance. Consider, as Henley suggests, who would touch whom—say, by putting one's arm on the other person's shoulder or by putting one's hand on the other person's back—in the following dyads: teacher and student, doctor and patient, master and servant, manager and worker, minister and parishioner, police officer and accused, businessperson and secretary. Most people brought up in our culture would say that the first-named person in each dyad would be more likely to touch the second-named person than the other way around. It is the higher-status person who is permitted to touch the lower-status person; in fact, it would be a breach of etiquette for the lower-status per-son to touch the person of higher status.

Henley further argues that in addition to indicating relative status, touch-ing also demonstrates the assertion of male power and dominance over women. Men may, says Henley, touch women in the course of their daily routine—in the restaurant, in the office, and in the school, for example—and thus indicate their "superior status." When women touch men, on the other hand, the interpretation that it designates a female-dominant relationship is found not acceptable (to men), and so this touching is explained and interpreted as a sexual invitation.

Who Touches Whom Where

A great deal of research has been directed at the question of who touches whom where. One of the most famous studies was that conducted by Sidney M. Jourard, a summary of whose findings is presented in Figure 14.1. In the first figure, labeled "Body for mother" we have the areas and frequency with which these areas of a male college student's body were touched by his mother. The second figure records the areas and frequency with which these areas were touched by the student's father, and so on. The key within the figure indicates the percentage of students who reported being touched in these areas.

Jourard reports that touching and being touched differ little between men and women. Men touch and are touched as often and in the same places as women. The major exception to this is the touching behavior of mothers and fathers. Mothers touch children of both sexes and of all ages a great deal more than do fathers, who in many instances go no further than touching the hands of their children. The studies that have found differences between touching behavior in men and women seem to indicate that women touch more than men do. For example, women seem to touch their fathers more than men do. Also, it seems that female babies are touched more than male babies. In an investigation of the wish to be held versus the wish to hold it was found that women report a greater desire to be held than to hold; and whereas men also report a desire to be held, it is not as intense as that of women. This, of course, fits in quite neatly with our cultural stereotypes of men being protectors (and therefore indicating a preference for holding) and women being protected (and therefore indicating a preference for being held).

A great deal more touching is reported among opposite-sex friends than among same-sex friends. Both male and female college students report that they touch and are touched more by their opposite-sex friends than by their same-sex friends. No doubt the strong societal bias against same-sex touching accounts, at least in part, for the greater prevalence of opposite-sex touching that most studies report. I suspect, however, that a great deal of touching goes on among same-sex friends but goes unreported, for at least two reasons. First, college students are often fearful that they might be thought homosexual if they admit to touching or being touched by same-sex partners, and homosexual students will often be "forced" by various pressures to play the role of the heterosexual and give even more heterosexually oriented responses than would heterosexuals themselves. Second, many people are unaware of touching same-sex partners; it is a behavior that is often engaged in without any conscious awareness, much as we are unaware of making slight movements with our head when we indicate a direction or of smiling when we are feeling good. Sexual touching, on the other hand, is often done with awareness—sometimes a planned awareness—and, at least in the early stages, with considerable self-consciousness.

The Jourard study was replicated 10 years later when support was found

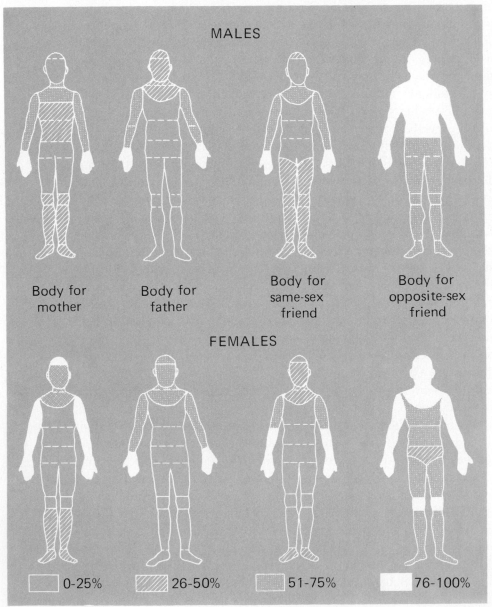

FIGURE 14.1
The amount of touching of the various parts of the body as reported by male and female college students. Source: From S. M. Jourard, "An Exploratory Study of Body-Accessibility," British Journal of Social and Clinical Psychology 5(1966):221–231.

MALES

Body for mother

Body for father

Body for same-sex friend

Body for opposite-sex friend

FEMALES

0-25%   26-50%   51-75%   76-100%

for all of Jourard's earlier findings, except that in the later study both males and females were touched more by opposite-sex friends than in the earlier study. In another similar study, college students in Japan and in the United States were surveyed. The results are presented in Figure 14.2. The results present a particularly dramatic case for cross-cultural differences; students from the United States reported being touched twice as much as did students from Japan.

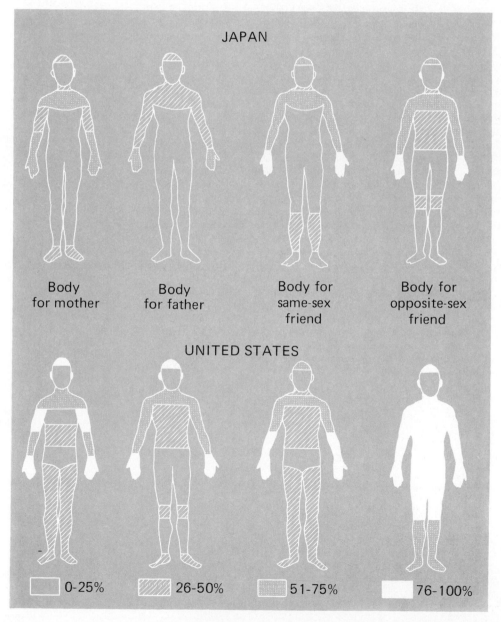

FIGURE 14.2 Areas and frequency of touching as reported by Japanese and United States college students. Source: From Dean C. Barnlund, "Communicative Styles in Two Cultures: Japan and the United States," in A. Kendon, R. M. Harris, and M. R. Key, eds., Organization of Behavior in Face-to-Face Interaction (The Hague: Mouton, 1975).

SOURCES

Perhaps the most authoritative source on body communication is Ray L. Birdwhistell, *Kinesics and Context: Essays on Body Motion Communication* (New York: Ballantine Books, 1970). This paperback contains 28 articles by Birdwhistell on body communication plus an extensive bibliography of research and theory in this area. Another interesting source is *Approaches to Semiotics*, edited by Thomas A. Sebeok, Alfred S. Hayes, and Mary Catherine Bateson (The Hague: Mouton, 1964). This volume also contains an excellent study by Weston LaBarre, "Paralinguistics, Kinesics, and Cultural Anthropology," and articles by Alfred S. Hayes and Margaret Mead which are particularly useful for the study of kinesics. The discussion and classification of types of body movements is from P. Ekman and W. V. Friesen, "The Repertoire of Nonverbal Behavior: Categories, Origins, Usage, and Coding," *Semiotica* 1 (1969): 49–98. Two works by Albert E. Scheflen are both interesting and informative: *Body Language and the Social Order* (Englewood Cliffs, N.J.: Prentice-Hall, 1972), and *How Behavior Means* (Garden City, N.Y.: Doubleday [Anchor Books], 1974). A general overview is provided in my "Kinesics—Other Codes, Other Channels," *Communication Quarterly* 16 (April 1968):29–32.

The studies referred to in this discussion of facial and eye communication are as follows: Albert Mehrabian, "Communication Without Words," in *Communication: Concepts and Processes*, rev. ed., Joseph A. DeVito, ed. (Englewood Cliffs, N.J.: Prentice-Hall, 1976); Paul Ekman, Wallace V. Friesen, and Phoebe Ellsworth, *Emotion in the Human Face: Guidelines for Research and an Integration of Findings* (New York: Pergamon Press, 1972); Paul Ekman, W. V. Friesen, and S. S. Tomkins, "Facial Affect Scoring Technique: A First Validity Study," *Semiotica* 3 (1971), 37–58; M. G. Cline, "The Influence of Social Context on the Perception of Faces," *Journal of Personality* 2(1956): 142–185; E. A. Haggard and K. S. Isaacs, "Micromomentary Facial Expressions as Indicators of Ego Mechanisms in Psychotherapy," in *Methods of Research in Psychotherapy*, L. A. Gottschalk and A. H. Auerbach, eds. (Englewood Cliffs, N.J.: Prentice-Hall, 1966). The Ekman, Friesen, and Carlsmith study may be found in *Emotions in the Human Face*, cited above.

For body touching, see Ashley Montague, *Touching: The Human Significance of the Skin* (New York: Harper & Row 1971); Frank A. Geldard, "Body English," in my *Communication: Concepts and Processes*; and, Lawrence Frank, "Tactile Communication," *Genetic Psychology Monographs* 56 (1957):209–255. For Jourard's studies on touching, see Sidney M. Jourard, *Disclosing Man to Himself* (New York: Van Nostrand Reinhold, 1968), and *Self-Disclosure* (New York: Wiley, 1971). Marc Hollender and Alexander Mercer conducted the study on holding: "Wish To Be Held and Wish To Hold in Men and Women," *Archives of General Psychiatry* 33 (January 1976): 49–51. On the role of touching in status and power relationships, see Nancy M. Henley, *Body Politics: Power, Sex, and Nonverbal Communication* (Englewood Cliffs, N.J.: Prentice-Hall, 1977). An interesting brief pamphlet on nonverbal communication and education is Genelle G. Morain, *Kinesics and Cross-Cultural Understanding* (Arlington, Va.: Center for Applied Linguistics, 1978).

The works referred to in Unit 13, especially those by Knapp, Leathers, and Rosenfeld and Civikly are appropriate here as well.

14.1 INSTRUCTING NONVERBALLY*

The purpose of this exercise is to heighten your awareness of nonverbal communication, particularly communication with one's body.

In this exercise the class is broken up into groups of five or six. One member from each group leaves the room for approximately 1 minute. When these "subjects" are out of the room, each group is given an instruction that they must communicate to the subject using only the nonverbal cue or cues to which they are restricted. All groups should of course be given the same instruction and be limited to the same verbal cue or cues so that the task will be equally difficult for all groups.

The first group to get the subject to comply with their instruction wins the round and gets 10 points. Then the process is repeated, this time with another subject chosen from the group, another instruction, and another nonverbal cue (or cues). The exercise is completed when one group wins 50 points, when time is up, or when some other predetermined point is reached.

Some sample instructions and types of nonverbal cues follow. Instructors may wish to compile their own list of instructions to ensure that they have not been seen by any member of the class.

Sample Instructions

Leave the room; give the teacher a pat on the back; shake hands with each member of the group; open (close) all the windows; open (close) the door; bring into the class someone who is not a member of the class; write the time on the board; find a red pen; raise your hand; clap hands; sit on the floor; put your shoes on the wrong feet; get a drink of water; hold up a notebook with a name of the school on it; comb your hair.

Nonverbal Cues

Vocal (but nonverbal) cues; hand and arm movements; eye movements (but not head movements); head movements; movements of the entire body; manipulation of the entire body; tactile cues; manipulation of objects in the room; leg movements (including feet movements).

*This exercise was adapted from one developed by my students in Interpersonal Communication. **211**

14.2 CONTROL BY NONVERBAL COMMUNICATION

Write the letters of a phrase or statement on pieces of typing paper or cardboard, one letter on each piece. Shuffle them randomly and distribute one to each student. (Select a phrase or statement that contains as many letters as there are students.)

Tell the students to form a phrase or statement without talking or writing anything. The students should attempt to arrange themselves so that the letters they are carrying spell out the phrase or statement. After the phrase or statement is formed, consider the following:

1. Did anyone emerge as leader?
2. What nonverbal behaviors were used by the leader to direct or control the behavior of the group members?
3. Did others attempt to take charge? When? In what way? With what nonverbal behaviors did they indicate a desire to take charge?
4. Were some members turned off? How did they signal this nonverbally?
5. How did you feel about being directed by other people without any talking taking place?

14.3 FACIAL COMMUNICATION

Working in dyads or small groups, test the conclusion of Ekman, Friesen, and Ellsworth that the face is capable of communicating the following eight "emotion categories": happiness, surprise, fear, anger, sadness, disgust, contempt, and interest.

On index cards write the names of these emotion categories, one to a card. Place the cards face down on the desk and have one person select a card at random and attempt to communicate the emotion using only facial gestures. Keep a record of accurate and inaccurate guesses. Play until each emotion has been demonstrated at least twice.

Then consider the following:

1. Do you agree with Ekman, Friesen, and Ellsworth that the face can communicate these eight emotion categories?
2. Are some emotions easier to communicate than others? Why do you suppose this is true?
3. Dale Leathers, in *Nonverbal Communication Systems,* suggests that in addition to the eight emotions noted above, the face is also capable of communicating bewilderment and determination. Test out this suggestion in any way that seems useful and valid to you.
4. Are some members of your small group better facial communicators (encoders) than others? Are some better decoders than others? How might you account for these differences in ability?

SPACE COMMUNICATION

Upon completion of this unit, you should be able to:
1. define *proxemics*
2. define *postural-sex identifiers, sociofugal-sociopetal orientation, kinesthetic factors, touch, vision, thermal factors, loudness,* and *smell*
3. identify and explain the four proxemic distances
4. give examples of the kinds of communications that would take place in each of the four proxemic distances
5. define *territoriality*
6. give examples of the operation of territoriality from your own experiences
7. explain how different surroundings might influence perception
8. explain the arbitrariness of color symbolism
9. explain at least five messages communicated by different seating arrangements

Like verbal behavior, spatial behavior communicates; space speaks just as surely and just as loudly as do words. A speaker who stands close to the listener, with his or her hands on the listener's shoulders and his or her eyes focused directly on those of the listener, clearly communicates something very different from the speaker who sits crouched in a corner with arms folded and eyes to the floor. Like verbal and body communication, spatial behavior is learned without any conscious or direct teaching by the adult community. Children are merely exposed to certain spatial relations which they internalize unconsciously, much as children seem to acquire the particular codes of speech or body motion.

In this unit we will explore several dimensions of spatial communication. First, we will discuss the general area of *proxemics*, or spatial communication—specifically, the several proxemic dimensions (or ways in which individuals treat space in interpersonal encounters) and the major proxemic distances (or the physical space between people in their interpersonal interactions). Second, we will look at the concept of *territoriality*—the possessive or ownershiplike reaction to an area of space or to a particular object. Third, we will consider the role of esthetics and color, that is, some of the ways in which space may be "decorated" to communicate different meanings.

PROXEMICS

Edward T. Hall, in the study he calls *proxemics*, provides much new and significant insight into nonverbal communication by demonstrating how messages from these different channels may be analyzed and by relating them to the spatial dimensions of communication. More formally, in "A System for the Notation of Proxemic Behavior," Hall defines *proxemics* as the "study of how man unconsciously structures microspace—the distance between men in the conduct of their daily transactions, the organization of space in his houses and buildings, and ultimately the layout of his towns."

Proxemic Dimensions

The best way to explain proxemics is to briefly present the eight general classes of proxemic behaviors and their more specific categories, as systematized by Hall.

1. *Postural-sex identifiers* refer to the posture and sex of the communication source and receiver. Hall divides this class into six possible categories: man prone, woman prone, man sitting or squatting, woman sitting or squatting, man standing, and woman standing.

2. *Sociofugal-sociopetal orientation*, referring to the physical directness of the communicators, specifies the relationship of one person's shoulders to the other person's shoulders. These positions are categorized on a 9-point scale, ranging from face-to-face communication in which the shoulders of both parties are parallel, through the situation in which the shoulders of the two parties form a straight line, to the situation in which there is back-to-back communication and the shoulders are again parallel. These nine positions are parallel face-to-face, at a 45° angle, 90°, 135°, 180°, 225°, 270°, 315°, and parallel back-to-back. As can be appreciated, this dimension gives us a good indication of how the positioning of the communicators' bodies may facilitate or inhibit social interaction.

3. *Kinesthetic factors* refer to the closeness of the two persons involved in communication and the potential that exists for the holding, grasping, or touching of each other. The four major categories are within body-contact distance, within touching distance with the forearm extended, within touching distance with the arm extended, and within touching distance by reaching.

4. *Touch*, referring to the amount and type of physical contact between the two parties, is quantified along a 7-point scale: caressing and holding, caressing and feeling, extended holding, holding, spot touching, brushing or accidental touching, and no contact.

5. *Vision*, the extent of visual contact between the two persons, is divided into four categories: sharp, focused looking at the other person's eyes; clear, focused looking at the person's face or head; peripheral, looking at the person in general but not focused on the head; and no visual contact.

6. *Thermal factors*, the amount of body heat of one person as perceived by the other, are categorized into four types: detection of conducted heat, detection of radiant heat, probable detection of some kind of heat, and no detection of heat.

7. *Loudness*, or vocal volume, is described on a 7-point scale: silent, very soft, soft, normal, somewhat above normal, loud, and very loud.

8. *Smell* is categorized into five types: detection of differentiated body odor, detection of undifferentiated odor, detection of breath odor, probable detection of some odor, and no detection.

These categories may appear at first to be somewhat rigid or too finely delineated. In analyzing proxemic behavior, however, adjacent categories can be combined to form more general ones, or if additional distinctions are needed, the categories may be further divided. Hall presents this system as a *tentative* strategy for analyzing proxemic behaviors.

Proxemic Distances

One of the earliest references to space as communication occurs in the Gospel of Luke (14:1–11):

> When thou are invited to a wedding feast, do not recline in the first place, lest perhaps one more distinguished than thou have been invited by him. And he who invited thee and him, come and say to thee, "Make room for this man"; and then thou begin with shame to take the last place. But when thou art invited, go and recline in the last place; that when he who invited thee comes in, he may say to thee, "Friend, go up higher!" Then thou wilt be honored in the presence of all who are at table with thee. For everyone who exalts himself shall be humbled, and he who humbles himself shall be exalted.

This brief passage illustrates one of the concepts or meanings that space communicates, namely, status. We know, for example, that in a large organization status is the basis for determining how large an office one receives, whether that office has a window or not, how high up the office is (that is, on what floor of the building), and how close one's office is to that of the president or chairperson.

Space is especially important in interpersonal communication, although we seldom think about it or even consider the possibility that it might serve a communicative function. Hall distinguishes four distances that he feels define the type of relationship permitted. Each of these four distances has a close phase and a far phase, giving us a total of eight clearly identifiable distances. These four distances, according to Hall, correspond quite closely to the four major types of relationships: intimate, personal, social, and public.

Intimate Distance

In *intimate distance,* ranging from the close phase of actual touching to the far phase of 6 to 18 inches, the presence of the other individual is unmistakable. Each individual experiences the sound, smell, and feel of the other's breath. The close phase is used for lovemaking and wrestling, for comforting and protecting. In the close phase the muscles and the skin communicate, while actual verbalizations play a minor role. In this close phase whispering, says Hall, has the effect of increasing the psychological distance between the two individuals. The far phase allows us to touch each other by extending our hands. The distance is so close that it is not considered proper in public, and because of the feeling of inappropriateness and discomfort (at least for Americans), the eyes seldom meet but remain fixed on some remote object.

Personal Distance

Each of us, says Hall, carries around with him or her a protective bubble defining our *personal distance,* which allows us to stay protected and untouched by others. In the close phase of personal distance (from 1.5 to 2.5 feet) we can still hold or grasp each other but only by extending our arms. We can then take into our protective bubble certain individuals—for example, loved ones. In the far phase (from 2.5 to 4 feet) two people can only touch each other if they both extend their arms. This far phase is the extent to which we can physically get our hands on things, and hence it defines, in one sense, the limits of our physical control over others. Even at this distance we can see many of the fine details of an individual—the gray hairs, tooth stains, clothing lint, and so on. However, we can no longer detect body heat. At times we may detect breath odor, but generally at this distance etiquette demands that we direct our breath to some neutral corner so as not to offend.

This distance is particularly interesting from the point of view of body odor and the colognes designed to hide it. At this distance we cannot perceive normal cologne or perfume. Thus it has been proposed that cologne has two functions: First, it serves to disguise the body odor or hide it; and second, it serves to make clear the limits of the protective bubble around the individual. The bubble, defined by the perfume, simply says you may not enter beyond the point where you can smell me.

Social Distance

At the *social distance* we lose the visual detail we had in the personal distance. The close phase (from 4 to 7 feet) is the distance at which we conduct impersonal business, the distance at which we interact at a social gathering. The far phase (from 7 to 12 feet) is the distance we stand when someone says, "Stand away so I can look at you." At this level business transactions have a more formal tone than when conducted in the close phase. In offices of high officials the desks are positioned so that the individual is assured of at least this distance when dealing with clients. Unlike the intimate distance, where eye contact is awkward, the far phase of the social distance makes eye contact essential—otherwise communication is lost. The voice is generally louder than normal at this level, but shouting or raising the voice has the effect of reducing the social distance to a personal distance. It is at this distance that we can work with people and yet not constantly interact with them and not appear rude. At certain distances, of course, one cannot ignore the presence of another individual. At other distances, however, we can ignore the other individual and keep to our own business.

This social distance requires that a certain amount of space be available. In many instances, however, such distances are not available; yet it is necessary to keep social distance, at least psychologically if not physically. For this we attempt different arrangements with the furniture. In small offices in colleges, for example, professors sharing an office might have their desks facing in different directions so that each may stay separated from the other. Or they may

Intimate, personal, social, and public distances echo our relationships with other people.

position their desks against a wall so that each will feel psychologically alone in the office and thus be able to effectively maintain a social rather than a personal distance.

Public Distance

In the close phase of *public distance* (from 12 to 15 feet) an individual seems protected by space. At this distance one is able to take defensive action should one be threatened. On a public bus or train, for example, we might keep at least this distance from a drunkard so that should anything come up (literally or figuratively) we could get away in time. Although at this distance we lose the fine details of the face and eyes, we are still close enough to see what is happening should we need to take defensive action.

At the far phase (more than 25 feet) we see individuals not as separate individuals but as part of the whole setting. We automatically set approximately 30 feet around public figures who are of considerable importance, and we seem to do this whether or not there are guards preventing us from entering this distance. This far phase is, of course, the distance from which actors perform on stage; consequently, their actions and voices will have to be somewhat exaggerated.

TERRITORIALITY

One of the most interesting concepts in ethology (the study of animals in their natural surroundings) is *territoriality*. For example, male animals will stake out a particular territory and consider it their own. They will allow prospective mates to enter but will defend it against entrance by others, especially other males of the same species. Among deer, for example, the size of the territory signifies the power of the buck, which in turn determines how many females he will mate with. Less powerful bucks will be able to hold on to only small parcels of land and consequently will mate with only one or two females. This is a particularly adaptive measure since it ensures that the stronger members of the society will produce most of the offspring. When the "landowner" takes possession of an area—either because it is vacant or because he gains it through battle—he marks it, for example, by urinating around the boundaries.

These same general patterns are felt by many to be integral parts of human behavior. Some researchers claim that this form of behavior is innate and is a symptom of the innate aggressiveness of humans. Others claim that territoriality is learned behavior and is culturally based. Most, however, seem to agree that a great deal of human behavior can be understood and described as territoriality regardless of its possible origin or development.

If we look around at our homes we would probably find certain territories that different people have staked out and where invasions are cause for at least mildly defensive action. This is perhaps seen most clearly with siblings who each have (or "own") a specific chair, room, radio, and so on. Father has his chair and mother has her chair. Archie and Edith Bunker always sit in the same chairs, and great uproars occur when Archie's territory is invaded. Similarly, the rooms of the house may be divided among members of the family. The kitchen, traditionally at least, has been the mother's territory. Invasions from other family members may be tolerated but are often not welcomed, and at times they are resisted. Invasions by members not of the immediate family, from a sister-in-law, mother-in-law, or neighbor, for example, are generally resented much more.

In the classroom, where seats are not assigned, territoriality can also be observed. When a student sits in a seat that has normally been occupied by another student, the regular occupant will often become disturbed and resentful and might even say something about it being his or her seat.

Like animals, humans also mark their territory (though generally not with urine). In a library, for example, you mark your territory with a jacket or some books when you leave the room. You expect this marker to function to keep others away from your seat and table area. Most of the time it works. When it does not work, there is cause for conflict.

The territory of humans (like that of animals) communicates status in various ways. Clearly the size and location of the territory indicates something about status. A townhouse on Manhattan's East Side, for example, is perhaps the highest-status territory for living in the country; it is large and at the same time located on the world's most expensive real estate. Status is also signaled by the unwritten law granting the right of invasion. High-status individuals have a right (or at least more of a right) to invade the territory of others than vice versa. The boss of a large company, for example, can invade the territory of a junior executive by barging into his or her office, but the reverse would be unthinkable. Similarly, a teacher may invade the personal space of a student by looking over his or her shoulder as the student writes. But the student cannot do the same in return.

ESTHETICS AND COLORS

The esthetics and color treatment of space communicate a great deal. On the basis of the ways in which space is "decorated," we make inferences about the individuals who occupy the space. Thus, oriental rugs, eighteenth-century oil paintings, and antique furniture communicate something very different from bare floors, unframed posters, and inflatable furniture. Similarly, a room painted bright red with a black ceiling and floor and all-white furniture communicates something quite different from a room painted beige with earth-color furniture. In addition, the esthetic and color variations influence one's behaviors within these spaces; in general, we function differently in differently decorated spaces.

Esthetics

That the decorations or surroundings of a particular place exert influence on us should be obvious to anyone who has ever entered a hospital with its sterile walls and furniture, or a museum with its imposing columns, glass-encased exhibits, and brass plaques.

Even the way in which a relatively ordinary room is furnished exerts considerable influence on us. In an insightful study on this question, Abraham Maslow and Norbett Mintz attempted to determine if the esthetic conditions or surroundings of a room would influence the judgments people made in these rooms. Three rooms were used; one was beautiful, one average, and one ugly.

The beautiful room had large windows, beige walls, indirect lighting, and furnishings that made the room seem attractive and comfortable. Paintings were on the walls, a large Navajo rug covered the floor, and drapes were on the windows. The average room was a professor's office with two mahogany desks and chairs, a metal bookcase, metal filing cabinets, and shades on the windows. The ugly room was painted battleship gray; lighting was provided by an overhead bulb with a dirty, torn shade. The room was furnished to give the impression of a janitor's storeroom in horrible condition. The ash trays were filled and the window shades torn.

In the three different rooms, students rated 10 art prints in terms of the fatigue-energy and displeasure-well-being depicted in them. As predicted, the students rated the prints in the beautiful room to be more energetic and to evidence more well-being. Those judged in the ugly room were rated as evidencing fatigue and displeasure, while those judged in the average room were perceived as somewhere between those two extremes.

In a follow-up study Mintz selected two of the subjects from the previous experiment and used them as "examiners." For a period of three weeks these two subjects tested other subjects for one hour per day, each alternating every day between the beautiful and the ugly room. After each hour the "examiners" were asked to rate the prints again, supposedly for measures of reliability.

It was found that the ratings of the prints were similar to that found in the first experiment. The subjects still rated the prints as more energetic and evidencing more well-being when in the beautiful room than when in the ugly room. Further, these results were consistent over the three weeks. The subjects did not adjust to the surroundings over time. The experimenter also tested the time spent by the "examiners" in testing their subjects. It was found that the testing in the ugly room was completed faster than that in the beautiful room 27 out of 32 times.

General observational conclusions show that the subjects did not want to test in the ugly room, became irritable and aggressive when they had to test in that room, and felt that time seemed to move more slowly when in the ugly room.

The implications of this type of finding seem extremely important. We are forced to wonder if the ghetto child studying in the tenement is able to derive the same benefits as the middle-class student studying in his or her own room. Can workers in an unappealing factory ever enjoy their job as much as workers in a pleasant office? What about prisons? Is aggressive behavior in prisons in part a function of the horrible surroundings prisoners are forced to live in? Is the higher crime rate in depressed areas, in part at least, a function of the "ugliness" of the surroundings? Questions such as these are not easy to answer, but they should be asked by any student of nonverbal communication.

Colors

When we are in debt we speak of being "in the red"; when we make a profit we are "in the black." When we are sad we are "blue," when we are healthy we are "in the pink," when we are jealous we are "green with envy," and when we are happy we are "tickled pink." To be a coward is to be "yellow" and to be inexperienced is to be "green." When we talk a great deal we talk "a blue streak," and when we talk to no avail we talk until we are "blue in the face." When we go out on the town we "paint it red," and when we are angry we "see red." Our language, especially as revealed through these time-worn clichés, abounds in color symbolism.

Henry Dreyfuss, in his *Symbol Sourcebook*, reminds us of some of the positive and negative meanings associated with various colors. Some of these are presented in Table 15.1. Dreyfuss also notes some cultural comparisons for

Color	Positive Messages	Negative Messages
red	warmth passion life liberty patriotism	death war revolution devil danger
blue	religious feeling devotion truth justice	doubt discouragement
yellow	intuition wisdom divinity	cowardice malevolence impure love
green	nature hope freshness prosperity	envy jealousy opposition disgrace
purple	power royalty love of truth nostalgia	mourning regret penitence resignation

Source: Adapted from Henry Dreyfuss, *Symbol Sourcebook* (New York: McGraw-Hill, 1971).

TABLE 15.1
Some Positive and Negative Messages of Colors

some of these colors. For example, red in China is a color for joyous and festive occasions, whereas in Japan it is used to signify anger and danger. Blue for the Cherokee Indian signifies defeat, but for the Egyptian it signifies virtue and truth. In the Japanese theater blue is the color for villains. Yellow signifies happiness and prosperity in Egypt, but in tenth-century France yellow colored the doors of criminals. Green communicates femininity to certain American Indians, fertility and strength to Egyptians, and youth and energy to Japanese. Purple signifies virtue and faith in Egypt, but grace and nobility in Japan.

In English it has been demonstrated that our connotative meanings for colors vary considerably. In Table 15.2 five color terms are presented with their average ratings on evaluation (for example, the good-bad, positive-negative dimension of language), potency (for example, the strong-weak, large-small dimension of language), and activity (for example, the active-passive, fast-slow dimension of language). The numbers are based on a 7-point scale ranging from +3 for the good, strong, and active sides of the scales through 0, which is the neutral position, to −3 for the bad, weak, and passive sides of the scale. As can be seen, red and blue are the most positive in terms of evaluation, and gray is the most negative. Red is the most potent and gray is the least potent. Red was judged as the most active and gray as the least active.

There is also some scientific evidence that colors affect us physiologically. For example, it has been found that respiratory movements increase with red light and decrease with blue light. Similarly, the frequency of eye blinks increases when eyes are exposed to red light and decreases when exposed to blue light. This seems consistent with our intuitive feelings about blue being more soothing and red being more active and also with the ratings noted in Table 15.2. And remember the difficult time that Bette Davis gave everyone in *Jezebel* because she insisted on wearing a red dress to a particularly staid ball. Had she insisted on a white or a blue dress, there would have been less of a problem, and probably even less of a story. In *Gone With the Wind*, Rhett Butler, upon hearing of Scarlett O'Hara's indiscretion with Ashley Wilkes, and knowing that everyone at the upcoming ball would be talking about Scarlett's

	Evaluation	Potency	Activity
yellow	.544	.212	−.637
red	1.256	1.012	−.050
green	.969	.706	−.619
gray	−.200	−.394	−1.362
blue	1.255	.812	−.375

Source: Adapted from James Snider and Charles E. Osgood, eds. "Semantic Atlas for 550 Concepts," in *Semantic Differential Technique: A Sourcebook* (Chicago: Aldine, 1969), pp. 625–636.

TABLE 15.2
Evaluation,
Potency, and
Activity Ratings
for Five Color
Terms

behavior, makes her wear a red dress—a color symbolic of her supposedly shameless and immoral behavior. Even the name "Scarlett" foretells something of her temperament and her future behavior. And in Nathaniel Hawthorne's *The Scarlet Letter,* Hester Prynne is forced to wear the letter *A* for "adultress," and it is no accident that the *A* is red.

Perhaps the most talked about (but least documented) communicative function of color is its supposed reflection of personality. Faber Birren argues that if you like red, your life is directed outward and you are impulsive, active, aggressive, vigorous, sympathetic, quick to judge people, impatient, optimistic, and strongly driven by sex. If, on the other hand, you dislike red, you also dislike the qualities in those people who like red, such as aggressiveness, optimism, and the like. You feel that others have gotten the better deal in life and you never feel really secure. Sexually, you are unsatisfied.

If you like blue you are probably conservative, introspective, and deliberate. You are sensitive to yourself and to others and have your passions under control. In your own communications you are cautious, your opinions and beliefs seldom change, and you question just about everything you do not understand. If you dislike blue you resent the success of others, and in fact enjoy their failures. You feel that your emotional and your intellectual lives are not fulfilled. You get irritated and are somewhat erratic in your own behavior.

This analysis was drawn from the many comments of Faber Birren in *Color in Your World.* Analyses of your personality based on your likes and dislikes of 11 colors as well as on conflicts (liking one color and disliking another color) are readily supplied by Birren and by various other writers, though there seems to be no hard evidence for these claims. The idea of analyzing someone's personality on the basis of color preferences seems intriguing, and yet the validity of such analyses is uninvestigated.

The messages that colors communicate about a culture are easily determined, while the personality traits that colors supposedly reveal are quite difficult and perhaps impossible to determine. As is true of so many aspects of nonverbal communication, we should be particularly cautious in drawing conclusions about people on the basis of their preferences for different colors.

SOURCES

For spatial communication the work of Edward T. Hall is perhaps the most well known and the most insightful. The discussion of proxemic dimensions comes from his "A System for the Notation of Proxemic Behavior," *American Anthropologist* 65 (1963):1003–1026. The discussion of proxemic distances comes from his *The Hidden Dimension* (New York: Doubleday, 1966). Hall's first popular work on spatial communication and still one of the most famous is *The Silent Language* (New York: Doubleday, 1959). Robert Sommer also deals with spatial communication, but from a somewhat different point of view. Particularly interesting are his *Personal Space: The Behavioral Basis of Design* (Englewood Cliffs, N.J.: Prentice-Hall, 1969), and *Design Awareness* (San Francisco: Rinehart Press, 1972). Experiential Vehicles 15.1 and 15.2 on seating positions are based on the work of Sommer summarized in *Personal Space.* On territoriality, see Robert Ardrey, *The Territorial*

Imperative (New York: Atheneum, 1966), a fascinating book on human territorial behavior. Also relevant here is the work of Edward Hall cited above.

The effects of surroundings are perhaps best explained in the work of Sommer cited above. The experiment on esthetic surroundings is described in A. H. Maslow and N. L. Mintz, "Effects of Esthetic Surroundings: I. Initial Effects of Three Esthetic Conditions upon Perceiving 'Energy' and 'Well-Being' in Faces," *Journal of Psychology* 41 (1956):247–254. Also relevant here is N. L. Mintz, "Effects of Esthetic Surroundings: II. Prolonged and Repeated Experience in a 'Beautiful' and 'Ugly' Room," *Journal of Psychology* 41 (1956):459–466. *The Lüscher Color Test*, I. A. Scott, ed. and trans. (New York: Pocket Books, 1971), and Faber Birren, *Color in Your World* (New York: Collier Books, 1962), are interesting attempts to relate color and personality and are useful for raising rather than answering questions.

15.1 SPATIAL RELATIONSHIPS AND COMMUNICATION FUNCTIONS

Presented below are diagrams of tables and chairs. Imagine that the situation is the school cafeteria and that this is the only table not occupied. For each of the eight diagrams place an X where you and a friend of the same sex would seat yourselves for each of the four conditions noted. Do this for both the round and the rectangular tables.

1. Conversing, for example, to talk for a few minutes before class

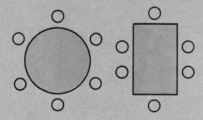

2. Cooperating, for example, to study together for the same exam or to work out a math problem

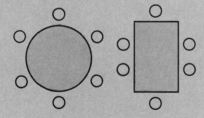

3. Co-acting, for example, to study for different exams

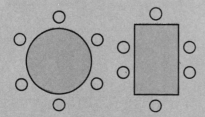

4. Competing, for example, to compete against each other in order to see who would be the first to solve a series of puzzles

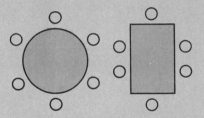

For Discussion

1. Why did you select the positions you did?
2. Explain the differences in the opportunity for nonverbal interaction that the different positions chosen allow.
3. How do these different positions relate to verbal communication?
4. Would you have chosen the same positions if you were romantically interested in the other person? Explain.
5. Compare your responses with the responses of others. How do you account for the differences in seating preferences?
6. Are there significant differences in choices between the round and the rectangular tables? Explain.

15.2 INTERPERSONAL INTERACTIONS AND SPACE

Presented below are diagrams of tables and chairs. Imagine that the situation is the school cafeteria and that this is the only table not occupied. In the space marked X is seated the person described above the diagram. Indicate by placing an X in the appropriate circle where you would sit.

1. A young man or woman to whom you are physically attracted and whom you would like to date but to whom you have never spoken

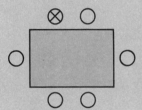

2. A person whom you find physically unattractive and to whom you have never spoken

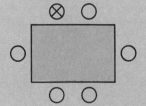

3. A person you dated once and had a miserable time with and whom you would never date again

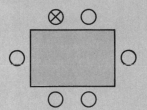

4. A person you have dated a few times and would like to date again

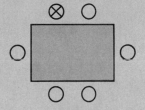

5. An instructor who gave you an *F* in a course last semester, which you did not deserve, and whom you dislike intensely

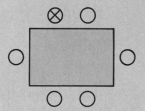

6. Your favorite instructor, whom you would like to get to know better

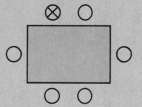

For Discussion

1. Why did you select the positions you did? For example, how does the position you selected enable you to better achieve your purpose?
2. Assume that you were already seated in the position marked X. Do you think that the person described would sit where you indicated you would (assuming the feelings and motives are generally the same)? Why? Are there significant sex differences? Significant status differences? Explain.
3. What does the position you selected communicate to the person already seated? In what ways might this nonverbal message be misinterpreted? How would your subsequent nonverbal (and perhaps verbal) behavior reinforce your intended message? That is, what would you do to ensure that the message you intended to communicate is in fact the message communicated and received?

15.3 *ESTHETIC AND COLOR COMMUNICATION*

The purpose of this exercise is to explore the influence that our physical environment has on interpersonal communication. Groups of five or six should be formed at random. The task of each group is to redesign your classroom so that it is more conducive to the aims of this course. Allow 15 to 20 minutes for the groups to come up with a new design. ("Redesign" should be taken to mean anything that is possible to do within the rules or restrictions imposed by the school and would include changing, adding, or removing any materials that may and can be changed, added, or removed by the group.)

After each group has planned the "new" classroom, the designs should be shared with the other members of the class. From all the suggestions, a composite redesigned classroom should be constructed and put into actual operation for at least a week of classes.

Before this design is put into effect, discussion should cover at least the following areas:

1. In what ways will this new design facilitate interpersonal communication? How? Be as specific as possible.
2. How would the classroom be designed if a party were to be held in it? Why? A formal lecture? Why?
3. If you could paint the classroom any color you wanted to, what color(s) would you select? Why?

SILENCE, PARALANGUAGE, AND TEMPORAL COMMUNICATION

Upon completion of this unit, you should be able to:

1. identify at least three functions of silence
2. define *paralanguage*
3. identify three or four major classes of paralinguistic phenomena
4. explain at least three messages that variations in paralinguistic phenomena might communicate
5. explain the communicative function of time
6. explain the relationship of time to culture, status, and appropriateness

We have seen how we can communicate by manipulating words and gestures. But we can also communicate with silence; by manipulating such paralinguistic factors as volume, rate, and pitch; and by our treatment of time. These three areas of nonverbal communication are the focus of this unit.

SILENCE

Don Fabun noted that "the world of silence may be a cold and bitter one; like the deep wastes of the Arctic regions, it is fit for neither man nor beast. Holding one's tongue may be prudent, but it is an act of rejection; silence builds walls—and walls are the symbols of failure." Thomas Mann, in one of the most-often quoted observations on silence, said, "Speech is civilization itself. The word, even the most contradictory word, preserves contact; it is silence which isolates." On the other hand, the philosopher Karl Jaspers observed that "the ultimate in thinking as in communication is silence," and Max Picard noted that "silence is nothing merely negative; it is not the mere absence of speech. It is a positive, a complete world in itself."

All of these are rather extreme statements on the nature and function of silence. Actually, I think all are correct—for some occasions, for some people, and for some times. The one thing on which all observations are clearly in agreement, and that needs to be stressed here, is that silence communicates. As we have seen, one of the universals of nonverbal behaviors is that they always

229

communicate, and this is no less true of silence. Our silence communicates just as surely and just as intensely as anything we might verbalize.

Functions of Silence

Perhaps the best way to approach silence is to consider some of the functions it might serve or the meanings it may communicate. One of the most frequent functions of silence is to allow the speaker time to think. In some cases, the silence allows the speaker the opportunity to integrate previous communications in order to make the necessary connections before the verbal communications may logically continue. In other instances it gives the speaker or the listener time for previous messages to sink in. This is seen most clearly after someone makes what he or she thinks is a profound statement, almost as if to proclaim that this message should not be contaminated by other, less significant and less insightful messages. At still other times the silence allows the individual to think of his or her future messages. Lecturers will often remain silent for short periods—though they might seem inordinately long to the lecturer as well as to the listeners—in order to think of what is to come next or perhaps to recall some fact or reference. In many instances people remain silent in order to prepare themselves for the intense communications that are to follow. It is rather like the calm before the storm. Before messages of intense conflict, as well as before messages confessing undying love, there is often silence. Again, the silence seems to prepare the receiver for the importance of the future messages.

Some people use silence to hurt others. Silence is used as a weapon, and we often speak here of giving someone "the silent treatment." After a conflict, for example, one or both individuals might remain silent as a kind of punishment. Children will often imitate their parents in this and will refuse to talk to playmates when they are angry with them. Silence to hurt others may also take the form of refusing to acknowledge the presence of another person; here silence is a dramatic demonstration of the total indifference one person feels toward the other. It is a refusal to recognize the person as a person, a refusal to treat him or her any differently than one would treat an inanimate object. Such silence is most often accompanied by blank stares into space, a preoccupation with a magazine or some manual task, or perhaps by feigning resting or sleeping. Here the nonverbal movements reinforce silence as a refusal to acknowledge the individual as a person.

Sometimes silence is used as a response to personal anxiety or shyness or threats. One might feel anxious or shy among new people and prefer to remain silent. By remaining silent the individual precludes the chance of rejection. It is only when the silence is broken and an attempt to communicate with another person is made that one risks rejection. At other times the silence may be a kind of flight response made to threats by another individual or group of individuals. A street gang that makes remarks as one passes is one example. By remaining silent, by refusing to engage in verbal contact, we attempt to remove ourselves psychologically from the situation.

Silence may be used to prevent the verbal communication of certain messages. For example, in conflict situations silence is sometimes used to prevent certain topics from surfacing and to prevent one or both parties from sticking their proverbial feet into their proverbial big mouths. We made the point earlier that verbal expressions can never be reversed; once said, something cannot be unsaid. In conflict situations silence often allows us time to cool off before uttering expressions of hatred, severe criticism, or personal attacks, and here it serves us to good advantage.

Silence may be used to prevent one from saying the wrong thing or from making a fool of oneself. "Keep quiet and people will think you a philosopher," a Latin proverb advises. The alternative, though, is perhaps what most people have in mind when they remain silent: "Talk and people will think you a fool."

Like the eyes or face or hands, silence can also be used to communicate varied emotional responses. Sometimes silence communicates one's determination to be uncooperative or one's defiance; by refusing to engage in verbal communication we defy the authority or the legitimacy of the other person's

Silence is often used to hurt other people, especially those very close to us.

position. In more pleasant situations, silence might be used to express affection or love, especially when coupled with long and longing stares into each other's eyes. In many religious ceremonies, for example, reverence is signaled by silence. Often the congregation remains silent throughout a religious ritual or verbalizes only responses. Silence is often used to communicate annoyance, usually coupled with a pouting expression, arms crossed in front of the and nostrils flared. In some of these situations silence is used because talk is perceived as superfluous or perhaps as less effective.

Of course, silence is often used when there is simply nothing to say, when nothing occurs to one to say, or when one does not want to say anything. James Russell Lowell expressed this best, I think: "Blessed are they who have nothing to say, and who cannot be persuaded to say it." Few would probably want to argue with Lowell. Yet, it is not very easy to determine exactly when there is nothing to say. For a radio commentator or announcer to have nothing to say and to remain silent would be unthinkable. Radio, and to only a somewhat lesser extent television, cannot afford to remain silent for anything but the shortest pause: air time is just too expensive. Also, silence on radio or television is so unexpected and seems so out of place that listeners would become annoyed and would probably change the station.

Silence also proves troublesome at parties, where it is taken as a sure sign of failure and even the most banal chatter would be a welcomed alternative. When meeting someone for the first time, when visiting someone at a hospital, or when attending a funeral, silence becomes particularly awkward and speaking particularly difficult. We know we should say something but just then can think of nothing. Even "weather talk" would be welcomed.

Cultural Relativity

The communicative functions of silence in the previous situations are not universal. The Apache, for example, regard silence very differently. Among the Apache mutual friends will not feel the need to introduce strangers who may be working in the same area or on the same project. The strangers may remain silent for several days. During this time they are looking each other over, attempting to determine if the other person is all right. Only after this period would the individuals talk. During the courting period, especially during the initial stages, Apache individuals remain silent for hours; if they do talk, they generally talk very little. It is only after a couple has been dating for several months that they will have lengthy conversations. These periods of silence by the men are generally attributed to shyness or self-consciousness. The use of silence is explicitly taught to the women, and they are especially discouraged from engaging in long discussions with their dates. Silence during courtship is to many Apache a sign of modesty. When a young woman speaks a great deal, she is thought to be betraying prior experience with men, and in some cases, it is seen as a sign of the woman's willingness to engage in sexual relations.

PARALANGUAGE

An old exercise used to increase a student's ability to express different emotions, feelings, and attitudes was to have the student say the following sentences while accenting or stressing different words: "Is this the face that launched a thousand ships?" Significant differences in meaning are easily communicated depending on where the stress is placed. Consider, for example, the following variations:

1.   IS this the face that launched a thousand ships?
2.   Is THIS the face that launched a thousand ships?
3.   Is this the FACE that launched a thousand ships?
4.   Is this the face that LAUNCHED a thousand ships?
5.   Is this the face that launched a THOUSAND SHIPS?

Each of these five sentences communicates something different. Each, in fact, asks a totally different question, even though the words used are identical. All that distinguishes the sentences is stress, one of the aspects of what is called paralanguage. *Paralanguage* may be defined as the vocal (but nonverbal) dimension of speech. Paralanguage refers to the manner in which something is said rather than to what is said.

Paralanguage Structure

An outline of a classification offered by George L. Trager is presented in Table 16.1. More important than the specifics of this table, though, is that paralanguage encompasses a great deal of vocal expression and can be classified and analyzed rather precisely for various different purposes.

The four major classes of paralinguistic phenomena are *voice qualities*, *vocal characterizers*, *vocal qualifiers*, and *vocal segregates*. The sounds used in vocal segregates are not the same as those same sounds when used in words— that is, the *sh* that means "silence!" is not the same as the same sound in *shed*. The "pause" noted as a vocal segregate is classified in a somewhat different area by many contemporary researchers. This area, generally referred to as "hesitation phenomena," is concerned with all forms of hesitations, the pause being only one of these. Some of the classifications are actually continuous scales; vocal lip control may be analyzed as ranging from "rasp" through "openness" rather than simply as either "rasp" or "open."

If we assume the validity of the proposition that nothing never happens, that all behavior serves a communicative function, then we must further assume that each of these paralinguistic features also communicates meaning. Thus the speaker who speaks quickly communicates something different from the one who speaks slowly. Even though the words might be the same, if the speed differs, the meaning we receive will also differ. And we may derive different meanings from "fast talk" depending on the speaker. Perhaps in one person we might perceive fear, feeling that he or she is hurrying to get the statement over with. In another we might perceive annoyance or lack of concern, inferring that he or she speaks rapidly so that not too much time is wasted. In still another we might perceive extreme interest, feeling that the person is speaking quickly so that he or she can get to the punch line and hear our reaction.

Paralanguage and Interpersonal Interaction

On the basis of paralinguistic cues, we form opinions about people: about their emotional states as well as about their status, their sex, and about various

TABLE 16.1
*Paralanguage: A
Classification*

I. Voice Qualities
  A. Pitch Range
    1. Spread
      a. Upward
      b. Downward
    2. Narrowed
      a. From above
      b. From below
  B. Vocal Lip Control
    1. Rasp
    2. Openness
  C. Glottis Control
    1. Sharp transitions
    2. Smooth transitions
  D. Pitch Control
  E. Articulation Control
    1. Forceful (precise)
    2. Relaxed (slurred)
  F. Rhythm Control
    1. Smooth
    2. Jerky
  G. Resonance
    1. Resonant
    2. Thin
  H. Tempo
    1. Increased from norm
    2. Decreased from norm
II. Vocalizations
  A. Vocal Characterizers
    1. Laughing/crying
    2. Yelling/whispering
    3. Moaning/groaning
    4. Whining/breaking
    5. Belching/yawning

B. Vocal Qualifiers
  1. Intensity
    a. Overloud
      (1) somewhat
      (2) considerably
      (3) very much
    b. Oversoft
      (1) somewhat
      (2) considerably
      (3) very much
  2. Pitch Height
    a. Overhigh
      (1) slightly
      (2) appreciably
      (3) greatly
    b. Overlow
      (1) slightly
      (2) appreciably
      (3) greatly
  3. Extent
    a. Drawl
      (1) slight
      (2) noticeable
      (3) extreme
    b. Clipping
      (1) slight
      (2) noticeable
      (3) extreme
C. Vocal Segregates
  1. Uh-uh
  2. Uh-huh
  3. Sh
  4. (Pause)

Source: Adapted from George L. Trager, "Paralanguage: A First Approximation," *Studies in Linguistics* 13 (1958):1–12; George L. Trager, "The Typology of Paralanguage," *Anthropological Linguistics* 3 (1961):17–21; and Robert E. Pittenger and Henry Smith, Jr., "A Basis for Some Contributions of Linguistics to Psychiatry," *Psychiatry* 20 (1957):61–78.

other characteristics; about potential conversational exchanges—when to talk and when to keep silent; and about whether to believe or not to believe the speaker. Each of these three issues will be examined.

Paralanguage and People Perception

We are a diagnostically oriented people, quick to make judgments about another's personality based on various paralinguistic cues. At times our judgments turn out to be correct, at other times incorrect. But the number of times our judgments are proved correct and incorrect does not seem to influence the frequency with which we make such judgments. We may, for example, conclude that speakers who speak so softly that we can hardly hear them have some kind of problem. Perhaps they feel inferior—they "know" that no one really wants to listen, "know" that nothing they say is significant, and so speak softly. Other speakers will speak at an extremely loud volume, perhaps because of an overinflated ego and the belief that everyone in the world wants to hear them as though what they have to say is so valuable that they cannot risk our not hearing every word. Speakers who speak with no variation, in a complete monotone, seem uninterested in what they are saying and seem to encourage a similar lack of interest from their listeners—if any are still around. We might perceive such people as having a lack of interest in life in general, as being rather bland individuals. All of these conclusions are, at best, based on little evidence. Yet this does not stop us from making such conclusions.

It is important for us to inquire into the relationship between paralanguage and impression formation. It does seem that certain voices are symptomatic of certain personality types, of certain problems, and specifically that the personality orientation leads to the vocal qualities. When listening to people speak—regardless of what they are saying—we form impressions based on their paralanguage as to what kind of people they are. Our impressions seem to consist of physical impressions (perhaps about body type and certainly about sex and age), personality impressions (they seem outgoing, they sound shy, they appear aggressive), and evaluative impressions (they sound like good people, they sound evil and menacing, they sound lovable, they have vicious laughs).

Much research has been directed to the question of the accuracy of these judgments—that is, how accurately we may judge a person on the basis of voice alone. One of the earliest studies on this question was conducted by T. H. Pear. Pear used nine speakers and had over 4000 listeners make guesses about these nine speakers. The sex and age of the speaker appeared to be guessed with considerable accuracy. However, the listeners were only able to guess the occupations of the clergyman and the actor.

Other studies pursued the investigation of the relationship between vocal characteristics and personal characteristics. Most studies suggest, in agreement with Pear, that sex and age can be guessed accurately on the basis of the voice alone. This is not to say that complete accuracy is possible, but age does seem capable of being guessed within relatively small ranges.

One of the most interesting findings on voice and personal characteristics is that listeners can accurately judge the status (high, middle, or low) of speakers from hearing a 60-second voice sample. In fact, many listeners reported that they made their judgments in less than 15 seconds. It has also been found that the speakers judged to be of high status were rated as being of higher credibility than those rated of middle and low status.

One important finding reported in a number of different studies is that on the basis of paralinguistic information, listeners agree about the personality of the speaker. The listeners' judgments, however, are very often in error. Listeners seem to have stereotyped ideas about how vocal characteristics and personality characteristics are related and utilize these stereotypes in their various judgments. Sometimes the stereotypes are of the groups to which the listeners themselves belong. For example, in a study of Scottish and English speakers, Scottish listeners judged the Scottish voices as belonging to persons of greater generosity, friendliness, good-heartedness, and likability. English listeners, on the other hand, judged the English voices as belonging to persons who were more intelligent, ambitious, self-confident, and apt to serve as leaders.

There is much greater agreement in the literature when we consider the question of identifying the emotional states of speakers from their vocal expression. Generally, in these studies the content of the speech is nonexistent or is held constant. Thus in a content-free situation the speaker would attempt to communicate anxiety, for example, by saying the alphabet or perhaps by reciting numbers. In the situation where the content is held constant, the speakers say the same sentences (generally rather unemotional ones) for all the emotions they are to communicate. It has been found that speakers can communicate or encode emotions through content-free speech or through content that is unrelated to the emotions, and listeners are able to decode these emotions. A typical study would involve speakers using numbers to communicate different emotions. Listeners would have to select the emotion being communicated from a list of 10 possible emotions. In situations like this listeners are generally effective in guessing the emotions.

Listeners vary in their ability to decode the emotions, speakers vary in their ability to encode the emotions, and the accuracy with which emotions are guessed depends on the emotions themselves. For example, while it may be easy to distinguish between hate and sympathy, it may not be so easy to distinguish between fear and anxiety. (This type of study is used as the basis for Experiential Vehicle 16.1)

To test your ability to decode emotions on the basis of verbal descriptions, try to "hear" the following voices and try to identify the emotions being communicated: affection, anger, boredom, or joy?

1. *This voice is soft, with a low pitch, resonant quality, a slow rate, a steady and slightly upward inflection. The rhythm is regular and the enunciation is slurred.*

2. *This voice is loud, with a high pitch, moderately blaring quality, a fast rate, an upward inflection and a regular rhythm.*

3. *This voice is loud, with a high pitch, a blaring quality, a fast rate, and an irregular up-and-down inflection. The rhythm is irregular and the enunciation clipped.*

4. *This voice is moderate to low in volume, with a moderate-to-low pitch, a moderately resonant quality, a moderately slow rate, and a monotone or gradually falling inflection. The enunciation is somewhat slurred.*

According to research by Joel Davitz, the first voice would communicate affection, the second joy, the third anger, and the fourth boredom.

Paralanguage and Conversational Exchange

Paralinguistic cues are widely used to signal conversational turns, the changing (or maintaining) of the speaker or listener role during the conversation. Perhaps the most obvious way in which paralinguistic cues are used in conversational turns is when the speaker uses them to maintain his or her speaking position. Thus, the speaker may in the course of conversation pause while vocalizing *-em*, *-er*, and the like. These vocalized pauses are insurance that no one else will jump in and take over the role of speaker; they announce to others in the conversation that this speaker is not finished but has more to say. In a somewhat more oblique way paralinguistic cues are used to maintain one's role as listener. This would take the form of vocalizing some reinforcing or approving type of sound while someone else is talking. This kind of positive feedback in effect tells the speaker to keep on going, to say more, and, perhaps most important, that this listener approves of what is being said.

One of the most important conversational functions paralinguistic cues serve is to announce to the others in the conversation that the speaker has finished and that it is now someone else's turn to speak. So, for example, the speaker may, at the end of a statement, add some paralinguistic cue such as *eh?*, which asks the others in the conversation to speak now. But notice that such paralinguistic cues do not give the new speaker carte blanche but relinquish the speaker's position to another one with specific stipulations. Thus, the speaker who says, "Schmedly gave me the *F* unfairly, eh?" is actually making three statements with this simple *eh?* First, the speaker is asking the other person to speak. Second, the speaker is asking that the other person speak specifically to the topic of the *F* grade. And third, the speaker is asking the new speaker to agree that the *F* was unfair. Of course, not all paralinguistic invitations to speak ask that the listener speak so specifically. Often, speakers will indicate that they have finished speaking by dropping their intonation or by a prolonged silence or by asking some general type of question. In these cases, the new speaker has considerably more freedom.

Still another function of paralinguistic cues is to indicate to the speaker that a listener would like to say something, that the listener would like to take his or her turn as speaker. Sometimes listeners do this by simply saying, "I would like to say something," but often it is done paralinguistically by uttering some vocalized -er or -um that tells the speaker (at least the sensitive speaker) that someone else would like to speak. (These vocalizations are in many instances indistinguishable from those the speaker uses to maintain the speaking position.) This request to speak is also often done with facial and mouth gestures. Frequently, a listener will indicate a desire to speak by opening his or her eyes and mouth wide as if to say something or just begin to gesture with a hand.

Paralanguage communications are not only taken for granted, but most people are unaware of the extent to which they quietly regulate our conversations and help to direct the conversational flow.

Paralanguage and Persuasion

The rate of speed at which people speak is the aspect of paralanguage that has received the most attention. It is of interest to the advertiser, the politician, and, in fact, to anyone who attempts to convey information or to influence others. This is especially so when time is limited or expensive. The research conducted on rate shows that in one-way communication situations (where one person is doing all or most of the speaking and the other person is doing all or most of the listening), persons who talk fast are more persuasive and are evaluated more highly than are persons who talk at or below normal speeds. This greater persuasiveness and higher regard holds true regardless of whether the individual talks fast or has his or her speech speeded up electronically (as in time-compressed speech).

In one experiment, for example, subjects were asked to listen to taped messages and then to indicate the degree to which they agreed with the message and their opinions as to how intelligent and objective they thought the speaker was. Rates of 111, 140, and 191 words a minute were used. (The average speaking rate is about 130 to 150 words per minute.) Subjects agreed most with the fastest speech and least with the slowest speech. Further, they rated the fastest speaker as being the most intelligent and the most objective and rated the slowest speaker as the least intelligent and the least objective. Even in experiments in which the speaker was demonstrated to have something to gain personally from persuasion (as would, say, a used car dealer), the speaker who spoke at the fastest rate was the more persuasive.

When we look at comprehension, rapid speech also has the advantage. Subjects who listened to speeches at different speeds had their comprehension measured by means of multiple choice tests. For example, using 141 words per minute as the average and considering comprehension at this rate as 100 percent, it was found that when the rate was increased to 201 words per minute the comprehension was 95 percent and when the rate was further increased to 282 words per minute (that is, double the normal rate) comprehension was still

90 percent. Even though the rates increased dramatically, the comprehension rates fell only slightly. These 5 percent and 10 percent losses are more than offset by the increased speed and thus make the faster rates much more efficient in communicating information. If the speech speeds are increased more than 200 percent, however, comprehension falls dramatically.

A somewhat faster than normal speed is also preferred by most listeners. For example, when subjects were able to adjust the speed at which they heard a message they adjusted it to approximately 25 percent faster than normal speed. Similarly, persons find commercials presented at approximately 25 percent faster than normal more interesting than commercials presented at normal speeds, and the level of attention (indexed by the amount of electrical activity measured by electrodes attached to the subject's frontalis muscle of the forehead) is greater for fast speeds than for normal or slow speeds.

We need to be cautious, however, in applying this research to the interpersonal communication situation. As John MacLachlan points out, during the time the speaker is speaking, the listener is generating and framing a reply. If the speaker talks too rapidly, there may not be enough time to compose this reply and resentment may therefore be generated. Furthermore, the increased rate may seem to be so unnatural that the listener may come to focus on the speed of speech rather than the thought expressed. But, in one-way communication situations, especially mass communication ones, it is clear that increased rates will become more and more popular. Already, increased speech rates are used extensively in direct-selling commercials which seem to be increasing almost daily. Their popularity will, it seems, influence other forms of mass media advertising and electronic communication in general.

TEMPORAL COMMUNICATION

In a manner much analogous to space, time too communicates. Consider, for example, some students who constantly arrive late for biology class. Their previous class is next door, and so difficulty in getting to the class is not the problem. Yet they consistently come late. (Consider what you would think if the biology teacher were always late for class.) For some reason they find themselves engaged in something else that invariably consumes more time than anticipated. These same students, however, are always early for their interpersonal communication class. Regardless of the reasons for being late and early, they communicate something to the instructors of both courses. To the biology teacher it might be that the students hate the class, that they are somehow disorganized, or that they have weak kidneys. To the communication teacher it might mean that they are anxious to get better acquainted with the other students, that they are interested in the course, or perhaps that they have nothing else to do. Regardless of what impression the teachers get, they do get impressions.

Time and Culture

The sense of time varies with different cultures and even with different subcultures. Edward Hall has pointed to the phenomenon of CPT—colored people's time. CPT is different from WPT—white people's time. CPT is approximate where WPT is exact. Waiting is nothing to get excited about in CPT but is an affront in WPT. This concept was used some years ago with considerable effect in the television series "Maude," in which Florida, Maude's black maid, tells her husband that he had better pick her up at nine o'clock, not CPT but WPT—that is, exactly nine. Some black students may be late for class or for appointments without feeling that any great tragedy has occurred. White teachers often have difficulty adjusting to this; they feel such "lateness" somehow shows disrespect or lack of interest. Actually, there is no desire to communicate disrespect; it is simply due to the fact that different people run on different clocks—some clocks are exact, others are approximate.

In different parts of the United States and in different parts of the world, there are wide variations in the treatment of time. In New York City, for example, time is treated reverently; being late is serious and is looked upon with considerable disdain. In San Francisco, on the other hand, people do not seem to worry so much about being "on time"; being late is seldom interpreted as a social catastrophe. Northern Europe seems to operate by a clock that is relatively exact, whereas southern Europe seems to operate by a clock that is more approximate. And, as in the United States, there are, of course, variations within each of these countries.

In our society, generally, it is permissible to be 5 or 10 minutes early or late for most appointments. For the most part our culture demands considerable clock watching. In other societies time is not looked at in the same way, and there is nothing wrong with being one or even two hours "late." Appointments are not made so that a specific block of time is set aside for you (as in our culture) but rather that you are expected to arrive sometime in the evening, for example, and the business or socialization will take place when you get there. This may cause considerable problems for Americans working in foreign countries as well as for foreigners working in America. Consider, for example, someone being one or two hours late for dinner and then entering without even attempting to make an apology. Surely we would assume that we have a right to be angry. Yet to the foreigner nothing inappropriate—and certainly nothing to offend the host—has occurred.

Within our culture, for example, consider what arriving or leaving early or late at a party might mean. On one level the time of arrival and departure might communicate something about interest or enjoyment. But such messages also communicate something about our willingness to socialize, our concern for the host, our level of frustration tolerance, our need to make a grand entrance or exit, and so on. Some persons seem particularly sensitive to the appropriateness of time, while other seem totally oblivious. Some persons consistently arrive late for dinner, for example, and then wonder why they are seldom invited back. Some seem totally unaware of when to leave. Although we may look at our watch several times, yawn three or four times at strategic places in the conversation, mention that there is a full day of work ahead of us tomorrow, and give any number of other cues, there seems to be no awareness of time with some people.

Time and Status

Time is especially linked to status considerations. For example, the importance of being on time varies directly with the status of the individual we are visiting. If the person is extremely important, we had better be there on time; in fact, we had better be there early just in case he or she is able to see us before schedule. As the individual's status decreases, it is less important for us to be on time. Students, for example, must be on time for conferences with teachers, but it is more important to be on time for deans and still more important to be on time for the president of the college. Teachers, on the other hand, may be late for conferences with students but not for conferences with deans or the president. Deans, in turn, may be late for teachers but not for the president. Within any hierarchy, similar unwritten rules seem to be followed in dealing with time. This is not to imply that these "rules" are just or fair. It is only to point out that they exist.

Even the time of dinner and the time from the arrival of guests to eating varies on the basis of status. Among lower-status individuals dinner is served relatively early and if there are guests, they eat soon after they arrive. For higher-status people dinner is relatively late, and a longer period of time elapses between arrival and eating—usually the time it takes to consume two cocktails.

Time and Appropriateness

Promptness or lateness in responding to letters, in returning telephone calls, in acknowledging gifts, and in returning invitations all communicate significant messages to other individuals. Such messages may be indexed on such scales as interest-disinterest, organized-disorganized, considerate-inconsiderate, sociable-unsociable, and so on.

The amount of time people live in one place, the time a professor stays at one school, or the time an individual remains with a particular doctor, lawyer, or therapist also communicate something about the individual and about the relationship between them.

There are also times during which certain activities are considered appropriate and other times during which they are considered inappropriate. Thus, it is permissible to make a social phone call during the late morning, afternoon, and early evening, but it is not permissible to call before eight or nine in the morning or during dinner time or after 11 at night. Similarly, in making dates an appropriate amount of notice is customary. When that acceptable amount of time is given as notice, it communicates a certain recognition of the accepted standards, perhaps respect for the individual, perhaps a certain social grace. Should any of these time conventions be violated, however, other meanings are perceived. For example, a phone call at an abnormal hour will almost surely communicate urgency of some sort; we begin to worry what could be the matter as we race toward the phone.

If, in asking for a date, the call is made the night before or even the same night as the expected date, it may communicate any number of things. Say, Chris calls Pat Saturday afternoon for a date that evening. Calling at that particular time may communicate, for example, that Chris had another date who canceled, or that Chris knew that Pat would be free and so there was no need to give notice, or that Chris was such a catch that Pat would welcome Chris regardless of the time called, and so on. In turn Pat's response or answer communicates significant meaning to Chris. Pat's acceptance might confirm Chris's expectation that Pat was free or that Pat would welcome Chris's call at any time. Pat's rejection, depending on the kind of ego Chris had, might communicate that Pat really wanted to date Chris but could not appear too eager, or that Pat didn't really want to date Chris and only used the short notice as an excuse, or that Pat had already made plans despite Chris's presumptuousness.

Any violation of accepted time schedules is determined; that is, it has a reason. As senders we may or may not be consciously aware of such reasons. As receivers we can only guess at the possible reasons based on whatever other cues are available.

Silence, paralanguage, and time are three elements of nonverbal communication that oftentimes function below the level of conscious awareness. Nevertheless, when a speaker or listener misuses any of these unstated rules, it frequently identifies the individual as one lacking in some social communication skill. It often distinguishes the person we enjoy interacting with from the person with whom we feel uncomfortable and ill at ease. Through an understanding of the ways in which these three dimensions affect our communications, we are less likely to break these small but socially significant rules of interpersonal interaction, and at the same time we will be better able to understand the problems generated by those who break these rules as well as the reactions of others when such nonverbal rules are broken.

SOURCES

On silence, see Max Picard, *The World of Silence* (Chicago: Gateway, 1952) for a philosophical perspective, and Irving J. Lee, "When to 'Keep Still,'" in *Language: Concepts and Processes,* Joseph A. DeVito, ed. (Englewood Cliffs, N.J.: Prentice-Hall, 1973) for a communications perspective. On silence among the Apache, see K. H. Basso, "'To Give up on Words': Silence in Western Apache Culture," in *Language and Social Context,* Pier Paolo Giglioli, ed. (Baltimore: Penguin Books, 1972). For a study on the discomfort of silence, see Helen M. Newman, "The Sounds of Silence in Communicative Encounters," *Communication Quarterly* 30 (Spring 1982):142–149.

For a classification of and introduction to paralinguistic phenomena, see George L. Trager, "Paralanguage: A First Approximation," *Studies in Linguistics* 13 (1958):1–12, and "The Typology of Paralanguage," *Anthropological Linguistics* 3 (1961):17–21. Mark Knapp, *Nonverbal Behavior in*

Human Interaction, 2d ed. (New York: Holt, Rinehart and Winston, 1978) provides an excellent summary of research findings. George F. Mahl and Gene Schulze likewise provide a thorough summary of the research and theory in this area. See their "Psychological Research in the Extra-linguistic Area," in *Approaches to Semiotics,* T. A. Seboek, A. S. Hayes, and M. C. Bateson, eds. (The Hague: Mouton, 1964). For a collection of research studies on paralanguage, see Joel R. Davitz, ed., *The Communication of Emotional Meaning* (New York: McGraw-Hill, 1964). For the study by T. H. Pear, see his *Voice and Personality* (London: Chapman and Hall, 1931). For a thorough review of paralanguage, see Ernest Kramer, "Judgment of Personal Characteristics and Emotions from Nonverbal Properties," *Psychological Bulletin* 60 (1963):408–420, Albert Mehrabian, *Silent Messages* (Belmont, Calif.: Wadsworth, 1971), in addition to Knapp, and Mahl and Schulze, cited above. An excellent review is provided by W. P. Robinson, *Language and Social Behaviour* (Baltimore: Penguin Books, 1972). The study of English and Scottish speakers and listeners can be found in W. M. Cheyne "Stereotyped Reactions to Speakers with Scottish and English Regional Accents," *British Journal of Social and Clinical Psychology* 9 (1970):77–79.

For the research reported in relation to speech rate, persuasion, and comprehension I relied on James MacLachlan, "What People Really Think of Fast Talkers," *Psychology Today* 13 (November 1979):113–117.

16.1 PARALÁNGUAGE COMMUNICATION*

In this exercise a subject recites the alphabet while attempting to communicate each of the following emotions:

> anger
> fear
> happiness
> jealousy
> love
> nervousness
> pride
> sadness
> satisfaction
> sympathy

The subject may begin the alphabet at any point and may omit and repeat sounds, but the subject may use only the names of the letters of the alphabet to communicate these feelings.

The subject should first number the emotions in random order so that he or she will have a set order to follow that is unknown to the audience, whose task it will be to guess the emotions expressed.

As a variation, have the subject go through the entire list of emotions: once facing the audience and employing any nonverbal signals desired and once with his or her back to the audience without employing any additional signals. Are there differences in the number of correct guesses depending on which method is used?

For Discussion

1. What are some of the differences between encoding and decoding "emotional meaning" and "logical meaning"?
2. Davitz and Davitz found the number of correct identifications for these emotions to be as follows: anger (156), nervousness (130), sadness (118), happiness (104), sympathy (93), satisfaction (75), love (60), fear (60),

*This exercise is based on J. R. Davitz and L. J. Davitz, "The Communication of Feelings by Content-Free Speech," *Journal of Communication* 9 (1959):6–13.

jealousy (69), and pride (50). Do these figures correspond to those you obtained? What conclusions would you draw about the relative ease or difficulty of expressing these emotions?

3. Do you think there is a positive relationship between encoding and decoding ability in situations such as this? Is the person who is adept at encoding the emotions also adept at decoding them? Explain.
4. What variables might influence encoding ability? Decoding ability?
5. What personality factors seem relevant to the encoding and decoding of emotions?

16.2 SOME NONVERBAL SEX DIFFERENCES*

The following statements summarize some of the research findings on sex differences in nonverbal communication. For each statement, insert *men* or *women* in each of the blank spaces. After completing all 15 statements, consider the ''Questions for Discussion.''

1. _____ seem to be slightly more accurate at judging emotions from observing facial expressions than _____ .
2. _____ seem better able to communicate emotions by facial expressions than _____ .
3. _____ smile more than _____ .
4. _____ are generally approached more closely than _____ .
5. _____ reveal their emotions facially more readily than _____ .
6. _____ extend their bodies, taking up greater areas of space, than _____ .
7. _____ maintain more eye contact than _____ in mixed sex dyads.
8. Both men and women, when speaking, look at _____ more than at _____ .
9. In mixed sex dyads, _____ interrupt _____ more often than the other way around.
10. Some research indicates that _____ speak with greater volume than _____ .
11. If a man and a woman are walking toward each other, the _____ will be more apt to move out of the _____ 's way than the other way around.

*Although most books on nonverbal communication discuss sex differences, I relied for this exercise on the excellent summaries in Judee K. Burgoon and Thomas Saine, *The Unspoken Dialogue* (Boston: Houghton Mifflin, 1978), and Barbara Eakins and Gene Eakins, *Sex Differences in Communication* (Boston: Houghton Mifflin, 1978).

12. Unattractive ——————— seem to be less accepted than are unattractive ——————— .
13. ——————— both touch and are touched more than ——————— .
14. ——————— engage in greater mutual eye contact with a same sex partner than ——————— .
15. Same sex pairs of ——————— sit more closely together than do same sex pairs of ——————— .

Questions for Discussion

1. On what basis did you think that the nonverbal behavior was more accurately ascribed to one sex rather than the other?
2. What do you think might account for the differences in nonverbal behavior?
3. Are there types of women or men in which these differences are especially pronounced? Almost absent? Totally absent? On what basis do you make these predictions?
4. How would you go about testing one of these statements for accuracy?
5. After learning the answers given by research findings, do these seem to be consistent with your own observations? Which one(s) is (are) not? How might you account for this discrepancy?

16.3 NONVERBAL TRUTHS AND FALSEHOODS: REVIEW QUIZ IV

Indicate whether each of the following statements is *True* or *False*. If a statement is false explain why it is false and rewrite it so that it is true.

1. All contradictory (or mixed) messages are double-binding.
2. Nonverbal behavior sometimes serves a metacommunicational function.
3. Emblems are nonverbal behaviors that translate words or phrases rather directly, for example, the O.K. or the peace signs.
4. Regulators are nonverbal behaviors that accompany and literally illustrate the verbal messages.
5. Generally, fathers touch their children more than do mothers.
6. College students report that they are touched more by their same-sex friends than by their opposite-sex friends.
7. The closest proxemic distance Edward Hall identifies is personal distance.
8. Territoriality refers to a possessive or ownershiplike reaction to an area of space.
9. All cultures seem to treat silence in the same way; all cultures seem to attribute the same meanings to silence.
10. Paralanguage is the verbal but nonvocal dimension of speech.

11. Generally, it has been found that slow talkers are more persuasive than fast talkers.

12. Two reasons why speakers should speak at a rate slower than normal are that comprehension is improved and that listeners prefer slower-than-normal speech.

13. Affect displays are always unintentional.

14. While verbal language is governed by rules, nonverbal communication is not.

15. The relative status of the individuals in a dyad has no influence on who is permitted to touch whom.

MESSAGE RECEPTION
PART FIVE

UNIVERSALS OF MESSAGE RECEPTION

Upon completion of this unit, you should be able to:
1. explain the active nature of the message-reception process
2. explain the subjective nature of message reception
3. give examples from your personal experiences of subjectivity in message reception
4. explain meaningfulness and consistency as principles of message reception
5. explain the cumulative nature of message reception
6. explain the partial and limited nature of message reception
7. explain the multichanneled nature of message reception
8. explain the role of conditioning in message reception
9. explain the law of least effort as it applies to message reception

The reception of messages—whether these are verbal or nonverbal—is not a simple, solitary act but rather a complex process consisting of a number of different but interrelated activities. After the message is sent, it is perceived in some way; the message is seen, felt, tasted, smelled, or heard. In Unit 18 we will focus on the processes and principles of perception, emphasizing people perception. Because of the importance of verbal messages in interpersonal communication, listening as one type of message reception is singled out for special consideration in Unit 19. During the reception of the message and after the message is received, part of the receiver's reaction feeds back to the source, informing the source as to how the message is being received and reacted to. In many cases this feedback serves as a stimulus for future messages. The concept of feedback and its role in interpersonal communication is also discussed in Unit 19. Our primary aims in Part Five are to describe the processes of verbal and nonverbal message reception and, hence, increase our understanding of them, and to provide the materials necessary for improving our own message-receiving abilities.

But before examining the specifics of each of the processes, we need to look at some of the universals of message reception—those characteristics that are universal or common to all forms of message reception and that define all processes of message reception.

251

MESSAGE RECEPTION IS AN ACTIVE PROCESS

Message reception is an active rather than a passive process. People are not containers into which information may be poured much as you would pour water into a glass. Rather they are active participants in the reception process. We work actively with the messages that we receive, altering them in ways that may better suit our expectations or our individual needs at the time.

We actively select the messages to which we will attend. The Republican will listen to Republican messages, and the Democrat will listen to Democratic messages. We also determine in part the effects that messages will have on us—for example, who we will believe and who we will not believe, those that we will allow to influence us significantly and those we will not allow to influence us.

This is not to say that all message reception is consciously controlled; much of it is regulated subconsciously. We may not even be aware of some messages we receive—at least not at the time of reception. But some time later, sometimes years later, they may surface and be found to have exerted considerable influence on our lives.

MESSAGE RECEPTION IS SUBJECTIVE

The message that occurs in the outside world is not the message that we receive. What we receive is actually a function of what occurs outside of us in combination with what occurs inside our skin. Message reception is not an objective process; it is in fact a highly subjective process. The same message (that is, the same message in the outside world) received by two different people is actually two different messages. Similarly, the same message received at two different times is actually two different messages since we have changed and what went on inside our skins last year is not what is going on now; hence the message is received differently.

Each of these propositions is verified in numerous ways every day of our lives. Consider, for example, going to a movie with a friend. You each see the same movie, but the reception is extremely different; one may find it exciting and entertaining and the other dull and boring. An editor told me that *Shampoo* was one of the best movies of all time and that I should be sure to see it. I saw it and had to struggle to stay awake and, in fact, actually fell asleep. The stimulus (the movie) was the same for both of us, but we were very different people with different things going on inside our heads; consequently, the messages received were, for all practical purposes, very different. The difference in perception caused by time is no less striking. Movies that I thought sensational a few years ago I may now view as trite and uninsightful. The movie itself has not changed; what has changed is what is going on inside my skin.

In perceiving people we do not simply perceive their individual bits of behavior; we perceive some structured whole. In interpersonal perception,

then, our expectations and our wants or needs will be particularly important.
We may have been told that Chris is honest and warm and that Pat is dishonest
and cold. If we then observe the exact same behaviors of these two individuals
we would probably perceive them in very different ways depending upon our
previous conceptions of what these people are like.

"Beauty is in the eye of the beholder," the old saying goes, and in terms
of perception theory, it clearly is. That is why the same individual can be perceived as ugly by one person and as beautiful by another, why the same person
can be perceived as humorous by one and as "sick" by another, why the same
person can be perceived as "encouraging students to use their full potential"
by one and as "unrealistic in his or her demands" by another.

The messages we receive and the ways in which we allow ourselves to
receive them are greatly influenced by our history of reinforcement and by our
present needs and wants. We receive messages and, in fact, actively seek out
messages that will reinforce us. We seek out messages that will provide us with
some kind of reward. If we are in need of peer approval, we will actively seek
out peer-approval messages.

Similarly, we will avoid messages that will cause pain or discomfort or
otherwise punish us. This may take the form of avoiding people who are usually
negative toward us, or avoiding advertisements extolling the pleasures of smoking after we have decided to quit, or avoiding articles about smoking causing
cancer when we smoke two packs a day.

In this respect message reception behavior is much like behavior in general. We seek out the rewards and we avoid the punishments, we approach
what will reinforce us and we avoid what will punish us. We are no fools.

MESSAGE RECEPTION ASSUMES
MEANINGFULNESS AND CONSISTENCY

In receiving verbal, nonverbal, or people messages we make the assumption that what we see or hear is meaningful and consistent in terms of our previous experience and knowledge.

Generally, we assume that people are sensible and that their behaviors
stem from some logical antecedent. We assume, in other words, a certain
degree of predictability in other people's behavior. We assume that they will
be consistent from one occasion to another, or at least relatively so. If you come
home one afternoon and find your father crying and you know that a close
friend of his died last night, you would perceive the crying to be related to the
death of the friend. Logically, of course, there could be any number of reasons
for his crying. If that same behavior were evidenced at a particularly sad movie
or while cooking onions or after receiving notice of being fired, you would perceive the crying as having different meaning. Thus, we attribute to the behavior
a meaning that seems most sensible in the total context in which it occurs.

To understand the concept of consistency (also referred to as *stability* or *invariance*), focus on an object at least 20 feet away, say, a picture or a book or a person. Now walk toward that object until you are a foot or less away. Physically, of course, the object did not change in size; it also did not change in size psychologically, despite the fact that the size of the image on the retina changed drastically as you approached it. Psychologically, we adjust our perceptions because we "know" from past experiences that things do not change in size as we get closer. We know how to adjust our perceptions of size on the basis of retinal image, distance, and object size.

In interpersonal perception we function in a very similar way. We perceive various behaviors of a friend as that friend is talking with a group of people. Naturally, this friend has never acted in this exact way before; no behaviors are ever repeated exactly. We do not focus our attention on the specific bits of behavior but on those aspects that are more or less unchanging, for example, his or her purposes, motivations, values. Consequently, our perception of these behaviors is relatively stable; we see the behavior of our friend as being consistent with our previous experience and knowledge.

Assume that you know several people who seem constantly to be praising themselves. At every turn they tell you how great they are. You might then label them as "egomaniacs" or as "egocentric." Now notice what effect that label will have on your perception of the future behaviors of these individuals. Upon seeing them again, the easiest way to structure your perception and make sense of it is to categorize it as egocentric. In doing this you are assuming that there is a certain stability to people's behavior and that there is a certain degree of invariance.

Our attempt to interpret incoming messages as meaningful and consistent is aided by the cumulative nature of message reception. When we receive messages, they are not simply taken in and stored in isolated compartments in our short-term and long-term memory systems. Rather, the messages that we receive today interact with the messages received the day before, and so on. And, of course, the messages—the data, the information, the concepts, the ideas, the theories, the beliefs, the attitudes, and so on—that we have stored in our memories up until now will influence the way in which all future messages will be received, remembered, and stored.

If, for example, you receive a message about your best friend, that message will be combined with all the other information that you have about your best friend, about the nature of friendship, and about various other related topics. The way in which it is evaluated, the extent to which you believe it to be true or false, the importance you assign to it, the way it makes you feel, the action you will base on it, and a host of other thoughts and behaviors will depend on how this new message relates to all the other information you have on this and related subjects. This cumulative nature of message reception is well illustrated in the spiral model presented earlier (Figure 2.3).

MESSAGE RECEPTION IS PARTIAL AND LIMITED

There are an infinite number of possible messages occurring right now in the outside world. The verbal messages alone usually number in the hundreds, to say nothing of the visual messages, olfactory messages, and so on. And yet out of this tremendous number we receive relatively few.

Clearly there are limits to our capacity to receive messages and to process information both in terms of its quantity and in terms of its complexity. We can only deal with so much information; when that amount is exceeded, we ignore the rest or simply go through the motions of receiving it when actually nothing is happening. For example, at a disco people will often go through the motions of hearing and responding to verbal messages when in fact they actually cannot make out what is being said. But apparently they get enough cues to know when a smile is appropriate, when a shake of the head is suitable, or when a look of intense concern is expected. Similarly, when messages get too complex, we may

There is no way we can attend to all the messages around us. We have to be selective and attend to those that seem most relevant, most interesting, and most powerful.

receive only the surface elements and ignore the rest. We may understand the words, for example, but their significance may go over our heads. This is seen quite clearly in someone who knows little about art or music when she or he views a painting or listens to a piece of music. Very little beyond the line and color, the words and arrangement, may be received.

In part, the limitations are imposed by our mental capacities. We have just so much ability to deal with messages and simply cannot push it beyond its limits. In part, our limitations are imposed by our own prejudices—our relative closed-mindedness or open-mindedness. A person who is extremely prejudiced against Martians, for example, will have difficulty receiving favorable messages about Martians. Instead, the messages may not be received or they may be distorted to the point where they become totally opposite to what the source may have intended.

MESSAGE RECEPTION IS MULTICHANNELED

Interpersonal message reception is multichanneled; interpersonal messages are received simultaneously through a number of different channels. For example, in talking face-to-face with one other person, we receive the auditory messages through our sense of hearing. At the same time, we receive gestural, facial, and eye messages through our sense of vision, tactile messages through our sense of touch, olfactory messages through our sense of smell, and at times, say, when kissing, gustatory messages through our sense of taste. Even when we are speaking on the telephone we are still receiving nonauditory messages, this time from our own immediate surroundings. We are constantly taking in visual messages from our immediate physical context, olfactory messages from the coffee on the stove, gustatory messages from the cake we are eating, and so on. In fact, we would have to construct a highly artificial communication situation if we wished to create single-channeled message reception. In real-life interpersonal interaction, single-channel message reception does not seem to exist.

The important implication of the multichanneled nature of message reception is that the messages coming in through the different channels may reinforce each other, contradict each other, or present us with simultaneous but unrelated information. Usually, the messages coming through the different channels reinforce each other; the verbal greeting, for example, is accompanied by a gestural greeting, a smile, or a handshake. At times, however, the messages contradict each other, as when the verbal greeting is accompanied by a pained expression, a sense of uneasiness, or a lack of direct eye contact. At still other times messages received at the same time may be unrelated, as when we are listening to what one person is saying but at the same time admiring the room or listening to still another conversation. Often we are busy receiving our own messages, as we rehearse what we are going to say next or when we are preoccupied with some problem or some decision we must make, or when we are concentrating on a toothache, hunger, or thirst. Although these messages may be unrelated to the message being received from the person with whom we are interacting, they nevertheless interfere to some extent with our reception of this "primary" message.

MESSAGE RECEPTION FOLLOWS THE LAW OF LEAST EFFORT

George Kingsley Zipf formulated a principle called "the law of least effort." Zipf's concern was actually with describing the ways in which language changes; his assumption was that language changes always followed the law of least effort. Pronunciation changes, for example, were always in the direction of less effort, as were changes in word meanings and in syntactic patterns. The principle, however, was applicable to a variety of issues in daily living and was soon applied widely.

I think it is especially applicable to message reception. Here it would refer to the practice of receiving those messages that require little effort and avoiding those messages that require us to expend much energy and effort. Probably the easiest messages for us to receive come from television, and perhaps this is one reason why we watch so much television. This is not to say that it is the only reason, but clearly it seems to be one reason why people spend more time watching television than they do reading.

Messages that are complicated and thus take a great deal of energy to decipher are less popular than are messages that require little effort. Newspapers—even the *New York Times* and the *Wall Street Journal*—make a great effort to simplify in order to enable a reader to go through the newspaper without expending much effort. Picture magazines like *People* and *Us* have become extremely popular largely because they require very little effort to go through. *Reader's Digest* is popular in part for the same reason; it requires less effort to read than the original articles or books.

One example we might relate to easily is this very book. I wrote it in units so that it would require less effort to get through than would longer chapters. My assumption was that you would be more apt to pick up the book if you could get through a unit in a relatively short period of time. When we face a chapter of 50 or 60 pages of tough prose, we are more likely to put it off until an examination forces us to face it. This principle of least effort may also be used to explain, at least in part, why first impressions persevere for so long. It is easier for us to formulate an impression and then filter all new information through this first impression. This is a great deal easier (though not very effective in the long run) than continuously revising our impressions as new information is provided. Further, our tendency to seek the path of least effort may also account for our failure to check the validity of our assumptions and our "facts." The result here is often misunderstanding and interpersonal conflict.

Other things being equal, then, we seem to receive those messages that require the least effort to interpret and the least expenditure of energy and to avoid those messages that will require a greater effort and energy expenditure.

SOURCES

One of the best sources on message reception is Wilbur Schramm and William E. Porter, *Men, Women, Messages, and Media: Understanding Human Communication,* 2d ed. (New York: Harper & Row, 1982). The principle of least effort may be found in two works by George Kingsley Zipf, *The Psycho-Biology of Language: An Introduction to Dynamic Philology* (Boston: Houghton Mifflin, 1935), and *Human Behavior and the Principle of Least Effort* (Cambridge: Harvard University Press, 1949).

17.1 THE STRANGER*

The purpose of this exercise is to explore the bases you use in perceiving and judging people you see for the first time. Since we all make judgments of people on seeing them, we need to investigate the ways and means we use in making these judgments.

A stranger (someone you have not seen before) will be brought into the class. Look the stranger over and answer the questions below. For this phase of the exercise, no interaction between you and the stranger should take place. Use the number "1" to mark your answers.

After answering all the questions you will be able to interact with the stranger for 5 or 10 minutes. Ask him or her any questions you wish, though none can be directly related to the questions asked below. The stranger should answer any questions posed as fully as he or she thinks necessary. The stranger should not, however, answer any questions that relate directly to the questions posed on the following pages. After this interaction, again answer the questions, this time using "2" to mark your answers.

After these answers have been recorded, the stranger or the instructor will go over each of the questions, specifying which answers the stranger thinks are most appropriate.

The stranger would most likely:

1. read
   - _____ a comedy
   - _____ a classic Russian novel
   - _____ a sex-improvement manual
   - _____ a philosophical essay
   - _____ a current popular novel
   - _____ a Gothic romance

2. see
   - _____ a mystery movie
   - _____ a romantic movie
   - _____ a western
   - _____ a comedy
   - _____ an erotic movie
   - _____ a foreign film

3. participate in
   - _____ baseball
   - _____ tennis
   - _____ golf
   - _____ skiing
   - _____ none of these

4. listen to
   - _____ classical music
   - _____ rock music
   - _____ country and western music
   - _____ popular music
   - _____ disco

*This exercise (though in a somewhat different form) was suggested by James C. McCroskey, Carl E. Larson, and Mark L. Knapp in their *Teacher's Manual* for *An Introduction to Interpersonal Communication* (Englewood Cliffs, N.J.: Prentice-Hall, 1971).

5. watch on television
   _____ a situation comedy
   _____ the news
   _____ an educational show
   _____ a detective show
   _____ a sports show
   _____ a soap opera

6. prefer to be
   _____ alone
   _____ in a crowd
   _____ with one person

7. go to
   _____ a rock concert
   _____ an art museum
   _____ a baseball game
   _____ an opera
   _____ a play
   _____ a movie

8. look for in a mate
   _____ intelligence
   _____ looks
   _____ personality
   _____ money

9. subscribe to
   _____ *Playboy/Playgirl*
   _____ *National Geographic*
   _____ *Time/Newsweek*
   _____ *Popular Mechanics*
   _____ *Modern Bride*

10. behave
    _____ as an extrovert
    _____ as an introvert
    _____ as an ambivert

11. act
    _____ aggressively
    _____ assertively
    _____ nonassertively

12. be
    _____ very energetic
    _____ very lazy
    _____ fairly energetic
    _____ fairly lazy

13. behave in most situations
    _____ very emotionally
    _____ very rationally
    _____ fairly emotionally
    _____ fairly rationally

14. What is the stranger's
    Age _____
    Occupation _____
    Educational level reached _____
    Marital status _____
    Financial status _____

Describe the stranger's personality in two, three, or four adjectives. How does the stranger feel now? Explain.

Discussion should focus on at least the following:

1. In what ways did the responses to the above questions illustrate the subjective nature of message reception?
2. Were the assumptions of meaningfulness and consistency evidenced in the responses? How?
3. Was the cumulative nature of message reception illustrated in the various responses? If so, in what ways?
4. Explain the active-passive nature of message reception in terms of this specific experience with the stranger.
5. In what ways was message reception partial and limited?

6. In what ways was message reception multichanneled?
7. Was the law of least effort evidenced in your responses? If so, how?

17.2 WHO?

The purpose of this exercise is to explore some of the verbal and nonverbal cues that people give off and that others receive and use in formulating assumptions about the knowledge, ability, and personality of another. The exercise should serve as a useful summary of the concepts and principles of verbal and nonverbal communication and of message reception.

The entire class should form a circle so that each member may see each other member without straining. If members do not know all the names of their classmates, some system of name tags should be used for this exercise.

Each student should examine the following list of phrases and should write the name of one student to whom he or she feels each statement applies in the column labeled "Who?" Be certain to respond to all statements. Although one name may be used more than once, the experience will prove more effective if a wide variety of names are chosen. Unless the class is very small, no name should be used more than 4 times.

Next to each student's name, record a *certainty rating* in the column labeled "CR," indicating how sure you are of your choices. Use a 5-point scale with 5 indicating great certainty and 1 indicating great uncertainty.

After the names and certainty ratings have been written down for *each* statement by *each* student, the following procedure may prove useful. The instructor or group leader selects a statement and asks someone specifically, or the class generally, what names were written down. (There is no need to tackle the statements in the order they are given here.) Before the person whose name was put down is asked if the phrase is correctly or incorrectly attributed to him or her, some or all of the following questions should be considered.

1. Why did you select the name you did? What was there about this person that led you to think that this phrase applied to him or her? What *specific* verbal or nonverbal cues led you to your conclusion?
2. What additional verbal and/or nonverbal cues would you need to raise your degree of certainty?
3. Is your response at all a function of a stereotype you might have of this individual's ethnic, religious, racial, or sexual identification? For example, how many women's names were put down for the questions or phrases about the saws or pistons? How many men's names were put down for the statements pertaining to cooking or using a sewing machine?
4. Did anyone give off contradictory cues such that some cues were appropriate for a specific phrase and others were not appropriate? Explain the nature of these contradictory cues.
5. How pleased or disappointed are the people whose names have been

proposed? Why? Were there any surprises? Why were some of these guesses unexpected?

6. How do you communicate your "self" to others? How do you communicate what you know, think, feel, and do to your peers?

Who?   *CR*

1. goes to the professional theater a few times a year
2. has taken a vacation outside the country in the last 12 months
3. likes to cook
4. watches soap operas on a fairly regular basis
5. wants lots of children
6. knows the function of a car's pistons
7. knows how to knit
8. would vote against the ERA
9. has a pet
10. has seen a pornographic (XXX rated) movie within the last 3 months
11. knows how to wire a lamp
12. has been to an opera
13. is a member of an organized sports team
14. watches television for an average of at least 3 hours per day
15. knows who played Superman in the television series
16. has cried over a movie in the last few months
17. fluently speaks a foreign language
18. is married
19. has many close friends
20. knows how potatoes should be planted
21. knows who Edward R. Murrow was
22. knows the differences among a hacksaw, a jigsaw, and a copingsaw
23. knows the ingredients for a bloody Mary
24. knows how to make a hollandaise sauce
25. knows the function of the spleen
26. knows what an armoire is
27. can name all 12 signs of the zodiac
28. has a car in his or her immediate family costing over $15,000
29. would come to the aid of a friend even at great personal sacrifice

30. is frequently infatuated (or in love)
31. would like, perhaps secretly, to be a movie star
32. knows how to play bridge
33. enjoys reading poetry
34. knows where Liechtenstein is
35. knows the legal status of Puerto Rico
36. keeps a diary or a journal
37. knows how many members are on a soccer team
38. knows what SALT stands for
39. knows who the heavyweight boxing champion is
40. knows what the prime rate means
41. was a member of the Boy Scouts or Girl Scouts
42. is very religious
43. would describe himself or herself as a political activist
44. wants to go to graduate, law, or medical school
45. would vote in favor of gay rights legislation
46. is planning to get married within the next 12 months
47. is going to make a significant contribution to society
48. is going to be a millionaire
49. is a real romantic
50. would emerge as a leader in a small group situation

INTERPERSONAL PERCEPTION

Upon completion of this unit, you should be able to:

1. define *interpersonal perception*
2. explain the three major stages in the perception process
3. explain the process of attribution and identify the operation of the three criteria used in making causal judgments
4. explain how self-attribution differs from other-attribution
5. define *self-serving bias* and explain its operation in causal attribution
6. explain at least three variables related to the accuracy of interpersonal perception
7. explain what is meant by an *implicit personality theory* and describe its influence on interpersonal perception
8. define and explain the relevance in interpersonal perception of the following: *self-fulfilling prophecy, perceptual accentuation, primacy, recency, consistency,* and *stereotype*

Perception is the process by which we become aware of objects and events in the external world through our various senses: sight, smell, taste, touch, and hearing. Perception is an active rather than a passive process. Our perceptions are only in part a function of the outside world; in large measure they are a function of our own past experiences, our desires, our needs and wants, our loves and hatreds. Hans Toch and Malcolm MacLean express the essence of this transactional view of perception most clearly. "Each percept [that which is perceived], from the simplest to the most complex, is the product of a creative act.... We can never encounter a stimulus before some meaning has been assigned to it by some perceiver.... Therefore, each perception is the beneficiary of all previous perceptions; in turn, each new perception leaves its mark on the common pool. A percept is thus a link between the past which gives it its meaning and the future which it helps to interpret." In this unit our concern is with explaining the nature of perception, particularly its role in interpersonal communication. First, we will consider the stages in the perception process and what happens between the occurrence of an event and a person's interpretation and evaluation of that event. Second, we will explore attribution—the process by which we attempt to understand behavior, especially the reasons or motivations for behavior. Third, we will focus on the issue of accuracy in interpersonal perception: How accurate are our perceptions of others? What characteristics make some people more accurate perceivers than others? Fourth, we will consider six major perceptual processes—the processes we use to perceive people and make inferences about them.

STAGES IN THE PERCEPTION PROCESS

The process of perception may be viewed as occurring in three stages or steps. These stages are not discrete and separate; in reality they are continuous and blend into one another.

Sensory Stimulation Occurs

At this first stage the sense organs are stimulated—we hear the Stones's new record, we see someone we have not seen for years, we smell perfume on the person next to us, we taste a juicy steak, we feel a sweaty palm as we shake hands.

We all have different abilities to hear, see, smell, taste, and feel and these different abilities influence what we perceive. Some people can hear very high-pitched sounds whereas others cannot. Similarly, some can see great distances whereas others have trouble seeing 10 feet away.

Even when we have the sensory ability to perceive stimuli, we do not always do so. For example, when you are daydreaming in class you do not hear what the teacher is saying until your own name is called. Then you wake up. You know your name was called, but you do not know why. This is a clear and perhaps too frequent example of our perceiving what is meaningful to us and not perceiving what is not meaningful (or at least what we temporarily judge to be meaningless).

An obvious implication of this is that what we do perceive is only a very small portion of what could be perceived. Much as we have limits on how far we can see, we also have limits on the quantity of stimulation that we can take in at any given time. One of the goals of education, or so it would seem, is to train us to perceive more of what exists, whether it be art, politics, music, communication, social problems, or any other conceivable source of sensory stimulation.

Sensory Stimulation Is Organized

At the second stage the sensory stimulations are organized in some way and according to some principles. Exactly how our sensory stimulations are organized and what principles such organization follows are not always agreed upon. The principles of proximity and resemblance, however, seem useful in interpersonal perception and will serve to illustrate how sensory stimuli might be organized. The *principle of proximity* states that persons who are physically close to one another (persons who are often seen together or who live close to each other) will be perceived as a group, as having some commonality. The *principle of resemblance* states that people who are similar in appearance (members of the same race or those who dress in similar ways) will also be grouped together and distinguished from those of a different race or who dress very differently.

Sensory Stimulation Is Interpreted-Evaluated

The third step in the perceptual process is interpretation-evaluation, terms that we hyphenate and consider together to emphasize that in reality they cannot be separated. This third step is inevitably a subjective process involving evaluations on the part of the perceiver. Our interpretations-evaluations, then, are not based solely on the external stimulus but rather are greatly influenced by our past experiences, our needs, our wants, our value systems, our beliefs about the way things are or should be, our physical or emotional states at the time, our expectations, and so on. It should be clear from even this very incomplete list of influences that there is here much room for disagreement among different people. Although we may all be exposed to the same external stimulus, the way it is interpreted-evaluated will differ with each person and from one time to another for the same person.

ATTRIBUTION

Perhaps the most interesting and most insightful theoretical approach to interpersonal perception is that of *attribution theory,* developed largely by E. E. Jones and K. E. Davis and expanded and clarified greatly by H. H. Kelley. Attribution is a process through which we attempt to understand the behaviors of others (as well as our own), particularly the reasons or motivations for these behaviors. Most of our inferences about a person's motivations—a person's reasons for behaving in various ways—come from our observations of the person's behaviors.

If our eventual aim is to discover the causes of another's behavior, then our first step is to determine if the individual is responsible for the behavior or if some outside factor is responsible. That is, we first have to determine if the cause of the behavior is *internal* (for example, if the behavior is due to the person's personality or to some such enduring trait) or if the cause of the behavior is *external* (for example, if the behavior is due to some situational factor). Internal and external are the two kinds of causality with which attribution theory is concerned.

Consider an example. We look at a teacher's grade book and observe that 10 *F*'s were assigned in cultural anthropology. In an attempt to discover what this behavior (assignment of the 10 *F*'s) reveals about the teacher, we first have to discover if the teacher was in fact responsible for the behavior or if it could be attributed to outside or external factors. If we discover that the examinations on which the grades were based were made up by a faculty committee and that the committee set the standards for passing or failing, we could not attribute any particular motives to this individual teacher since the behavior was not internally caused. Rather, it was externally caused (in this case by the department committee in conjunction with each student's performance on the examination).

On the other hand, let us assume that the following occurred: This teacher made up the examination without any assistance from other faculty and no department or university standards were used; the teacher made up his or her own standards for passing and failing. Now we would be more apt (though perhaps not fully convinced) to attribute the 10 *F*'s to internal causes. We would be strengthened in our beliefs that there was something internalized within this teacher, some personality characteristic, for example, that led to this behavior if we discovered that (1) no other teacher in anthropology gave out nearly as many failures, (2) this particular teacher frequently gives out lots of *F*'s in cultural anthropology, and (3) this teacher frequently gives many *F*'s in other courses as well. These three bits of added information would lead us to conclude that there was something in this teacher that motivated the behavior. These three new items of information each represent one of the three principles we use in making causal judgments in interpersonal perception: (1) consensus, (2) consistency, and (3) distinctiveness. We use each of these principles every day in making judgments about people though we talk about them with a different jargon.

Consensus

When we focus on the principle of *consensus* we ask essentially, "Do other people react or behave in the same way as the person on whom we are focusing?," that is, are they acting in accordance with the general consensus? If the answer is "no," then we are more likely to attribute the behavior to some internal cause. In the teacher example, we were strengthened in our belief that there was something internal causing the *F*'s when we learned that other teachers did not do this—there was low consensus. When only one person acts contrary to the norm, we are more likely to attribute that person's behavior to some internal motivation. If all teachers gave a great number of *F*'s (that is, if there was high consensus), we would be more likely to look for causality outside the individual teacher and conclude, for example, that the anthropology department uses a particular curve in determining grades, that the students were not very bright, or any other reason external to the specific teacher.

Consistency

When we focus on the principle of *consistency* we ask if this person repeatedly behaves the same way in similar situations. If the answer is "yes," there is high consistency, and we are likely to attribute the behavior to the person, to some internal motivation. The fact that this teacher frequently gives lots of *F*'s in cultural anthropology leads us to attribute cause to the teacher rather than to outside sources. If, on the other hand, there was low consistency—that is, if this teacher rarely gives *F*'s—then we would be more likely to look for reasons external to the teacher. We might consider, for example, the possibility that this specific class was not terribly bright or that the department required the teacher to start giving out failures, and so on. That is, we would look for causes external to the teacher.

Distinctiveness

When we focus on the principle of *distinctiveness*, we ask if this person reacts in similar ways in different situations. If the answer is "yes," there is low distinctiveness and we are likely to conclude that there is an internal cause. A low distinctiveness indicates that the situation is not distinctive and that this person reacts in similar ways in different situations. The fact that the teacher reacted the same way (gave lots of *F*'s) in similar situations led us to conclude that this particular class was not distinctive and that the reason or motivation for the behavior could not be found in this unique situation. We further concluded that this behavior must be due to the teacher's inner motivation. Consider the alternative: Assume that this teacher gave all high grades and no failures in all other courses (that is, that the cultural anthropology class situation was highly distinctive), then we would conclude that the motivation for the failures was to be found in sources outside the teacher and for reasons unique to this class.

Low consensus, high consistency, and low distinctiveness lead us to attribute a person's behavior to internal causes. High consensus, low consistency, and high distinctiveness lead us to attribute a person's behavior to external causes. A summary with a specific example is presented in Table 18.1.

Of course, not all behaviors are equally revealing of internal motivations. Some behaviors tell us a great deal about an individual while other behaviors fail to separate this person from thousands of others. First, behaviors that are produced by one motivation are more revealing than are behaviors produced by various and numerous motivations. And, second, behaviors that are uncommon or are drastically different from those produced by others are more revealing than are behaviors common to everyone.

Consider attempting to account for the reason why a friend took a position with Hulk Industries. The job is a boring one, the work required is physically demanding and unpleasant, but it pays well. Further, our friend has turned down easier and more exciting jobs that did not pay well. From this we would likely conclude that this individual was motivated by money. The behavior of taking the position with Hulk Industries could only be accounted for (assuming we had all the facts) on the basis of the money factor. This behavior is therefore more revealing of motivation than would taking a position with Wonder, Inc. where the job was interesting, the work was easy and pleasant, and the money was good. Here we would not be able to make a strong inference concerning which motive operated to produce the given behavior.

Likewise, uncommon behaviors are more revealing than common behaviors. Consider the mother who buys her children new clothes, sees that they go to bed on time, and supervises their homework. These are the functions of many mothers and hence would not be particularly revealing; they would not enable us to separate this mother from thousands of other mothers. However, take the mother who beats her child for hanging her new dress on a wire hanger—as the book and film *Mommie Dearest* depicted (accurately or falsely I do not know). This bit of behavior is uncommon enough for us to find it revealing; this behavior tells us something about this particular individual and enables us to distinguish her from thousands of other mothers.

A Note on Self-Attribution

In *self-attribution*—the attempt to account for our own behaviors—we follow the same general patterns with two main differences. First, there is a general tendency to see the behaviors of others as internally caused but our own behaviors as externally caused. In part this seems due to the fact that in accounting for our own behaviors, we have a great deal more information than we do when accounting for the behaviors of others. For example, we know that we have acted differently in other situations and therefore can more easily attribute this specific behavior to this specific situation. Also, since we cannot focus directly on our own behaviors and see them as objectively as we see the behaviors of others, we focus most of our attention on the environment or situation. Both of these tendencies, then, lead us to attribute the majority of the causes of our own behaviors to situational factors.

Situation:	A student is observed complaining about a grade received in a philosophy course. On what basis will we conclude whether this behavior is internally or externally caused?

Internal If:

1. No one else complained. (Low Consensus)

2. Student has complained in the past. (High Consistency)

3. Student has complained to other teachers in other courses. (Low Distinctiveness)

External If:

1. Many others have complained. (High Consensus)

2. Student has never complained in the past. (Low Consistency)

3. Student has never complained to other teachers. (High Distinctiveness)

TABLE 18.1
A Summary of Consensus, Consistency, and Distinctiveness in Causal Attribution

The second major difference in self-attribution involves what has been called the *self-serving bias*. Generally, this self-serving bias leads us to take credit for the positive and to deny responsibility for the negative. Thus, when attempting to account for our negative behaviors, we would be more apt to attribute them to situational or environmental factors, and when accounting for our positive behaviors, we are likely to attribute them to internal factors.

Generally, then, in self-attribution, we attribute our behaviors to situational factors—especially when they are negative. When our behaviors are positive, the self-serving bias tends to have greater force and leads us to attribute the cause to some internal factor, to our positive personality characteristics.

ACCURACY IN INTERPERSONAL PERCEPTION

*Children can tell what a person is really like, even though adults might
  have difficulty.*
Women are just naturally better judges of people than men.
*He or she is so popular with everyone; he or she must be an excellent
  judge of people.*
*After going on an encounter weekend, we should be able to judge people
  more accurately.*

These statements reflect our concern with accuracy in interpersonal perception. Some of these statements seem logical on the basis of our experience. Some seem logical because of some rule of analogy—we went on an encounter weekend, improved our accuracy, and therefore conclude that encounter weekends improve perception accuracy for people in general. Some seem logical because some authority told us so.

Actually much experimental research, clearly synthesized by Mark Cook, has been directed at testing these and similar statements to determine the characteristics of persons who are particularly accurate in interpersonal perception. Some of the prominent factors or variables are age, sex, intelligence, popularity, personality characteristics, and training.

Contrary to the popular notion that children can tell what a person is really thinking or really like, accuracy of interpersonal perception increases with age rather than decreases. For example, it has been found that judgments of emotion from facial and vocal cues as well as sociometric judgments increase in accuracy with age. The popular notion that women are more accurate interpersonal perceivers than men has some—but not overwhelming—support. Differences on the basis of sex have not been found in most studies. In the few studies that have found differences, women have performed at a slightly higher level than men. It is interesting to note that the emotions of women are perceived more accurately than the emotions of men. This may be due to the fact that women have been "allowed" to express emotion more freely than have men in our culture. Consequently, the expression of emotion in women may have been more complete and less inhibited than its expression in men. Or perhaps because of women's more frequent expressions of emotions, they have learned emotional expression better than have the men.

Although intellectual brilliance does not ensure interpersonal perceptual accuracy, generally the more intelligent the person, the better he or she is at accurately judging other people. This is due in part to the fact that those of superior intelligence generally have more categories—more names and labels—for describing people. They, therefore, are less apt to group people into broad and general (and inaccurate) classes as much as will those with fewer categories. Having a great number of categories for describing people's personalities and behaviors probably assists us in focusing our attention on small differences that others, without these finely differentiated categories, might not see. Surely it enables those with these extra categories to appear to be more accurate and more sophisticated in their interpersonal perceptions.

It is generally assumed that people who are popular and socially favored have achieved their standing because they are accurate judges of people. A number of studies have sought to investigate this, but no definite conclusions seem warranted. At times, of course, accurate perception may prove a hindrance to popularity if this skill enables the individual to see all the faults in others. On the other hand, if it gives an individual better insight into other people, then it probably functions to improve social relationships. A great deal of research has focused on the personality characteristics of accurate perceivers. Are accurate perceivers more sociable or less sociable, more empirically oriented or less empirically oriented, more independent or more dependent? Here there is much confusion. Generally the personality characteristics of accurate judges include sociability, toughmindedness, empiricism, nonconformity, independence, strong will, and dominance. When the sex of the judge is controlled, however, a somewhat different picture emerges. "The picture of the good male judge that emerges," says Cook "is rather unexpected. The good male judge of males is described as a rather insensitive aggressive person while the good male judge of females is described as very ineffectual. The good female judges are described slightly more favorably."

Training, it is assumed, will increase one's ability at almost anything. We seem to have an undying faith in the ability of individuals to be educated to the point where they can do just about anything. With interpersonal perception, however, training has not been found to be effective, at least not generally. Interpersonal perception has been improved when judges were given immediate knowledge of results, but T-groups and clinical training, for example, have not resulted in improved interpersonal perception. It should be noted that such training does provide people with a host of new labels and terms, and this makes it appear that their accuracy has improved. Actually, however, it has not. Or so say the experimental studies.

Perceiving the characteristics or traits of another is a particularly complex and difficult task, and it should come as no surprise that generally we are not very good at it. We are especially poor in perceiving those who are very different from us and are at our best in perceiving those who are very similar to us.

PERCEPTUAL PROCESSES

There are a number of significant processes that govern interpersonal perception. These processes greatly influence what we observe and what we fail to observe, what we infer and what we fail to infer about another person. These processes help to explain the reasons why we make some predictions and why we decline to make other predictions about people. These processes help us to impose some order on the enormous amount of data that impinges on our senses. They enable us to simplify and categorize the vast amount of information around us. In some cases, as is noted in the following discussions, they lead to oversimplification and to a distortion of information. Here the operation of six major perceptual processes is identified and described: implicit personality theory, the self-fulfilling prophecy, perceptual accentuation, primacy-recency, consistency, and stereotyping.

Implicit Personality Theory

We each have a theory of personality. Although we may not be able to verbalize it, we nevertheless have the rules that constitute a theory of personality. More specifically, we have a system of rules that tells us which characteristics of an individual go with which other characteristics. Consider, for example, the following brief statements. Note the characteristic in parentheses that best seems to complete the sentence:

> *John is energetic, eager, and (intelligent, stupid).*
> *Mary is bold, defiant, and (extroverted, introverted).*
> *Joe is bright, lively, and (thin, fat).*
> *Jane is attractive, intelligent, and (likeable, unlikeable).*
> *Susan is cheerful, positive, and (attractive, unattractive).*
> *Jim is handsome, tall, and (flabby, muscular).*

It is not important which words you selected. And certainly there are no right and wrong answers. What should be observed, however, is that certain of the words "seemed right" and others "seemed wrong." What made some seem right was our *implicit personality theory*, the system of rules that tells us which characteristics go with other characteristics. The theory tells us that a person who is energetic and eager is also intelligent, not stupid, although there is no logical reason why a stupid person could not be energetic and eager.

The widely documented and previously discussed "halo effect" is a function of our implicit personality theory. If we know an individual to possess a number of positive qualities, we make the inference that she or he also pos-

sesses other positive qualities. There is also a "reverse halo effect" which operates in a similar way. If we know a person to possess a number of negative
qualities then we are more likely to infer that she or he also possesses other
negative qualities. Implicit personality theories, with their halo and reverse
halo effects, often lead to self-fulfilling prophecies.

The Self-Fulfilling Prophecy

A *self-fulfilling prophecy* is a phenomenon that occurs when we make a
prediction or formulate a belief that comes true because we have made the
prediction and acted on it as if it were true. Identifying the four basic steps in
the self-fulfilling prophecy should clarify this important concept and its implications for interpersonal perception.

1. We make a prediction or formulate a belief about a person or a
   situation. (For example, we make a prediction that Pat is awkward in
   interpersonal encounters.)
2. We act toward that person or situation as if that prediction or belief was
   in fact true. (For example, we act toward Pat as if Pat was in fact
   awkward.)
3. Because we act as if the belief is true, it becomes true. (For example, because of the ways in which we act toward Pat, Pat becomes tense and
   manifests awkwardness.)
4. We observe *our* effect on the person or the resulting situation and what
   we see strengthens our beliefs. (For example, we observe Pat's
   awkwardness and this reinforces our belief that Pat is in fact awkward.)

If we expect people to act a certain way or if we make a prediction about the
characteristics of a situation, our predictions will frequently come true because
of the self-fulfilling prophecy phenomenon.

A widely known example of the self-fulfilling prophecy is the Pygmalion
effect. In one study of this effect teachers were told that certain pupils were
expected to do exceptionally well—that they were late bloomers. The names of
these students were actually selected at random by the experimenters; however, the results were not random. Those students whose names were given to
the teachers actually did perform at a higher level than did the other students.
In fact, these students even improved in I.Q. score more than did the other
students.

Eric Berne, in *Games People Play*, and Thomas Harris, in *I'm O.K., You're
O.K.*, both point out the same type of effect but in a somewhat different context.
These transactional psychologists argue that we live by the scripts that are given
to us by our parents, and that we essentially act in the way in which we are told
to act. Much like the children who were expected to do well, we all, according
to transactional psychology, live by the scripts given to us as children.

Consider, for example, people who enter a group situation convinced that
the other members will dislike them. Almost invariably they are proven right;

the other members do dislike them. What they may be doing is acting in such a way as to encourage people to respond negatively. The person made a prophecy and then fulfilled it.

We must consciously monitor our perceptions and the manner in which we act on them to ensure that we are not creating for ourselves and others stumbling blocks to accurate and effective interpersonal perception.

Perceptual Accentuation

"Any port in a storm" is a common enough phrase which in its variants appears throughout our communications. To many, even an ugly date is better than no date at all. Spinach may taste horrible, but when you are starving, it can taste like filet mignon. And so it goes.

In a classic study on need influencing perception, poor and rich children were shown pictures of coins and later asked to estimate their size. The poor children estimated the size as much greater than did the rich children. Similarly, hungry people perceive food objects and food terms at lower recognition thresholds (needing fewer physical cues) than people who are not hungry.

Perhaps the most important factor to influence our interpersonal perceptions is who we are.

In terms of interpersonal perception, this process, called *perceptual accentuation*, leads us to see what we expect to see and what we want to see. We see people we like as being better looking than people we do not like; we see people we like as being smarter than people we do not like. The obvious counterargument to this is that we actually prefer good-looking and smart people—not that people whom we like are seen as being handsome and smart. But perhaps that is not the entire story.

In a study reported by Zick Rubin, male undergraduates participated in what they thought were two separate and unrelated studies that were actually two parts of a single experiment. In the first part each subject read a passage; half the subjects were given an arousing sexual seduction scene to read, and half were given a passage about seagulls and herring gulls. In the second part of the experiment subjects were asked to rate a female student on the basis of her photograph and a self-description. As might be expected, the subjects who read the arousing scene rated the woman as significantly more attractive than did the other group. Further, the subjects who expected to go on a blind date with this woman rated her more sexually receptive than did the subjects who were told that they had been assigned to date someone else. How can we account for such findings?

Although this experiment was a particularly dramatic demonstration of perceptual accentuation, this same general process occurs every day. We magnify or accentuate that which will satisfy our needs and wants. The thirsty person sees a mirage of water, the sexually deprived person sees a mirage of sexual satisfaction, and only very rarely do they get mixed up.

Primacy–Recency

Assume for a moment that you are enrolled in a course in which half the classes are extremely dull and half the classes are extremely exciting. At the end of the semester you are to evaluate the course and the instructor. Would the evaluation be more favorable if the dull classes constituted the first half of the semester and the exciting classes constituted the second half of the semester or if the order were reversed? If what comes first exerts the most influence, we have what is called a *primacy effect*. If what comes last (or is the most recent) exerts the most influence, we have a *recency effect*.

In an early study on the effects of primacy-recency in interpersonal perception, Solomon Asch read a list of adjectives describing a person to a group of subjects and found that the effects of order were significant. A person described as "intelligent, industrious, impulsive, critical, stubborn, and envious" was evaluated as more positive than a person described as "envious, stubborn, critical, impulsive, industrious, and intelligent." The implication here is that we utilize early information to provide us with a general idea as to what a person is like, and we utilize the later information to make this general idea or impression more specific. Numerous other studies have provided evidence for the effect of first impressions. For example, in one study subjects observed a student (actually a confederate of the experimenter) taking a test. The task of the subject was to estimate the number of questions the student got right and to predict how well he would do on a second trial. The confederate followed two different orders. In one order, the descending order, the correct answers were all in the beginning. In the ascending order, the correct answers were toward the end. In each case, of course, there were the same number of correct and incorrect answers. Subjects judged the descending order to contain more correct responses. They also estimated that students in the descending order would do better on a second trial and judged them to be more intelligent.

The obvious practical implication of primacy-recency is this: The first impression you make is likely to be the most important. It is through this first impression that others will filter additional information to eventually formulate a picture of who you are. At the same time, we should recognize that our first impressions of others may not be accurate descriptions of the entire person. Hence, we should try to keep an open mind and not allow our first impressions to blind us to further incoming data or lead us to misinterpret additional (and perhaps contradictory) information.

Consistency

There is a rather strong tendency to maintain balance or consistency among our perceptions. As so many of the current theories of attitude change demonstrate, we strive to maintain balance among our attitudes; we expect certain things to go together and other things not to go together. On a purely intuitive basis, for example, respond to the following sentences by noting the expected response.

1. I expect a person I like to (like, dislike) me.
2. I expect a person I dislike to (like, dislike) me.
3. I expect my friend to (like, dislike) my friend.
4. I expect my friend to (like, dislike) my enemy.
5. I expect my enemy to (like, dislike) my friend.
6. I expect my enemy to (like, dislike) my enemy.

According to most consistency theories, our expectations would be as follows: We would expect a person we liked to like us (1) and a person we disliked to dislike us (2). We would expect a friend to like a friend (3) and to dislike an enemy (4). We would expect our enemy to dislike our friend (5) and to like our other enemy (6). All of these should be intuitively satisfying.

Further, we would expect someone we liked to possess those characteristics that we liked or admired. And we would expect our enemies not to possess those characteristics that we liked or admired. Conversely, we would expect persons we liked to lack unpleasant characteristics and persons we disliked to possess unpleasant characteristics.

In terms of interpersonal perception this tendency for balance and consistency may influence the way in which we see other people. It is easy to see our friends as being possessed of fine qualities and our enemies as being possessed of unpleasant qualities. Donating money to the poor, for example, can be perceived as an act of charity (if from a friend) or as an act of pomposity (if from an enemy). We would probably laugh harder at a joke told by a well-liked comedian than at that very same joke if told by a disliked comedian.

Stereotyping

One of the most frequently used shortcuts in interpersonal perception is stereotyping. Originally *stereotype* was a printing term that referred to the plate that printed the same image over and over again. A sociological or psychological stereotype is a fixed impression of a group of people. We all have stereotypes, whether they be of national groups, religious groups, or racial groups, or perhaps of criminals, prostitutes, teachers, plumbers, or artists.

When we have these fixed impressions we will often, upon meeting a member of a particular group, see that person primarily as a member of that group, and all the characteristics we have in our minds for members of that group are applied to this individual. If we meet someone who is a prostitute, for example, we have a host of characteristics for prostitutes that we are ready to apply to this one person. To further complicate matters, we will often see in this person's behavior the manifestation of various characteristics that we would not see if we did not know that this person was a prostitute. Stereotypes distort our ability to accurately perceive other people. They prevent us from seeing an individual as an individual; instead the individual is seen only as a member of a group.

SOURCES

A thorough summary of perception is contained in Mark Cook, *Interpersonal Perception* (Baltimore: Penguin, 1971), on which I relied heavily for the entire unit. A more thorough and scholarly presentation of this area is Renato Tagiuri, "Person Perception," in *The Handbook of Social Psychology*, 2d ed., G. Lindzey and E. Aronson, eds. (Reading, Mass.: Addison-Wesley, 1969). Standard reference works in this area include Michael Argyle, *Social Interaction* (London: Methuen, 1969), and Renato Tagiuri and Luigi Petrullo, eds., *Person Perception and Interpersonal Behavior* (Stanford, Calif.: Stanford University Press, 1958). A brief but insightful account of interpersonal perception is provided by Albert Hastorf, David Schneider, and Judith Polefka in *Person Perception* (Reading, Mass.: Addison-Wesley, 1970). I found Zick Rubin, *Liking and Loving: An Invitation to Social Psychology* (New York: Holt, Rinehart and Winston, 1973), a most useful source. Much of the discussion of the perceptual processes is based on the insights provided by Rubin. The cited study by Solomon Asch is "Forming Impressions of Personality," *Journal of Abnormal and Social Psychology* 41 (1946):258–290. The cited study on forming impressions of exam-taking students was conducted and reported by Edward E. Jones, Leslie Rock, Kelley G. Sharver, and Lawrence M. Ward, "Pattern of Performance and Ability Attribution: An Unexpected Primacy Effect," *Journal of Personality and Social Psychology* 10 (1968):317–340. Both of these studies are discussed by Rubin. On the role of perception in interpersonal communication, see Don E. Hamachek, *Encounters with Others: Interpersonal Relationships and You* (New York: Holt, Rinehart and Winston, 1982).

On attribution theory see E. E. Jones and K. E. Davis, "From Acts to Dispositions: The Attribution Process in Person Perception," in *Advances in Experimental Social Psychology*, vol. 2, L. Berkowitz, ed. (New York: Academic Press, 1965), pp. 219–266. H. H. Kelley offers several works: "Attribution Theory in Social Psychology," in *Nebraska Symposium on Motivation*, D. Levine, ed.

(Lincoln: University of Nebraska Press, 1967), pp. 192–240, "The Process of Causal Attribution," *American Psychologist* 28 (1973): 107–128, and *Personal Relationships: Their Structures and Processes* (Hillsdale, N.J.: Erlbaum, 1979). For recent reviews of attribution theory see, for example, Harold H. Kelley and John L. Michela, "Attribution Theory and Research," in *Annual Review of Psychology*, M. R. Rosenzweig and L. W. Porter, eds. (Palo Alto, Calif.: Annual Reviews, 1980):457–501, and David R. Siebold, "Recent Books on Social Cognition: The Mind/Society Circle," *Quarterly Journal of Speech* 67 (November 1981):416–427.

The self-fulfilling prophecy was originally formulated by Robert K. Merton in *Social Theory and Social Structure* (New York: Free Press, 1957). For the original Pygmalion studies see R. Rosenthal and L. Jacobson, *Pygmalion in the Classroom* (New York: Holt, Rinehart and Winston, 1968). Although a number of studies failed to replicate these original findings, the most recent studies seem now to again support the Pygmalion effect. See, for example, W. B. Seaver, "Effects of Naturally Induced Teacher Expectancies," *Journal of Personality and Social Psychology* 28 (1973): 333–342. An excellent collection of articles on the self-fulfilling prophecy may be found in Paul M. Insel and Lenore F. Jacobson, eds., *What Do You Expect? An Inquiry into Self-Fulfilling Prophecies* (Menlo Park, Calif.: Cummings, 1975).

18.1 PERCEIVING OTHERS

List the name of the person in this class who you would most like to:

1. have a date with
2. go into business with
3. have dinner with
4. have meet your family
5. discuss your inner feelings with
6. work on a class project with
7. have at a party
8. have as a group leader
9. borrow money from
10. room with
11. drive cross-country with
12. be happy with
13. be sad with
14. be locked in a jail cell with
15. go camping with

Class members should discuss their results as a whole. Specifically, consider the following:

1. What cues did the people give that led you to feel as you did about them?
2. What quality of the person named led you to select him or her for that purpose?
3. Think of (but do not verbalize) the persons with whom you would least like to do the 15 things listed. Why? That is, what cues did these people give that led you to feel as you did about them?
4. What quality of the person led you to reject him or her for that purpose?
5. For which purposes do you think other people would select you? What qualities do people see in you that would lead them to select you for one or more of these 15 items?

18.2 PERCEIVING MY SELVES

The purposes of this Experiential Vehicle are to get us to better understand how we perceive ourselves, how others perceive us, and how we would like to perceive ourselves. In some instances and for some people these three perceptions will be the same; in most cases and for most people, however, they will be different.

Following this brief introduction are 11 lists of items (animals, birds, colors, communications media, dogs, drinks, water creatures, foods, music, sports, and transportation). Read over each list carefully, attempting to look past the purely physical existence of the objects to their "personalities" or "psychological meanings."

Instructions

1. First, for each of the 11 lists indicate the one item that best represents how you perceive yourself—not your physical self, but your psychological-philosophical self. Mark these items *MM* (Myself to Me).
2. Second, for each of the 11 lists select the one item that best represents how you feel others perceive you. By "others" is meant acquaintances—neither passing strangers nor close friends, but people you meet and talk with for some time—for example, people in this class. Mark these items *MO* (Myself to Others).
3. Third, for each of the 11 lists select the one item that best represents how you would like to be. Put differently, what items would your ideal self select? Mark these items *MI* (Myself as Ideal).

After all 11 lists are marked three times, discuss your choices in groups of five or six persons in any way you feel is meaningful. Your objective is to get a better perspective on how your self-perception compares with the perceptions of others and your ideal perception. In discussions you should try to state as clearly as possible why you selected the items you did and specifically what each selected item means to you at this time. You should also welcome any suggestions from the group members as to why they think you selected the items you did. You might also wish to integrate consideration of some or all of the following questions into your discussion.

1. How different are the items marked *MM* from *MO*? Why do you suppose this is so? Which is the more positive? Why?
2. How different are the items marked *MM* from *MI*? Why do you suppose this is so?
3. What do the number of differences between the items marked *MM* and the items marked *MI* mean for personal happiness?
4. How accurate were you in the items you marked *MO*? Ask members of the group which items they would have selected for you.
5. Which of the three perceptions (*MM, MO, MI*) is easiest to respond to? Which are you surest of?
6. Would you show these forms to your best same-sex friend? Your best opposite-sex friend? Your parents? Your children? Explain.

ANIMALS

_____ bear
_____ cobra
_____ deer
_____ fox
_____ hyena
_____ leopard
_____ lion
_____ monkey
_____ rabbit
_____ turtle

BIRDS

_____ albatross
_____ chicken
_____ eagle
_____ hawk
_____ ostrich
_____ owl
_____ parrot
_____ swan
_____ turkey
_____ vulture

COLORS

_____ black
_____ blue
_____ brown
_____ green
_____ gray
_____ pink
_____ purple
_____ red
_____ white
_____ yellow

COMMUNICATIONS MEDIA

_____ body language
_____ book
_____ film
_____ fourth-class mail
_____ gossip
_____ radio
_____ smoke signals
_____ special delivery letter
_____ telephone
_____ television

DOGS

_____ Afghan
_____ boxer
_____ Dalmatian
_____ Doberman pinscher
_____ German shepherd
_____ greyhound
_____ husky
_____ mutt
_____ poodle
_____ St. Bernard

DRINKS

_____ beer
_____ champagne
_____ coffee
_____ milk
_____ prune juice
_____ scotch
_____ sherry
_____ water
_____ wine
_____ hot chocolate

WATER CREATURES

_____ angelfish
_____ blowfish
_____ dolphin
_____ eel
_____ goldfish
_____ mermaid
_____ piranha
_____ shark
_____ whale
_____ Portuguese
man of war

FOODS

_____ apple pie
_____ Big Mac
_____ caviar
_____ filet mignon
_____ french fries
_____ ice cream sundae
_____ gelatin
_____ peanut butter
_____ tossed salad
_____ fiber cereal

MUSIC

_____ broadway/film
_____ country and western
_____ disco
_____ folk
_____ hymns
_____ jazz
_____ opera
_____ popular
_____ rock
_____ synthesized
(computerized)

SPORTS	TRANSPORTATION
_____ auto racing	_____ bicycle
_____ baseball	_____ bus
_____ boxing	_____ jet plane
_____ bullfighting	_____ horse and wagon
_____ chess	_____ kiddy car
_____ fishing	_____ motorcycle
_____ ice skating	_____ Rolls Royce
_____ skydiving	_____ skateboard
_____ tennis	_____ van
_____ yachting	_____ Volkswagen

18.3 PERCEPTION AND SIGNIFICANT OTHERS

All six interpersonal perceptual processes pertain to the ways in which we make judgments about people on the basis of insufficient evidence. These judgments, then, are inferential rather than factual statements about others. Of course, we never do have *all* the evidence, and because of this it is extremely important that our judgments be based on an accurate reading of at least the insufficient evidence. Since we will not stop making almost instant judgments of people, we should at least make these judgments as logically as possible. This exercise is designed to increase our awareness of the ways in which the six perceptual processes considered in this unit operate in us, and to raise questions pertaining to the logic of our judgments.

Instructions

The exercise may be completed in small groups of five or six students or with the entire class. Each member is supplied with a number of index cards. From the following Group Categories list, the group leader or instructor should select one and ask that each student write down five or six judgments they might make about members of this group. Students should not attempt to write down "logical" or "intellectually motivated" responses but rather the judgments they would probably make upon meeting or hearing about a member of this group. No names should be put on these cards, and no attempt should be made to discover the author of any particular card. The cards should be collected and read aloud by the group leader or instructor.

Discussion should center on the ways in which judgments are made and the ways in which the six perceptual processes discussed in this unit operate. Specifically, attention should be focused on the following:

1. The roles of primacy and recency in the formation of judgments about these groups

2. the operation of the self-fulfilling prophecy
3. the influence of perceptual accentuation
4. the nature of our implicit personality theory and the influence it exerts on our judgments of these groups
5. the operation of our tendency to maintain or establish consistency or balance
6. the role of stereotyping

After judgments for this group have been considered, another group category should be selected and the process repeated.

GROUP CATEGORIES

alcoholics	evangelists	Protestants
automobile mechanics	farmers	psychoanalysts
bartenders	feminists	psychologists
blacks	homosexuals	religious leaders (priests,
cartoonists	interior decorators	ministers, rabbis)
Catholics	Jews	rock singers
chefs	lawyers	stewardesses and stewards
children	lesbians	telephone operators
cocktail waitresses	movie stars	television repairpersons
comedians	musicians	textbook authors
communists	nurses	theater critics
construction workers	opera singers	thieves
convicts	pimps	truck drivers
delivery persons	police officers	unmarried men
doctors	politicians	unmarried women
dress designers	professors	whites
drug addicts	prostitutes	

18.4 CAUSAL ATTRIBUTION

For each of the following examples, indicate whether you think the behavior of the individual was due to *internal* causes—for example, personality characteristics and traits or various personal motives—or to *external* causes—for example, to the particular situation one is in, to the demands of others who might be in positions of authority, or to the behaviors of others. The behavior in question appears underlined.

1. Pat has just quit his job. No one else that we know has quit that job. Pat has quit a number of jobs in the last 5 years and has in fact quit this same job once before.

2. Mary has just failed her chemistry test. A number of other students (in fact, some 40 percent of the class) have also failed the test. Mary has never failed a chemistry test before and, in fact, has never failed any other test in her life.

3. *Liz tasted the wine, rejected it, and complained to the waiter.* No one else in the place seemed to complain about the wine. Liz has complained about the wine before and has frequently complained that her food was seasoned incorrectly, that the coffee was not hot enough, and so on.

4. *Russel took the children to the zoo.* Russel works for the Board of Education in a small town and taking the children on trips is one of his major functions. All people previously in the job have taken the children to the zoo. Russel has never taken any other children to the zoo.

5. *John ran from the dog.* A number of other people also ran from this dog. I was surprised to see John do this because he never ran from other animals before and never from this particular dog.

6. *Donna received all* A's *on her film projects.* In fact, everyone in the class got A's. This was the first A that Donna ever received in film and in fact the first A she ever received in any course.

After you have responded to all six examples, identify the information contained in the brief behavioral descriptions that enabled you to make judgments concerning (1) consensus, (2) consistency, and (3) distinctiveness. What combination of these three principles would lead you to conclude that the behavior was internally motivated? What combination would lead you to conclude that the behavior was externally motivated?

INTERPERSONAL LISTENING AND FEEDBACK

Upon completion of this unit, you should be able to:

1. define *listening*
2. list and explain the five obstacles to effective listening
3. list and explain the five guides to effective listening
4. identify and explain the three basic processes in sequential listening
5. define *feedback*
6. diagram and explain the model of the feedback cycle
7. distinguish between positive and negative feedback
8. identify at least four qualities of giving effective feedback
9. identify at least four qualities of receiving effective feedback
10. explain the concept of feedforward

Interpersonal communication can only exist to the extent that someone somewhere is listening. If we did not assume that someone was listening—attentively and with sensitivity—we would probably stop talking. Interpersonal communication is a two-way process; a listener is just as important as a speaker. At the same time that we are listening, we are also responding, we are also sending messages of response back to the speaker. These are feedback messages. Here, then, we continue to address the issue of message reception in terms of listening and feedback.

THE IMPORTANCE OF LISTENING

There can be little doubt that we listen a great deal. Upon awakening we listen to the radio. On the way to school we listen to friends, to people around us, and perhaps to screeching cars, singing birds, or falling rain. In school our listening day starts in earnest, and we sit in class after class listening to the teacher, to comments by other students, and sometimes even to ourselves. We listen to friends at lunch and return to class to listen to more teachers. We arrive home and again listen to our family and friends. Perhaps we then listen to records, radio, or television. All in all, we listen for the entirety of our waking day.

Numerous studies have been conducted to determine the percentage of **285** our communication time devoted to listening as compared with speaking, reading, and writing. In one study it was found that adults in a variety of occupations spent approximately 70 percent of their day in one of the four communication activities. Of that time, approximately 42 percent was spent in listening, 32 percent in talking, 15 percent in reading, and 11 percent in writing. Listening percentages for students were even higher.

That we listen a great deal of the time, then, can hardly be denied. Whether we listen effectively or efficiently, however, is another matter. For some reason we do not feel that it is necessary to improve our listening or that it is even possible. If you search through your catalogue, you will find numerous courses designed to improve writing skills. And, of course, you will even find courses designed to improve your tennis, golf, and fencing abilities. Yet you will probably not find a single course in listening, despite its importance and its pervasiveness. The one exception to this general rule is found in music departments, where courses in listening to music will be offered. If it is useful to teach "music listening," wouldn't a similar concern for language and speech be logical? It seems to be assumed that because we listen without a great deal of effort, we open our ears somewhat as we open a drain. But this view, as we shall see, is far from accurate.

In actual practice most of us are relatively poor listeners, but our listening behaviors could be made more effective and more efficient. Given the amount of time we engage in listening, the improvement of that skill would seem well worth the required effort. And it does take effort. Listening is not an easy matter; it takes time and energy to listen effectively.

Although the prevailing attitude is that listening benefits the listener—and certainly it does—it benefits the speaker as well. When we listen to someone we generally demonstrate supportiveness and in so doing provide the individual with the environment necessary to continue communicating without fear of criticism or negative evaluation. The supportive listener, then, helps the speaker to pursue an issue or line of argument unhindered by defensiveness or fear. Listening also helps us to build meaningful relationships. Here the benefits accrue to both speaker and listener. As Carl R. Rogers and Richard E. Farson point out, listening "builds deep, positive relationships and tends to alter constructively the attitudes of the listener. Listening is a growth experience." And, it should be emphasized, this growth experience refers to the person who is being listened to as well as to the listener.

A Definition of Listening

By *listening* we mean an active process of receiving aural stimuli. Contrary to popular conception, listening is an active rather than a passive process. Listening does not just happen; we must make it happen. Listening takes energy and a commitment to engage in often difficult labor. Rogers and Farson define *listening* as an active process in the following way: "It is called 'active' because the listener has a very definite responsibility. He does not passively absorb the words which are spoken to him. He actively tries to grasp the facts and the feelings in what he hears, and he tries, by his listening, to help the speaker work out his own problems."

Listening involves receiving stimuli and is thus distinguished from hearing as a physiological process. The word *receiving* is used here to imply that stimuli are taken in by the listener and are in some way processed or utilized. For at least some amount of time, the signals received are retained by the listener.

Listening involves aural stimuli, that is, signals (sound waves) received by the ear. Listening therefore is not limited to verbal signals but encompasses all signals sent by means of fluctuations in air—noises as well as words, music as well as prose.

That listening deals with aural stimuli should not be taken to imply that it is uninfluenced by nonverbal factors. Obviously it is. Nonverbal sources of interference include, for instance, extreme beauty or extreme ugliness, which will often distract our attention from listening, as would peculiar facial or body movements; and the esthetics of the surroundings—whether appealing or unappealing—will often divert attention from listening as we concentrate on the famous painting over the fireplace, the patches of dirt on the floor, or the smell of food. I often wonder how elementary school students can concentrate on what the teacher is saying when the room is covered with pictures, maps, penmanship directions, flags, word cards, arithmetic examples, holiday decorations, and all sorts of other stimuli competing for attention. Equally significant are nonverbal factors that facilitate listening. Comfortable (but not too comfortable) and close (but not too close) seating for conversation helps us in listening. Consistent facial and body movements—those that do not call attention to themselves—also help.

OBSTACLES TO EFFECTIVE LISTENING

Listening is at best a difficult matter. Yet it may be made easier, more pleasant, and more efficient if some of the obstacles or barriers to effective listening are eliminated. Although many such obstacles could be identified, five general classes of obstacles are considered here.

Prejudging the Communication

Whether in an auditorium listening to a lecture or in a small group of people, there is a strong tendency to prejudge the communications of others as uninteresting or irrelevant to our own needs or to the task at hand. Often we compare these communications with something we might say or with something we might be doing instead of "just listening." Generally, listening to others comes in a poor second.

By prejudging a communication as uninteresting we are in effect lifting the burden of listening from our shoulders. If we have already determined that the communication is uninteresting, then there is no reason to listen. So we just tune out the speaker and let our minds drift back to last Saturday night.

Most communications are, at least potentially, interesting and relevant. If we prejudge them and tune them out, our preconceptions will never be proven wrong. At the same time, however, we close ourselves off from potentially useful information. Perhaps most important is that we do not give the other person a fair hearing.

Rehearsing a Response

For the most part we are, as Wendell Johnson put it, our own most enchanted listeners. No one speaks as well or on such interesting topics as we do. If we could listen just to ourselves, listening would be no problem.

Particularly in small group situations, but also in larger settings, the speaker may say something with which we disagree; for the remainder of that speaker's time we rehearse our response or rebuttal or question. We then imagine his or her reply to our response and then our response to his or her response and so on and on. Meanwhile, we have missed whatever else the speaker had to say—perhaps even the part that would make our question unnecessary or irrelevant or that might raise other and more significant questions.

Filtering Out Messages

I once had a teacher who claimed that whatever he could not immediately understand was not worth reading or listening to; if it had to be worked at, it was not worth the effort. I often wonder how he managed to learn, how he was intellectually stimulated, if indeed he was. Depending on our own intellectual equipment, many of the messages that we confront will need careful consideration and in-depth scrutiny. Listening will be difficult, but the alternative— missing out on what is said—seems even less pleasant than stretching and straining our minds.

Perhaps more serious than filtering out difficult messages is filtering out unpleasant ones. None of us want to be told that something we believe in is untrue, that people we care for are unpleasant, or that ideals we hold are self-destructive. And yet these are the very messages we need to listen to with great care. These are the very messages that will lead us to examine and reexamine our implicit and unconscious assumptions. If we filter out this kind of information, we will be left with a host of unstated and unexamined assumptions and premises that will influence us without our influencing them. That prospect is not a very pleasant one.

A different type of message, but one that presents many listeners with considerable difficulty, is the expression of positive feelings. Many people become awkward and ill at ease when listening to such expressions and in turn often make the speaker uncomfortable as well. The result of this reciprocal awkwardness is the general suppression of expressions of positive emotions, of warmth, of caring—a state of affairs that no one really wants to encourage.

Much as we have to learn to listen to and respond to negative expressions, we also have to learn to listen to and respond to positive expressions. One of the best ways to improve our ability to deal with such pleasant and reinforcing expressions is to engage in an experience such as the "Positive Words" exercise in Experiential Vehicle 25.2.

Using the Thought–Speech Time Differential Inefficiently

It should be obvious that we can think much more quickly than a speaker can speak. Consequently, in listening to someone our minds can process the information much more quickly than the speaker can give it out. At communication conventions it was especially interesting to listen to Ralph Nichols, a nationally known expert on listening. Unlike most speakers, Nichols would speak very rapidly. At first, his speech sounded peculiar because it was so rapid. Yet it was extremely easy to understand; our minds did not wander as often as they did when listening to someone who spoke at a normal speed. I would not recommend that we all speak more rapidly since there are various side effects that are difficult to control. But it is important to realize that listening results in a great deal of time left over; only a portion of our time is used in listening to the information in the messages.

Given this state of affairs, we are left with a number of possibilities—from letting our minds wander back to that great Saturday night to utilizing the time for understanding and learning the message. Obviously, the latter would be the more efficient course of action. With this extra time, then, we might review concepts already made by the speaker, search for additional meanings, attempt to predict what the speaker will say next, and so on. The important point is that we stay on the topic with the speaker and don't let our thoughts wander to distant places from which they will not return.

Focusing Attention on Language or Delivery

It is difficult for many people not to concentrate on the stylistic peculiarities of an individual. In hearing a clever phrase or sentence, for example, it is difficult to resist the temptation to dwell on it and analyze it. Similarly, it is difficult for many not to focus on various gestures or particular aspects of a voice. Focusing on these dimensions of communication only diverts time and energy away from the message itself. This is not to say that such behaviors are not important but only that we can fall into the trap of devoting too much attention to the way the message is packaged and not enough to the message itself.

GUIDES TO EFFECTIVE LISTENING

Listening ability—like speaking, reading, and writing ability—can be improved. In each case there are no easy rules or simple formulas. There are, however, some guidelines that should be of considerable value.

Listen Actively

Perhaps the first step to listening improvement is the recognition that it is not a passive activity; it is not a process that will happen if we simply do nothing to stop it. We may hear without effort, but we cannot listen without effort.

Listening is a difficult process; in many ways it is more demanding than speaking. In speaking we are in control of the situation; we can talk about what we like in the way we like. In listening we are forced to follow the pace, the content, and the language set by the speaker.

Perhaps the best preparation for active listening is to act as an active listener. This may seem trivial and redundant. In practice, however, this may be the most often abused rule of effective listening. Students often, for example, come into class, put their feet up on a nearby desk, nod their head to the side, and expect to listen effectively. It just does not happen that way. Recall, for example, how your body almost automatically reacts to important news. Almost immediately you assume an upright posture, cock your head to the speaker, and remain relatively still and quiet. We do this almost reflexively because this is how we listen most effectively. This is not to say that we should be tense and uncomfortable, but only that our bodies should reflect an active mind.

Listen for Different Levels of Meaning

In Shakespeare's *Julius Caesar* Marc Antony, in giving the funeral oration for Caesar, says: "I come to bury Caesar, not to praise him. / The evil that men do lives after them, / the good is oft interred with their bones." And later: "For Brutus is an honourable man; / So are they all, all honourable men." But Antony, as we know, did not come to bury Caesar and certainly not to convince the crowd that Brutus was, in fact, an honorable man. Instead he came to incite the crowd to avenge the death of Caesar, his friend.

In most messages there is an obvious meaning that a literal reading of the words and sentences enable us to derive. But there is often another level of meaning; sometimes, as in *Julius Caesar*, it is the opposite of the expressed literal meaning; sometimes, it seems totally unrelated to the literal meaning of the verbalized messages. In reality few messages have only one level of meaning; messages that do have only one meaning seem the exception. Most messages function on at least two or three levels at the same time. Consider some of the frequently heard messages: A friend asks you how you like his new haircut. Another friend asks you how you like her painting. On one level, the meaning is clear: Do you like the haircut? Do you like the painting? But it seems reasonable to assume that on another level, and perhaps a more important level, they are asking you to say something positive about them—about his appearance, about her artistic ability. They seem to be asking for positive stroking, asking you to say something pleasant and positive. The parent who verbalizes how hard he or she has worked at the office or in the home may well be asking for some expression of appreciation rather than merely complaining as it may at first appear. The child who complains about the unfairness of the children in the playground may be asking for affection and love, for some expression of caring, for some indication that you understand. The college student who expresses the desire to quit school and get a full-time job may be asking for encouragement or perhaps for some understanding of the soon-to-be-received, not-so-great grades.

In interpersonal listening we have to be particularly sensitive to the different levels of meaning because if we respond only to the surface level communication (to only the literal meaning), we will miss the opportunity to make meaningful contact with the other person's feelings and real needs. If we say to the parent, "You're always complaining. I bet you really love working so hard," we are failing to meet the needs of this call for understanding and appreciation.

Deciphering the Message

In attempting to decipher the different levels of meaning, a few previously considered principles might prove useful. Meaning is communicated both verbally and nonverbally, by what is said as well as by what is done with the face, the eyes, the hands, and so forth. Sweating hands, shaking knees, a limp handshake, a wink of the eye, the avoidance of direct eye contact, when used in conjunction with verbal messages, alter those verbal messages in significant ways and clue us into the likelihood that there is more to this message than the mere literal meaning. Further, we should recognize that the meaning of a communication lies also in what is omitted. The parents of teenagers who talk about the teenage drug problem of everyone else's teenagers but never once mention their own children (and may never even think of their own children in this connection) are communicating some important information that deserves looking into.

Earlier we noted that all messages have a content and a relationship dimension. Listening for different levels of meaning will be aided if we focus on both relational and content aspects. The student who constantly criticizes or challenges the teacher is on one level communicating disagreement over content; the student is debating the issues. On another level—the relationship level—however, the student may well be voicing objections to the instructor's authority or perhaps to the instructor's authoritarianism. If the instructor is to deal effectively with the student, both types of messages must be listened to and both must receive a response.

We also previously considered the quality of immanent reference—the inevitability of talking about one's immediate situation and about oneself. In listening for the different levels of meaning, we need to recognize that one inevitably talks about oneself, from one's own point of view, colored by one's needs, wants, and desires, on the basis of one's own previous experiences, and so on. Whatever a person says is, in part, a function of who that person is, and to listen for the different levels of meaning is to attend to those personal, self-referential messages.

All this is not to say that we should disregard the literal meaning of inter-personal messages or that we should constantly focus attention on what else the speaker might be attempting to communicate. If we do this, we will quickly find that our listening problems are over; no one will be talking with us anymore. We need to walk a reasonable line between the literal and the underlying meanings in the messages we receive. We need to become sensitive to the underlying meanings in many messages but not preoccupied with them to the point that we see and hear nothing else. We need to be ready to respond to the underlying messages while not becoming obsessed with uncovering everyone's hidden meanings. Perhaps the best guideline to use is to respond to the various levels of meaning in the messages of others as you would like others to respond to yours—sensitively but not obsessively, ready but not overanxious.

Listen with Empathy

It is relatively easy to learn to listen for understanding or for comprehension. But this is only a part of communication. We also need to feel what the speaker feels; we need to empathize with the speaker.

To empathize with others is to feel with them, to see the world as they see

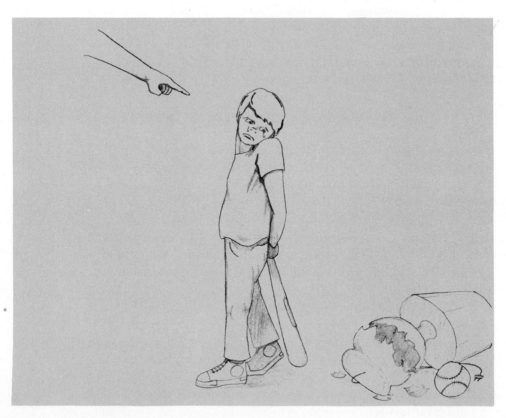

Sometimes it is difficult to listen with empathy.

it, to feel what they feel. Only when we achieve this will we be able to fully understand another's meaning. Carl Rogers calls this "listening with understanding," which means "to see the expressed idea and attitude from the other person's point of view, to sense how it feels to him, to achieve his frame of reference in regard to the thing he is talking about." In a similar vein, Charles Kelly notes that "empathic listening" occurs "when the person participates in the spirit or feeling of his environment as a communication receiver. This does not suggest that the listener is uncritical or always in agreement with what is communicated, but rather that his primary interest is to become fully and accurately aware of what is going on." There is no fast method for achieving empathy with another individual; but it is something we should work toward. It is important that we see the teacher's point of view, not from that of our own but from that of the teacher. And it is equally important for the teacher to see the student's point of view from that of the student.

So often we witness behavior of others that seems to us foolish and ridiculous. Popular college students might intellectually understand the reasons for the depression of the unpopular student, but that will not enable them to emotionally understand the feelings of depression. What popular students need to do is to put themselves in the position of the unpopular student, to role play a bit, and begin to feel his or her feelings and think his or her thoughts. Then these students will be in a somewhat better position to "really understand," or to empathize.

Rogers suggests that one way to improve our empathic ability when in an argument or a heated discussion is to institute the rule that each person may speak for himself or herself only after he or she has first restated both the ideas and the feelings of the previous speaker to that speaker's satisfaction. Then and only then may the individual speak for himself or herself.

Listen with an Open Mind

Listening with an open mind is extremely difficult. In counseling students one of the most difficult tasks is to make them realize that even though they may dislike a particular teacher, they can still learn something from him or her. For some reason many people will attempt to punish the people they dislike by not listening to them. Of course, if the situation is that of teacher and student, then it is only the student who suffers by losing out on significant material.

We also need to learn to continue listening fairly even though some signal has gone up in the form of an out-of-place expression or a hostile remark. Listening often stops when such a remark is made. Admittedly, to continue listening with an open mind is a difficult matter, yet here it is particularly important that listening continue.

Listen Critically

Although we need to emphasize that we should listen with an open mind and with empathy, it should not be assumed that we should listen uncritically.

Quite the contrary. We need to listen fairly but critically if meaningful communication is to take place. As intelligent and educated citizens, it is our responsibility to critically evaluate what we hear. While it is very easy simply to listen to a friend and nod agreement, it is extremely important that what is said be evaluated and critically analyzed. Friends have biases, too; at times consciously and at times unconsciously these biases creep into discussions. They need to be identified and brought to the surface by the critical listener. Contrary to what most people will argue, the vast majority of our friends will appreciate the responses of critical listeners. It demonstrates that someone is listening.

FEEDBACK AS A REGULATOR

Feedback is information concerning the progress or lack of progress being made by the communication source. On the basis of this information the source may or may not adjust, modify, strengthen, deemphasize, or change the content or form of his or her messages.

The most popular and perhaps most logical way to explain feedback in communication is with a mechanical analogy. The clearest mechanical feedback system is the thermostat. Let us say that we set the thermostat at the desired temperature of 68 degrees. When the temperature rises above 68 degrees, the thermostat sends information in the form of an electrical signal to the heat-producing mechanism, which decreases the heat production. When the temperature falls below 68 degrees, the thermostat sends information that results in an increase in the heat production. In this way the temperature is maintained at about 68 degrees. This is an example of a negative feedback mechanism; information about the room temperature is fed back to the heat-producing mechanism when the temperature deviates from the predetermined desired level. This negative feedback serves a corrective function. Now consider a thermostat that works in the opposite way: when the temperature rises above 68 degrees, the thermostat sends information to the heat-producing mechanism that raises the temperature. This higher heat then leads the thermostat to send additional information to raise the heat even more, and so on. Alternatively, consider the situation in which the temperature falls below 68 degrees. This would trigger the thermostat to send information to the heat-producing mechanism to lower the heat production, which would further lower the temperature in the room. This then leads the thermostat to instruct the heat-producing mechanism to further lower the heat output, and so on. The result would be either extreme heat or extreme cold. This is an example of a positive feedback system; information about the room temperature is fed back to the heat-producing mechanism to increase the deviation from the established predetermined level.

A Model of the Feedback Cycle

Feedback in human communication is similar to, though by no means identical with, the feedback in the mechanical system of the thermostat. The model presented in Figure 19.1 illustrates the concept of feedback in human communication. The solid arrows going from source to receiver represent the *object messages,* that is, the messages about the people, objects, and events in the world. The dotted arrows going from the receiver to the source represent the messages about the object messages, or the *metamessages.* These messages we call feedback. *Feedback* messages are information sent back by the receiver to the source; they are the receiver's responses to the messages of the source. The short arrows going back to the source represent the feedback that the source gets from his or her own message production; for example, we hear ourselves when we speak, we feel ourselves when we gesture.

The model is intended to represent visually a number of different characteristics concerning feedback. First, feedback is constantly occurring; it is not something that happens at the end of a public speech or after the television program is over or after we say goodnight. Rather feedback is being emitted throughout the communication encounter in much the same way that object messages are emitted throughout the encounter.

The continuous lines are used to emphasize the fact that the feedback influences the object message, which influence the subsequent feedback message, which in turn influences the next object message, and so on. Object messages and metamessages are interdependent; each influences the other.

The model also illustrates that the feedback from the receiver and the feedback from the self, both of which may be received simultaneously or sequentially, are distinguishable by the source. A normal source does not confuse feedback from the self with that from receivers. Pathological sources frequently do make this confusion, the paranoid being the clearest example.

Finally, the juxtaposition of the object messages and the feedback messages is intended to indicate that feedback may be understood and analyzed in the same general way as object messages. Feedback, like object messages, may come through all channels—auditory, visual, and so on. Feedback is also subject to noise interference and distortion. Feedback represents only a part of the

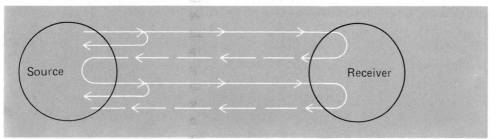

*FIGURE 19.1
A Model of the
Feedback Cycle.*

receiver's total response to the object messages, just as the object messages represent only a part of the source's thoughts and ideas.

Positive and Negative Feedback

Both positive and negative feedback occur in other types of systems. Negative feedback is seen clearly in biological systems. When your blood pressure rises, receptors in certain arteries are stretched and send nerve impulses to the brain. The brain then sends signals to dilate the blood vessels, which reduces the blood pressure. Conversely, if blood pressure falls below the acceptable level, messages are sent to constrict the blood vessels and thus to speed up the heart and raise the blood pressure to an acceptable level. One of the most common manifestations of positive feedback is the snowball effect. As a small snowball rolls, it collects snow and becomes larger. In its larger size it collects even more snow. As it grows its capacity to collect more snow also grows. The cycle is a continuous positive one. Now consider the operation of negative and positive feedback in interpersonal communication.

Negative feedback in interpersonal communication may be manifested in numerous ways, such as looks of disapproval, a lack of interest, negative verbalizations, and disagreements. The major function of negative feedback is to provide the source with information that the message deviates from the predetermined desired effect. This negative feedback provides the source with the information that he or she needs to modify, change, alter, redirect, or revise the messages being sent. Negative feedback also has other effects on the source. For example, when negative feedback is received, mistakes on the part of the source increase (there are more false starts, more sentence changes, more stutters, and more omitted syllables). There are more linguistic errors—errors of pronunciation, articulation, semantics, and syntax. There are more frequent shifts in topic and focus and a general increase in defensiveness. There is a decrease in the number of verbalizations; the source becomes less willing to talk or communicate in general.

Positive feedback, on the other hand, consists of such manifestations as looks of approval, looks of interest, positive verbalizations, and expressed or implied agreement. When the source receives positive feedback, he or she is in effect informed that the message is being received as intended and that no significant deviations from this intended goal are apparent. On the basis of this information the source may intensify, strengthen, continue, or enlarge upon the message he or she is already sending. The other effects of positive feedback are basically the opposite of those of negative feedback. There is a decrease in blunders and an increase in the number of verbalizations. There is a decrease in linguistic errors and a tendency to continue with the topic and focus that originally led to the positive feedback. There is also a corresponding decrease in defensiveness.

EFFECTIVE FEEDBACK

Like all message reception processes, feedback may be ineffective, effective, or anywhere in between these two extremes. In an effort to strengthen the chances of our feedback being effective, some suggestions are offered here both for the giving of feedback and for the receiving of feedback.

Giving Feedback Effectively

The process of giving effective feedback seems characterized by at least five qualities: immediateness, honesty, appropriateness, clarity, and informativeness.

Immediateness. The most effective feedback is that which is most immediate. Ideally, feedback is sent immediately after the message is received. Feedback, like reinforcement, loses its effectiveness with time; the longer we wait to praise or punish, for example, the less effect it will have. To say to children that they will get punished when Daddy comes home probably does little to eliminate the undesirable behavior simply because the punishment or feedback comes so long after the behavior.

Honesty. Feedback should be an honest reaction to a communication. To say this is not to provide license for overt hostility or cruelty but to say that feedback should not merely be a series of messages that the speaker wants to hear and that will build up his or her ego. Feedback concerning one's understanding of the message as well as one's agreement with the message should be honest. We should neither be ashamed or afraid to admit that we did not understand a message, nor should we hesitate to assert our disagreement.

We can, of course, consistently give speakers the feedback they want. You can shake your head, indicating understanding, as the teacher spouts incomprehensible drivel and nod agreement with his or her equally incomprehensible theories. This may make the teacher feel that you are intelligent and clever. But note the effect that this kind of behavior has: It reinforces the behavior of the teacher. It will lead that teacher to continue addressing classes with this same incomprehensible drivel. In effect, you have told the teacher that he or she is doing a good job by your positive feedback. The same is true with any speaker in any type of communication situation.

The quality of teaching, and in fact of all the communicative arts, is in large part a reflection of the listeners; we are the ones who keep the levels of communication where they are.

Appropriateness. Feedback should be appropriate to the general communication situation. For the most part we have learned what is appropriate and what is not appropriate from observing others as we grew up. And so there is no need for spelling out what is and what is not appropriate here. We should recognize, however, that appropriateness is a learned concept; consequently, what is appropriate for our culture is not necessarily appropriate for another culture. Thus, for students to stamp their feet when a teacher walks in might signal approval or respect in one culture but might signal hostility in another.

We should also note that feedback to the message should be kept distinct from feedback to the speaker. We need to make clear, in disagreeing with speakers, for example, that we are disagreeing with what they are saying and not necessarily rejecting them as people. We may dislike what a person says but like the person who is saying it.

Clarity. Feedback should be clear on at least two counts. It should be clear enough so that speakers can perceive that it is feedback to the message and not just a reflection of something you ate that did not agree with you. Feedback should also be clear in meaning; if it is to signal understanding, then it should be clear to the speaker that that is what you are signaling. If you are disagreeing, then that, too, should be clear.

Informativeness. The feedback you send to speakers should convey some information; it should tell them something they did not already know.

In any classroom there are always some students who sit with the same expression on their faces regardless of what is going on. You could lecture on the physics of sound or you could show a stag film and their expression would remain unchanged—or at least relatively so. These people communicate no information and serve only to confuse the speaker.

Similarly, to always respond in the same way conveys no information. To communicate information, responses must be, in part at least, unpredictable. If speakers are able to completely predict how you will respond to something they say, then your response conveys no information and does not serve any useful feedback function.

Receiving Feedback Effectively

Just as we can use guidance in how to give feedback, we can also use guidance in how to receive feedback. In fact, it probably takes a great deal more effort and ingenuity to respond appropriately to feedback than to give feedback to others. The process of receiving feedback effectively is characterized by sensitivity, supportiveness, open-mindedness, helpfulness, and specificity.

Sensitivity. Perhaps the first step in receiving and responding to feedback is to develop a sensitivity to it—a sensitivity that will enable us to perceive feedback in situations where it might normally go unnoticed. Feedback is given to us at all times, through both verbal and nonverbal means. Most often the feedback comes in the form of nonverbal messages—the puzzled face, the wide smile, the limp handshake, and so on. These are examples of feedback to which we have to learn to become sensitive. And, of course, verbal feedback also comes in many forms. At times the verbal feedback is obvious; it is said directly and without any attempt at subtlety: "Your humor is gross," "You walk like an elephant," "When you look at me that way, I want to kiss you." But most often verbal feedback comes to us in more subtle ways—the quick, almost throwaway remark about your method of approaching someone; the slow, belabored effort to say something good about your newly decorated apartment. Feedback may also be given by silence, as when someone would normally be expected to say something but says nothing. When you ask someone for a date and at three different times there are three different excuses and the person does not suggest an alternative time, then perhaps there are no time conflicts after all. Perhaps the person is saying "no" in an imperfect and indirect way.

Supportiveness. We need to be supportive of the person giving the feedback in order to avoid, or at least suspend, any defensive responses. Your own responsiveness to the feedback will in large measure determine the comprehensiveness and depth of the feedback you receive. Defensiveness is usually taken as a sign to stop giving feedback. If the feedback is stopped, we stand to lose a great deal of insight that we might otherwise have gained. Often, for example, in hearing negative feedback there is a tendency to respond in kind: "If you think I come on strong, you should have seen yourself last night." This, of course, does nothing to help the cause of responsible and helpful feedback. If we make the assumption that the person giving the feedback has our own betterment in mind, and this seems a reasonable enough assumption, and if we keep this clearly in mind, our defensiveness should be lessened.

Open-Mindedness. We need to learn to listen to feedback with an open mind. If the feedback is negative, and especially if it centers on some issue of high ego involvement, then it becomes particularly difficult to accept and we tend to block it out very quickly, even before we hear the entire message. We obviously need to listen to the entire feedback message and to suspend judgment until we have heard it all and understood it all. This is not to say that we must therefore uncritically accept everything anyone else says about us; certainly we should not. We need to evaluate critically what is said, accept what seems reasonable and useful, and reject what seems unreasonable and not useful. But we should only make these decisions after we have fully listened to and fully understood what the individual is saying.

Helpfulness. It seems strange to advise someone to help out the person giving the feedback, especially if that feedback is negative. And yet that is exactly what we must do. The task of giving feedback is a difficult one, and the person giving us the feedback needs to be helped along. Often initial feedback will be given in general and highly abstract terms. In this form the feedback is not very useful. Yet most of these general and abstract comments can be made more specific and more useful, and hence some energy may be profitably

devoted to enabling the person giving the feedback to become more specific.
And so, for example, it might help if, in hearing the feedback, we would say,
"Do you mean when I said . . . ?" or "Are you referring to the time I . . . ?" This
type of behavior will also demonstrate supportiveness, and the feedback giver
will probably be more anxious and more willing to supply additional and more
specific feedback. We need also to be helpful to the feedback giver in an
encouraging way. We need to provide the conditions conducive to the giving of
clear and honest feedback.

Specificity. A principle closely related to helpfulness is specificity. When
listening to feedback we need to translate it into very specific, preferably
behavioral, terms. We need to think of the feedback in terms of what it means
to our own specific behavior—today's and tomorrow's. That is, we need to ask
what we can learn on the basis of this feedback: How can we adjust our interpersonal verbal and nonverbal messages on the basis of this feedback?

FEEDFORWARD

When the distinguished literary critic, author, and semanticist I. A. Richards was asked by *Saturday Review* to contribute to its "What I Have Learned"
series—a series of articles in which leading theorists were asked to record their
most important insights and learnings—he chose to write on feedforward. "I
am not sure I have learned anything else as important," noted Richards. "I have
been able to realize what a prime role what I have come to call 'feedforward'
has in all our doings."

Whereas feedback is information that is sent back to the source informing
him or her as to the effects of the messages, *feedforward* is information that is
sent prior to the regular messages telling us something about future messages.
Feedforward messages are predictions we make concerning what will take
place. Perhaps the most important type of feedforward is the information we
tell ourselves about the messages we expect to receive or how we expect our
own messages to be received by others. For example, whenever we approach
an interpersonal communication situation, we make certain predictions: they
won't like me; I'm going to convince mother to give me the car tonight; I'm sure
he'll go out with me on Saturday night. These predictions are feedforward. We
are in effect identifying for ourselves what messages we expect to receive in
the near future.

When we meet someone we often make predictions about the behaviors
and qualities we expect these people to evidence. Often we make these predictions even before we say "hello." We say to ourselves: she's a snob, he's guilty,
she's honest, he has a sense of humor, she seems warm and friendly, and so on.
After we get to know the person a bit more, we then match what the person
says or does against our initial predictions—the feedforward messages—and

we evaluate how accurate we have been. At times we do this consciously: most often we do it without conscious awareness.

In scientific analysis and research, feedforward may be seen as the hypothesis-making step in scientific inquiry. The actual results or findings are the feedback that confirm or deny the feedforward predictions or hypotheses. In writing this book, I had certain goals or aims in mind; I wanted to accomplish certain things. These goals and the outline of the text were my feedforward; they were my guides. As I produced each unit, I compared the completed unit (the results) with this initial feedforward to see if I had indeed accomplished what I set out to do. The completed unit provided me with feedback concerning how close I came to my feedforward predictions. The feedforward was my plan; the feedback was information about the results or outcomes. I used the feedforward to guide my behaviors and I used the feedback to see how well I did.

We also send feedforward messages to others to inform them as to what kinds of messages are to follow and even to provide some guidelines for them in interpreting the messages that do follow. Such examples of feedforward would include a smile as you approach someone at a party which tells that person that the future messages will be positive ones; a scowl on your face as you wait at the door for your spouse to return home communicates that future messages will be unpleasant and negative; a friendly "hello" tells someone that you are pleased to see him or her and wish to communicate further. Feedforward messages are metacommunicational; they are comments on other messages, on messages that are yet to be sent.

Feedforward is sometimes only vaguely conceptualized, as when we approach someone with the subconscious thought of being responded to positively (or negatively), or when we walk into a classroom on the first day of the term and, upon seeing the teacher, settle back to a predicted relaxing and enjoyable experience (or brace for a tedious and boring one). At other times feedforward is finely and completely detailed—as when an author may develop a thorough outline of an article to be written with every idea to be developed in the article noted in the outline.

Feedforward is not something that we may or may not choose to use. It is inevitable. The question that should concern us is how we can use feedforward most effectively. Some guidelines may be suggested. First, it helps if we maintain an awareness that we consciously and subconsciously make these predictions and that these predictions influence our perceptions. If we make a prediction that someone is a snob, we tend to activate a self-fulfilling prophecy. What we need to realize is that had we made a different prediction—say that the person was shy—then we would very likely have interpreted the behaviors differently. Feedforward influences what we perceive—almost invariably, we see what we want to see and what we expect to see. It is wise to keep in mind that these may be illusions.

When we do make such interpersonal predictions, they should be made with a tentativeness rather than a certainty. We should make them so that we are prepared to see contradictory evidence. We should be psychologically ready to have our predictions fail to materialize. This is not to say that we should expect our feedforward predictions to be erroneous, but merely that we should be ready to deal with the possibility that we have made inaccurate predictions.

It helps to develop a feedforward plan in some detail when dealing with long messages—with speeches, compositions, essays, articles, and books. When we do this we will have a clearer focus for our behaviors and will know where we are in our plan at any given moment, where we have to go next, and where we eventually want to wind up.

Lastly, all feedforwards—whether of the vaguely conceived or of the detailed type—should be kept flexible. We should be ready to revise our plan in light of new ideas and new evidence. When a person's behavior does not confirm our feedforward hypothesis, we should be careful not to say too readily, as so many people do, that the observed behavior is not typical. Rather, we should consider the possibility that our feedforward needs to be revised and that maybe this person is not a snob, is not warm, is not honest, and so on. Even when we make detailed plans, we need to realize that these too should be kept flexible and that as we pursue our goals, our methods may need to be changed and that even the goals themselves may change.

When you entered college you made certain plans and certain predictions about what you wanted to study and what you wanted to become. After exposure to varied courses, ideas, and philosophies you may wish to revise your plans and strategies for attaining your goals. When your plans are tentative rather than certain, detailed rather than vague, and flexible rather than rigid, you will be much better able to institute useful and productive changes and will be better able to accept them.

SOURCES

On the nature of listening and for numerous studies, see Larry L. Barker, *Listening Behavior* (Englewood Cliffs, N.J.: Prentice-Hall, 1971), and Carl Weaver, *Human Listening: Processes and Behavior* (Indianapolis: Bobbs-Merrill, 1972). Perhaps the classic in the area is Ralph Nichols and Leonard Stevens, *Are You Listening?* (New York: McGraw-Hill, 1957). Listening from the point of view of auditory attention is covered in Neville Moray, *Listening and Attention* (Baltimore: Penguin, 1969). Ella Erway, *Listening: A Programmed Approach,* 2d ed. (New York: McGraw-Hill, 1979), covers the nature of listening, its importance, and the ways in which it can be improved. An insightful and practical view of listening is presented in Ernst G. Beier and Evans G. Valens, *People Reading: How We Control Others, How They Control Us* (New York: Warner Books, 1975).

The obstacles to effective listening covered here are also covered in a number of books on listening, such as those noted above. Similarly, the guides to effective listening presented here are also considered in other texts in different ways. A useful overview is Ralph Nichols, "Do We Know How to Listen? Practical Helps in a Modern Age," *Communication Education* 10 (1961):118–124. This article contains 10 suggestions for improving listening. Most of the suggestions for improving listening—those presented here as well as those presented in other texts—owe their formulation to the work of Ralph Nichols. See also *Are You Listening?*, cited above. Another useful and informative source is Wendell Johnson, *Verbal Man* (New York: Colliers, 1969).

On empathic listening, see Carl R. Rogers, "Communication: Its Blocking and Its Facilitation," in *Communication: Concepts and Processes*, rev. ed., Joseph A. DeVito, ed. (Englewood Cliffs, N.J.: Prentice-Hall, 1976), and Charles M. Kelly, "Empathetic Listening," in *Small Group Communication: A Reader*, 3d ed., Robert S. Cathcart and Larry A. Samovar, eds. (Dubuque, Iowa: Brown, 1979). One of the most insightful discussions on listening is provided by Carl R. Rogers and Richard E. Farson, "Active Listening," in *Communication: Concepts and Processes*, 3d ed., Joseph A. DeVito, ed. (Englewood Cliffs, N.J.: Prentice-Hall, 1981). An approach to listening similar to that advocated in this unit may be found in Baxter and Corinne Geeting, *How to Listen Assertively* (New York: Monarch, 1976).

For serial (or sequential) communication, read William V. Haney, "Serial Communication of Information in Organizations," in *Communication: Concepts and Processes*, cited above, and *Communication and Organizational Behavior: Text and Cases*, 3d ed. (Homewood, Ill.: Irwin, 1973). On feedback, see John Keltner, *Interpersonal Speech Communication: Elements and Structures* (Belmont, Calif.: Wadsworth, 1970), and Barrie Hopson and Charlotte Hopson, *Intimate Feedback* (New York: New American Library, 1973). The concept of feedforward owes its formulation to I. A. Richards; see particularly *Speculative Instruments* (Chicago: University of Chicago Press, 1935), and "The Secret of 'Feedforward,'" *Saturday Review* 51 (February 1968):14–17. Bess Sondel provides a useful summary of Richards's contributions in *The Humanity of Words: A Primer of Semantics* (New York: Harcourt Brace Jovanovich, 1958). Edward DeBono's brief discussions are most insightful; see his *Wordpower* (New York: Harper & Row, 1977); a number of the feedback examples used come from DeBono. For an analysis of the concept of feedback as used in communication by the different theoretical perspectives, see B. Aubrey Fisher, *Perspectives on Human Communication* (New York: Macmillan, 1978).

19.1 SEQUENTIAL COMMUNICATION

This exercise is designed to illustrate some of the processes involved in what might be called "sequential communication," that is, communication that is passed on from one individual to another.

This exercise consists of both a visual and a verbal part; both are performed in essentially the same manner. Taking the visual communication experience first, six subjects are selected to participate. Five of these leave the room while the first subject is shown the visual communication. He or she is told to try to remember as much as possible, as he or she will be asked to reproduce it in as much detail as possible. After studying the diagram, the first subject reproduces it on the blackboard. The second subject then enters the room and studies the reproduced diagram. The first diagram is then erased, and the second subject draws his or her version. The process is continued until all subjects have drawn the diagram. The last reproduction and the original drawing are then compared on the basis of the processes listed below.

The verbal portion is performed in basically the same way. Here the first subject is read the statement once or twice or even three times; the subject should feel comfortable that he or she has grasped it fully. The second subject then enters the room and listens carefully to the first subject's restatement of the communication. The second subject then attempts to repeat it to the third subject, and so on until all subjects have restated the communication. Again, the last restatement and the original are compared on the basis of the processes listed below.

Members of the class not serving as subjects should be provided with copies of both the visual and the verbal communications and should record the changes made in the various reproductions and restatements.

Special attention should be given to the following basic processes in sequential communication.

1. *Omissions.* What kinds of information are omitted? At what point in the chain of communication are such omissions introduced? Do the omissions follow any pattern?
2. *Additions.* What kinds of information are added? When? Can patterns be discerned here, or are the additions totally random?
3. *Distortions.* What kinds of information are distorted? When? Are there any patterns? Can the types of distortions be classified in any way? Are the distortions in the direction of increased simplicity? Increased

304

complexity? Can the sources of or reasons for the distortions be identified?

Nonverbal Communication

Verbal Communication

A verbal communication that works well comes from William Haney's "Serial Communication of Information in Organizations":

> *Every year at State University, the eagles in front of the Psi Gamma fraternity house were mysteriously sprayed during the night. Whenever this happened, it cost the Psi Gams from $75 to $100 to have the eagles cleaned. The Psi Gams complained to officials and were promised by the president that if ever any students were caught painting the eagles, they would be expelled from school.*

19.2 FEEDBACK ON THE SELF

In this exercise you are asked to participate in dyadic interaction, using the sentence-completion task as a model. The major purpose of this interaction is to provide you with an opportunity both to give and to receive relatively immediate feedback of a relatively personal nature.

Form a dyad with a person who does not know you very well. One person (A) reads the first sentence from the list below, and the other person (B) repeats the sentence and completes it in one or more ways. All the responses should focus on the way the individual feels now. The process is continued for all five sentences and is then repeated with A serving as the respondent and B reading the sentences.

After both individuals have responded to all the sentences, each person should write a short paragraph about his or her impressions of the other person. These paragraphs should focus on the information that was derived from the sentence-completion interactions. Information derived from other cues should be identified as such—for example, cues from nonverbal behaviors, from the way the person is dressed, from the tone of voice, and so on.

After the paragraphs have been completed, exchange and discuss them in any way that seems meaningful to you.

SENTENCES FOR COMPLETION

1. My major strengths and weaknesses are . . .
2. When I think of love, the feelings and thoughts going through my mind are . . .
3. My interactions with others might best be characterized as . . .
4. My major hopes for the future, for myself and for those who are meaningful to me, are . . .
5. If I could have any three wishes come true, the wishes would be . . .

19.3 FEEDBACK IN COMMUNICATION

The purpose of this exercise is to illustrate the importance of feedback in communication. The procedure is to have a listener at the blackboard and a speaker prepared to communicate under various different conditions.

The object of the interactions is for the speaker to communicate to the listener instructions for reproducing a diagram. The different conditions under which this task is attempted should enable you to investigate the importance of feedback in communication. Members of the class not participating as speaker or listener should see the diagrams.

First Condition
The speaker is given a diagram that is neither too complex nor too simple. With his or her back to the listener, the speaker must communicate instructions for reproducing the diagram. The listener is not allowed to speak.

Second Condition
The speaker is given another diagram and must tell the listener how to reproduce it. This time the speaker may observe what the listener is doing and may comment on it. The listener is not allowed to speak.

Third Condition
The speaker is given a third diagram and must tell the listener how to reproduce it. The speaker may again observe what the listener is doing and

may comment on it. This time, however, the listener may ask any questions he or she wishes of the speaker.

Discussion

Discussion should center on the accuracy of the drawings and the confidence the listeners had in their attempts at reproducing the diagrams. Which is the most accurate? Which is the least accurate? To what extent did the feedback, first visual and then both visual and auditory, help the listener reproduce the diagram?

19.4 SCRAMBLED ANSWERS: REVIEW QUIZ V

Unscramble the answers to complete the following sentences.

1. Message reception is BJUCVIETES.
2. The law stating that behavior generally follows the easiest path is called the law of OELTAEFFTRS.
3. The process through which we attempt to understand the behaviors of others (as well as our own) is called BIOTTRUNIAT.
4. When we ask "Do other people react or behave in the same way as the person on whom we are focusing?" we are using the principle of NESNUSCOS.
5. When we are concerned with whether the person reacts in similar ways in different situations, we are using the principle of VIISNISDENSTTCE.
6. When our focus is on whether the person repeatedly behaves the same way in similar situations, we are using the principle of CENTSONYSIC.
7. The bias that leads us to take credit for the positive and to deny responsibility for the negative is referred to as the SLESREGFINV bias.
8. If what comes first exerts more influence than what comes last, we have what is called a RAYCIMP effect.
9. A fixed impression of a group of people is referred to as a ETSROPETYE.
10. We need to feel what the speaker feels; we need to listen with PEMTAYH.
11. Information concerned with telling the speaker the progress or lack of progress she or he is making is referred to as EDBEKCAF.
12. Information that is sent prior to the primary messages telling us something about future messages is referred to as DERRAWDOFFE.

INTERPERSONAL RELATIONSHIPS
PART SIX

UNIVERSALS OF INTERPERSONAL RELATIONSHIPS

OBJECTIVES

Upon completion of this unit, you should be able to:
1. explain the nature of interpersonal relationships
2. explain the five-stage model of relationships
3. explain the ways in which relationships are multidimensional
4. explain the complexities characteristic of interpersonal relationships
5. explain at least two implications of the complexity of interpersonal relationships
6. define the concepts of breadth and depth as used in the theory of social penetration
7. illustrate how the concepts of breadth and depth can be used to describe interpersonal relationships
8. explain the uniqueness and constant-change characteristics of interpersonal relationships

Our relationships are perhaps the most important part of our social world. These relationships define not only what we do and who we do it with, but they define in large part who we are and what we think of ourselves. Our relationships can lead us to rejoice or to sink into depression; they can make us happy or can make us cry; they can help us develop and progress or they can limit and, in some cases, destroy us. It is not surprising, therefore, that a large part of interpersonal communication should be devoted to relationships—their development, their maintenance, and their deterioration.

In Part Six, then, the focus will be on this most important dimension of interpersonal communication—relationships between people. In the following units some of the ways in which people relate to one another will be examined. Specifically, we cover relational development, or the ways in which relationships are established and maintained (Unit 21); interpersonal attraction, or the factors that account for attraction between people (Unit 22); conflict (Unit 23); friendship (Unit 24); love (Unit 25); the family (Unit 26); and relational deterioration (Unit 27).

Before we examine each of the different relationships, it would be useful
to characterize interpersonal relationships generally and explain some of the
universals of interpersonal relationships. In this way we will be able to spell
out the characteristics that all interpersonal relationships have in common,
avoid unnecessary repetition in the discussions that follow, and provide essential background information. It should be clear at the start that interpersonal
relationships are in a very real sense communication events. For the most part
these relationships are established by and maintained through communication,
and in many instances they deteriorate and terminate because of a lack of communication. Without interpersonal communication these relationships would
lose their very essence—love or friendship without verbal or nonverbal communication would be inconceivable.

Because relationships are essentially communication events, they have an
effectiveness dimension. Much as we can learn to deliver a more effective public speech, to write more effective short stories, or to direct a film more effectively, we can learn to make our interpersonal relationships more effective,
more productive, and more satisfying. It is hoped that the discussions presented
here and in the following units will provide an increased understanding of the
varied dimensions of interpersonal relationships and will thus enable you to
develop and maintain more effective relations.

RELATIONSHIPS ARE ESTABLISHED IN STAGES

Most relationships, possibly all, are established in stages. We do not
become intimate friends immediately upon meeting someone but rather we
grow into an intimate relationship gradually, through a series of steps or stages.
And the same is probably true with most other relationships as well. "Love at
first sight" seems to create a problem for a stage model of relationships and so
rather than argue that such love cannot occur (my own feeling is that it can and
frequently does), it seems wiser to claim that the stage model of relationships
characterizes *most* relationships for *most* people *most* of the time.

The five-stage model presented in Figure 20.1 seems a suitable one for
describing at least some of the significant stages in the development of relationships. For each specific relationship, you might wish to modify and revise
the basic model in various ways. Yet, as a general description of relationship
development, the stages seem fairly standard.

The Five Stages

At the first stage we make *contact*, there is some kind of sense perception—we see the person, we hear the person, we smell the person. This is the
stage of "Hello, my name is Joe"—the stage where we exchange basic infor-

mation that is generally preliminary to any more intense involvement. According to some researchers, it is at this stage—within the first 4 minutes of initial interaction—that we decide if we want to pursue the relationship or if we want to get out. It is at this stage that physical appearance is so important because it is the physical dimensions that are most open to sensory inspection. Yet, qualities such as friendliness, warmth, openness, and dynamism are also revealed at this stage as well. If we like the individual and want to pursue the relationship we proceed to the second stage, the stage of involvement.

The *involvement* stage is the stage of acquaintances, the stage at which we commit ourselves to getting to know the other person better and also to revealing ourselves to the other person. If this is to be a romantic relationship, then we might date at this stage; if it is to be a friendship relationship, we might share our mutual interests—go to the movies or to some sports event together.

At the third stage, that of *intimacy*, we commit ourselves still further to the other person and, in fact, establish a kind of primary relationship where this individual becomes our best or our closest friend, lover, and/or companion. This commitment may take many specific forms; for example, it may be a marriage commitment, it may be a commitment to help the person or to be with him or her, or a commitment to reveal our deepest secrets. The type of commitment will naturally vary with the relationship and with the individual, but the important characteristic is that the commitment made is a special one; it is a commit-

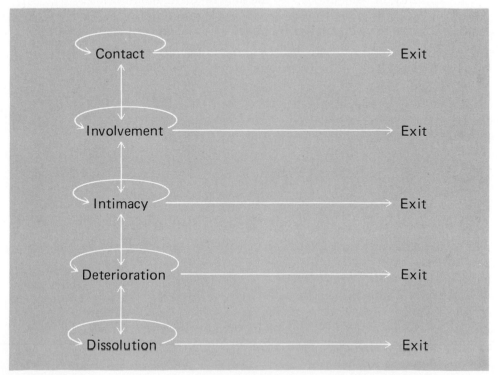

FIGURE 20.1
A Five-Stage
Relationship
Model.

ment that we do not make to everyone but only to a select few. This intimacy stage is reserved for very few people—sometimes just one and sometimes two, three, or perhaps four. Rarely do we have more than four intimates, except, of course, in a family situation.

The next two stages are the other side of the progression and represent the weakening of bonds between the parties in the relationship. At the *deterioration* stage we begin to feel that this relationship may not be as important as we had previously thought. We grow further and further apart. We share less of our free time together and when we do there are awkward silences, less self-disclosures, and in general, a self-consciousness in our communication exchanges. At this stage we are not exactly sure what to call our "intimate." The person is not quite a lover or an ex-lover, not really a close friend but not an ex-friend either. This deterioration stage is that awkward in-between stage of neither here nor there. If this deterioration stage continues unaltered, we enter the stage of dissolution.

The *dissolution* stage is the cutting of the bonds tying the individuals together. If a marriage, then the dissolution is symbolized by a divorce, although the actual relational dissolution takes the form of establishing separate and different lives away from each other. This is the point of "goodbye"—the point at which we become ex-lovers, ex-friends, ex-husbands, ex-wives, and so on. At times this is a stage of relief and relaxation—finally it is over and done with. At other times this is a stage of intense anxiety and frustration—of recriminations and hostility, of resentment over the time ill-spent and now lost. In more materialistic terms, it is the stage where property is divided, where legal battles ensue over who should get the Mercedes and who should get the Rolls Royce. It is the time of child custody battles. But it is also the time during which the individuals must look to the establishment of a new and different life—either alone or with another person. Some people, it is true, will continue to live psychologically with a relationship that has already been dissolved: they will frequent the old meeting places, they will reread old love letters, they will daydream about all the good times, and, in general, will fail to extricate themselves from this relationship that has died in every way except in their minds.

Movement Among the Stages

Figure 20.1 contains three types of arrows. The Exit arrows indicate that each stage offers the opportunity to exit the relationship. After saying "hello" we can say "goodbye" and exit. The vertical or "movement" arrows going to the next stage and back again represent the fact that we can move to another stage, either one that is more intense (as say from involvement to intimacy) or one that is less intense (say from intimacy to deterioration). We can also go back to a previously established stage. For example, you may have established an intimate relationship with someone but did not want to maintain it at that level. At the same time you were relatively pleased with the relationship and so it was not really deteriorating. Rather you just wanted it to be somewhat less intense and so you might go back to the involvement stage and reestablish the relationship at that more comfortable level. Similarly, if in the stage of deterioration, problems and differences are worked out, the people may reestablish themselves into an intimate relationship again. And of course we may skip stages, although instances of this are probably not as common as one might think. Often people in a relationship may appear to be skipping a stage when they are merely passing through a particular stage very quickly. Often, for example, we see a couple skip from the initial stage of contact to the stage of intimacy. It is not that they have bypassed involvement; it is instead that the involvement stage lasted for only a very short time and to outsiders was not apparent. This is not to say, however, that in certain instances a stage could not be skipped. The stages, then, may last for different periods of time, but there is no fixed time period that any stage must occupy. Stages may be extremely short or extremely long in duration.

The "self-reflexive" arrows—the arrows that return to the beginning of the same level or stage—signify that any relationship may become stabilized at any point. We may, for example, continue to maintain a relationship at the intimate level without the relationship deteriorating or going back to the less intense stage of involvement. Or we might remain at the "Hello, how are you" stage—the contact stage—without getting involved any further.

RELATIONSHIPS ARE MULTIDIMENSIONAL

Interpersonal relationships are not unitary but exist as different types and on different levels. That is, in addition to differing in degree, relationships also differ in kind. Our relatively limited vocabulary for describing interpersonal relationships forces us to use the same term when perhaps there should be different labels for each of the different types or levels of relationships.

By different *types* of relationships I mean basically that the relationship can focus on different classes of persons. Most obviously, we should note that each of the relationships may focus on another person or on oneself. Although we may call the friendship for another person and the friendship for oneself by the same label, they are really two different kinds of relationships—related, to be sure, and yet significantly different as well. Love is perhaps the clearest example. We may have love for our family—our parents or our children, for example. We may also have love for a friend, for a political or religious leader, for a Good Samaritan, or for a sexual partner. All of these loves are quite different from one another; consequently, our attitudes, our emotions, and our behaviors are all quite different depending on the type of love we have.

By different *levels* I mean that each of these relationships can focus primarily on one or more aspects of ourself—emotional, physical, and intellectual at the very least. Each of the interpersonal relationships may focus primarily on one or more of these dimensions. Thus, for example, we may have a love for an individual that is primarily emotional or primarily physical or primarily intellectual. Similarly, cooperation, conflict, attraction, or friendship may focus primarily on one or more of these dimensions. This is not to say that any relationship can be centered exclusively on one of these dimensions. Rather, any given relationship consists of a unique combination of the various levels, and although one level may predominate at any given time, all levels are involved in varying degrees, thus the multidimensional nature of relationships.

The recognition that there are numerous different kinds of love, friendship, conflict, and so on, and that each of these involves the different dimensions of the self in different proportions will enable us to better understand and to deal more effectively with our own interpersonal relationships.

RELATIONSHIPS ARE COMPLEX

Few persons would attempt to argue that interpersonal relationships are simple. But it is perhaps not so obvious why they are complex and what the implications of this complexity are. I think that interpersonal relationships are complex for the same reasons that communication is complex. Each person in the relationship (as in communication generally) consists of a unique collection

Universals of interpersonal relationships.

of experiences, thoughts, abilities, needs, fears, desires, and so on, and these greatly influence how he or she interacts with another person, who in turn also possesses a unique set of experiences, thoughts, abilities, and so on. The interaction of these unique, multifaceted, and constantly changing individuals itself causes additional changes. In short, there are a multitude of variables influencing the relational processes, and because these are in a state of constant change, the relationship is extremely complex.

More important than the complexity itself are the implications of the complexity. One of the most important of these implications is that our understanding or analysis of any interaction is necessarily limited and partial. We can never hope to understand fully any interpersonal relationship, whether it is one in which we are involved personally or one to which we are a third party. Our analysis, therefore, should also always be tentative and our conclusions stated with a clear recognition that we may well be wrong. Our point of view is subjective and is only one among many. As our view is limited, so is everyone else's; no one can speak with absolute authority about any relationship. This is particularly true and frequently forgotten, I think, in conflict situations, in which each individual is certain that he or she is correct. The unstated assumption here is that one can know all there is to know about the conflict and can therefore conclude who is right and who is wrong. Once that assumption is recognized as false, a more appropriately modest response may take the place of definite conclusions. And when conclusions are advanced as tentative rather than definitive, there is a much greater likelihood that the conflict will be resolved.

Everything has multiple causes. It is true that there may be immediate causes, that some causes may immediately precede the effect and may therefore seem more like *the* cause than others. However, all interpersonal interactions and relationships are the result of multiple causation. The love that develops between two people, the conflict that tears a marriage apart, the friendship that emerges between former strangers, the attraction one feels for another, and so many other relationships are all caused by numerous factors, and to attempt to find the one cause is foolhardy. Consider, for example, the couple who have a fight over one of them being late for an appointment. If they assume that their conflict was caused only by the lateness, they are probably never going to resolve the conflict and are only avoiding facing other issues, for example, Why is the lateness so important? Why is it a source of conflict now when it was not two weeks ago? Why does the conflict take the form of hurting each other? Why is the lateness of someone else not conflict-provoking?

Another implication of the complexity of interpersonal interactions is that our ability to predict and to control relationships is limited. As a relationship increases in complexity, our ability to predict its course decreases. This is understandable; there are so many factors to consider that it becomes impossible to predict what will happen when one factor changes or when a new factor is introduced. When we cannot predict what will happen in a relationship, we lose our ability to control it. This inability to completely control an inter-personal relationship is at once both unfortunate and comforting. It is unfortunate in the sense that we are not such masters of our fate as we would like to be: we cannot make someone love us if that person does not want to; or, alternatively, we may not be able to stop loving someone even though we may feel that the love is destructive; we may not be able to win the friendship of a particular person; we may not be able to resolve important conflicts between ourselves and the people we love. Although we can in many instances improve the situation, we must recognize that there are limits to what we can do.

That we cannot completely control these relationships is comforting in the sense that our responsibility ends at some point; we need not emotionally beat ourselves to death when a relationship fails. We can only control so much and no more. It seems to me that we need only hold ourselves responsible for what we can influence—for what we *can* control.

RELATIONSHIPS VARY IN TERMS OF BREADTH AND DEPTH

Relationships may be described in terms of the number of topics talked about and the degree of "personalness" to which these topics are pursued. The number of topics about which the individuals communicate is referred to as *breadth*. The degree to which the inner personality, the inner core of an individual is penetrated in the interpersonal interaction is referred to as *depth*.

Let us represent an individual as a circle and divide that circle into various parts. These parts would represent the topics or areas of interpersonal communication or breadth. Further, visualize the circle and its parts as consisting of concentric inner circles. These would represent the different levels of communication or the depth. Representative examples are provided in Figure 20.2. In order to provide specific examples, the circles are all divided into eight topic areas (identified A through H) and five levels of intimacy (represented by the concentric circles). Note that in circle A only three of the topic areas are penetrated. Two of these are penetrated only on the first level and one of them is penetrated to the second level. In this type of interaction, three topic areas are talked about and they are discussed at rather superficial levels. This is the type of relationship that we might have with an acquaintance. Circle B represents a more intense relationship, a relationship that is broader (here four topics are discussed) and in which the topics are discussed to a deeper level of penetration. This is the type of relationship we might have with a friend. In circle C we have a still more intense relationship. Here there is considerable breadth (seven of the eight areas are penetrated) and depth (note that most of the areas are penetrated to the deepest levels). This is the type of relationship we might have with a lover, a parent, or a child.

All relationships—friendships, loves, families—may be profitably described in terms of these concepts of breadth and depth—concepts which are central to the theory of *social penetration* developed by Irwin Altman and Dalmas Taylor. In its initial stage a relationship would normally be characterized by narrow breadth (few topics would be discussed) and shallow depth (the topics that are discussed would be discussed only superficially). If early in a relationship topics are discussed to a depth which would normally be reserved for intimates, we would probably experience considerable discomfort. As already noted (Unit 7, "Self-Disclosure"), when intimate disclosures are made early in a relationship we feel something is wrong with the disclosing individual. As the relationship grows in intensity and intimacy, both the breadth and the depth increase and these increases are seen as comfortable, normal, and natural progressions.

When a relationship begins to deteriorate, the breadth and depth will, in many ways, reverse themselves—a process of *depenetration*. For example, while in the process of terminating a relationship, you might eliminate certain topics from your interpersonal interactions and at the same time discuss the topics you discuss in less depth. You would, for example, reduce the level of your self-disclosures and reveal less and less of your innermost feelings. This reversal does not always work, of course. In some instances of relational deterioration, both the breadth and the depth of interaction increase. A good example of this is seen in the film *Making Love*. Here the relationship between Michael Ontkean and Kate Jackson is breaking up because after 8 years of marriage he realizes that he is attracted to men. But during the breakup, we see a process of penetration rather than depenetration; they each reveal themselves to each other to a much greater depth and discuss more topic areas than they had previously. Usually, however, relational deterioration is characterized by a decrease in both breadth and depth.

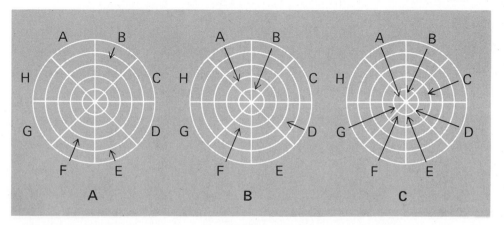

FIGURE 20.2
*Social Penetration
with (A) Acquaintance, (B) Friend,
and (C) Intimate.*

RELATIONSHIPS ARE UNIQUE AND CONSTANTLY CHANGING

The characteristics of uniqueness and constant change seem even more true of interpersonal relationships than of communication in general. Take the example of friendship. Each friendship we have is unique and different from every other friendship. We have no two friendships we could say are identical; each friendship is at least a little bit different from each other friendship.

Each friendship is also constantly changing. Never are interpersonal relationships static; they are always in a state of change. Friendship may improve and get stronger or deteriorate and get weaker. But it never stays the same.

In addition to the interpersonal relationship constantly changing, we, as people, are changing and our memories of the relationship are changing as well. Therefore, even past relationships—relationships that are over and terminated—change because our memories of them change and we ourselves change. We easily forget the pain in a relationship and easily remember the pleasures; relationships seem, therefore, to have a way of getting better over time, at least in our memories. And we change. What we considered important 5 years ago we may consider unimportant now, and a harm done to us 5 years ago that helped to sever a relationship may seem incidental and minor now, and we may wonder why we allowed that incident to end what was otherwise a happy and productive relationship. To assume sameness and consistency in any relationship is unrealistic; all relationships are different from one moment to another, and although not all differences make a difference, we can be sure that there are differences and changes.

Relationships can never, therefore, be duplicated or repeated. A relationship that you have had in the past will never come again. Better ones or worse ones may take its place, but the same one will never be repeated.

SOURCES

In approaching the study of interpersonal relationships you may wish to consult the following works to gain an additional and somewhat different perspective: Murray S. Davis, *Intimate Relations* (New York: Free Press, 1973), and Mark L. Knapp, *Social Intercourse: From Greeting to Goodbye* (Boston: Allyn & Bacon, 1978). For different views on the stages of a relationship see, for example, Knapp's *Social Intercourse;* Clifford H. Swensen, *Introduction to Interpersonal Relations* (Glenview, Ill.: Scott, Foresman, 1973); Linda Krug, "Alternative Lifestyle Dyads: An Alternative Relationship Paradigm," *Alternative Communications* IV (May 1982):32–52; and Julia T. Wood, "Communication and Relational Culture: Bases for the Study of Human Relationships," *Communication Quarterly* 30 (Spring 1982):75–83. On social penetration see Irwin Altman and D. Taylor, *Social Penetration: The Development of Interpersonal Relationships* (New York: Holt, Rinehart, and Winston, 1973). On different relationships and the names we use to label them, see Mark L. Knapp, Donald G. Ellis, and Barbara A. Williams, "Perceptions of Communication Behavior Associated with Relationship Terms," *Communication Monographs* 47 (November 1980):262–278.

20.1 EXTRAORDINARY PEOPLE: RELATIONAL ANALYSIS

The following dialogue is an abbreviated account of the development and dissolution of a relationship. The five stages of relationships, for example, are consequently easy to see and are quite clearly differentiated from each other. In reality and in longer dialogues, these divisions would not be so obvious. The main purpose of this dialogue is to provide a focus for the discussion and analysis of the universals of interpersonal relationships considered in this unit.

Examine the dialogue and identify the five universals of interpersonal relationships. Respond to the following questions with references to specific phrases in the dialogue as much as possible.

1. *Relationships are established in stages.*
   Identify the stages in the dialogue. What specific conversational phrases in the dialogue cue you to the stage of the relationship?
2. *Relationships are multidimensional.*
   What evidence can you find in the dialogue that exhibits the relationship's multidimensional nature (type and levels)?
3. *Relationships are complex.*
   What factors might you point to that make this relationship complex? It might help you to appreciate complexity if you try to answer such questions as: What information not included in the dialogue would help you to better understand the couple and their relationship? What do they fail to understand about each other? What factors might have accounted for the relationship originally developing? Progressing? Deteriorating?
4. *Relationships vary in terms of breadth and depth.*
   What would you expect the breadth and depth of the relationship to be at each of the five stages? At what stage is there greatest breadth? At what stage is there greatest depth?
5. *Relationships are unique and constantly changing.*
   In what way is this relationship unique? How has the relationship changed throughout the five stages? What changes might you predict will occur subsequent to this breakup? How might change have been a factor in the deterioration of the relationship?

Pat: *Hi. Didn't I see you in English last semester?*
Chris: *Yeah. I'm surprised you noticed me. I cut that class more than I attended. I really hated it.*
Pat: *So did I. Higgins never did seem to care much about whether you learned anything or not.*
Chris: *That's why I think I cut so much. Your name's Pat, isn't it?*
Pat: *Yes. And you're Chris. Right?*
Chris: *Right. What are you doing in Interpersonal Communication?*
Pat: *I'm majoring in communication. I want to go into television production—maybe editing or something like that. I'm not really sure. What about you?*
Chris: *It's required for engineering. I guess they figure engineers should learn to communicate.*
Pat: *You gonna have lunch after this class?*
Chris: *Yeah. You?*
Pat: *Yeah. How about going over to the Union for a burger?*

[*At the Union Cafe*]

Chris: *I'm not only surprised you noticed me in English, I'm really flattered. Everyone in the class seemed to be interested in you.*
Pat: *Well, I doubt that but it's nice to hear.*
Chris: *No, I mean it. Come on. You know you're popular.*
Pat: *Well, maybe . . . but it always seems to be with the wrong people. Today's the exception, of course.*
Chris: *You sure know the right things to say.*
Pat: *O.K. then let me try another. What are you doing tonight? Want to go to a movie? I know it's late and all but I thought just in case you had nothing to do.*
Chris: *I'd love to. Even if I had something else planned, I'd break it.*
Pat: *That makes me feel good.*
Chris: *That makes me feel good too.*

[*Six months later*]

Pat: *I hope that this doesn't cause problems but I got you something.*
Chris: *What is it?*
Pat: *Take a look. I hope you like it.*
Chris: [Chris opens the package and finds a ring.] *I love it. I can't believe it! You know, a few weeks ago when we had to write up a recent fantasy for class, I wrote one I didn't turn in. And this was it. My very own fantasy coming true. I love you.*
Pat: *I love you . . . very much.*

[*Chris and Pat have now been living together for about two years.*]

Pat: *It's me. I'm home.*
Chris: *So am I.*
Pat: *That's not hamburgers I smell is it?*

Chris: *Yes, it is. I like hamburgers. We can afford hamburgers. And I know how to cook hamburgers. Make something else if you don't want to eat them.*

Pat: *Thanks. It's nice to know that you go to such trouble making something I like. I hate these damn hamburgers. And I especially hate them four times a week.*

Chris: *Eat out.*

Pat: *You know I have work to do tonight. I can't go out.*

Chris: *So, shut up and eat the burgers. I love them.*

Pat: *That's good. It's you for you. Whatever happened to us and we?*

Chris: *It died when I found out about your little side trips upstate.*

Pat: *But I told you I was sorry about that. That was six months ago anyway. I got involved, I know, but I'm sorry. What do you want to do, punish me for the rest of my life? I'm sorry, damn it. I'm sorry!*

Chris: *So am I. But I'm the one who was left at home alone while you were out fooling around.*

Pat: *Is that why you don't want to make love? You always have some kind of excuse.*

Chris: *It's not an excuse. It's a reason. And the reason is that I've been lied to and cheated on. How can I make love to someone who treats me like dirt.*

Pat: *But I don't. I love you.*

Chris: *But I don't love you. Maybe I never have.*

Pat: *I will eat out.*

[*Two weeks later*]

Pat: *Did you mean what you said when you said you didn't love me?*

Chris: *I think I did. I just lost my feelings. I can't explain it. When I learned about your upstate trips I just couldn't deal with it. And I guess I tried to protect myself and, in the process, lost my feelings for you.*

Pat: *Then why do you stay with me? Why don't you leave?*

Chris: *I don't know. Maybe I'm afraid to be alone. I'm not sure I can do it alone.*

Pat: *So, you're going to stay with me because you're afraid to be alone? That's crazy. Crazy. I'd rather see us break up than live like this—a loveless relationship where you go out on Tuesdays and I go out on Wednesdays. What kind of life is that?*

Chris: *Not much.*

Pat: *Then let's separate. I can't live with someone who stays with me out of fear of being alone, who doesn't want to be touched, who doesn't want to love me. Let's try to live apart and see what happens. Maybe we need some distance. Maybe you'll want to try it again.*

Chris: *I won't but I guess separation is the best thing.*

Pat: *Why don't you stay here and I'll go to my brother's place tonight. I'll pick up my things tomorrow when you're at work. I don't think I can bear to do it when you're here.*

Chris: *Goodbye.*

DEVELOPMENT OF INTERPERSONAL RELATIONSHIPS

Upon completion of this unit, you should be able to:

1. identify some of the contact substitutes our culture has established
2. identify at least four reasons for the development of interpersonal relationships
3. explain social exchange theory as it relates to relationship development
4. identify at least five ways in which verbal contact may be made
5. define *phatic communion* and explain its importance in initial verbal contact
6. identify and explain at least four means of making nonverbal contact
7. explain at least three guides and obstacles to relational development

There is probably nothing as important to you or me or indeed to anyone as contact with another human being. So important is contact with another person that when this is absent for prolonged periods of time, depression sets in, self-doubt surfaces, and one finds it difficult to conduct even the very basics of daily living. Desmond Morris, in *Intimate Behaviour*, notes that contact with other humans is so important that our culture has established all sorts of substitutes so that when human contact is absent, all may not be totally lost. There are, according to Morris, professional contact persons like doctors, nurses, and masseurs who are often seen not because of some physical ailment but because of the need for contact.

An obvious substitute for human contact is animal contact. People keep dogs and cats as pets, sometimes even dressing them up in elaborate and expensive outfits and talking to them as if they had normal human comprehension. There is also contact with objects—pillows, bedcovers, clothing, jewelry, and so on. Linus's security blanket is a good example. Then, of course, there is auto-contact, or self-touching. We touch our hair, our faces, our legs, our arms, and often this is done as a substitute for the contact of others. The numerous substitutes for human contact, however, are just that—substitutes—and in the final analysis are usually poor and inadequate substitutes.

324

In this unit we explore some of the dimensions of establishing contact with another person, concentrating on first encounters. Specifically, we look at some of the reasons for starting relationships—the reasons why we seek contact with other people. The ways of making verbal contact, including that most important aspect, phatic communion, will then be examined. Next, ways of making nonverbal contact will be explored. And finally, I consider possible guides and obstacles to first encounters—what can go wrong and what might be done to facilitate successful first encounters.

REASONS FOR RELATIONAL DEVELOPMENT

Each person pursues a relationship or desires contact for unique and individual reasons; no two relationships are pursued for exactly the same reason. Consequently, there are millions of reasons for seeking contact. Here we consider just four.

To Alleviate Loneliness

One reason that comes to mind easily is that contact with another human being helps to alleviate loneliness. At times we experience loneliness because

Loneliness makes us more eager to develop new interpersonal relationships and makes us less selective.

we are physically alone, although being alone does not necessarily produce loneliness. Many can experience closeness with others though separated by long distances. At other times we are lonely because we have a need for close contact—sometimes physical, sometimes emotional, and most often both— which is, at least at the time, unfulfilled. From a different perspective, Chester Bennett makes a similar observation: "Psychological studies of ship-wrecked sailors and prisoners in solitary confinement, experimental investigations of people who are closeted with their own thoughts for relatively brief periods of time, show how difficult it is for most of us to cope with isolation. We like solitude in small doses—if we can find a place to be alone in today's world. But mostly we seek companionship. We want to share experiences, even the private ones, with someone."

We want to feel that someone cares, that someone likes us, that someone will protect us, that someone ultimately will love us. And perhaps close relationships with another person assure us that someone does care, does like us, and will just be there when we need human contact.

Some people, in an attempt to alleviate loneliness, seek always to surround themselves with numerous acquaintances. Sometimes this helps; often it only serves to make the loneliness all the more real. One close relationship usually works a lot better. Most of us know this, and that is why we seek to establish relationships.

To Secure Stimulation

Human beings, not unlike experimental monkeys and rats, need stimulation; if they are not stimulated, they withdraw; sometimes they die. Human contact is one of the best ways—though clearly not the only way—to be stimulated. We are composites of many different dimensions, and all of our dimensions need stimulation. We are intellectual creatures, and so we need intellectual stimulation. We talk with people about ideas, we attend classes, we argue about different interpretations of a film or novel. We thus exercise our reasoning, our analytical, and our interpretative abilities. In so doing we improve, sharpen, and expand them.

But we are also physical creatures and need physical stimulation as well. We need to touch and be touched; we need to hold and be held; we need to look at people and have them look at us—not through us or around us or at our new jacket, but at us. Perhaps we need to be assured that we are physical beings. College classrooms have consistently failed to take into consideration the physical stimulation needed for growth and development. A hand on our shoulder, a tight hug, or a warm handshake may help us more than being told our interpretation of Kant was correct. Put in terms of *social exchange theory*, we would say that we develop relationships in which our rewards or profits will be greater than our costs. We involve ourselves in relationships that will provide us with rewards or profits—basically, those things that fulfill our needs for security, sex, social approval, financial gain, status, and so on. But rewards or profits involve some cost or "payback." For example, in order to acquire the reward of financial gain an individual might have to give up some degree of freedom. The cost of gaining parental approval might be a loveless marriage or giving up a relationship that provided other types of rewards or gains. Using this basic economic-oriented model, the social exchange theory puts into clearer perspective our tendency to seek profit (gain or reward) while incurring the least cost (punishment or loss). If you think about your current or past relationships, you will be able to see quite clearly that the relationships you pursued and maintained have been those that provided you with greater profit and greater need fulfillment than cost. Those relationships you did not pursue or that you terminated were probably those whose costs or losses exceeded the rewards or profits; these were the relationships where there was more dissatisfaction than satisfaction, more unhappiness than happiness, more problems than pleasures.

We are also emotional creatures and need emotional stimulation. We need to laugh and to cry. We need to feel hope and surprise, to experience warmth and affection. We need exercise for our emotions as well as for our intellectual capacities. In our culture men have been taught that it is wrong to cry or to be fearful. And women have been taught that it is wrong to be aggressive or to feel sexual. Both sexes need to be retaught—each also needs the emotions at one time assigned only to the other sex.

To Establish Contact for Self-Knowledge

We need contact with other human beings because through them we learn about ourselves; we acquire that essential knowledge of self largely through interaction with others. In the discussion of self-disclosure in Unit 7, I tried to make the point that we see ourselves in part through the eyes of others. If our friends see us as warm and generous, for example, we will probably also see ourselves as warm and generous. Our self-perceptions are greatly influenced by what we think others think of us, and so contact with others enables us to see ourselves in a somewhat different way, from a somewhat different perspective.

To Maximize Pleasures and Minimize Pains

The most general reason why we establish relationships, and one that could include all the others, is that we seek human contact so that our pleasures may be maximized and our pains minimized. We seem to have a need to share our good fortune with other people—perhaps to earn their praise, perhaps to assure us that we are in fact fortunate; perhaps to participate with us in enjoying the newfound pleasures. We also have a need to seek out relationships when we are in emotional or physical pain. Perhaps this goes back to when we were children and ran to mother to kiss our wounds or tell us everything was all right. We now find it difficult to run to mother, and so we go to others, generally to friends who will provide us with the same kind of consolation that mother did.

A significant complication is introduced when we realize that in the satisfaction of one need, another need may of necessity go unsatisfied. For example, consider the person who forms a close primary relationship out of a need for security, social status, and economics but who also needs to be independent and to interact intimately with a number of different people. The two classes of needs contradict each other. If one of these groups of needs is satisfied, the other must go unsatisfied. Whether one develops and maintains the relationship or terminates it depends on how strong the various needs are. For example, some of us have a very strong need to affiliate with others; some of us have a strong need for independence. Which needs will prevail and whether the relationship develops or deteriorates will depend on the relative strength of these needs. But the fact that our needs so often do conflict is perhaps one of the reasons why so few people are entirely satisfied with their relationships. Often such dissatisfaction is not the "fault" of our partner or of ourselves, but is simply in the nature of our complicated and often conflicting system of needs.

VERBAL CONTACT

In *How to Pick Up Girls,* the author lists 50 opening lines which are offered to the unsuspecting reader interested in "picking up a girl." Among these 50 are, "How long do you cook a leg of lamb?," "Didn't I meet you in Istanbul?," and "Who's your dentist?" I confess to never having used any of these myself, and fortunately I do not know of anyone who has and so cannot attest to their usefulness or uselessness. But the prominence given to opening lines and ways of starting verbal contact in the various manuals and popular magazine articles says something about its perceived importance. The opening line is perhaps the most difficult sentence to say, and yet if it goes unsaid, there is little chance of a relationship developing. In fact, the opening few lines are regarded by some researchers as being crucial in that they determine whether the relationship will be developed or terminated.

Our approach is not to provide you with one-liners to use to pick up girls or boys, women or men, but rather to explain the various ways of making verbal contact.

Seven Paths to Verbal Contact

I think it is profitable to approach the ways of making verbal contact by reference to some of the basic elements of the communication act. Specifically, we consider seven ways of making verbal contact: self-references, other references, relational references, contextual references, displacement references, metacommunicational references, and combination references.

Self-References

Self-references are statements made about the speaker himself or herself. Such references may be descriptive—the name, rank, and serial number type of statement of simply "I'm from Oregon. Where are you from?" They may be attitudinal: "I hate cocktail parties," "I love interpersonal communication courses." At times the statements may be self-disclosing—although in the initial stages of verbal contact these are not very common. At other times—on the first day of class, for example—students will say such things as, "I'm worried about this class," "I flunked this course last semester; I hope I can make it through this time," or simply, "I'm nervous."

Other References

By other references I mean statements made about the other person in the encounter rather than about other people generally. Perhaps the most common type of other reference is to ask a question. The answer to the question is not important; what is important is that verbal contact has somehow been made. And so, for example, we might ask someone for a light even though we have matches or for the time even though we have a watch. Questions may be addressed to a variety of issues, and so we may ask questions about other people ("Are you a friend of Bertha's?," "Do you know Harry?"), about events ("Was there a party here last night?"), about objects ("Is this the right book for this course?"), about attitudes, values, and opinions ("Do you think you'll like this course?"), about past behaviors ("Have you taken a course with this teacher before?"). References to the other person can be as simple as a brief compliment ("You have nice eyes"). Similarly, references to something observed may also serve the same purpose, for example, "Your smile reminds me of . . . " or "You look just like . . . "

Relational References

Statements of relational reference make some comment on the encounter between the two people, either on the relationship to be developed or on some activity in which both might engage, for example, "May I buy you a drink?," "Would you like to dance?," or "May I join you?" These statements are particularly interesting because they force the other person to comment on the relationship as well. Thus, to a statement such as, "Is this the right book for the course?" the other person may answer "yes" or "no" without any commitment concerning the development of a relationship. And again the burden falls on the initiator. But a statement such as, "May I buy you a drink?" calls for an answer that says something about the person's reaction to the questioner.

Contextual References

Statements about the context are among the most common opening lines. As we noted in Unit 1, there are at least three major variables in the communication context: social-psychological, temporal, and physical. Thus, one may comment on any of these aspects, for example, "This is an awfully threatening environment" or, "This place seems so friendly" (social-psychological context), "It's getting late" (temporal context), "I like this painting" (physical context). Perhaps most comments on the physical context would be made in reference to other people.

Displacement References

Earlier we noted that the human language characteristic of displacement enabled us to refer to things not in the immediate perceptual field. Displacement references, then, are statements concerning people, events, objects, and relations that are not in the immediate context. Such references may be to the future ("What will you do this weekend?"), the past ("Was that you at the movie on Saturday night?"), to the real ("What are you majoring in?"), and to the imagined ("What would you do if you had $1 million?"). Displacement references are often used to establish commonalities between two people: Did you read . . . ? Did you see . . . ? Did you take a course in . . . ? and so on, and are attempts to establish common ground.

Metacommunicational References

Another characteristic of human language we considered earlier was metalinguistic capacity—language can be used to talk about language. Metacommunication is simply the more general term and refers to messages about messages, whether verbal or nonverbal. "I have difficulty talking with new people" or "I feel awkward saying this" are metacommunicational references. They are messages about messages. Not as obvious, but nevertheless still metacommunication, are the statements made about nonverbal messages, for example, "You look bored," "You seem to be having a great time the way you're smiling," or "I'm surprised you look so confident."

Combination References

Finally, we have references that combine two or more types of references. For example, the proverbial, "What's a nice person like you doing in a place like this?" combines other reference with contextual reference. "This course sounds a lot better than the one I had last period" combines contextual and displacement references. "I usually have difficulty talking with strangers, but you're different" combines self, other, and metacommunicational references.

Phatic Communion

No discussion of verbal contact can omit phatic communion—the small talk that precedes the big talk, the talk that opens the channels of communication so that the important and significant issues may be discussed.

In terms of content, phatic communion is trivial—"Hello," "How are you?," "Fine weather, isn't it?," "Have a nice day," and the like; but in terms of establishing and maintaining relationships, phatic talk is extremely important.

For one thing, phatic communication assures us that the social customs are in effect; the general rules of communication that we expect to operate will operate here also. The teacher who says, "Turn to Chapter Three" before saying "Hello" clues us into a situation in which the normal rules seem not to operate.

In first encounters, phatic communion enables us to reveal something of ourselves and at the same time to gain some preliminary information about the other person. Even if it is only to hear the tone or quality of voice, something is gained. Sometimes the important benefit is that phatic talk allows us time to look each other over and to decide on our next move. Phatic communion also shows us that the other person is willing to communicate, that in fact the channels of communication are open, that there is some willingness to pursue the interaction.

Phatic communion, by its nature and because of the purposes it serves, is noncontroversial; with phatic talk there is little chance for conflict or fighting. Similarly, the topics considered are unemotional and hence not ego-involving. They are neither intellectually demanding nor are they too personal. In phatic talk the parties avoid extreme positions; rather, they seem to engage in what appears to be rather bland, innocuous, inane chatter. But we need to see that what on the surface is shallow is actually a foundation for later and more significant communication.

An important point implied throughout this discussion is that all of the ways of making verbal contact may well sound trite and unoriginal, but they are for the most part examples of phatic communion. They are messages whose importance and usefulness should not be measured by their originality or their profundity; they should rather be taken simply as an attempt to establish some kind of verbal contact.

The person who says, "Haven't I seen you here before?" is probably asking not if you have been here before but rather "Would you like to talk with me?" To answer the literal question and fail to respond to the underlying and more significant question is a clear example of miscommunication.

NONVERBAL CONTACT

The ways of making contact nonverbally are probably more numerous and more varied than the ways of making contact verbally. Again, no complete catalogue is attempted here. Rather, we mention just a few of the more popular nonverbal behaviors used in making initial contacts.

An obvious one is the *nonverbal "hello,"* the slight head nod which is often used to say hello when you do not want to raise your voice. The head nods with a slight smile while the eyes stay with the person. If that nod is ignored, the nonverbal "hello" has either been too subtle and not correctly perceived or it has been perceived but rejected—not unlike responses to the verbal "hello."

Another nonverbal means is *spatial proximity*, or placing ourselves physically close to the person with whom we wish to make contact. At a crowded bar or disco this is one of the most frequently used techniques. The mere physical proximity provides the initial, though not sufficient, step for interpersonal contact.

Approval gestures such as a smile or a wink are frequently used to indicate one's desire to make interpersonal contact. The smile seems permitted to both men and women. Although women are supposed to be more subtle in indicating an interest in another person, they are permitted to smile—though faintly. The wink, however, seems restricted to the male—at least for initial encounters.

In all cultures the time during which strangers may engage in *direct eye contact* is rigidly defined and deeply imbedded in our unconscious. As we were growing up we learned that staring was wrong and that we should especially not stare at strangers—at least not when they can see us. Even in conversing with someone we do not maintain direct eye contact for long periods of time. Rather, we look at each other and then glance away, then look back at each other and then glance away, and so on. When the time rule is broken and the eye contact is direct and prolonged, we are generally signaling some desire to make interpersonal contact. If the direct and prolonged eye contact is returned, then the desire seems mutual. If it is not returned, again you have probably been misunderstood or rejected.

In an interactional setting where there are different people and various activities going on, you may concentrate your attentions on one person and thus signal that you are desirous of establishing contact. Most of the time this *concentrated attention* takes the form of direct eye contact. But often it is more of a general body orientation, in which we face the individual, ignore all others and follow the person's movements and actions with our eyes. Sometimes we imitate their movements, smile when they smile, shake our head as they do, even light a cigarette when and as they do.

The most direct method of establishing contact nonverbally is obviously actual *physical contact*. The type of direct physical contact permitted and encouraged varies greatly depending on the context, the persons involved, and the encouragement given in return. Usually direct physical contact comes after some of the other nonverbal overtures have been accepted and perhaps returned in kind. E.T., the extraterrestrial, for example, did not touch his earthling companion until a relationship was established and his touching seemed to mark the beginning of a more advanced stage in their relationship.

GUIDES AND OBSTACLES TO RELATIONAL DEVELOPMENT

Initial encounters fail or succeed largely for the same reasons that well-established relationships fail or succeed. And so perhaps the best answer to the question of what makes some attempts successes and others failures is contained in this book. After all, interpersonal communication is interpersonal communication. In Unit 3 we considered positiveness, openness, equality, empathy, and supportiveness as the five characteristics of effective interpersonal communication. These same five qualities will go a long way in making first encounters successful as well. But there are also other factors more specific to initial encounters, and these will be considered here. These characteristics should be looked at as additions to those postulated for effectiveness in interpersonal communication generally.

In this discussion the guides are considered together with the obstacles because they seem here to be opposite ends of the same qualities.

Perceived Interest and Lack of Interest

All of us want to be thought of as being of interest to someone. We want to be told, verbally as well as nonverbally, that someone is interested in us. And we want to be told that someone is interested in us for ourselves—not for what he or she can get out of us, whether it be a job, money, sex, or whatever. And surely when someone attempts to make contact, he or she almost inevitably demonstrates some kind of interest; otherwise, why would the person want to make contact? This sounds logical until we begin to observe initial encounters and are forced to come to the conclusion that many people simply do not know how to demonstrate interest in another person. Perhaps it is because they are not genuinely interested in the first place. But perhaps they are interested and simply do not know how to express this interest.

A clear example of this occurs frequently at crowded singles bars or discos. One person may go up to another and begin a conversation, but he or she continues to look around and fails to maintain the eye contact that says, "I am interested in you," and fails psychologically and physically to exclude the others in the bar. Instead you get the feeling that the person is engaged in this conversation but still on the lookout for someone better to come along.

Interest and lack of interest can be demonstrated in many different ways. Direct eye contact and the exclusion of others, already mentioned, are obvious examples. But our general body posture also says a great deal about our interest in another person. The individual who keeps his or her body at a 90 degree angle to the body of the other person seems to be demonstrating a decided lack of interest. Similarly, the totally passive individual seems to be saying, "I'm here, but I'm not really interested—at least not enough to get really involved." The failure to listen to what the other person is saying—perhaps because we want to hear the conversation of the party next to us or the music—seems almost too obvious to mention, yet it seems to occur with extremely high frequency.

Self Versus Other Orientation

People who are preoccupied with themselves usually wind up staying by themselves. Except to themselves, they are bores. Each of us wants to feel that the other person wants to hear about us, wants to listen to what we have to say. I suspect that the time spent talking about oneself versus talking about the other person would provide us with reasonably good indications of the success or failure of the initial encounter. The person who talks only about himself or herself impresses nobody. A reasonable balance between talk and listening, between self and other orientation, is needed.

There is a danger in going to the other extreme, however, and concentrating so much on the other person that we do not reveal anything about ourselves. And although the other person may conclude that we are mysterious and fascinating, he or she may also conclude that we are shallow, having nothing to contribute, and live a very dull existence. Or more realistically, he or she may conclude—more often subconsciously than consciously—that we do not want to give of ourselves and do not want to share anything about ourselves with anyone.

Acceptance and Nonacceptance

In the discussion of supportiveness, we pointed out that evaluative statements increase defensiveness. To the extent that a person feels evaluated and tested, she or he will become defensive. In initial encounters this same kind of situation manifests itself. The concepts of acceptance and nonacceptance, however, seem more appropriate here. We want to feel that we are being accepted as a unique and significant individual. We want to feel that our attitudes, our values, and our opinions are accepted. We want to know that our feelings are accepted as valid expressions of what we are experiencing. We want to be accepted as equals.

This is not to say that we expect the other person to believe as we do, to hold the same values and opinions as we do, or to feel as we feel. Rather, we expect the other individual to recognize our right to believe as we do, to feel as we feel. Thus, I can disagree with your opinions or I can feel totally different about the same incident or person; yet I should still be able to see that your opinions and your feelings are valid for you.

To the extent that we feel accepted rather than challenged or rejected, we feel free to express ourselves. And perhaps this is what we really look for in a relationship—an opportunity to express ourselves as we wish without fear of rejection, without fear that love will be withdrawn, without fear that we will be punished.

Need Fulfillment Versus Need Nonfulfillment

We began this unit with some of the reasons why we seek contact and relationships with other people. One of the major reasons noted in a number of different contexts was that interpersonal contact fulfills needs—to alleviate loneliness, to be stimulated, to gain knowledge of the self, and so on. Even in the initial phases those needs are paramount, and to the extent that they are fulfilled, or at least to the extent that there seems some promise that they might be fulfilled, the interpersonal encounter will be developed and maintained. To the extent that these needs are not fulfilled or are thwarted, the interpersonal encounter will not be pursued or will be terminated if it is already developed.

Naturally, not everything is so clear-cut. It would be foolhardy to assume that a logical analysis such as this actually goes on in the minds of the individuals engaged in the interpersonal interaction. Far from it. Rather, one probably senses in some vague and general way the extent to which the interaction is enjoyable or unenjoyable, and it is on this basis that relationships are continued or terminated. The perceived enjoyment or unenjoyment is in turn related closely to the extent to which the interaction is fulfilling of our significant needs.

SOURCES

Murray S. Davis, *Intimate Relations* (New York: Free Press, 1973) and Mark L. Knapp, *Social Intercourse: From Greeting to Goodbye* (Boston: Allyn & Bacon, 1978) are both useful on relational development. Also see Chester C. Bennett, "Secrets Are for Sharing," *Psychology Today* 2 (February 1969):31–34. Textbooks in interpersonal communication also cover relational development. See, for example, Kenneth L. Villard and Leland J. Whipple, *Beginnings in Relational Communication* (New York: Wiley, 1976), and Michael D. Scott and William G. Powers, *Interpersonal Communication: A Question of Needs* (Boston: Houghton Mifflin, 1978). For social exchange theory see, for example, J. W. Thibaut and H. H. Kelley, *The Social Psychology of Groups* (New York: Wiley, 1959) and H. H. Kelley and J. W. Thibaut, *Interpersonal Relations: A Theory of Interdependence* (New York: Wiley/Interscience, 1978).

21.1 RELATIONAL DEVELOPMENT ANALYSIS

In an attempt to relate the concepts concerning relational development more closely to you as an individual, the following questions are offered as stimuli for discussion. First, respond to each of the questions individually. Respond as fully and as specifically as you can. Second, in small groups or with the class as a whole, consider each of the questions.

1. Why do you seek to develop interpersonal relationships? That is, identify the reasons *you* seek relationships with others.

2. If you are currently in a relationship, why do you continue with it? What factors are operating to maintain the relationship? What purpose or purposes is the relationship serving? Are there any purposes that an ideal relationship would serve for you that your current relationship is not serving? How might your relationship be realigned to better serve this currently unserved purpose?

3. How do you attempt to make verbal contact with another person? Do you have a general mode of making contact or do you act differently in each situation? With what type of verbal contact are you most comfortable? Least comfortable?

4. How do people make verbal contact with you? How do you respond to such attempts? What factors influence the way in which you respond? Consider, for example, what there is about you that leads you to respond as you do. What is there about the other person that influences how you respond?

5. How do you make nonverbal contact with others? With what approach are you most comfortable? Least comfortable?

6. How do others make nonverbal contact with you? How do you respond to the varied approaches? That is, do you respond positively to some and negatively to others? Explain.

7. What type of verbal and/or nonverbal approaches seem most effective? Least effective? Why?

8. What guidelines would you offer for interpersonal contact? That is, if you were advising a friend on how to go about meeting someone or establishing a relationship with someone, what would you tell her or him? What obstacles would you identify and suggest that your friend seek to avoid? On what bases do you offer these suggestions? That is, what reasons could you advance to support your suggestions?

9. What one rule for relationship contact do you feel is the most important? **336**

ATTRACTION IN INTERPERSONAL RELATIONSHIPS

Upon completion of this unit, you should be able to:
1. define *interpersonal attraction*
2. define *attractiveness* and explain its influence in interpersonal attraction
3. explain the relativity of physical and personality attractiveness
4. identify some of the sex differences in attractiveness
5. define *proximity* and explain the ways in which it influences interpersonal attraction
6. explain the "mere exposure" hypothesis
7. define *reinforcement* and explain how it enters into interpersonal attraction
8. explain the "gain-loss" theory of attraction
9. define *similarity* and explain how it operates in interpersonal attraction
10. explain the "matching" hypothesis
11. define *complementarity* and explain the ways in which it influences interpersonal attraction

We are all attracted to some people and not attracted to others. In a similar way, some people are attracted to us and some people are not. This seems to be the universal human condition. If we were to examine the people we are attracted to and the people we are not attracted to, we would probably be able to see patterns in the decisions or judgments we make. Even though many of these decisions seem subconsciously motivated, we can nevertheless discern patterns in the interpersonal choices we make.

We are all probably attracted to a "type" of person or to "types" of people. This ideal type (which differs for each person) can probably be found, in varying degrees, in each of the people we are attracted to and its opposite, in varying degrees, in each of the people we are not attracted to. It has been found that most people are interpersonally attracted to others on the basis of five major variables: attractiveness (physical and personality), proximity, reinforcement, similarity, and complementarity.

ATTRACTIVENESS (PHYSICAL AND PERSONALITY)

Attractiveness comes in at least two forms. When we say, "I find that person attractive," we probably mean either (1) that we find that person physically attractive or (2) that we find that person's personality or ways of behaving attractive. For the most part we tend to like physically attractive people rather than physically ugly people, and we tend to like people who possess a pleasant personality rather than an unpleasant personality. Few would find fault with these two generalizations. The difficulty arises when we try to define "attractive." A good way to illustrate this difficulty is to look at some old movies, newspapers, or magazines and compare the conceptions of beauty portrayed there with those popular now. Or examine the conceptions of beauty in different cultures. At some times and in some cultures people who are "fat" by our standards would be considered attractive, but in other cultures they would be considered unattractive. At one time fashion models were supposed to be extremely thin (remember Twiggy?), whereas they are now allowed to have some flesh on their bones. The same difficulty besets us when we attempt to define *pleasant personality*. To some people this would mean an aggressive, competitive, forceful individual, whereas to others it might mean an unassuming, shy, and bashful individual.

Similarly, we probably look for different physical and personality characteristics depending on the situation in which we are interacting. In a classroom it might be important to sit next to someone who knows all the answers, so regardless of this person's physical appearance, this "answer machine" is perceived as attractive. To go on a swimming date, however, we might select someone with a good body and not be too concerned with his or her intellectual abilities. When inviting someone to join a football team we might choose someone heavy and strong.

Although attractiveness (both physical and personality) is difficult, if not impossible, to define universally, it is possible to define it for any one individual for specific situations. Thus if a certain person were interested in dating someone, he or she would choose someone who possessed certain characteristics. For this person, then, in this situation, these are the characteristics that are considered "attractive." And in all probability, given this same person in another, similar situation, he or she would again look for someone who possessed these same characteristics. That is, we seem relatively consistent in the characteristics we find "attractive."

We also have a tendency to attribute positive characteristics to people we find attractive and negative characteristics to people we find unattractive. If people were asked to predict which qualities a given individual possessed, they would probably predict the possession of positive qualities if they thought the person attractive and negative characteristics if they thought the person unattractive. Numerous studies have supported this commonsense observation. In one study it was found that physically attractive people even get better treatment from therapists. In a Vanderbilt University Study it was found that young male psychologists who were training to be therapists responded with greater warmth and supportiveness to attractive than to unattractive women. These soon-to-be therapists also judged that the less attractive clients would more likely discontinue therapy. Perhaps we have here wishful thinking that develops into a self-fulfilling prophecy.

In another investigation of attractiveness and ugliness in mental adjustment, the researchers compared the attractiveness of hospitalized women with university employees and shoppers. It was found that lower levels of adjustment (for example, general satisfaction with life and with personal relationships) characterized the early lives of ugly subjects. The researchers concluded that "it is not mental illness that makes people ugly, but rather ugliness and its social consequences that drive some of them crazy."

When photographs of men and women varying in attractiveness were viewed by both men and women who were asked to assess these persons, the more attractive persons were judged to be sexually warmer and more responsive, more sensitive, kinder, more interesting, stronger, more poised, more modest, more sociable, more outgoing, to make more competent husbands and

Attraction often leads to strange (sometimes extreme) behaviors.

wives, to have happier marriages, and to secure more prestigious jobs. The less attractive persons were judged to make better parents.

When 400 teachers were shown identical report cards but with different pictures attached (some were of attractive and some were of unattractive persons), the teachers rated the report cards with the attractive persons' pictures attached as having higher educational potential, higher IQs, better social relationships with peers, and to have parents who were more interested in their education.

Even children have prejudices and are the object of attractiveness bias. For example, children between the ages of 4 and 6 believed that aggressive, antisocial behavior was more characteristic of unattractive than of attractive children. And female students, given a written description of some delinquent act and a photograph of the person who supposedly commited the act, judged the unattractive child as having more antisocial impulses and as being more likely to misbehave in the future. Attractive female college students received more favorable evaluations from fellow male students on essays they supposedly wrote and higher overall gradepoint averages in college than did unattractive females.

When students were asked to rate a man in terms of intelligence, self-confidence, likeability, and talent, he was rated more favorably on all four variables when he was pictured with an attractive girlfriend than when the very same man was pictured with an unattractive girlfriend.

It seems clear from these few studies and from the hundreds of others that might have been cited that attractiveness is an asset for both men and women but is especially important for women. It also seems clear that this is·a cultural phenomenon; we have been conditioned throughout our lives to look at women in terms of attractiveness and at men in terms of ability. This difference is well illustrated in one study in which men and women were asked to rate the qualities they find most important in the opposite sex. The results are presented in Table 22.1.

TABLE 22.1
Qualities Judged Most Important in a Potential Partner

For Men	For Women
1. achievement	1. physical attractiveness
2. leadership	2. erotic ability
3. occupational ability	3. affectional ability
4. economic ability	4. social ability
5. entertaining ability	5. domestic ability
6. intellectual ability	6. sartorial ability
7. observational ability	7. interpersonal understanding
8. common sense	8. art appreciation
9. athletic ability	9. moral and spiritual understanding
10. theoretical ability	10. art and creative ability

Source: From R. Centers, "The Completion Hypothesis and the Compensatory Dynamic in Intersexual Attraction and Love," *Journal of Psychology* 82 (1972):111–126.

It also seems clear that such findings as these (as well as the findings reported earlier on the relative importance of attractiveness in both men and women) are undergoing considerable change and will in the next decade or two change even more. Women are now beginning to be evaluated more in terms of their abilities and men more in terms of their physical attractiveness. And this trend seems likely to continue. Whether it will eventually equalize to the point where sex differences are totally erased (or even reversed, with attractiveness being more important for men) cannot be predicted on the basis of what we now know.

PROXIMITY

Some 200 years ago Henry Carey, in *Sally in Our Alley,* expressed the concept of proximity:

> Of all the girls that are so smart
> There's none like pretty Sally;
> She is the darling of my heart,
> And lives in our alley.

If we look around at the people we find attractive, we would probably find that they are the people who live or work close to us. This is perhaps the one finding that emerges most frequently from the research on interpersonal attraction. In one of the most famous studies Leon Festinger, Stanley Schachter, and Kurt Back studied friendships in a student housing development. They found that the development of friendships was greatly influenced by the distance between the units in which the people lived and by the direction in which the units faced. The closer the students' rooms were to each other, the better the chances were that they would become friends. It was also found that the students living in units that faced the courtyard had more friends than the student who lived in units facing the street. The people who became friends were the people who had the greater opportunity to interact with each other.

In college dormitories and in city housing projects with a number of floors, it is found that most friendships develop between people living on the same floor and that few develop between people on different floors. In fact, proximity influences not only who become friends but also how close the friendships come to be: the closer the living quarters, the closer the friendships. It is interesting to note that the vast majority of marriages are between people who have lived very close to each other physically.

Cadets at the Training Academy of the Maryland State Police who were asked to name their friends named persons whose last names came from the same part of the alphabet as did theirs. The practice at the Academy was to assign seats and rooms on the basis of alphabetical order, and so the persons with names from the same part of the alphabet were exposed to each other more and had a greater opportunity for interaction than persons whose names came from different parts of the alphabet. Again, it appears that proximity leads to attraction.

As might be predicted, physical distance is most important in the early stages of interaction. For example, during the first days of school, proximity (in class or in dormitories) is especially important. It decreases (but always remains significant) as the opportunity to interact with more distant others increases.

The importance of physical distance also varies with the type of situation one is in. For example, in anxiety-producing situations we seem to have more need for company and hence are more easily attracted to others than when we are in situations with low or no anxiety. It is also comforting to be with people who have gone through (or who will go through) the same experiences as we have. We seem especially attracted to these people in times of stress. We would also be more susceptive to being attracted to someone else if we have previously been deprived of such interaction. If, for example, we were in a hospital or prison without any contact with other people, we would probably be attracted to just about anyone. Anyone seems a great deal better than no one. We are also most attracted to people when we are feeling down or when self-esteem is particularly low.

When we attempt to discover the reasons for the influence that physical closeness has on interpersonal attraction, we can think of many. We seem to have positive expectations of people and consequently fulfill these by liking or being attracted to those we find ourselves near. Proximity also allows us the opportunity to get to know the other person—to gain some information about him or her. We come to like people we know because we can better predict their behavior, and perhaps because of this they seem less frightening to us than complete strangers.

Still another approach argues that *mere exposure* to others leads us to develop positive feelings for them. In one study women were supposedly participating in a taste experiment and throughout the course of the experiment were exposed to other people. The subjects were exposed to some people 10 times, to others 5 times, to others 2 times, to others 1 time, and to others not at all. The subjects did not talk with these other people and had never seen them before this experiment. The subjects were then asked to rate the other people in terms of how much they liked them. The results showed that they rated highest those persons they had seen 10 times, next highest those they had seen 5 times, and so on down the line. How can we account for these results except by "mere exposure"? Consider another study. Three groups of rats were selected at random. One group listened to recordings of Mozart for 12 hours a day for 52 days. Another group listened to recordings of Schoenberg for 12 hours a day for 52 days. A third group listened to no music at all. After these 52 days, each rat was placed in a specially designed cage so that it could select the music it wished to listen to. The music selected by the rats was written by the same composer as the music they had been exposed to for the 52-day period. Thus the rats raised on Mozart selected Mozart; the rats raised on

Schoenberg selected Schoenberg. Mozart was also preferred by the rats raised without music. To make this experiment more unbelievable, we should emphasize that the music the rats heard during the 52-day period was not the same as that selected by the rats in the specially designed cages; it was only written by the same composer. Again, can we account for these findings in any way other than mere exposure?

Of course, if our initial interaction with a person is unpleasant, then repeated exposure may not increase attraction. Mere exposure seems to work when the initial interaction is favorable or even neutral; in these cases exposure increases attraction. When the initial interaction is negative, however, mere exposure may actually decrease attraction.

Connected to this "mere exposure" concept is the finding that the greater the contact between people, the less they are prejudiced against each other. For example, whites and blacks living in housing developments became less prejudiced against each other as a result of living and interacting together. It is interesting to speculate on the influence that architects could have on interpersonal interaction, attraction, prejudice, and the like.

The most obvious reason for the effects of proximity seems to be simply that people are basically attractive. By interacting or being exposed to them, we realize this and are thus drawn to them. Put differently, perhaps we are attracted to people because they are attractive.

REINFORCEMENT

The most obvious statement we could make about interpersonal attraction is that we like those who like us and dislike those who dislike us. Naturally there are exceptions; there are some who love people who do not love them, and there are those who hate those who love them. For most of us, most of the time, however, we like those who like us. Put in more behavioral terms, we tend to like those who reward or reinforce us. The reward or reinforcement may be social, as in the form of compliments or praise of one sort or another or it may be material, as in the case of the suitor whose gifts eventually win the hand of the beloved.

But reward can backfire. When overdone, reward loses its effectiveness and may even lead to negative responses. The people who reward us constantly soon become too sweet to take, and in a short period we come to discount whatever they say. Also, if the reward is to work, it must be perceived as genuine and not motivated by selfish concerns. The salesperson who compliments your taste in clothes, your eyes, your build, and just about everything else is not going to have the effect that someone without ulterior motives would have. In all probability the salesperson is acting out of selfish concerns; he or she wants to make the sale. Hence this person's "reinforcements" would not lead us to be attracted to him or her since they would not be perceived as genuine.

The order in which reinforcement occurs and whether or not it is coupled with negative evaluations also affects its influence. Researchers investigated this issue by having subjects "overhear" conversations by others about themselves. Four conditions were established, each consisting of overhearing seven conversations. In the positive condition, all seven conversations the subjects overheard were positive. In the negative condition, all conversations were negative. In the negative-positive condition, the first three conversations were negative and the last four were positive. In the positive-negative condition, the first three conversations were positive and the last four were negative. After overhearing these conversations, the subjects were asked to indicate the extent to which they liked the "gossiping" individual on a scale ranging from -10 to $+10$. That is, the concern was which form of rewards and punishments would lead to the greatest amount of liking. It was found that the most-liked persons were the ones who first spoke negatively and then spoke positively; that is, the negative-positive condition produced the greatest amount of attraction ($+7.67$). The next most-liked persons were those in the positive condition ($+6.42$). The third most-liked were the persons in the negative condition ($+2.52$). The least liked were the persons who first spoke positively and then spoke negatively, that is, the positive-negative condition ($+0.87$).

Elliot Aronson has proposed that a *gain-loss theory* can account for such findings as these. Basically, the theory states that increases in rewards will have greater impact than will constant invariant rewards. We will like a person more if that person's liking (rewards) for us increases over time than if that person constantly rewards us indiscriminately. This holds true even if the number of rewards given by the person who always likes us are greater than those given by the person whose liking for us increases over time. Conversely, decreases in rewards have a greater impact than constant punishments; we will dislike the person whose rewards decrease over time more than the person who always punishes us or who never has anything good to say about us.

Intuitively this seems satisfying. We seem to have a greater attraction for the person who changes his or her mind toward us, as long as the final evaluation is positive. The person who first evaluates us positively and then negatively may well be perceived as a traitor, as an ally who later deserts us, and as such is less liked than the person who speaks consistently of us in the negative.

There is another dimension to reinforcement that should be mentioned here: we become attracted to persons we reward. We come to like people for whom we do favors. Although our initial reaction might be to say that we give rewards to people because we like them—and this is certainly true—it also works in reverse. Giving others rewards increases our liking for them as well. It seems we justify going out of our way by convincing ourselves that the person is worth the effort and is a likeable person generally. In an experiment in which subjects won money, one-third were asked to give it back as a special favor to the experimenter, another third were asked to give it back for the psychology department's research fund, and another third were not asked to return it at all. The subjects were later tested on how much they liked the experimenter. The subjects who gave back the money to the experimenter indicated the greatest liking for him. By liking him, the subjects justified giving back the money they won. You may have noticed this same phenomenon in your own interactions. You have probably increased your liking for persons after buying them an expensive present, going out of your way to do them a special favor, seeing a movie you did not want to see, and so on. In these and numerous similar instances, we justify our behavior by believing that the person was worth our efforts; otherwise, we would have to admit to being poor judges of character and to spending our money and our time on those who do not deserve it.

SIMILARITY

If people could construct their mates they would look, act, and think very much like themselves. By being attracted to people like ourselves we are in effect validating ourselves, saying to ourselves that we are worthy of being liked, that we are attractive. Although there are exceptions, we generally like people who are similar to ourselves in color, race, ability, physical characteristics, intelligence, and so on. We are often attracted to mirror images of ourselves.

If you were to ask a group of friends, "To whom are you attracted?," they would probably name very attractive people; in fact, they would probably name the most attractive people they know. But if we were to observe these friends, we would find that they go out with and establish relationships with people who are quite similar to themselves in terms of physical attractiveness. The *matching hypothesis* is useful in this connection and states that although we may be attracted to the most physically attractive people, we date and mate people who are similar to ourselves in physical attractiveness. Intuitively this, too, seems satisfying. In some cases, however, we notice discrepancies; we notice an old man dating an attractive younger partner or an unattractive woman with a handsome partner. In these cases, we will probably find that the less attractive partner possesses some quality that compensates for his or her lack of physical attractiveness. Prestige, money, intelligence, power, and various personality characteristics are obvious examples of qualities that may compensate for being less physically attractive.

Similarity is especially important when it comes to attitudes. We are particularly attracted to people who have attitudes similar to our own, who like what we like, and who dislike what we dislike. This similarity is most important when dealing with salient or significant attitudes. For example, it would not make much difference if the attitudes of two people toward food or furniture differed (though even these can at times be significant), but it would be of great significance if their attitudes toward children or religion or politics were very disparate. Marriages between people with great and salient dissimilarities are more likely to end in divorce than are marriages between people who are very much alike.

Generally, by liking people who are similar to us and who like what we like, we maintain balance with ourselves. It is psychologically uncomfortable to like people who do not like what we like or to dislike people who like what we like. And so our attraction for similarity enables us to achieve psychological balance or comfort.

Agreement with ourselves is always reinforcing. The person who likes what we like in effect tells us that we are right to like what we like. Even after an examination it is helpful to find people who wrote the same answers we did. It tells us we were right. Notice the next time you have an examination how reinforcing it is to hear that others have put down the same answers.

Another reason we are attracted to similarly minded people is that we can predict that since they think like us, they will like us as well. And so we like them because we think they like us.

We have often heard people say that the pets of people come to look and

The matching hypothesis.

act like their owners. This misses the point. Actually, the animals do not change. Rather, the owners select pets that look like them at the start. Look around and test this out on people who have dogs and cats.

COMPLEMENTARITY

Although many people would argue that "birds of a feather flock together," others would argue that "opposites attract." This latter concept is the principle of complementarity.

Take, for example, the individual who is extremely dogmatic. Would he or she be attracted to those who are high in dogmatism or to those who are low in dogmatism? The similarity principle predicts that this person will be attracted to those who are like him or her (that is, high in dogmatism), while the complementarity principle predicts that this person will be attracted to those who are unlike him or her (that is, low in dogmatism).

It may be found that people are attracted to others who are dissimilar only in certain situations. For example, the submissive student may get along especially well with an aggressive teacher rather than a submissive one but may not get along with an aggressive fiancé or spouse. The dominant wife may get along with a submissive husband but may not relate well to submissive neighbors or colleagues.

Theodore Reik in *A Psychologist Looks at Love* argues that we fall in love with people who possess characteristics that we do not possess and that we actually envy. The introvert, for example, if displeased with being shy, might be attracted to an extrovert.

There seems intuitive support for both complementarity and similarity and certainly neither can be ruled out in terms of exerting significant influence on interpersonal attraction. The experimental evidence, however, seems to favor similarity. Glenn Wilson and David Nias, in their *The Mystery of Love*, review evidence demonstrating that similarity in attitudes, physical attractiveness, self-esteem, race, religion, age, and social class seem to increase attraction and, therefore, support the similarity theory that people are attracted to people like themselves. But even here the correlations among these variables and attraction are weak and the evidence is certainly not as extensive as would be liked.

Complementarity finds less support. The most obvious instance of complementarity is found in the fact that most persons are heterosexual and are attracted to persons of the opposite sex. One of the most interesting supports for complementarity appears in the finding that when one person in a relationship is "witty" the other person is "placid." It seems so much easier being witty with a placid listener than with a competing wit—something we have probably all observed in our own interpersonal relationships.

SOURCES

The area of interpersonal attraction is thoroughly surveyed in Ellen Berscheid and Elaine Hatfield Walster, *Interpersonal Attraction* (Reading, Mass.: Addison-Wesley, 1969). I relied heavily on the review and the insights provided by Patricia Niles Middlebrook in *Social Psychology and Modern Life* (New York: Random House, 1974). Zick Rubin, *Liking and Loving: An Invitation to Social Psychology* (New York: Holt, Rinehart and Winston, 1973), covers the area of interpersonal attraction in an interesting and insightful manner. The experiments on "mere exposure" (the women in the taste experiment and the rats listening to music) are discussed by Rubin. The original references are in Susan Saegert, Walter Swap, and Robert B. Zajonc, "Exposure, Context, and Interpersonal Attraction," *Journal of Personality and Social Psychology* 25 (1973):234–242, and Henry A. Cross, Charles G. Halcomb, and William W. Matter, "Imprinting or Exposure Learning in Rats Given Early Auditory Stimulation," *Psychonomic Science* 7 (1967):233–234. The most authoritative source for the "mere exposure" hypothesis is Robert B. Zajonc, "Attitudinal Effects of Mere Exposure," *Journal of Personality and Social Psychology Monograph Supplement* 9, no. 2 (1968):Part 2. The studies cited in the discussion of attractiveness may be found in *Human Behavior* 7 (July 1978):26; in Glen Wilson and David Nias, *The Mystery of Love* (New York: Quadrangle/The New York Times Book Co., 1976); and in M. W. Segal, "Alphabet and Attraction: An Unobtrusive Measure of the Effect of Propinquity in a Field Setting," *Journal of Personality and Social Psychology* 30 (1974):654–657.

The analysis of attractiveness and the comparison between similarity and complementarity owes much to the Wilson and Nias discussion. The study of friendships in college housing was conducted by Leon Festinger, Stanley Schachter, and Kurt W. Back, *Social Pressures in Informal Groups: A Study of Human Factors in Housing* (New York: Harper & Row, 1950). Also see L. Nahemow and M. P. Lawton, "Similarity and Propinquity in Friendship Formation," *Journal of Personality and Social Psychology* 32 (1975):205–213 and E. B. Ebbesen, G. L. Kjos, and V. J. Konecni, "Spatial Ecology: Its Effects on the Choice of Friends and Enemies," *Journal of Experimental Social Psychology* 12 (1976):505–518. For the study on the influence of the order of reinforcement and the gain-loss theory, see E. Aronson and D. Linder, "Gain and Loss of Esteem as Determinants of Interpersonal Attractiveness," *Journal of Experimental Social Psychology* 1 (1965):156–171, and Elliot Aronson, *The Social Animal,* 3d ed. (San Francisco, Calif.: W. H. Freeman, 1980). On the matching hypothesis see, for example, Elaine Walster and G. William Walster, *A New Look at Love* (Reading, Mass.: Addison-Wesley, 1978). A useful overview of attraction from the point of view of the psychologist is provided in Herbert Harari and Robert M. Kaplan, *Psychology: Personal and Social Adjustment* (New York: Harper & Row, 1977).

The study on doing favors for others in increasing attraction may be found in Jon Jecker and David Landy, "Liking a Person as a Function of Doing Him a Favor," *Human Realations* 22 (1969):371–378, and is discussed in Aronson, *The Social Animal.* Also see the articles on attraction, dealing with some of the issued discussed in this unit, in Elliot Aronson, ed., *Readings About The Social Animal,* 3d ed. (San Fancisco, Calif.: Freeman, 1981), pp. 341–406.

22.1 THE QUALITIES OF INTERPERSONAL ATTRACTION

In order to test the principles and findings discussed in this unit, complete the following questionnaire and answer the two questions that follow it before reading any further.

CHARACTERISTICS OF THE PERSON TO WHOM YOU WOULD BE MOST ATTRACTED

Age

Sex

Height

Weight

General physical attractiveness

Race

Religion

Nationality

Intelligence

Years of formal education

Profession or professional goal

Religious attitudes

At least three major personality characteristics

1. List the names of five people to whom you are very attracted.
2. List the names of five people to whom you are not attracted.

Consider the following questions relevant to your responses.

1. Concerning the characteristics of the person you chose as being most attractive:
   a. Would the person whose characteristics you described be considered physically attractive? Physically unattractive? Would this person have an attractive personality? An unattractive personality?
   b. What specific characteristics did you emphasize in terms of attractiveness (physical or personality)?
   c. How similar are the characteristics you see yourself as possessing?
   d. Were the attitudinal characteristics especially important?
   e. Could instances of complementarity be identified? That is, did you list characteristics that would complement your own?

349

2. Concerning the persons you listed as being very attracted to:
   a. Are these persons attractive in terms of physical and personality characteristics?
   b. Do they live or work close to you?
   c. Do they reinforce you frequently? Socially? Materially?
   d. Are they similar to you in what they like and what they dislike? Are they similar to you in terms of physical and personality characteristics? Especially, are their attitudes toward significant issues similar to yours?
   e. Do they complement you in any way? How are they different from you? Are these differences complementary?
3. Concerning the persons you listed as being not attracted to:
   a. Are they generally unattractive? Physically? In terms of personality? What specific behaviors do you find unattractive?
   b. How does proximity enter into your choices? Do any of the persons listed live or work very close to you?
   c. Do these people reinforce you? If so, how do they do this? Why does their "reinforcement" not have a positive effect?
   d. How similar or dissimilar to you are the persons listed? Physically? Intellectually? Attitudinally?
   e. In what ways are you and they complementary? That is, do these persons have characteristics that would complement your own?
4. How valuable are the five variables discussed in this unit in explaining the bases for those you find interpersonally attractive? What other variables seem significant to you?

22.2 HEROES

At the end of this exercise is a list of 100 noted personalities currently in the news. Some of these persons you will recognize and will probably know a great deal about. Others, however, may seem totally unfamiliar. Your task is to select the five persons you would nominate for your personal hall of fame. This is, select the five people you feel could serve as your personal heroes.

Either of two general procedures will prove useful. After each person has selected five people from the list, the names should be written on index cards and collected anonymously. A tabulation of the number of votes for each person should be made, and the 10 persons receiving the highest number of votes should be noted. This method will provide an anonymous procedure and will probably result in a much more candid final list.

An alternative procedure is to form groups of five or six after each person has selected his or her own choices from the list. The task of each group is to select a final list of five persons that the group would nominate for its personal hall of fame. After each group has selected its "heroes," the names should be put on the blackboard. This procedure, although the easier and more efficient to follow, does not allow for anonymity and hence will probably result in the selection of more socially acceptable heroes.

DO NOT READ ANY FURTHER UNTIL YOU HAVE WRITTEN DOWN AND TURNED IN THE FIVE NAMES.

Discussion may then center on some or all of the following questions:

1. The "Heroes" list contains 50 male and 50 female names. Are there more men or women represented in the final list(s)? If there are differences, how do you account for them? Is the original list weighed unfairly in terms of one sex rather than the other by having more prominent males than females or vice versa? If so, how might that imbalance have been corrected? Did anyone feel an obligation to select both males and females? An obligation to select only one sex? Explain.

2. Did the male and female voter patterns differ significantly? If so, why do you think this happened?

3. On the "Heroes" list of 100 people there are 15 blacks. How did blacks do in the final list(s)? Explain. What other blacks might have been included on the list?

4. If sexual preference (gay or straight) had been listed along with the name, or if the information had been known (as with sex and race), would the gays have been selected? Do not accept a simple "yes" or "no" for this question. A "yes" may be a socially acceptable response among college students, but a deeper analysis might reveal different attitudes.

5. What areas of accomplishment are represented most frequently in the final list(s)? Why do you feel this is so?

6. How do you think the votes given here would differ if, say, your parents or your teachers did the voting? Explain.

7. Of the names on the "Heroes" list, which were the least well known? From what areas of accomplishment are these? How do you account for this?

8. What values do the class members hold that can be deduced from the final list of heroes? Are there any surprises?

HEROES

Bella Abzug	Marlon Brando	Salvador Dali
Muhammad Ali	Leonid Brezhnev	Angela Davis
Idi Amin	Helen Gurley Brown	Sammy Davis, Jr.
Neil Armstrong	Anita Bryant	Doris Day
Joan Baez	Carol Burnett	Jeane Dixon
F. Lee Bailey	Truman Capote	Queen Elizabeth
Pearl Bailey	Jimmy Carter	Werner Erhard
James Baldwin	Cesar Chavéz	Jane Fonda
Christiaan Barnard	Julia Child	Betty Friedan
Julian Bond	Shirley Chisholm	Indira Gandhi

Nikki Giovanni
Billy Graham
Patty Hearst
Lillian Hellman
Xaveria Hollander
Lee A. Iacocca
Mick Jagger
Elton John
Erica Jong
Barbara Jordan
Ted Kennedy
Billie Jean King
Coretta King
Jeane Kirkpatrick
Ayatollah Khomeini
Sophia Loren
Charles Manson
Paul McCartney
Rod McKuen
Shirley MacLaine
Maharishi Mahesh Yogi
Liza Minelli
Sun Myung Moon

Mary Tyler Moore
Patricia Murphy
Ralph Nader
Richard Nixon
Joyce Carol Oates
Sandra Day O'Connor
Jacqueline Kennedy Onassis
Dolly Parton
Pope John Paul II
Norman Vincent Peale
Isabel Perón
Sylvia Porter
Ayn Rand
Ronald Reagan
Vanessa Redgrave
Harry Reems
Jonas Salk
Phyllis Schlafly
Arnold Schwartzenegger
George P. Shultz
Bobby Seale
Tom Seaver
Fulton J. Sheen

Brooke Shields
Carly Simon
O. J. Simpson
Frank Sinatra
B. F. Skinner
Margaret Chase Smith
Alexander Solzhenitsyn
Steven Spielberg
Sylvester Stallone
Elizabeth Taylor
Shirley Temple
Mother Teresa
Margaret Thatcher
John Travolta
Pauline Trigère
Margaret Truman
Abigail van Buren
Gore Vidal
Barbara Walters
Lina Wertmuller
Roy Wilkins
Tennessee Williams
Stevie Wonder

CONFLICT IN INTERPERSONAL RELATIONSHIPS

Upon completion of this unit, you should be able to:
1. define *conflict*
2. provide at least three examples of conflict situations
3. state at least three conditions under which conflict is likely to occur
4. explain some of the effects that conflict has on communication
5. explain some of the principles of communication that are relevant to conflict and its resolution
6. explain at least four pseudoconflict resolution methods
7. explain the five stages in conflict resolution

Some years ago, a group of 11-year-old boys at a summer camp unknowingly became subjects in a most interesting study of conflict. There were three main stages in this simulated war devised by Muzafer Sherif and his colleagues. In the first stage the boys were divided into two groups and each group was isolated from the other. The boys developed close interpersonal relations with members of their own group and a strong feeling of group cohesiveness. The groups called themselves the Eagles and the Rattlers.

The second stage involved the creation of friction between the two groups. The groups were placed in a number of competitive and mutually frustrating activities. A high level of intergroup hostility was thus developed.

The third stage focused on attempts to reduce the conflict. At first the experimenters brought the groups together for mutually satisfying activities such as seeing a movie, eating, and participating in a series of experiments. The effect of these activities was to produce outward displays of conflict and hostility, both verbal and nonverbal. The experimenters then set up a series of goals that required mutual cooperation between the groups. In one situation the researchers staged a water shortage. The cooperation of all the boys was needed if the water was to be turned on again. In another situation both groups had to contribute to pay to obtain a movie they all wanted to see but for which neither group had enough money by themselves. In the third situation the two groups were removed from the camp and had to perform a number of cooperative tasks such as using their combined efforts to start a stalled truck.

The outcome of these situations was that the hostility between the two **353** groups was significantly reduced, and this was attributed by the experimenters to the interpersonal experiences of cooperation between the two groups. It seems universally agreed that if conflict is to be reduced, it is to be reduced through interpersonal interaction. The corollary to this seems equally agreed upon: If conflict is to be generated and maintained, it is to be done through interpersonal interaction as well. Conflict, both its generation and its resolution, seems largely an interpersonal communication process.

In this unit we examine conflict from a number of different perspectives. First, we will inquire into the nature of conflict, the ways in which it is manifested, and some of the problems (as well as some of the values) to be derived from conflict. Second, we will focus on the relationship between conflict and communication, considering the effect of conflict on communication and of communication on conflict. Third, we will look at conflict resolution, both the pseudomethods of resolution and the stages that might go into a model of conflict resolution.

THE NATURE OF CONFLICT

Conflict is one of the most complex of all interpersonal processes and consequently it is necessary to examine what conflict is and how it might be manifested. More specifically, we will explore conflict in terms of its locus and its negative and positive dimensions.

The Locus of Conflict

Using concepts developed earlier we may distinguish between content conflict and relationship conflict. *Content conflict* centers on objects, events, and persons in the world that are usually (but not always) external to the parties involved in the conflict. These include the millions of issues that we argue and fight about every day—the value of a particular movie, what to watch on television, the validity of a grade received on a term paper, the fairness of the last examination, the job promotion, the way to spend our savings, and how our false teeth look.

Relationship conflicts are equally numerous and include the conflict between two brothers that develops because the younger brother does not obey the older brother, the conflict between husband and wife because each wanted to have an equal say before vacation plans were made, and the conflict between mother and daughter when each wants to have the final say concerning the daughter's life-style. Here the conflicts are not so much concerned with the outside world or with some external object, but rather with the relationships between the individuals—with such issues as who is in charge, the equality of a marital relationship, and who has the right to set down rules of behavior.

Content and relationship conflicts are always easier to separate in a textbook than they are in reality where many conflicts contain elements of both content and relationship conflict. Yet, it helps a great deal if we can recognize which issues pertain to content and which to relationship. Only by doing this will we be able to understand the conflict well enough to manage it effectively and productively.

The Negative and the Positive Aspects of Conflict

In its most insidious form, conflict is war between individuals or nations. The object of the "game" is to bring the enemy to surrender. To accomplish this, anything goes. In sports, boxing perhaps comes closest to real conflict. Although disguised as competition and supported as analogous to baseball or football, the object of boxing is to harm your opponent to the point where he surrenders or is rendered incapacitated for 10 seconds. The greater the harm a fighter inflicts on his opponent, the closer he is to winning the bout and being proclaimed a hero. Verbal abuse is also conflict. It is a kind of verbal version of the boxing ring, as, for example, in slander or libel.

Conflict is likely to occur when both parties want or perhaps need the same thing—a particular river, grazing land, a protective mountain, a desirable job, an important promotion—and the only way to secure the desired object is to defeat any other person or group intent on taking it for themselves. Conflict is also likely to occur when someone is threatened. When a young boy is threatened and cannot extricate himself in a socially acceptable manner without actually fighting he often delivers the first blow. In more mature versions the same basic pattern is followed, but the threats are more subtle and more sophisticated and the consequences more lethal. Even among nations the same general pattern is followed. First the threats are verbal; then they are physical, but on a small scale, for example, blockading ships or shooting down a plane. When the threats can no longer be ignored—for physical, psychological, or social reasons—actual full-scale conflict results.

Naturally, conflict is more likely to occur among persons who dislike or hate each other, though there is also much conflict in marriage and among supposed lovers. And this suggests another condition under which conflict is likely to occur, namely, when one person has been hurt. When this happens, he or she is often likely to hurt back. If, for example, the husband hurts the wife by not responding favorably to her advances, she in turn may attempt to hurt him. As a result, he in turn may attempt to hurt her. As a result, she in return may attempt to retaliate and hurt him, and he again may respond in kind. The process of conflict spirals, with one response serving as the stimulus for another. Each attack becomes more and more deadly.

Although the usual view is that conflict is negative, as the examples above indicate, there are also a number of values or benefits to be derived from conflict. Alan Filley, in his *Interpersonal Conflict Resolution*, considers four major values of conflict.

1. Many conflict situations have the effect of diffusing more serious conflicts. This is especially the case when the conflicts (perhaps more

accurately described as competitive exchanges) are played out according to a system of rules. The disagreements that result often reduce the probability of more significant conflicts arising.

2. Conflict situations lead us to acquire new information, new ways of looking at things. They energize our creativity and force us to explore new ideas and new ways of behaving.

3. When the conflict is an intergroup one, then conflict functions to increase group cohesiveness. One of the most powerful ways to encourage members of a group to interact cooperatively and efficiently is to put the group into conflict with another group.

4. Conflict provides an opportunity for individuals or groups to measure their power, strength, or ability, since it is in conflict situations that such qualities are mobilized to their peak.

Brent Ruben affirms the view of conflict as having both positive and negative dimensions: "Although conflict may be associated with feelings of stress and pain, it must nevertheless be viewed as a *sine qua non* of learning, creativity, and biological and psychological growth and differentiation for the individual. And, as social conflict may be a precondition for war and political and economic strife, so, also, should it be regarded as the lifeblood of social change, choice, and social revolution."

When there is conflict within an interpersonal relationship and when we attempt to resolve that conflict, we are saying in effect that the relationship is worth the effort. To confront such a conflict we must care, at least to some degree, about the relationship; otherwise we would walk away from it. Although there may be exceptions—as when we confront conflict to save face or to gratify some ego need—it seems generally true that confronting a conflict indicates a degree of concern, of commitment, of a desire to preserve the relationship.

CONFLICT AND COMMUNICATION

As we have noted, the generation as well as the resolution of conflict are essentially communication processes. Consequently, there are two general areas concerning conflict and communication that need to be explored. The first concerns the effects that conflict has on communications. The second concerns the principles of communication that may be relevant to conflict resolution, or the effects that communication has on conflict.

The Influence of Conflict on Communication

Conflict leads to increased negative regard for the opponent. At times this negative feeling is passed down from generation to generation, as with warring families, tribes, or nations. Generally, the more conflict, the deeper the negative regard. Again, there is a spiral effect here. The conflict leads to negative regard, which leads to still more conflict, and so on. Conflict often leads to a waste of time and energy for both sides. Most obviously, conflict can lead to serious damage, physical or psychological, or death. Even in the most ritualized of all conflict situations—the boxing ring—men have died. But they also die in gang fights and in wars.

Conflict leads us to close ourselves off from the other individual—which seems a reasonable defensive strategy; it would not be to our advantage to reveal our weaknesses to our enemy. Conflict is at times the opposite of supportiveness; conflict often leads to destructiveness. We seek not to help but to destroy our opponent. In some cases conflict may lead people to develop an increased positiveness for themselves; perhaps the idea of glory due the conquering hero is still with us. But most reasonable people, it seems, would not take pride in killing. Conflict attempts to eliminate whatever equality may have been present at the start. If equality were to remain, there would be a constant stalemate. By harming or thwarting or destroying the other, we are in effect establishing superiority over them. Empathy, on the other hand, is perhaps increased in times of conflict. The only person who can empathize with the fighter who gets knocked out cold in the first round seems to be another fighter who went through the same or similar experience. So perhaps the victim and the victor are not so far apart in their feelings.

The Influence of Communication on Conflict

Our goal in the study of communication should be to provide insight into how conflict might be resolved through the application of principles of effective communication. In Unit 3 five characteristics of effective interpersonal communication were considered: (1) openness, (2) empathy, (3) supportiveness, (4) positiveness, and (5) the equality of both parties. These five principles might well be repeated here as guides to effective conflict management, but there are other principles that can be advanced that are unique to conflict situations and their resolution.

As was already mentioned, conflict is not necessarily bad. Similarly, we should realize that conflict resolution is not synonymous with the elimination of differences. There will always be differences and even disagreements among people. These are as natural as they are inevitable. In conflict resolution we wish to lessen the destructive and unproductive fighting, not to eliminate difference and diversity.

In conflict situations communication has, to an extent, already broken down, and consequently we need to move quickly to repair the damage done. One of the first tasks must be to reestablish mutual trust since it is likely that trust has long been abandoned. A special attempt should be made in conflict resolution to focus on the issues rather than on the personalities involved. Although we can never communicate objectively about the world without communicating about ourselves, we need to make a special effort in conflict situations to distinguish between these communications because there is a strong tendency to blame some one person for the conflict and to refocus the conflict onto this person.

In any conflict there are areas and issues of agreement. In any discussion of conflict we need to capitalize on these agreements and perhaps use them as a basis to gradually approach disagreements and impasses. Little is accomplished by emphasizing disagreement and minimizing agreement. We may have to journey far from the actual field of conflict to find such areas of agreement; in most cases, however, we will find them in the midst of the actual conflict.

We must also recognize that flexibility and a willingness to compromise are especially important in conflict situations. If we wish to resolve a conflict, we cannot approach it with the idea that things must be seen our way. There will be little hope of agreement and there is a good chance that the conflict will escalate. A willingness to change, to bend, to compromise seems essential in any attempt at conflict resolution.

Remember that conflict cannot be resolved unless the communication channels are kept open. To walk out on conflict situations or to refuse to confront the issues creates more problems than it solves. This is not to say we should constantly verbalize or that periodic moratoriums are not helpful. Rather, it is to emphasize that we need to be willing to *communicate*—to say what is on our minds and to listen to what the other person is saying.

CONFLICT RESOLUTION

In dealing with conflict resolution, it is wise to keeep in mind the following law of conflict: *Any conflict is easier to create than to resolve.* This law (advanced as a tribute to Murphy's original law, *If anything can go wrong, it will*) is simple enough, but there are some rather spiteful corollaries. For example, the time it takes to create an interpersonal conflict is always shorter than the time it takes to resolve the conflict. Alternatively, the energy expenditure needed to create a conflict is often minor; to resolve that conflict the energy expenditure is major.

There are two main approaches in conflict resolution: the unproductive and the productive. The *unproductive approach* seems to focus on hiding or covering up the conflict rather than on dealing with it directly to resolve it. The *productive approach* focuses on systematically examining the problem and its possible solutions. Each of these approaches is considered here. The unproductive methods are considered "pseudomethods" of resolution and the productive approach is considered under "Stages in Conflict Resolution."

Pseudomethods of Resolution

Although many such pseudomethods might be identified, we concentrate here on the five that seem the most important. Understanding these unproductive fight strategies will enable us to deal more effectively with them when they occur in the behavior of others and to eliminate them from our own conflict resolution arsenal.

Avoidance or Redefinition. One of the most frequently employed methods of conflict "resolution" is to avoid the conflict. This may take the form of actual physical flight (whereby the individual leaves the scene of the conflict), falling asleep, or just mentally withdrawing. Or it may take the form of emotional or intellectual avoidance, whereby the individual leaves the conflict psychologically by not dealing with any of the arguments or problems raised.

Avoidance often takes the form of changing the subject, or by talking about the problem so abstractly or in such incomprehensible language that mutual understanding is impossible. A similar method is to redefine the conflict so that it becomes no conflict at all or so that it becomes irrelevant to the individuals and hence unnecessary to deal with.

Force. Perhaps the most common picture of a pseudomethod of conflict resolution is that involving physical force. When confronted with a conflict, many prefer not to deal with the issues but rather simply to force his or her

Conflict patterns are learned early and often stay with us throughout our lives.

decision or way of thinking or behaving on the other by physically overpowering the individual, or at least by the threat of such physical force. At other times the force used is more emotional than physical. In either case, however, the issues are avoided and the individual who "wins" is the individual who exerts the most force. This, of course, is the technique of warring nations and spouses.

Minimization. Sometimes we deal with conflict by making light of it, by saying and perhaps believing that the conflict, its causes, and its consequences are really not important. We might argue that if left alone, time will resolve it. But time does absolutely nothing; over time *we* may do something, but time itself never acts in one way or the other.

Sometimes we minimize the conflict with humor and may literally laugh at it. Sometimes it is obvious, however, that our laughter is prompted by fear, embarrassment, or personal inadequacy in dealing with the conflict situation. But in many instances the humor seems logical enough; it eases the tension and, at least for a time, makes for more effective interpersonal relations. The problem is that the laughter does nothing to get at the root of the problem, and when the laughter dies the conflict is still very much alive.

Blame. Sometimes conflict is caused by the actions of one individual; sometimes it is caused by clearly identifiable outside forces. Most of the time, however, it is caused by such a wide variety of factors that any attempt to single out one or two factors is doomed to failure. And yet a frequently employed fight strategy is to avoid dealing with the conflict by blaming someone for it. In some instances we blame ourselves. This may be the result of a realistic appraisal of the situation, or it may be an attempt to evoke sympathy or to gain pity from the other individual. More often, however, we blame the other person. If a couple has a conflict over a child's getting into trouble with the police, for example, the parents may start blaming each other for the child's troubles instead of dealing with the conflict itself. As can easily be appreciated (at least when we are not parties to the conflict), blaming solves nothing other than temporarily relieving a degree of intrapersonal guilt.

Silencers. One of the most unfair but one of the most popular fight strategies is the use of silencers—a wide variety of fighting techniques that literally silence the other individual. One frequently used silencer is crying. When confronted by a conflict and unable to deal with it or when winning seems unlikely, the individual cries and thus silences the other person. Another technique is to hurt the other individual to the extent that he or she is silenced. This might involve bringing up some embarrassing inadequacy or some physical or personality problem. "You should be put back in the mental hospital" or "How can you talk when you can't even get a job and support your family?" may be totally irrelevant to the specific conflict but may go a long way toward silencing the other person.

Stages in Conflict Resolution

Any conflict situation may be approached as would a problem requiring a decision. The methods suggested for dealing with conflict are very similar to the methods of reflective thinking long taught as educational techniques and in small group communication classes. Here are distinguished five principal stages in conflict resolution. A diagram of these essential stages is presented in Figure 23.1. This diagram and the discussion that follows should not be taken to imply that all conflicts may be resolved in this way or in any other prescribed way. Some conflicts may not be amenable to solution; some differences may be irreconcilable. Communication can help us to understand and to resolve many conflicts but unfortunately not all.

1. Define the Conflict. Defining the conflict is perhaps the most essential step of conflict resolution, and yet many omit this stage entirely. We need to ask ourselves what the specific nature of the conflict is and why this conflict exists. It is at this stage that we should collect as much relevant data and as

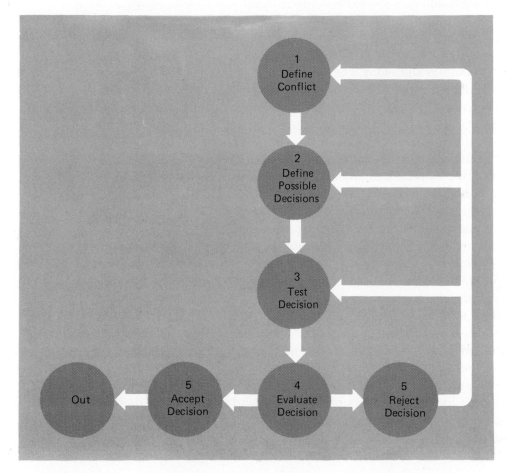

FIGURE 23.1
*Stages in Conflict
Resolution.*

many opinions as we possibly can. Special care should be taken to ensure that we collect data and opinions that may disagree with our position as well as the more supportive data and opinions.

In defining the conflict we should attempt to "operationalize" it to make it as concrete as possible. Conflict defined in the abstract is difficult to deal with and resolve. Thus, for example, the husband who complains that his wife is "cold and unfeeling" is defining the problem in such abstract terms that it will be difficult to reach agreement as to the nature of the conflict let alone its resolution. There should be an attempt to deal with conflicts in behavioral terms if possible. It is one thing for a husband to say that his wife is "cold and unfeeling" and quite another to say she does not call him at the office or kiss him when he comes home or hold his hand when they are at a party. These behaviors can be dealt with, whereas the abstract "cold and unfeeling" will be most difficult to handle. Further, it is useful to operationalize our conflicts because it forces us to be specific and to spell out exactly what we are fighting about. For a wife to say that her husband does not make her feel attractive but then fails to provide concrete examples of such behaviors is saying something quite different from the wife who can easily rattle off 20 recent specific situations in which he criticized her appearance, laughed at her clothes, whistled at other women, and so on.

2. Define Possible Decisions. For any conflict there are a number of possible decisions that can be made. In some instances any one of three or four possible decisions will resolve the conflict; in other cases only one possible decision will work. But in all cases we need first to analyze all possible alternatives.

The word *decision* is used deliberately instead of the more common *solution*. To say that we will find a solution to a conflict assumes that we will eliminate the conflict. Very probably this is not what will happen—we actually strive to lessen the conflict. To imply that we will actually solve a conflict as we solve a mathematical equation is assuming too simplistic a view of human behavior and human interpersonal relationships. More likely we are attempting to make a decision so that future interactions may be undertaken in a somewhat more productive setting. For example, if a husband discovers that his wife is having an affair with a neighbor and they move to another city or neighborhood, they have not "solved" the problem; rather, they have made a decision so that future interactions may take place in a more productive atmosphere. In short, the word *decision* seems more descriptive of what actually goes on in conflict resolution.

In analyzing the possible decisions to resolve the conflict we should attempt to predict the consequences of each of them. This is impossible to do with complete accuracy, yet some attempt should be made in this direction. We should guard against any tendency to dismiss possible decisions before we give them a fair hearing. Many excellent decisions are never put into operation because they at first seem strange, incorrect, or too difficult to implement.

3. Test the Decision. The true test of any decision can only be made when the decision is put into operation. And so we play the odds—we select the decision that seems the most logical and try it out. Although each decision put into operation should be given a fair chance, we should recognize that if a particular decision does not work, another decision should be put to test. It is self-destructive to put a decision into operation with the idea that if it does not work, then conflict resolution is impossible.

4. Evaluate the Decision. When the decision is in operation we need to evaluate it, examining the ways in which it helps to resolve (or aggravate) the conflict. Does it feel right? Does it make for improved interpersonal communication? Does it significantly lessen the conflict?

5. Accept or Reject the Decision. As a result of our evaluation we move to accept or reject the decision. If we accept the decision we move to "Out" and we are ready to put the decision into operation or perhaps to move on to consider other conflict situations and problems. If we move to reject the decision there are three alternatives: First, we might attempt to test another decision. Perhaps the decision we ranked as number two will prove more satisfactory, and again we try it out. A second possibility is to redefine the various decisions and then test one of them. The third course of action is to go back and reanalyze and redefine the conflict itself. That is, we can reenter the conflict resolution process at any of the first three stages. In any case, another decision must eventually be put into operation, which it is hoped will work better than the previous one. And perhaps we will have learned something from the last decision-making process that will prove useful in subsequent conflict resolution attempts.

SOURCES

An excellent overview of conflict is provided by David Dressler, *Sociology: The Study of Human Interaction* (New York: Knopf, 1969). A more detailed overview is Alan C. Filley, *Interpersonal Conflict Resolution* (Glenview, Ill.: Scott, Foresman, 1975). Two works relating conflict and communication are Fred E. Jandt, *Conflict Resolution Through Communication* (New York: Harper & Row, 1973), a collection of 16 articles, many of which are helpful in conceptualizing the role of conflict in communication and the role of communication in conflict, and *Perspectives on Communication in Social Conflict*, Gerald R. Miller and Herbert W. Simons, eds. (Englewood Cliffs, N.J.: Prentice-Hall, 1974), which contains eight thorough and perceptive articles on communication and conflict. This work also contains a bibliography of over 500 items.

George R. Bach and Peter Wyden, *The Intimate Enemy* (New York: Avon Books, 1968), is a popular, well-written, and insightful account of conflict and productive and unproductive ways of fighting.

The study of the boys at camp can be found in M. Sherif, O. J. Harvey, B. J. White, W. E. Hood, and C. W. Sherif, *Intergroup Conflict and Cooperation: The Robber's Cave Experiment* (Norman: University of Oklahoma Book Exchange, 1961).

For an analysis of the relationship between conflict and communication, see Robert J. Doolittle, "Conflicting Views of Conflict: An Analysis of Basic Speech Communication Textbooks," *Communication Education* 26 (March 1977):121–127, and Brent D. Ruben, "Communication and Conflict: A System-Theoretic Perspective," *Quarterly Journal of Speech* 64 (April 1978):202–210. An overview of conflict and communication may be found in Joyce Frost and William Wilmot, *Interpersonal Conflict* (Dubuque, Iowa: Brown, 1978).

The Red and Blue Game (Experiential Vehicle 23.2) owes its formulation to the Prisoner's Dilemma game. See Anatol Rapoport, *Fights, Games, and Debates* (Ann Arbor: University of Michigan Press, 1960).

EXPERIENTIAL VEHICLES

23.1 SANDY

Sandy is a beautiful young woman, age 21, and a senior in college. Sandy is majoring in biology and is an honor student; she plans to work toward her master's degree in biology at night while teaching high school during the day.

At the high school where Sandy has applied for a job, a committee of five members plus the school principal make all the hiring decisions. After reviewing Sandy's record—outstanding in every respect—the committee asks her in for a personal interview. This is a standard procedure with this high school. In this case, however, because Sandy's records and recommendations are so outstanding, the personal interview is regarded by the members of the committee and the principal as a formality. They are clearly eager to hire Sandy. Although there are other qualified applicants, none seems as outstanding as Sandy.

At the specified time Sandy appears to meet the committee. The members look at each other in shocked amazement; it seems obvious to them that Sandy is _____.* There is just no doubt that Sandy is, in fact, _____.*

Thinking quickly, the principal, as committee chairperson, tells Sandy that the committee has fallen behind schedule and that they will see her in 15 minutes. Sandy leaves the room and sits outside, waiting to be called back in. Sandy is well aware of their reactions and knows why they asked her to wait outside. She has seen those reactions before and is not surprised. She is _____,* and as she sits waiting she ponders what the committee will do.

The committee, now alone for 15 minutes, comes quickly to the point. The applicant is _____.* "What should we do?" the principal asks.

Students should role play members of the committee and reach a decision as to what they should do with regard to Sandy. The members of the committee are:

Mrs. Markham, the school principal
Mr. Ventri, the biology department chairperson
Miss Colson, teacher of physical education
Mr. Garcia, teacher of chemistry

*Your instructor will fill in these spaces.

Ms. Goldstein, teacher of Romance languages
Mr. Jackson, teacher of art

Approximately 10 to 20 minutes should be allowed for the discussion. After this time, the class members should discuss the interactions that took place in the role-playing session in terms of conflict and conflict resolution as discussed in this unit. This discussion should have no rigid structure and may focus on any of the concepts considered under conflict and conflict resolution.

23.2 RED AND BLUE GAME

For this exercise the class should be divided into dyads. One student is designated as Player 1 and the other student as Player 2. All players should inspect the accompanying matrix which contains the payoffs for each player, for each move. More specifically: Each player can play either RED or BLUE. (Follow this explanation while referring to the matrix below.) The moves of Player 1 determine whether the payoffs come from the top two quadrants (if RED is played) or the bottom two quadrants (if BLUE is played). The moves of Player 2 determine whether the payoffs come from the left two quadrants (if RED is played) or the right two quadrants (if BLUE is played). The numbers before the slashes are the payoffs for Player 1 and numbers after the slashes are the payoffs for Player 2. If both players play BLUE, each player loses 5 points (−5). If both players play RED, each player wins 5 points (+5). If Player 1 plays RED and Player 2 plays BLUE, Player 1 loses 10 points (−10) and Player 2 wins 10 points (+10). If Player 1 plays BLUE and Player 2 plays RED, Player 1 wins 10 points (+10) and Player 2 loses 10 points (−10). (The Summary Table of Choices and Payoffs will help the game move faster and easier.) The maximum amount of time allowed for each decision is 1 minute.

RED AND BLUE GAME MATRIX

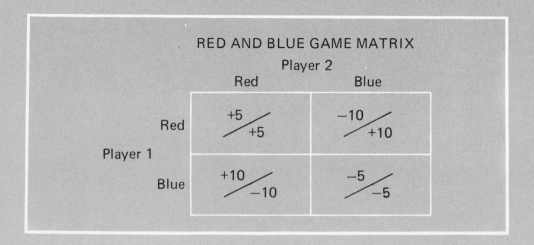

RED AND BLUE GAME MATRIX

Player 2

	Red	Blue
Red	+5 / +5	−10 / +10
Blue	+10 / −10	−5 / −5

Player 1

The game is played for 10 rounds and is recorded on a Score Sheet like the one provided. (Each player will need a Score Sheet.) Players reveal their decisions (that is, whether they choose BLUE or RED) only after they have entered them on the score sheet. Players must also record the amount won or lost and their cumulative balances in the spaces provided.

SUMMARY TABLE OF CHOICES AND PAYOFFS

The four choice combinations with their corresponding payoffs for each player are summarized in the following table.

Player 1: Red	Wins 5 points
Player 2: Red	Wins 5 points
Player 1: Red	Loses 10 points
Player 2: Blue	Wins 10 points
Player 1: Blue	Loses 5 points
Player 2: Blue	Loses 5 points
Player 1: Blue	Wins 10 points
Player 2: Red	Loses 10 points

SCORE SHEET FOR RED AND BLUE GAME

Round	Decision	Amount Won or Lost	Balance

TOTAL _____

After the game is played, discussion should center on some or all of the following issues:

1. How was the game perceived in terms of conflict?
2. How was conflict manifested in the actual playing of the game?

3. What were the goals of the players in playing the game?
Were these goals perceived as conflicting? Why?

4. How did your own history of conditioning influence the way in which you played the game and the way in which you responded to winning or losing the game?

5. How does the "winner" feel?

6. How does the "loser" feel?

7. If you were playing for real stakes (for example, money or grades), how would your behavior have differed?

8. What general implications can be drawn from this experience?

23.3 WIN AS MUCH AS YOU CAN*

This exercise is designed to explore some issues in conflict considered in this unit. "Clusters" of eight persons are formed. Each cluster consists of four teams of two members each. Visualizing the area as a clock, the four teams are placed at 12, 3, 6, and 9 o'clock. The teams should be far enough apart from each other so that they can communicate without the other teams' hearing them.

The game consists of 10 rounds. In each round each team selects X or Y. The selection is made on the basis of each team's prediction of what the other teams will select and the itemized "payoffs" as presented in the following "Payoff Table." For each round each team must select either X or Y. Both team members must agree on which letter to select.

The sequence of events should follow the "Score Sheet" (presented following the Payoff Table). For each round the teams are allowed a certain amount of time (listed in the column headed "Time") in which to make their selection of X or Y. After they reach their decision, the X or Y is recorded in the column headed "Choice." Only after each team has recorded its choices are the choices revealed. When the choices are revealed, refer to the Payoff Table to determine how many points each team wins or loses. For example, if two teams selected X and two teams selected Y, then according to the Payoff Table the teams selecting X would each win 2 points and the teams selecting Y would each lose 2 points. Another example: if one team selected Y and three teams selected X, the team that selected Y would lose 3 points and the teams that selected X would win 1 point each.

The amount won or lost for each round should be noted in the appropriate column, and a balance should be noted in the column headed "Balance."

Note that for rounds 5, 8, and 10 the game is played a bit differently.

*This exercise owes its formulation to an exercise by William Gellerman in *A Handbook of Structured Experiences for Human Relations Training,* vol. 2, J. William Pfeiffer and John E. Jones, eds. (LaJolla, Calif.: University Associates, 1974).

Before conferring with one's partner, all teams in the cluster confer for three minutes. Here the teams may talk about anything they wish, but they may not mark their choices at this time. They can only mark their choices after private consultations with their partners, which take place immediately after the cluster conferences. Note also that these three rounds are bonus rounds; the amount won or lost in that round is multiplied by 3 in round 5, by 5 in round 8, and by 10 in round 10.

PAYOFF TABLE

4 X's	lose 1 point each
3 X's 1 Y	win 1 point each lose 3 points
2 X's 2 Y's	win 2 points each lose 2 points each
1 X 3 Y's	win 3 points each lose 1 point each
4 Y's	win 1 point each

SCORE SHEET

Round	Time	Conference	Choice	Points Won	Points Lost	Balance
1	2 min.	partner				
2	1 min.	partner				
3	1 min.	partner				
4	1 min.	partner				
5	3 min. 1 min.	cluster partner		× 3 =	× 3 =	
6	1 min.	partner				
7	1 min.	partner				
8	3 min. 1 min.	cluster partner		× 5 =	× 5 =	
9	1 min.	partner				
10	3 min. 1 min.	cluster partner		× 10 =	× 10 =	Total =

Only consider the following questions *after* you have played the game.

1. How would you describe the behavior of the members of the cluster? How would you describe your own behavior?

2. Is this behavior typical? That is, did you behave here as you would in a real-life situation?

3. How do you feel about the way you played the game? Are you pleased? Disappointed? Sorry? Guilty? Explain the basis for your feelings.

4. If you were playing for points on an examination or even for points toward your final grade in the course, would you have played differently? Explain. What if you were playing for money—say, $1 per point?

5. Were you surprised at the way in which other members of your cluster played? Explain.

FRIENDSHIP IN INTERPERSONAL RELATIONSHIPS

OBJECTIVES

Upon completion of this unit, you should be able to:
1. define *friendship*
2. identify the functions that friendships serve
3. define the types of friendships identified by either Aristotle or Reisman
4. explain the three conceptualizations of friendship identified by James and Savary
5. identify the five stages of friendship development

When we were children, say around 3 to 7 years of age, our friendships might have been characterized as "momentary playmateship," where we valued friends for what they had (the ball, the rope, the tree house) and what they could do (play ball, run fast, jump rope). At this stage of development friends (as we think of them now) really did not exist. As we grew older, say between the ages of 4 and 9, we still had no real understanding of the mutual assistance nature of friendship. A friend, in the young "one-way assistance" relationship, was valued or desired basically for what he or she could give us or for doing what we wanted. Later, around the ages of 6 to 12, we entered our "two-way fair-weather cooperation" stage where friendship existed to serve our own self-interests rather than interests that were mutually beneficial. Around ages 9 to 15 we developed "intimate, mutually shared relationships"; we were able to step outside the friendship and view it as a third entity—a thing of value for its own sake. Friendship now became a collaborative effort that was entered into in order to achieve some common goals. Here we shared not only objective information but our feelings as well, and we helped each other with problems and conflicts. But at this stage, we were also possessive and resented third parties disturbing these friendships. Still later, from the ages of 12 to adulthood, we developed "autonomous interdependent friendships." These friendships—the ones we now have and the ones from the recent past, were developed and maintained to give mutual emotional and psychological support. Unlike the previous stage, however, the friendships here are not possessive and exclusive; rather, each friend is seen as able to develop other independent relationships and these relationships do not affect the basic structure of the original friendship.

These several stages, identified by psychologists Robert L. and Anne P. Selman, illustrate the development and growth from immature to mature and productive friendships and provide an excellent starting point for examining friendship as an interpersonal relationship.

Like love, friendship is something that poets, novelists, and artists of all kinds treat at great length. In the movies and on television friendships have become almost as important as romantic pairings—E. T. and Elliott, Rocky Balboa and Apollo Creed, Admiral Kirk and Mr. Spock, Laverne and Shirley, Hawkeye and B. J., and Trapper and Gonzo illustrate how important we think friendship is. It is paradoxical, then, that a topic of such obvious importance and of such popular appeal has been so neglected by social scientists. It is unfortunate that we have so little scientific data on friendships—their structures and functions, their development and maintenance.

Throughout our lives we meet numerous people, but out of this wide array we develop relatively few relationships we could call friendships. At times we seem afraid to develop friendships, afraid to extend ourselves, afraid to risk the possibility that we will be rebuffed and rejected in our overtures of friendship. Our increased mobility—in terms of both living and working—has contributed further to the difficulty in establishing friendship relationships, which admittedly take considerable time to develop. This difficulty is seen most clearly in college classrooms, in which you may develop a relationship with an individual in one class and then not have another opportunity to interact with that person for two or three semesters. In the discussion that follows I will begin with a definition of friendship and attempt to isolate the elements that constitute the essence of this type of relationship. Then three approaches to, or theories of, friendship are examined in order to further clarify the nature of friendship. Next, I will focus on some of the functions friendships serve, which are at the same time the reasons we develop friendships. Finally, an attempt will be made to define the stages of friendship development from the initial meeting to the creation of an intimate friendship. Throughout these discussions I will focus on friendship as a relationship between two people who may be of the same sex or of the opposite sex, of the same age or separated by generations. Sexual interests may or may not be present.

FRIENDSHIP: DEFINITIONAL ASPECTS

Everyone seems to know what a friend is and how one may be distinguished from a nonfriend or an enemy. And perhaps for most purposes this kind of intuitive feeling for what a friend is or how a friend behaves is sufficient. But for analyzing friendships generally and for suggesting specifically how friendships are developed and maintained, we need something a bit more precise. In order to achieve this needed precision we consider a working definition of *friendship* and some types of friendship.

A Working Definition

Friendship may be defined as an interpersonal relationship between two persons that is mutually productive, established and maintained through perceived mutual free choice, and characterized by mutual positive regard.

Friendship, as defined here, is an interpersonal relationship. (Although later we will note instances of imaginary and nonhuman "friends," we are really talking about relationships between people.) And because the relationship is an interpersonal one, communication interactions must have taken place between the people. Further, as Paul Wright notes, the interpersonal relationship involves a "personalistic focus." The individuals see and react to each other as complete persons, as unique, genuine, and irreplaceable individuals. Although we may view ourselves as having established a bond of friendship with the entire human race or with some subgroup, this is a different kind of bond and is probably more correctly designated as "concern," "regard," or even "universal love."

Friendships must be mutually productive. I include this qualifier to emphasize that friendship by definition cannot be destructive either to oneself or to the other person. Once destructiveness enters into a relationship, it can no longer be characterized as one of friendship. Love relationships, marriage relationships, parent-child relationships, and just about any other possible relationship can be destructive or productive. But friendship can only be productive. By definition, friendship enhances the potentials of the individual.

Friendships are established and maintained through perceived mutual free choice. At least they seem to be established through our perceived free choice; we think we are choosing freely. Sometimes we may be justified in this assumption; at other times it may be an illusion. This is a particularly troublesome concept. We do not choose our brothers and sisters, our aunts and uncles, our parents, and sometimes even our marital partners. Similarly, we do not have complete choice in the people we work with or live next to or go to school with. We tend to think, however, that we select our friends through free choice. But there are probably unconscious factors that exert some influence on our selection of friends, and so it may be misleading to say that friendships are established entirely by free choice. This notion of free choice (or perceived free choice) applies not just to the establishment of the relationship but also to its day-to-day interactions. As Paul Wright notes, "Good friends often contrive to spend time together even if it entails 'arranging' or inconvenience. They allow their lives to overlap; the plans, decisions, and activities of one person are contingent upon those of the other. A high level of voluntary interdependence is one mark of a strong friendship."

Finally, friendships are characterized by mutual positive regard. Liking people is essential for our calling them friends. Although this surely seems a reasonable inclusion, it seems that most definitions omit it entirely—perhaps because of their failure to distinguish true friendships from those merely bearing the label.

Types of Friendships

Another way of approaching friendship is to look, at least briefly, at some of the different types of friendships that have been defined. We know that not all friendships are the same, but we are often vague on how one friendship differs from another. I discuss here the friendship types as distinguished by Aristotle, Reisman, and James and Savary in order to give you a clear picture of the variety of friendships that can and do exist. In reviewing these varied friendship types, you should be able to see more clearly how you function as a friend and how your friends function with you.

Aristotle: Utility, Pleasure, Virtue

In his *Nicomachean Ethics*, Aristotle identified three kinds of friendly relationships, each of which was motivated by a different purpose. Friendships based on *utility* were those in which the individuals formed a relationship in order to profit from the association, for example, financial advantage, prestige, professional advancement, and so on. Self-interests rather than mutual interest motivated the friendship. Friendships based on *pleasure* were those in which the individuals associated for the purpose of increasing their pleasures—whether physical, emotional, intellectual, sexual, and so on. Both of these types of friendships, of course, are motivated by the desire to gain something. Friendships based on *virtue*, however, were those that grew out of a recognition by each person of the good qualities (the virtues) of the other. When we see a person's essential goodness, we grow to like them and wish to form a bond of friendship with them.

Reisman: Reciprocity, Receptivity, Association

John M. Reisman, in his *Anatomy of Friendship*, also distinguishes three types of friendships. The friendship of *reciprocity* is the ideal type of friendship—the kind we think of when we visualize an ideal friendship. It is characterized by loyalty, self-sacrifice, by mutual affection, and generosity. A friendship of reciprocity is a friendship based on equality, where each individual shares equally in the giving and in the receiving of the benefits and rewards of the relationship. The friendship of *receptivity*, on the other hand, is characterized by an imbalance of giving and receiving; one person is the primary giver and one person is the primary receiver. This imbalance, however, is a positive one because each person gains something from the relationship—the person who receives affection and the person who gives affection both have their individual (but different) needs satisfied. This is the friendship that often develops between a teacher and a student or between a doctor and a patient; in fact, a difference in status is, according to Reisman, an essential factor for the friendship of receptivity to develop. The friendship of *association* is a transitory one, sometimes more aptly described as a friendly relationship rather than a friendship. These associative friendships are the kind we have with fellow classmates or with various neighbors or even with coworkers. There is here no great loyalty, no great trust, no great giving or receiving. Rather, it is an association that is cordial but not very intense.

James and Savary: Half-to-Whole, Nourishment, Third Self

Muriel James and Louis Savary, in their insightful *The Heart of Friendship*, distinguish among three viewpoints or theories concerning the nature and effects of friendship. These viewpoints provide considerable insight into what friendship is and what it does to people.

The first approach, which we might label the *half-to-whole view*, conceives of friendship as a process of making people whole. People without friends, in this view, are incomplete individuals, and it is only through the establishment of a friendship that these people are made whole. Friendship changes you; it makes you complete. But at the same time, it also leads the individual to supplant his or her own identity. Traditional marriages are often viewed in this way; the husband and wife become one; they are no longer as much individuals as they are a team. Here there is no "I" or "you"; there is just "we" and "us."

The second approach, which we might label the *nourishment view*, conceives of friendship as enhancing, developing, and nourishing each individual. According to this view, friendship does not destroy individuality but rather heightens it. This approach, as James and Savary note, is clearly typified in the famous and often-repeated observation of Fritz Perls from *Gestalt Therapy Verbatim*:

> I do my thing, and you do your thing. I am not in this world to live up to your expectations, and you are not in this world to live up to mine. You are you, and I am I: if by chance we find each other, it's beautiful. If not, it can't be helped.

Whereas traditional views of marriage aligned themselves with the half-to-whole approach, Perls's view of friendship allows the uniqueness and the individuality of each person to grow and to progress. Here they remain "I" and "you."

The third view that James and Savary distinguish is called the *third-self theory* and views friendship as having a life of its own. It is an extension of the nourishment point of view and is not incompatible with it. When two persons experience friendship, a third self emerges—a metaself, a higher-order self. In this view friendship does not destroy or even detract from the uniqueness and individuality of each person but actually enhances it; at the same time, a new self—a third self—emerges. A similar situation occurs with individual notes played on a piano. Each is unique and individual, but when they are played together something new emerges without destroying the integrity or individuality of the individual notes.

According to this view—which James and Savary feel is the most meaningful—each friendship should be treated like a new person, much as a corporation is treated legally as a person. This is similar to teams and gangs having their own identity and even their own names.

One of the implications of this view is that concern and attention must be directed not only to each other but to the relationship as well, that is, to the metaself, the third self. The problem created by the neglect of this third self is seen clearly in those parent-child relationships in which the parent cares for the child's biological and physical needs but ignores the relationship between them. This relationship—this third self—must be cared for and acknowledged just as the individual must be. In this view there are "I," "you," and "we" (the third self).

These different types of friendships may also be seen in the responses of people who were asked to identify the qualities they felt most important in a friend. The responses, presented in Table 24.1 are derived from a *Psychology Today* survey of 40,000 respondents. If you examine the list, you will find it easy to fit each one of these qualities into one of the types of friendship noted above.

Before concluding this journey through various definitions, some mention should be made of imaginary and nonhuman "friendships." If you look around you, you will probably be surprised at the number of nonhumans classified as friends. In the Mary Chase play, *Harvey,* Elwood P. Dowd's best friend is an imaginary 6-foot rabbit named Harvey. Although everyone else dismisses him,

Friendship Qualities	Percentage of Respondents
1. Keeps confidence	89%
2. Loyalty	88
3. Warmth; Affection	82
4. Supportiveness	76
5. Frankness	75
6. Sense of humor	74
7. Willingness to make time for me	62
8. Independence	61
9. Good conversationalist	59
10. Intelligence	57%

Source: Based on Mary Brown Parlee and the Editors of *Psychology Today,* "The Friendship Bond," *Psychology Today* 13 (October 1979):43–54, 113.

TABLE 24.1
The 10 Most Frequently Mentioned Qualities of a Friend

Harvey is quite "real" to Elwood. Harvey is not unlike the inner voices that many people hear and that guide their behaviors. Whether these voices are the results of inner conflicts, inner guidance, suppressed desires, or unfulfilled fantasies, they take on the qualities of friends. Cartoon figures, knights on white horses, and the imaginary playmates so popular with children would also be classified as "friends" by many.

We also have other kinds of friends. To Lorelei Lee in *Gentlemen Prefer Blondes*, "Diamonds Are a Girl's Best Friend," and in the song of this name she gives numerous reasons for her choice. Dogs are our "best friends," we are told, and they are in many instances treated as best friends—given the best food, the best chair, and in various other ways the treatment we would normally reserve for close or intimate friends. Cats, birds, fish, and various other animals are also often afforded the very best treatment. Not long ago thousands of people bought rocks in a box as "pets." Plants are common "friends." The child's doll seems a most logical kind of friend. The doll is always available, never refuses to play, and otherwise does what its owner wants. All of these imaginary and nonhuman "friends" serve important functions for the individual. Our concern here, however, is with interpersonal human friendships and the functions they serve.

FRIENDSHIP FUNCTIONS

In the previously mentioned *Psychology Today* survey, the 40,000 respondents indicated from a wide number of activities which ones they had engaged in over the past month with friends. Table 24.2 presents the 10 most frequently noted activities. As can be appreciated from this list, friendship seems to serve the same functions that all relationships serve but in a unique way. Friendships serve the functions of alleviating loneliness; providing physical, intellectual, and emotional stimulation; and presenting an opportunity to gain self-knowledge. Two general functions—need satisfaction and pleasure/pain functions—

Friendship Activities
1. Had an intimate talk
2. Had a friend ask you to do something for him or her
3. Went to dinner in a restaurant
4. Asked your friend to do something for you
5. Had a meal together at home or at your friend's home
6. Went to a movie, play, or concert
7. Went drinking together
8. Went shopping
9. Participated in sports
10. Watched a sporting event

Source: Based on Mary Brown Parlee and the Editors of *Psychology Today*, "The Friendship Bond," *Psychology Today* 13 (October 1979):43–54, 113.

TABLE 24.2
The 10 Most Frequently Identified Activities Shared with Friends

are considered by most theorists as basic functions of friendship. These, then, are the functions that friendships serve, as well as the reasons we develop and maintain them.

Need Satisfaction

Friendships develop and are maintained to satisfy those needs that can only be satisfied by certain people. We select as friends those who, on the basis of our experiences or our predictions, will help to satisfy our basic needs or growth needs, and we cultivate and strive to preserve these relationships.

Selecting friends on the basis of need satisfaction is similar to our choosing a marriage partner, an employee, or any person who may be in a position to satisfy our needs. Thus, for example, if we have the need to be the center of attention or to be popular, we select friends who provide fulfillment of these needs—that is, people who allow us, and even encourage us, to be the center of attention or who tell us, verbally and nonverbally, that we are popular.

As our needs change as we grow older or develop in different ways, the functions that we look for in our friendships also change, and in many instances

"Life is so much more enjoyable now that you're here."

old friends are dropped from our close circle to be replaced by new friends who better serve these new needs.

Psychologist Paul H. Wright has identified more specifically the needs that we seek to have satisfied through friendships. We establish and maintain friendships, Wright observes, because they provide us with certain "direct rewards."

First, friends serve a *utility value*. A friend may have special talents, skills, or resources that may prove useful to us in achieving our specific goals and needs. We may, for example, become friends with someone who is particularly bright because such a person might assist us in getting better grades, in solving our personal problems, or in getting a better job.

Second, friends serve an *affirmation value*. The behavior of a friend toward us acts as a reflecting mirror that serves to affirm our personal value and enables us to recognize our positively valued self-attributes. A friend may, for example, help us to recognize more clearly our leadership abilities, our athletic prowess, or our sense of humor.

Third, friends serve an *ego-support value*. By behaving in a supportive, encouraging, and helpful manner, friends enable us to more easily view ourselves as worthy and competent individuals.

Fourth, friends serve a *stimulation value*. A friend introduces us to new ideas and new ways of seeing the world and helps us to expand our world view. A friend enables us to come into contact with issues and concepts with which we were not previously familiar—with modern art, foreign cultures, new foods, and hundreds of other new, different, and stimulating things.

Pleasure/Pain Functions

The other function of friendship is to maximize pleasure and minimize pain. This view is actually a special case of the need-satisfaction function.

If you were to ask people to complete the statement, "I most need a friend when . . .," I think they would answer in two ways. One would be to say, "I most need a friend when I'm down," "I most need a friend when I'm feeling sorry for myself," or "I most need a friend when I'm depressed." Such statements typify the function that friendships serve in the avoidance or the lessening of pain. We want a friend to be around when we are feeling down so that he or she will make us feel a little better, lift our spirits, or in some way alleviate the pain we are feeling.

The other would be to say, "I most need a friend when I'm happy," " . . . when I want to share my good news," or " . . . when I want someone to enjoy something with me." These statements typify the general function friendships serve to augment one's pleasure. A great part of the pleasure in winning a game, in receiving good news, and in experiencing some good fortune is in telling someone else about it and in many cases sharing it with them.

In the scientific terminology of operant conditioning we would say that we have friends because friends provide reinforcement. Friends may provide us with positive reinforcement by complimenting us, giving us presents, and providing social support for our ideas and our decisions. Or friends may provide negative reinforcement by removing painful stimuli, nursing us when we are sick, getting us out of our depressions, alleviating loneliness, and in general minimizing our pain. Goethe expressed much the same idea when he wrote:

> The world is so empty
> if one thinks only
> of mountains, rivers, and
> cities; but to know someone
> who thinks and feels with me,
> and who, though distant
> is close to me in spirit,
> this makes the earth for me
> an inhabited garden.

If you carefully examine your own friendships, I think you will find personal evidence of these two general functions.

STAGES IN FRIENDSHIP DEVELOPMENT

Friendship at first sight is even more rare than love at first sight—if it is possible at all. While you may like a person at first sight, you could hardly call that person a friend, at least not until there has been some opportunity for interaction and communication. Friendship, like most things worthwhile, takes time to develop. It may be described according to a number of stages or phases and is best viewed as existing on a continuum. At one end are "strangers" or "the initial meeting of two persons," and at the other end are "intimate friends." We need to consider what happens in between these two extremes so that we might be in a better position to move from initial meetings to real friendships, to encourage the growth of friendship in the right direction, and to introduce correctives in the process should problems, obstacles, or breakdowns occur.

The labels we use for these various stages are, like all labels, arbitrary. It is important to emphasize this point, however, because while we may label a person an "acquaintance" in our thoughts, we might actually call him or her a casual friend. The labels are not important; what is important is that we see the progression, the gradual development toward intimacy that may take place.

Another important point to note is that many friendships stabilize themselves at some stage before reaching what we call the intimate stage. The friendship does not progress or deteriorate; it reaches a level that seems mutually satisfying for both individuals and remains at that level, with neither person caring to dissolve it or to see it grow beyond this level. This type of situation is seen often among college students, especially among those who commute to school. The two students may be good friends within the context of college; they may take courses together and perhaps study and eat lunch together, but after the school day, they each go their own ways. One may spend nonschool time with a boyfriend or girlfriend, while the other may stay with neighborhood friends. People who work together often develop friendships that stabilize themselves in this same way. It should be easy to appreciate the potential conflict that may arise should one individual want the relationship to progress when the other is content with its current stage.

Initial Contact

The first stage of friendship development is obviously an initial meeting of some kind. It may be a meeting by accident or by strategy, planned or unplanned, self-initiated or brought about by some third-party introduction, face-to-face or by letter or telephone. In any event, some interpersonal encounter must take place. This does not mean that what has happened prior to the encounter is unimportant—quite the contrary. In fact, one's prior history of friendships, one's personal needs, and in short, one's readiness or lack of readiness for friendship development is extremely important in determining whether a relationship will develop into a close friendship, will end soon after the first encounter, or will continue for a long period as a mere acquaintanceship. At this stage physical attraction is particularly important, and I think this is true for same-sex as well as for opposite-sex friendships or whether sex is at issue at all.

The ways in which such meetings may take place have already been considered in our discussion of relational development (Unit 21). What is important is that at the meeting stage, some interpersonal communication has taken place.

Acquaintanceship

If the initial meeting proves at all productive, the individuals progress to the acquaintanceship stage. At this stage personality attractiveness becomes significant and in fact greatly determines whether or not the relationship will progress to or beyond this point. The dimension of physical attractiveness, however, probably never fades completely.

At this stage there is a clear recognition of each other, a consistent exchange of phatic messages, and a definite memory for name, face, and other identifying data. Put differently, at this stage each person is clearly defined in the mind of the other person and clearly distinguished from other persons.

At the acquaintanceship stage, and in fact at all subsequent stages, a process of testing goes on which most people seem reluctant to admit to. At this stage we attempt to determine whether this acquaintanceship should be developed into a closer relationship or whether it should be terminated. The entire dating system of our culture is essentially one in which each person tests the other person and attempts to determine whether a long-term or even a lifetime relationship should be established.

The communications at this stage are essentially impersonal. There is little attempt to talk about personal problems, about fantasies and unfulfilled desires, about family problems, about one's financial situation. In short, there is little attempt to engage in self-disclosure of any significance. In fact, should significant self-disclosures occur, they immediately call attention to themselves and seem intuitively out of place.

Casual Friendship

This stage is very much like the previous one, except that now we have what we might call a dyadic consciousness. There is a sense of "we-ness," a sense of togetherness. At this stage the individuals participate in activities as a unit rather than as separate individuals. Most importantly, each person sees the dyad as a unit—as a whole. At this stage communications begin to get personal, although significant self-disclosure does not usually take place until the next stage.

The casual friend is the one we would call to go to the movies, the one we would sit with in the cafeteria or in class, or the one with whom we would ride home from school. The loss of such a friendship would disturb us, but only for a relatively short period of time. We might feel diminished, but only slightly so.

Close Friendship

The close friendship is an intensification of the casual friendship; it is a logical progression along the lines of intimacy from the casual friendship. In the close friendship stage significant self-disclosure takes place. We feel that whatever we say about ourselves will not only be kept in confidence but will be accepted. The friendship is felt to be strong enough that our disclosures will not weaken it or damage it in any significant way. This is not to say that we are not at times proven wrong; certainly there are such times. But generally we correctly make the assumption that we will be accepted and that the relationship will withstand any disclosures. As Santayana has put it, "One's friends are that part of the human race with which one can be human."

At this stage the individuals are able to predict the behaviors of each other with considerable accuracy. In part our predictions are based on our having seen the other person in similar situations, and assuming some consistency on his or her part, we make the prediction that the person will again behave in the same way. But in part our predictions are based on knowing things about the person that enable us to extrapolate beyond anything we have ever observed. We may know the person's values, attitudes, and opinions about specific issues, and so when decisions are to be made or when actions are to be taken, we use our knowledge of his or her values and attitudes to predict his or her behaviors. Empathy is developed to a significant degree at this point. We can put ourselves into the shoes of the other person quite easily and begin to feel as he or she feels.

At this stage we become willing to make significant sacrifices for the other person. We will go far out of our way for the benefit of this friend, and the friend in turn does the same. Touching becomes an accepted part of our nonverbal behavior. Depending on the sex of the individuals, close friends may kiss, hug, slap each other on the back or on the buttocks, put their arms around each other's shoulders, and so on. The touching is not uncomfortable as it often is with a stranger or a mere acquaintance. Instead, it serves a comforting function for both parties; it assures each of the individuals that they are in fact close. It is nonverbal testimony that this is indeed a close friendship.

Intimate Friendship

An intimate friendship possesses all the qualities of the close friendship but goes beyond these. The amount of self-disclosure is even greater; the disclosures themselves are more revealing; greater acceptance is expected and is received; and there is even less of a perceived threat to the friendship when such disclosures are made. "A friend," said Ralph Waldo Emerson, "is a person with whom I may be sincere. Before him I may think aloud."

Empathy is at its height in the intimate friendship. We feel what the other person is feeling with greater intensity and greater likeness or similarity. If he or she fails a course or loses a job or has a fight with his or her parents, we know what the other person is going through because we can feel as he or she feels.

The sacrifices each friend is willing to make at this stage are more extreme than those normally seen at the close friendship stage. A classic example of this is found in the Old Testament, in Ruth's expression of friendship for Naomi (Ruth 1:16–17):

> *Do not ask me to abandon or forsake you! For wherever you go I will go, wherever you lodge I will lodge, your people shall be my people, and your God my God. Wherever you die I will die, and there be buried. May the Lord do so and so to me, and more besides, if aught but death separates me from you!*

The touching that is permitted among close friends is naturally permitted here, as is more intimate touching, again, depending for specifics on the sex of the individuals. Touching between intimates may be more prolonged and more frequent and may focus on more intimate body parts. We may touch each other's faces, breasts, thighs, and so on without any self-consciousness, without any granting of permission. In fact, the societal rules that govern touching behavior in our culture, as well as the rules governing other forms of verbal and nonverbal behavior, are disregarded by intimates. Intimates create their own rules of interpersonal interaction. The rules are formed from mutual agreement rather than societal edict. And even the rules that the intimates themselves create may be broken, normally without fear of offending.

As with all relationships, friendship relationships are unique: no two are ever the same. Consequently, the five stages should be regarded as general phases that a relationship might pass through and not as essential and fixed positions that all relationships must follow.

SOURCES

A cross-cultural perspective on friendship is provided by Robert Brain, *Friends and Lovers* (New York: Basic Books, 1976). Muriel James and Louis Savary, *The Heart of Friendship* (New York: Harper & Row, 1976), provides some interesting insights into friendship relations. Jerry Gillies, *Friends: The Power and Potential of the Company You Keep* (New York: Barnes & Noble Books, 1976), covers the various aspects of friendship thoroughly and provides useful and interesting experiences for investigating our own friends and friendship relationships. For more scholarly accounts of friendship, see S. B. Kurth, "Friendships and Friendly Relations," and G. D. Suttles, "Friendship as a Social Institution," in *Social Relationships*, G. J. McCall, ed. (Chicago: Aldine, 1970), pp. 136–170 and 95–125. For an excellent summary of theory and research on friendship, see Paul H. Wright, "Toward a Theory of Friendship Based on a Conception of Self," *Human Communication Research* 4 (Spring 1978):196–207. The stages in friendship development were taken from Robert L. Selman and Anne P. Selman, "Children's Ideas About Friendship: A New Theory," *Psychology Today* 13 (October 1979):71–80, 114. For an insightful analysis of close friendships, see William K. Rawlins, "Negotiating Close Friendship: The Dialectic of Conjunctive Freedoms," *Human Communication Research* (in press). A useful well-written overview is provided in Alan Loy McGinnis, *The Friendship Factor* (Minneapolis, Minn.: Augsburg Publishing House, 1979).

24.1 FRIENDSHIP FEELINGS

This experiential vehicle asks you to examine your feelings about being a friend. In responding to this "quiz," try to avoid thinking of what would be the "right" or the "best" choices and answer with your true feelings. Select only one alternative for each question. Respond to these questions now, before reading any further.

1. If Friend won a $1 million lottery, you would
   a. be extremely pleased.
   b. be pleased but feel it should have been you.
   c. be displeased but not exceptionally so.
   d. be resentful.

2. If you and Friend—who knew about the same as you—studied together for an examination and Friend got an *A* and you got a *C,* you would
   a. be pleased that Friend did so well but displeased that you did not do so well.
   b. be displeased at the wide discrepancy in grades.
   c. be resentful that Friend did well and you did not.

3. If Friend called you up in the middle of the night because Friend was depressed, you would
   a. listen as long as Friend wanted you to.
   b. tell Friend that you were sleeping and that you will call back in the morning.
   c. tell Friend that this is not an appropriate time to call and hang up.

4. If Friend called you up in the middle of the night because Friend wanted to share the good news that Friend was going to be married, you would
   a. listen as long as Friend wanted you to.
   b. tell Friend that you were sleeping and that you would call back in the morning.
   c. tell Friend that this is not an appropriate time to call and hang up.

5. If you were anxious to see a particular movie but Friend wanted to see another film, you would
   a. insist on seeing the movie you preferred.
   b. express your preference but give in to Friend's choice.
   c. discuss the merits of each movie and be amenable to whichever one seems best.

    d.   do not express your preference but simply agree to see the movie of
Friend's choice.

6.   If Friend sought you out for an hour or so, you would be most responsive,
helpful, willing to spend the time with Friend

    a.   in sharing Friend's joy at having just received an important
promotion.

    b.   in consoling Friend over just being fired.

    c.   in helping Friend accomplish some important work-related task.

Unlike most tests there are no correct or incorrect answers here. These
questions were designed to assist you in bringing to a more conscious
awareness some of your feelings about what friendship entails. Each response
entails a very different definition of what a friend is and what a friend should
be. For example, in number 6 I think the "best" choice is *a* because I think that
the most important function a friend can serve is to unselfishly share a friend's
joy. Alternative *c,* I think, is the next best choice since we are again helping a
friend to do something that will benefit only Friend. Alternative *b,* while still a
respectable and worthwhile choice, is the least defining of friendship largely
because it is relatively easy to console someone. In fact, we readily console
people who are not our friends. Many take a kind of pleasure in sharing the
grief of another; we have been conditioned to do this since we were children.
But our competitive natures have led us to compete even with our closest
friends. Therefore, to select either alternative *a* or *b* means that we must put our
friend above this very natural, well-learned competitive response. Obviously
with different assumptions about friendship, different alternatives will be
selected.

    In a manner similar to that offered for question 6, in groups of four to six,
consider each of the alternatives for each of the questions.

24.2 FRIENDSHIP BEHAVIORS

Six specific situations are presented below. For each situation you are asked to
indicate (1) how you, as a friend, would respond, by writing the word *would* in
the appropriate space, (2) how you think a good friend should respond, by
writing *should* in the appropriate space, and (3) the qualities or characteristics
you feel a good friend should have relevant to these six situations, by
completing the sentence, " . . . because a good friend should . . ."

    After completing all six situations, respond to the questions presented at
the end of this exercise—alone, in dyads, or in small groups of five, six, or
seven persons.

FRIENDSHIP AND LOVE

    *Two of your close friends have been going together for a few months.
They seem to care for each other a great deal, and the relationship seems*

to be a mutually productive one. The only problem is that you are in love with one of them. At times you feel the love is returned, but perhaps because you have been silent about your feelings, nothing has been said. You wonder what you should do.

------ ------   a. Confess your love to the one you love.
------ ------   b. Say nothing.
------ ------   c. Confess your love to both friends.
------ ------   d. Confess your love to the friend you are not in love with and see the reaction before doing anything else.
------ ------   e. (Other—you suggest an alternative.)

. . . because a good friend should . . .

FRIENDSHIP AND MONEY

Your closest friend has just gotten into serious debt through some misjudgment. You have saved $2500 over the past few years and plan to buy a car on graduating from college. Your friend asks to borrow the money, which could not be repaid for at least four or possibly five years. Although you do not need the car for work or for any other necessity, you have been looking forward to the day when you could get your own car. You've worked hard for it and feel you deserve the car, but you are also concerned about the plight of your friend who would be in serious trouble without the $2500 loan. You wonder what you should do.

------ ------   a. Lend your friend the money.
------ ------   b. Tell your friend that you have been planning to buy the car for the last few years and that you cannot lend him or her the money.
------ ------   c. Give your friend the money and tell your friend that there is no need to pay it back; after all, your friend already has enough problems without having to worry about paying it back.
------ ------   d. Tell your friend that you already gave the $2500 to your brother but that you would certainly have lent him or her the money if you still had it.
------ ------   e. (Other—you suggest an alternative.)

. . . because a good friend should . . .

FRIENDSHIP AND ADVICE

Two friends, Pat and Chris, have been dating for the past several months. They will soon enter into a more permanent relationship after graduating from college. Pat is now having second thoughts and is currently having *an affair with still another friend, Lee. Chris tells you that there is probably an affair going on (which you know to be true) and seeks your advice. You are the only one who is friendly with all three parties. You wonder what you should do.*

_____ _____ a. Tell Chris everything you know.

_____ _____ b. Tell Pat to be honest with Chris.

_____ _____ c. Say nothing; don't get involved.

_____ _____ d. Suggest to Chris that the more permanent relationship planned should be reconsidered, but don't be specific.

_____ _____ e. (Other—you suggest an alternative.)

. . . because a good friend should . . .

FRIENDSHIP AND DEPRESSION

One of your close friends has been having problems and seems to be constantly depressed. For the past month your friend has been calling you or visiting you to tell you all about these problems and depression, asking your advice, and rehashing everything imaginable. These discussions have succeeded only in depressing you, but this seems to have gone unnoticed by your friend. Although you have recommended professional help, your friend won't listen. You wonder what you should do.

_____ _____ a. Continue to listen in the hope that the depression will lessen.

_____ _____ b. Tell your friend that you just cannot continue to listen to all these problems because they are depressing you and getting nothing accomplished.

_____ _____ c. Tell your friend to seek professional help or you will withdraw from the relationship.

_____ _____ d. Lay some of your depression on your friend and see what happens.

_____ _____ e. (Other—you suggest an alternative.)

. . . because a good friend should . . .

FRIENDSHIP AND CHEATING

Your anthropology instructor is giving a midterm and is grading it on a curve. Your close friend somehow manages to secure a copy of the examination a few days before it is scheduled. Since you are a close friend, the examination is offered to you as well. You refuse to look at it. The examination turned out to be even more difficult than you had anticipated, with the highest grade being a 68 (except for your friend, who received a 96). According to the system of curving used by this instructor, each grade will be raised four points. But this means that the highest grade (aside from your friend's) will be only a 72, or a C—. A few students will receive C—, about 30 to 40 percent will receive D, and the rest (over 50 percent) will receive F. Although only you and your friend know what happened, you know that the instructor and the entire class are wondering why this one student—never a particularly outstanding student—did so well. After curving, your grade is 70 (C—). You wonder what you should do.

		a. Tell your friend to confess or you will tell the instructor yourself (although you could not prove it).
		b. Tell the instructor what happened (even though you could not prove anything).
		c. Say nothing; don't get involved.
		d. (Other—you suggest an alternative.)

. . . because a good friend should . . .

FRIENDSHIP AND MARRIAGE

You are very close friends with a couple, Jane and James, who are engaged and who plan to marry within the next few months. It is clear to you, however, that Jane does not love James and is only planning to go through with the marriage because of James's money, which is considerable. You wonder what you should do.

		a. Tell James that Jane is not in love with him but is only interested in his money.
		b. Tell Jane that you know her plans and that she should change her ways and her plans.
		c. Say nothing; don't get involved.
		d. Suggest to James that he should reconsider his relationship and his plans of marrying Jane without being specific.
		e. (Other—you suggest an alternative.)

. . . because a good friend should . . .

For Discussion

1. Were there significant differences between the *would* and the *should* responses? How do you account for these differences?
2. What values or standards or models did you use in making the *should* responses? Why did you choose them?
3. With which situation did you experience the greatest difficulty in making a decision as to what you would do? Can you explain why?
4. Does friendship necessarily entail the willingness to make sacrifices?
5. How would you define *friend?*

LOVE IN INTERPERSONAL RELATIONSHIPS

Upon completion of this unit, you should be able to:
1. identify the five dimensions or variables of love identified by Pitirim Sorokin
2. define *ludus, storge, mania, pragma, eros,* and *agape*
3. explain the relationship between infatuation and love and between jealousy and love
4. explain at least three conditions under which love is more likely to occur
5. explain the theory of love as *labeled arousal*
6. explain the theory of love as imprinting
7. explain at least three ways in which women and men differ in their loving behavior
8. explain the relationship between loving and communication

Of all the types of interpersonal relationships, none seems as important as love. "We are all born for love," noted Disraeli; "It is the principle of existence and its only end." Cyril Bibby, in his essay "The Art of Loving," suggests that *loving* may be a better term to use than *love* and in so doing gets at some of the important qualities of this interpersonal relationship. So long as love is treated as a thing, to be built up mechanically by the addition of this piece of social relationship to that piece of amatory technique, it can never really flourish. To make the most of the human capacity for loving, it is necessary to treat it as an activity of the whole person, in which body and mind and emotions are all actively involved. This is not to deny the importance of social factors or of sexual techniques but merely to put them in their proper place as aids to an essentially outgiving activity.

THE NATURES OF LOVE

Loving and *love* are not easy terms to define. Unlike concepts such as attraction or conflict, which can be defined and measured with some ease, *love* and *loving* resist such approaches. On the one hand, we have poets who extol love's virtues: "Come live with me and be my love, And we will all the pleasures prove," wrote Christopher Marlowe, and who could resist the promise of such a reward? On the other hand, there are cynics, spoken for eloquently by Ambrose Bierce in *The Devil's Dictionary*. Love, says Bierce, is "a temporary insanity curable by marriage or by removal of the patient from the influences under which he incurred the disorder. This disease, like caries and many other ailments, is prevalent only among civilized races living under artificial conditions; barbarous nations breathing pure air and eating simple food enjoy immunity from its ravages."

Perhaps it's the variety of ways in which people may love that makes definition difficult. In *How Do You Feel?* four different approaches to loving are presented. Among the words the writers use in describing the feelings and the behaviors of loving are: *warmth, contentment, excitement, oneness, limitless, infinite, boundless, totally encompassing, lucky, faith, trust, dynamic, effort, commitment, tender, multicolored, active, healthy, energetic, courageous, forward-looking, patient, robust, openness, honesty, understanding,* and *fun.* Throughout these words there is a clear emphasis on activity rather than passivity. Loving is an active process. Larry Carlin, in one of the essays in *How Do You Feel?*, puts it this way: "When I feel loving it seems like I can't keep what's inside inside; I have to reach out, touch, embrace, hold, kiss."

Pitirim Sorokin further explains love by identifying five major dimensions or variables.

1. *Intensity.* Loving feelings or behavior can vary in intensity from nothing to slight to some undefined extreme. Love can vary in intensity from giving a dime to a beggar to sacrificing one's life for one's loved ones.
2. *Extensity.* Love can vary in terms of the degree to which it extends from outside the individual and may be solely a love of oneself (low extensity) or may range to the love of all humankind (high extensity).
3. *Duration.* Like any emotion, loving can vary in duration from seconds to a lifetime.
4. *Purity.* By "purity" Sorokin means the degree to which the love is motivated by considerations for the self or by considerations for the other person. "Impure" love, in this system, refers to love motivated by selfish considerations without concern for the other person. Pure love is the love of an individual for the sake of the beloved.
5. *Adequacy.* Love may vary from wise to blind. In inadequate or blind love there is a huge difference between the purposes or motives in loving and the consequences. An example of inadequate or blind love might be the excessive love a father and a mother have for their child which leads the child to become totally dependent upon them. Adequate or wise love, on the other hand, has consequences that are positive for the beloved.

These five dimensions give just a glimpse of the complexity of love. Additional qualities or dimensions of love are noted in Figure 25.1 Each of these

Figure 25.1 Some Qualities or Dimensions of Love

LOVE

Quality		Opposite
supportive		nonsupportive
open		closed
empathic		unempathic
positive		negative
equal		unequal
intense		weak
extense		nonextense
pure		impure
long in duration		short in duration
adequate		inadequate
need fulfilling		need nonfulfilling
sexual		nonsexual
rational		irrational
possessive		nonpossessive
selfish		unselfish
productive		destructive
singular		mutual
friendly		unfriendly
honest		dishonest
romantic		unromantic
happy		unhappy
satisfying		unsatisfying
jealous		non-jealous
trusting		distrusting
growing		shrinking
comfortable		uncomfortable
public		private
approved		disapproved
interesting		uninteresting
accepted		resisted
conditional		unconditional
spontaneous		strategic
provisional		certain
temporary commitment		long-term commitment
dynamic		static
adult-like		child-like
aware		unaware
symmetrical		complementary
ethical		unethical
cooperative		competitive

392

individual scales represents a different aspect of love, and each position on the scale represents a different degree of intensity of that aspect. Any love may be defined by indexing it along these various dimensions. Still this would not be a complete definition.

TYPES OF LOVE

In addition to describing love in terms of its significant dimensions or variables, we may also describe love in terms of a kind or type. In *The Colors of Love*, John Alan Lee distinguishes a number of types or kinds of love: ludus, storge, mania, pragma, eros, and agape as well as various combinations of these. A brief explanation of these various types should help to clarify further the nature of love.

Ludus

Ludus love is experienced as a game. The ludic lover sees love as fun, as a game to be played. The better he or she can play the game, the more the love is enjoyed. To the ludic lover, love is not to be taken too seriously; emotions are to be held in check lest they get out of hand and make trouble; passions never rise to the point where they get out of control. Ludic love is a self-controlled love—a love that the lover carefully manages and controls rather than allowing it to control him or her. This lover is consciously aware of the need to remain in control and uses this awareness to guide his or her own behaviors.

The ludic lover retains a partner only so long as he or she is interesting and amusing. When the partner is no longer interesting enough, then it is time to change. And ludic lovers do change partners frequently. Perhaps because love is a game, sexual fidelity is not something that is of major importance in a ludic love relationship. The ludic lover expects his or her partner to have had (and probably to have in the future) other partners and does not appear to get too upset if occasional partners are experienced during their relationship.

The dating patterns that we have seem greatly influenced by ludic conceptions of love. In ludic love (as in dating) there is no mutual claim and no long-time commitment agreed upon by the partners. Instead it is experienced because it is fun and when it stops being fun, the relationship is terminated. Like one would rate a date (on the currently popular 10-point scale, for example), one would also rate one's ludic partner. When one's rating gets too low or when others are available with higher ratings, the ludic relationship is ready to come to an end.

Storge

Like ludus, *storge* lacks passion and intensity. But whereas the ludic lover is aware of passion but keeps it under control, the storge lover is unaware of any intensity of feeling. The storgic lover does not set out to find a lover but rather seems to establish a storge relationship with someone who he or she knows and with whom he or she enjoys similar interests and activities. Storgic love just seems to develop over a considerable period of time rather than happen in one mad burst of passion. As might be expected, sex in storgic relationships comes late, but even when it comes it never seems to assume any great importance. One great advantage of this is that storgic lovers are not plagued by sexual difficulties as are so many other types of lovers.

Storgic lovers rarely say "I love you" or even remember what many would consider romantic milestones such as the first date, the first weekend alone, the first time we said "I love you" and so on. Storgic love is a gradual process of unfolding one's thoughts and one's feelings; the changes seem to come so slowly and so gradually that it is often difficult for the individuals involved—and of course for outsiders—to properly and accurately define exactly where the relationship is at any point in time. Storgic love is sometimes difficult to separate from friendship; it is often characterized by the same qualities we would use to characterize friendship: mutual caring, compassion, respect, and concern for the other person.

Not only is storgic love slow in developing and slow burning, it is also slow in dissolving. Storgic lovers can, for example, endure long periods of time away from each other without feeling that there is any problem with the relationship. Similarly, they may endure long periods of relative inactivity or lack of excitement without feeling there is any relationship problem.

Mania

Manic love differs greatly from both ludus and especially storge in numerous ways. But perhaps the most obvious quality of mania which separates it from all others, is its extremes of both highs and lows, of ups and downs. The manic lover loves intensely but at the same time intensely worries and fears the loss of the love. And this intense fear prevents the manic lover in many cases from deriving as much pleasure as might be derived from the relationship. At the slightest provocation, for example, the manic lover experiences extreme jealousy. Manic love is obsessive; the manic lover has to possess his or her lover completely—in all ways, at all times. And in return the manic lover wishes to be possessed, to be loved intensely. It seems almost as if the manic lover is driven to these extremes by some outside force or perhaps by some inner obsession that cannot be controlled.

Manic lovers are often unhappy with life and so devote a great deal of energy to being in love. The manic lover's poor self-image seems only capable of being improved by having someone love him or her; self-worth seems to come only from being loved rather than from any sense of inner satisfaction. Because love is so important to the manic lover, danger signs in a relationship are often ignored; the manic lover really believes that if there is love between them, nothing else matters.

There is a spiral effect in the manic relationship brought on by the manic lover's need to possess and be possessed completely and wholly. When, for example, the manic lover expresses commitment and an intensity of feelings, he or she expects more intense expression of commitment in return. This is responded to with further increased commitment and so on. The manic lover needs to give and to receive constant attention and constant affection. When this is not given or when an expression of increased commitment is not returned, depression, jealousy, self-doubts, or similar reactions are often experienced and can lead to the extreme lows characteristic of the manic lover.

Pragma

The *pragma* lover is the practical lover who seeks a relationship that will work. Pragma lovers seek compatibility and a relationship in which their important needs and desires will be satisfied. Computer matching services seem based largely on an assumption of pragmatic love. Compatibility is emphasized, so the computer will match persons on the basis of similar interests, attitudes, personality characteristics, religion, politics, hobbies, and a host of other likes and dislikes. The assumption here is that persons who are similar will be more apt to establish relationships than will persons who are different. This assumption is generally supported by the research on interpersonal attraction.

In its extreme, pragma love may be seen in the person who writes down the qualities he or she wants in a mate and actively goes about seeking someone to match these stated qualities. As might be expected, the pragma lover is concerned with the social qualifications of a potential mate even more so than with personal qualities; family and background are extremely important to the pragma lover who does not rely on feelings as much as on logic. The pragma lover wants to marry and settle down and get on with the business of living. In pragma, a love relationship is clearly a means to the achievement of other ends, unlike the manic lover to whom the love relationship is the end and all else are means to its attainment. The pragma lover views love as a necessity—or certainly as a useful relationship—that makes the rest of life somewhat easier. And so the pragma lover will ask such questions of a potential mate as "Will this person earn a good living?," "Can this person cook?," and "Will this person help me advance in my career?"

Not surprisingly, relationships rarely deteriorate among pragma lovers. This is true in part because pragma lovers have chosen their mates carefully and have emphasized similarities. Perhaps they have intuitively discovered what experimental research has recently confirmed, namely that relationships between similar people are much less likely to break up than are relationships among those who are very different. Another reason for the less frequent breakups seems to be that their romantic expectations are not unrealistic. They seem willing to settle for less and, consequently, they are seldom disappointed.

Eros

One version of the Narcissus legend is that Narcissus, a beautiful Greek boy, fell in love with his own reflection in the water. So absorbed was he with his own beauty that he ignored the love of the beautiful nymph, Echo. One day, while admiring his own reflection and attempting to get closer and closer to it, he fell into the water and died. Another way of looking at this legend, as John Lee suggests, is to look at Narcissus as the classic erotic lover. In this view Narcissus was punished for his total absorption with a beauty and perfection that he could never possess. His own reflection was more beautiful than the fountain nymph Echo, or than anyone else he could possibly love. The erotic lover focuses on beauty and physical attractiveness, sometimes to the exclusion of qualities we might consider more important and more enduring. And like Narcissus, the erotic lover often has an ideal image of beauty that is unattainable in reality. Consequently, the erotic lover often feels unfulfilled. Erotic lovers are particularly sensitive to physical imperfections in their beloveds—a nose that is too long, a complexion that is blemished, a figure that is a bit too full, and so on—all cause difficulties for the eros lover. And this is one reason why the erotic lover wants to experience the entire person as quickly in the relationship as possible.

Eros is an ego-centered love, a love that is given to someone because that person will return the love. It is in this sense a utilitarian, rational love because it is a calculated love with an anticipated return. Eros is essentially hedonistic; it is a sensual love of the physical qualities of an individual. In eros physical attraction is paramount; there is a definite sensual feeling for the other person's body.

Eros is a discriminating type of love; it is selective in its love objects. It is directed at someone because he or she is valuable and can be expected to return the love in kind.

Agape

Agape is a compassionate love; it is an egoless, self-giving love. Agape is nonrational and nondiscriminative. Agape creates value and virtue by its love rather than bestowing love only on that which is valuable and virtuous. The agapic lover will love even those he or she does not have any close ties with. This lover will love the stranger on the road, and the fact that they will probably never meet again has nothing to do with it. Jesus, Buddha, Gandhi, and similar people practiced and preached agape rather than eros, an unqualified love rather than the qualified love of eros.

Agape is a spiritual love. One cannot love altruistically if one loves with the thought that one will be rewarded in some way for this love or compassion. Agapic love is offered with no concern for any kind of personal reward or gain. The agapic lover loves without even expecting that the love will be returned or reciprocated.

The agapic lover gives to the other person the kind of love the person needs even though there may be great difficulties or personal hardships involved. Thus, for example, if one person in a love relationship would prefer to be free and to be living with another person, the true agapic lover will leave the relationship for the sake of the beloved with no thought that this altruistic act will result in his or her love being returned. Furthermore, the true agapic lover will want this new relationship to succeed and will be hurt if it brings unpleasantness or unhappiness to the beloved. Most often when relationships break up and one of the parties is hurt, the hurt individual wants the new relationship to fail, as a kind of punishment for the hurt suffered. Similarly, when someone hurts you, you often want them hurt in return. But the agapic lover responds differently; even if hurt, the agapic lover wants only the best for the beloved.

In one sense agape is more of a philosophical kind of love than a love that most of us have the strength to achieve. In fact, John Lee notes that "unfortunately, I have yet to interview any respondent involved in even a relatively short-term affiliative love relationship which I could classify without qualification as an example of agape. I *have* encountered brief agapic episodes in continuing love relationships."

Each of these loves can combine with others to form new and different patterns. These six, however, should be sufficient to delineate some of the major types of love and to illustrate the complexity of a love relationship. It is perhaps obvious to say that different people are satisfied by different things—that each person seeks satisfaction in a somewhat unique way. When it comes to love, however, this "obvious" point needs to be highlighted. The love that may seem to you to be "lifeless" or "crazy" or "boring" may to someone else be ideal. At the same time, another person may see the very same negative qualities in the love you are seeking that you might see in theirs. With a knowledge of these various kinds of love, we may become a bit more tolerant and empathic. A real problem does arise, of course, when a person seeking one type of love falls in love with a person seeking a vastly different type of love—to this there seems no easy way to a mutually productive relationship.

INFATUATION AND JEALOUSY

As can be appreciated from its varied definitions, dimensions, and kinds, love is not a concept that is easy to pin down; it seems to go in numerous directions all at once. To make matters even more difficult, a number of misconceptions about love add even more complexity. Two of the most important are considered here: (1) the assumption that infatuation and love are two different emotions and should be treated differently and (2) the assumption that jealousy is a sign of intense love.

Infatuation

One of the most often discussed issues concerning love is the distinction between love and infatuation. The assumption seems to be that love is real, whereas infatuation only appears real; love is lasting, whereas infatuation passes quickly; love is mature, whereas infatuation is immature; love is comforting, whereas infatuation is anxiety provoking; love is meaningful, whereas infatuation is foolish. These distinctions are neatly written into our dictionaries: the *Random House Dictionary* defines *love* as "a profoundly tender, passionate affection for a person," "a feeling of warm personal attachment or deep affection," "sexual passion or desire, or its gratification," *Infatuation,* on the other hand, is defined as "foolish or all-absorbing passion" and *to infatuate* is defined as "to inspire or possess with a foolish or unreasoning passion."

Rational emotive therapists Albert Ellis and Robert Harper in *A Guide to Successful Marriage* discuss a study of the "loves" and "infatuations" of 500 college women. In reporting their relationships, these women used the term "infatuation" to describe those of their relationships that were past and unenduring and "love" to describe their present relationships. As Ellis and Harper explain, "In our monogamously oriented society, evidently, we make our young people so ashamed of falling in love frequently and then falling promptly or eventually out of love again—which my study showed that they actually do most of the time—that they are loath to confess, even to themselves, how often they do love. They consequently divide amorous attachments into 'loves' and 'infatuations,' and call their past loves infatuations and their present infatuations loves."

I would agree with Ellis and Harper that the best thing to do with the term *infatuation* is to drop it entirely and to recognize that to distinguish between infatuation and love creates more confusion than clarity. What we need to recognize is that there are many kinds of love and there are many styles of loving. We may love mildly or intensely, for a short time or for the rest of our lives, selfishly or altruistically, realistically or unrealistically, heterosexually or homosexually, monogamously or plurally, productively or destructively, sexually or nonsexually, and no doubt in numerous other ways as well. What is right for one person may be entirely wrong for another person; what produces satisfaction for one person may produce dissatisfaction for another.

Jealousy

Another misconception is the assumption that jealousy is a sign of intense love. It is often assumed that if there is no jealousy, there is no love, and it is under this assumption that people often encourage jealous responses in their partners. In this way, they feel, they will be shown how deeply they are loved.

Let us say that someone shows considerable interest in your partner and that your partner returns the interest. How would you respond? On the one hand, you can respond with thoughts and words reflecting your admiration for this person's good taste and your general satisfaction with your mate's being concerned with other people and his or her responsiveness to the needs or desires of other people. On the other hand, you can respond with dissatisfaction with yourself for your loss of attractiveness, with your partner for his or her neglect of you, and with this third party for attempting to steal what you believe is rightfully yours.

Clearly the first response is the more mature and the more productive, though it may be much more difficult. The second response is the jealous response triggered by a fear of being excluded, of being an outsider rather than an insider, or by a fear of losing one's mate or perhaps one's own sex appeal. The greater the loss, the greater the jealousy; the greater the need to belong, the greater the jealousy at being excluded.

Jealousy is a feeling of dissatisfaction and displeasure occasioned by the fear that a person's sexual partner or lover will be lost to another. Jealousy may also be brought on by the belief (whether real or imagined) that one's lover is having an affair with another person.

One of the major problems with jealousy is that it leads to an increase in insecurity, which in turn leads us to perceive potential loss in more situations, which in turn stirs up more jealousy, which in turn leads to an increase in insecurity, and so on. "Jealousy is not a barometer by which the depth of love may be read," noted Margaret Mead. "It merely records the degree of the lover's insecurity. It is a negative, miserable state of feeling, having its origin in a sense of insecurity and inferiority."

At times there is good reason to feel insecure, and perhaps it is jealousy that warns us of forces that might endanger our security. At other times jealousy can provide us with the motivation and the justification for "letting go," for saying what we have been wanting to say, and perhaps for retaliating with behavior we might have been repressing. Insofar as jealousy motivates a more honest reaction to a disturbing situation, it can facilitate communication that is open and honest. When the jealousy is denied or when the behaviors it motivates are dishonest reflections of a poorly understood emotional reaction, it can be destructive of a relationship and of a positive self-image.

In Freudian theory jealousy is a defense mechanism against one's own impulses to be unfaithful and the impulse to engage in homosexual activities. One must then wonder if when homosexual lovers experience jealousy, it is due to the impulse to engage in heterosexual activities. Most contemporary theorists, I think, would argue that jealousy is a learned mode of behavior which is greatly dependent upon the culture in which one is raised. We have probably learned to respond to certain situations with jealousy much as we have learned to respond to some situations with anxiety and to others with openness, hostility, or friendliness. Regardless of what theoretical position is taken, it seems to be agreed that jealousy is motivated by a concern for the self. Jealousy is not a sign of love for another person; it reflects more accurately one's own insecurity and perhaps one's degree of self-absorption or self-love.

THE DEVELOPMENT OF LOVE

Love is an extremely difficult emotion to deal with in terms of its development or the conditions conducive to its occurrence. How do you make someone love someone? What makes one person love another? It would be a gross understatement to say that these are difficult questions. And so it is with considerable hesitancy that an attempt is made here to characterize the ways in which love develops. First, I offer some tentative propositions concerning the conditions under which love is more likely to occur. Second, two theories concerning the development of love are offered.

Conditions Conducive to the Development of Love

Loving, it seems, is more likely to occur under the following general circumstances.

1. *When there is mutual respect.* Both research and folk wisdom attest to the difference between loving and liking. One can be present without the other. We can like someone we do not love, and we can also love someone we do not like. Yet it seems that in most situations we like and respect the person we love, with the liking and respecting coming first.

2. *When the individuals have positive self-images.* I assume here that for a person to engage in a loving relationship, it is easier if he or she first has a positive self-image. If one dislikes oneself, then it will be extremely difficult—if not impossible—to love another.

3. *When there is a physical attraction.* Although I am considering both sexual and nonsexual love, it seems that there is a physical component in any love relationship. At best, we have to want to be with someone to love him or her, and generally we choose not to be with people we find unattractive. And attractiveness and unattractiveness are at least in part physical.

4. *When the individuals are relatively free of significant problems.* It is difficult to love or be loving when we have nothing to eat and no prospects of getting a job, for example. If we are on the verge of being convicted and being sentenced to jail for life, it is understandable that we would think very little, if at all, about love and loving. We may, of course, worry about our loved ones and what will happen to them, but we would not be in a very good position to establish a new love relationship. These examples are purposely far removed from our own experiences. But consider individuals who constantly worry about and plan for their businesses. Their available energy for love is greatly reduced. The students who think only about grades have little time and energy for loving.

Theories on the Development of Love

While literary and poetic explanations of love and loving are varied and numerous, there are few scientific explanations that seem to have any merit. Two exceptions to this general rule are discussed here with the intention of stimulating you to reflect on the nature of love in interpersonal relationships rather than convince you that these are in fact the ways in which love develops.

Love as Labeled Arousal

One of the most interesting theories of emotion, proposed by Stanley Schachter, hypothesizes that there are two factors essential for emotion. The first factor is physiological arousal which may take various forms, for example, increased heart rate, sweating, increased breathing rate, facial flush, and so on. The second essential factor is that this physiological arousal has to be labeled or named in terms of its cause. So, if you experience intense physiological arousal when someone forces you to address an audience of several hundred people, you might label that as *fear*. Neither factor by itself is sufficient for the development of emotion; both arousal and labeling must be present.

A number of researchers have attempted to apply this basic theory to love. One such example is that of Ellen Berscheid and Elaine Walster who expanded the two-factor theory to three factors. Three factors (or three components) are necessary, say Berscheid and Walster, for love to develop. First, there has to be some knowledge of how the culture defines love, that is, one has to know what love is. By knowing what love is—even if the individual has not yet experienced it—the person is in a ready state to find it, to recognize it, and perhaps to expect it. The more one thinks about love, it appears, the greater the chances for experiencing love. Second, there must be some appropriate person available to whom this love can be directed. (Naturally it helps if this available person possesses those qualities that you find attractive or that meet with your expectations.) Third, there must be some physiological arousal that has been labeled *love*.

The process of the development of love, then, would have three stages: we know what love is, are looking for it, and are ready to experience it. We spot a likely love object; we experience a physiological arousal that we label *love*. (The arousal may be stimulated by some love-related activity like kissing, or perhaps from some unrelated activity like running or fighting.)

One of the interesting implications of this theory is that love may be encouraged by disco dancing, viewing a boxing match, seeing a horror movie, hearing a rock concert, or winning or losing money on the horses. All will lead to physiological arousal. However, the individual must then label the arousal as *love*. Needless to say, this labeling is more likely to take place when the initial physiological arousal seems logically related to what we normally think of as love.

This theory very satisfactorily explains why women are reportedly more prone to fall in love after an intense relationship than are men. The intense relationship, we may assume, will lead to physiological arousal of both sexes, and so the first factor is present for both. But note that women have been conditioned to associate this type of arousal with love and so will be more apt to label the experience as *love* than will males, who traditionally have been taught that there is a definite separation between physiological arousal and love. These sex differences are growing smaller, but, some difference still survives and perhaps accounts—at least in part—for the different love experiences of males and females.

Love as Imprinting

The concept of imprinting was developed by Konrad Lorenz, who used it to refer to the behavior of ducklings who would follow just about any object that walked in front of them as they hatched. Normally this is the mother duck, but when it was Lorenz himself, the ducklings treated him as if he were their mother and even in the presence of the natural mother would nevertheless follow Lorenz.

Imprinting is in some respects like one-shot conditioning; it occurs once, and apparently the behavior is learned for all time. First, there is a specific time in the life of the individual in which imprinting occurs. The time varies with the behavior and with the specific animal, but there seem to be critical periods for different behaviors. Second, imprinting does not seem to be influenced by rewards or punishments extrinsic to the behavior; apparently an animal may be imprinted even if it is being punished at the same time. Third, the imprinting occurs without rewards or punishments occurring after the behavior is emitted. The behavior itself is apparently the reward.

Edward Brecher has argued that this concept of imprinting and particularly these three characteristics may be used to explain love. According to Brecher, falling in love is essentially an imprinting process. It occurs not so much because of the individual one meets but rather because of the time in the life of the individual. Usually a boy or girl will fall in love at puberty, and the object of the love is not particularly relevant. What is important is that he or she was at the right time in life to fall in love and so did so. As Brecher put it, "Just as the mallard duckling follows the first moving object that happens by when it is thirteen hours old, so the boy or girl freshly arrived at adolescence falls in love with the first potential love object who happens past at the critical period of puberty. The object imprinted may be too old or too young, too fat or too thin, too bashful or too domineering; it doesn't much matter if he or she comes past when the moment for falling in love is ripe."

This theory seems to explain well why it is that we never seem to get over our first love, why our first love and our first lover always seem to have a special place in our thoughts and in our feelings.

If we attempted to combine these two positions, we would propose a five-factor theory which would take the "labeled *arousal*" theory as a basis and add to it two "imprinting" elements: (1) the actual presence of the appropriate love object or some clear symbolic representation, for example, a photograph or film, and (2) a specific time in life that love is apt to develop most readily. According to this synthesized theory, then, the entire process would go something like this:

1. We learn about love from our culture; we know what love is; we look for love; we expect love to happen to us.
2. We reach a particular point in our lives when we are ready for love—we are at the stage where imprinting is possible.
3. We see an appropriate love object or some symbolic representation.
4. We are physiologically aroused from kissing, fighting, or some other physical activity.
5. We label the physiological arousal *love* and attribute that arousal—that love—to the "appropriate love object."

SEX DIFFERENCES IN LOVING

In our culture, the differences between men and women in love are considered great. In poetry, in novels, and in the mass media women and men are depicted as acting very differently when falling in love, in being in love, and in ending a love relationship. Women are seen as totally absorbed with love whereas men are seen as relegating love to one part of their lives. Or, as Lord Byron put it in *Don Juan*, "Man's love is of man's life a thing apart,/'Tis woman's whole existence." Women are portrayed as being emotional whereas men are portrayed as being logical. Women are supposed to love intensely while men are supposed to love with some detachment. Noted the military leader Giorgio Basta: "Man loves little and often, woman much and rarely." While the folklore on sex differences is extensive, the research is meager.

In their responses to a questionnaire designed to investigate love, social psychologist Zick Rubin found that men and women were quite similar; men and women seem to experience love to a similar degree. Women do, however, indicate greater love for their same-sex friends than do men. This may reflect a real difference between the sexes or it may be a function of the greater social restrictions under which men operate. Men are not supposed to admit their love for another man, lest they be thought homosexual or somehow different from their fellows. Women are permitted a greater freedom to communicate their love for other women.

In an attempt to investigate the number of romantic experiences and the ages at which these occur, sociologist William Kephart surveyed over 1000 college students from 18 to 24 years of age. The women indicated that they had been infatuated more times than the men. The median times infatuated for women was 5.6 and for men was 4.5. For love relationships, there is greater similarity. The median number of times in love for these same women was 1.3 and for the men was 1.2. As expected, women had their first romantic experiences earlier than men. The median age of first infatuation for women was 13 and for men was 13.6; median age for first time in love for women was 17.1 and for men was 17.6.

In this same study men, contrary to popular myth, were found to place more emphasis on romance than women. For example, the college students were asked the following question: "If a boy (girl) had all the other qualities you desired, would you marry this person if you were not in love with him (her)?" Approximately two-thirds of the men responded "no," which seems to indicate that a high percentage were concerned with "love" and "romance." However, less than one-third of the women responded "no." Further, when sociologist D. H. Knox surveyed men and women concerning their views on love—whether it is basically realistic or basically romantic—it was found that married women had a more realistic (less romantic) conception of love than did married men. It is also interesting to note that married persons had a more realistic view of love than did unmarrieds.

Popular myth would have us believe that when love affairs break up, the breakups are the result of the man developing some outside affair. But the

Contrary to much popular folklore, men appear to daydream about a broken affair more than women.

research does not seem to support this. When surveyed on the reasons for breaking up, only 15 percent of the men indicated that it was because of their interest in another partner, but 32 percent of the women noted this as a reason for the breakup. And these findings are consistent with the perceptions of the partners regarding the causes of the breakups as well: 30 percent of the men but only 15 percent of the women noted that their partner's interest in another person was the reason for the breakup. The most popular reason reported was a mutual loss of interest: 47 percent of the men and 38 percent of the women noted this as a reason for breaking up.

In their reactions to broken romantic affairs there are both similarities and differences between women and men. For example, both women and men tended to remember only the pleasant things and to revisit places with past remembrances about equally. On the other hand, men engaged in more dreaming about the lost partner and in more daydreaming generally as a reaction to the breakup.

What will happen in the next decades with regard to sex differences in loving is hard to gauge. On the one hand, as the sexes become more equal socially and economically, the differences in love and loving may be lessened considerably, maybe even eliminated. On the other hand, as the socioeconomic differences are eliminated, the sexual-romantic-loving differences may be accentuated and may well take on added significance and relevance.

LOVING AND COMMUNICATION

Herbert A. Otto, one of the leaders in the human potential movement, notes in *Love Today* the paradoxical conclusions made about communication in love. Communication in love, says Otto, is characterized by two features: "(1) confusion and lack of clarity; and (2) increased clarity and comprehension." While some lovers note the extreme difficulty in understanding what the other person means, many others note the exceptional ability they now seem to possess in understanding the other person. Related to this is Truman Capote's definition of love as not having to finish your sentences.

Ron Lunceford, in *How Do You Feel?*, expresses clearly the strong desire to communicate love and the difficulties in doing so.

> The one thing I think I wish for myself is that I could express my love more. I can express my love, but sometimes I have the fear of talking about it too much. I like being loved and I like giving love and sometimes talking about it changes that feeling for me. Sometimes too it is sad for me to talk about love and loving feelings to people who don't have someone to love or anyone to love them; that's sad.
>
> I want to say sometimes to people, "Hey, you can love me and we don't have to make promises to each other." Some people can handle that and some can't. Some just need permission to express love and be open to it; sometimes it helps to begin to take that risk.
>
> But for me, I want to say, "I love you" more. I don't want anyone I love to go without knowing that.

But loving implies the taking of risks, as Lunceford mentions. We run the risk of not having our love returned or being rejected outright. The alternative we often take is to conceal our love or perhaps never even admit it to ourselves. Communicating our love also involves the risk of self-disclosure. In any love relationship mutual self-disclosure is important. As Otto says, "This helps to establish a relationship characterized by optimal personality growth for both lovers."

Much as loving relationships are helped by self-disclosure, love also encourages openness and honesty. We seem to have a need to express ourselves, to let other people know who we "really" are. And yet perhaps because of the fear of rejection, we conceal our "true selves." In a love relationship we have someone to whom we can reveal ourselves without fear of being rejected or thought foolish. Not every relationship is quite so simple, of course. In many instances it is with the people we love that we are most on guard. If, for example, we initially pretended to be strong, we might conceal weakness for fear that it was our strength that made us attractive. It is often with people we love that we hide aspects of ourselves that we might readily reveal to strangers if we were sure of never meeting them again.

Empathic communication is naturally increased in any love relationship since, on the basis of our more open communication, we can understand how the other feels and want to feel what he or she feels. In many ways, to love someone is to support him or her. We naturally support those we love, in part because we want them to be secure and unafraid. Our supportiveness helps them and theirs helps us. Love is an emotion that is not only good to receive but good to give as well; it makes us feel pleased to love and, consequently, the positiveness we feel for ourselves, for our beloved, and for the relationship itself is increased. Normally, we love persons whom we respect and regard as good; we like them as well as love them. If we love someone, we want to become a part of him or her. This is perhaps the best way to encourage the feeling of equality.

SOURCES

Pitirim A. Sorokin, "Altruistic Love," and Cyril Bibby, "The Art of Love," in *The Encyclopedia of Sexual Behavior*, Albert Ellis and Albert Abarbanel, eds. (New York: Hawthorn Books, 1967), were particularly helpful in defining and characterizing love and loving. *How Do You Feel?*, John Wood, ed. (Englewood Cliffs, N.J.: Prentice-Hall, 1974), contains interesting articles by Ron Lunceford and Larry and Kay Carlin, both cited here, as well as by John Wood and Bill and Audry McGraw. All four articles, and in fact the entire book, are worth reading. Zick Rubin, *Liking and Loving* (New York: Holt, Rinehart and Winston, 1973), is especially insightful.

For types of love, see John Alan Lee, *The Colors of Love* (New York: Bantam Books, 1977). For the theories of love as physiological arousal, see Stanley Schachter, "The Interaction of Cognitive and Physiological Determinants of Emotional State," in *Advances in Experimental Social Psychology*, vol. 1, Leonard Berkowitz, ed. (New York: Academic Press, 1964), and the explanation of the Berscheid-Walster adaptation in Robert A. Baron and Donn Dyrne, *Exploring Social Psychology*, 2d ed. (Boston: Allyn & Bacon, 1982). Also see Ellen Berscheid and Elaine Walster, "A Little Bit about Love," in *Foundations of Interpersonal Attraction*, T. L. Huston, ed. (New York:

Academic Press, 1974). For the theory of love as imprinting, see Edward M. Brecher, *The Sex Researchers* (Boston: Little, Brown, 1969). Herbert A. Otto, "Communication in Love," in *Love Today: A New Exploration*, Herbert A. Otto, ed. (New York: Dell [Delta Books], 1972), is perhaps the best single source on love and communication. Two excellent works offer thorough summaries of research on love and insight into our own loving behavior: Elaine Walster and G. William Walster, *A New Look at Love* (Reading, Mass.: Addison-Wesley, 1978) and Glenn Wilson and David Nias, *The Mystery of Love* (New York: Quadrangle/The New York Times Book Co., 1976).

The studies reported on sex differences in loving were taken from Glen Wilson and David Nias, *The Mystery of Love*. Original references are as follows: William M. Kephart, "Some Correlates of Romantic Love," *Journal of Marriage and the Family* 29 (1967):470–479; D. H. Knox, "Concepts of Love by Married College Students," *College Student Survey* 4 (1970):28–30; and, for the study on frequency and age of first romantic experiences, see C. Kirkpatrick and T. Caplow, "Courtship in a Group of Minnesota Students," *American Journal of Sociology* 51 (1945):114–125.

EXPERIENTIAL VEHICLES

25.1 GIFT GIVING

This exercise is an excellent one to use at the end of the semester as a kind of final parting "gift" that one member of the class gives to another.

In groups of five or six persons, each member indicates a "gift" that he or she would wish to obtain for each of the other members of the group. (It is sometimes helpful to write down the names of each person in the group and the gift you would want these people to have next to their names.)

These gifts are symbolic gifts and are not actually given. Rather, they are wished for the other person. As such the gifts may be material or spiritual, concrete or abstract, expensive or inexpensive, general or specific. In all cases, however, they must be positive gifts.

Discussion may center on the reasons for the selections made, for appropriateness or inappropriateness, what they say about the person for whom the gift is intended, what they say about the relationship between the persons, and so on.

25.2 POSITIVE WORDS

This exercise is performed by the entire class. One person is "it" and takes a seat in the front of the room or in the center of the circle. (It is possible, though not desirable, for the person to stay where he or she normally sits.) Going around in a circle or from left to right, each person says something positive about the person who is "it."

For this exercise only volunteers should be chosen. Students may be encouraged but should not be forced to participate. Although this exercise is perhaps more appropriate to the content of the earlier units, it is best done when the students know each other fairly well. For this reason, it is introduced here.

Persons must tell the truth, that is, they are not allowed to say anything about the person that they do not believe. At the same time, however, all statements must be positive. Only positive words are allowed during this exercise. Persons may, however, "pass" and say nothing. No one may ask why something was said or why something was not said. The positive words may refer to the person's looks, behavior, intelligence, clothes, mannerisms, and so on. One may also say, "I don't know you very well, but you seem friendly," or

"You seem honest," or whatever. These statements, too, must be believed to be true.

After everyone has said something, another person becomes "it." After all volunteers have been "it," consider the following questions individually.

1. Describe your feelings when thinking about becoming "it."
2. How did you feel while people were saying positive words?
3. What comments were the most significant to you?
4. Were you "it"? If so, would you be willing to be "it" again? If not, why not?
5. How do you feel now that the exercise is over? Did it make you feel better? Why do you suppose it had the effect it did?
6. What implications may be drawn from this exercise for application to everyday living?
7. Will this exercise change your behavior in any way?

After you have completed all these questions, share with the entire class whatever comments you would like to make.

PRIMARY RELATIONSHIPS, FAMILIES, AND INTERPERSONAL COMMUNICATION

Upon completion of this unit, you should be able to:
1. define *family* and *primary relationship*
2. identify five characteristics common to all primary relationships
3. identify five of the reasons discussed here for the maintenance of primary relationships
4. define and explain the four communication patterns that characterize primary relationships
5. identify at least seven reasons for conflicts within primary relationships or families
6. explain the operation of manipulation, nonnegotiation, emotional appeal, personal rejection, and empathic understanding as conflict strategies in primary relationships
7. identify and explain the five suggestions for improving communication within the primary relationship and the family

All of us are now or were at one time part of a family. Some of our experiences have been pleasant and positive and are recalled with considerable pleasure. Other experiences have been unpleasant and negative and are recalled only with considerable pain. Part of the reasons for the pleasure or the pain involved in these experiences rests with the interpersonal communication patterns that operate within such a small tightly knit group. This unit is designed to provide a better understanding of the interpersonal communication patterns that operate within the family and, hopefully, some insight into how these interactions can be made more effective and more productive.

Five issues relating to these goals are discussed. First, we consider the nature and characteristics of families and primary relationships in order to spell out some of the universals common to these relationships. Second, we look into the reasons why people establish and maintain such relationships. Third, we will identify the patterns of communication that operate within these interpersonal units. Fourth, the nature of conflict within primary relationships and families is considered—the reasons such conflicts develop and some of the interpersonal conflict strategies that can be employed to eliminate them. Fifth, some suggestions are offered for improving interpersonal communication within primary relationships and families.

PRIMARY RELATION-
SHIPS, FAMILIES, AND
INTERPERSONAL
COMMUNICATION

411

PRIMARY RELATIONSHIPS AND FAMILIES: NATURE AND CHARACTERISTICS

If you had to write a definition of what constitutes a family, you would probably note that a family consists of a husband, a wife, and one or more children. When pressed you might also note that some of these families also consist of other relatives—in-laws, brothers and sisters, grandparents, aunts and uncles, and so on. But there are other types of relationships that are, to its own members, "families." Perhaps the most obvious example is people living together in a marriagelike state but who are not in fact married. For the most part, they live as if they were married. There is, for example, an exclusive sexual commitment, there may be children, there are shared financial responsibilities, shared time and space, and so on. These relationships are like traditional marriage unions except that in one case the union is recognized by church and/or state and in the other it is not. Another obvious example is the gay male or lesbian couple who live together as "lovers" with all of the other characteristics of a "family" but who are not legally married. Many of these unions too have children from previous heterosexual unions or by adoption.

The communication principles that apply to the traditional nuclear family (the mother-father-child family) also seem to apply to these nonmarried relationships as well. In the following discussion the term *primary relationship* is used to designate the two principal parties involved—the husband and wife, for example—and the term *family* to designate the broader constellation which would include children, relatives, and assorted significant others. All primary relationships have a number of characteristics in common and these will be identified.

Defined Roles

There is a relatively clear perception of the roles each person is expected to play in relation to each other and to the relationship as a whole. Each knows approximately what his or her obligations, duties, privileges, and responsibilities are. This does not mean that the individuals do not fight over the roles or that they are completely satisfied with them, just merely that the roles are fairly clear to the parties. Such roles might include wage earner, cook, house cleaner, child watcher, social secretary, home decorator, plumber, carpenter, food shopper, money manager, and so on. At times the roles may be shared, but even in the sharing it is generally assumed that one person has primary responsibility for certain tasks and the other person for others.

Commitment to Preservation

In primary relationships there is a commitment to the preservation of the relationship. Again, this does not mean that each party is always satisfied with the relationship or that there are not times when they wish they were alone or with someone else. Rather, it is to imply that the individuals usually have an intellectual and emotional commitment to maintain this particular relationship. They seek its preservation, its continuance. Along with this commitment is a strong bond between the individuals; generally they care for and like (perhaps even love) each other.

Recognition of Responsibilities

The parties see themselves as having certain obligations and responsibilities to each other. In the "single" state the individual does not have the same kind of obligations to another person that he or she does in a primary relationship where individuals have an obligation to help each other financially—on a day-to-day basis as well as on a more long-term basis, for example, in insurance, hospitalization, and retirement planning. Relationships today are more than ever characterized by this economic interdependence. As inflation and recession erode our earnings and savings and as the desire to accumulate goods and to improve one's living conditions increase, this economic interdependence will become even more significant in defining our primary relationships.

There are also emotional responsibilities: to comfort the individual when distressed, to take pleasure in their pleasures, to feel their pain, and to raise their spirits. Temporal obligations must also be considered since each person is obligated to reserve some large block of time for the other. This does not mean that the parties are obligated to spend all of their time together but rather to recognize that time-sharing is important to the relationship. Each couple will naturally define this differently. With some couples these temporal commitments and obligations are extensive; they do everything together and rarely do anything alone or with third or fourth parties. Other couples sleep together but do little else with each other. Between these two extremes lie most primary relationships. Sexual obligations are another factor: the individuals in a primary relationship are more or less committed to achieving a substantial part of their sexual gratification with each other.

Shared History and Future

One of the most important characteristics of primary relationships is that they have a shared history and the prospect of a shared future. For a relationship to become a primary one there must be some history, some significant past interactions. Primary relationships do not emerge fully grown but rather develop over a period of time, though certainly the period of time varies greatly from one relationship to another. During this time the members get to know each other, to understand each other a little better, and ideally to like and even love each other. Similarly, the parties in such an interpersonal relationship view the relationship as having a potential future. In fact, this is one of the main reasons why relationships are developed—so that each individual will have a special partner tomorrow, the day after that, and perhaps forever. In contrast, casual sexual encounters do not have a history and usually do not have a prospect of the future—at least this is not the individuals' primary orientation. In such casual encounters the object is a purely sexual-emotional one and does not involve the same temporal commitment or the same mutuality that a primary relationship does. This is not to say that casual relationships cannot be intense or satisfying; nor is it to say that such casual relationships may not develop into significant and lasting relationships—some can and do. Nevertheless, at the point of the encounter, the casual relationship does not have a significant shared past or a prospect of a shared future, which in itself functions to alter the relationship a great deal. When individuals in a primary relationship have a shared history and a commitment to a shared future, they respond to each other, to relational problems, to significant others in very different ways than do partners who have no history or prospect for a future.

Shared Living Space

In our culture, persons in primary interpersonal relationships usually share the same living space. When living space is not shared, it is generally seen as "abnormal" or as temporary by both the culture as a whole and by the individuals involved in the relationship. For example, one of the parties may work out of town, may be in prison, in the armed forces, or in a hospital. But this situation is generally seen as a deviation from the normal pattern. There are cases, of course, where a man or woman who lives with a partner, parents, with children or even alone may have a lover on some "back street" with whom they may not share the same living space. Even though they do not share their living space, they probably perceive that as the ideal and, in fact, usually do share some special space at least part of the time.

In some cultures men and women do not share the same living space— the women may live with the children while the men live together in a commune-type arrangement. Today, in our culture many couples are choosing to live apart with each maintaining his or her own apartment. Usually they do this with a view to sharing the same space at some more appropriate time, for example, when the level of commitment of one or both parties is higher or when other problems or difficulties have been resolved. So while this shared space notion applies to most primary relationships, it is not a universal of the same order as those previously discussed. Rather, it is a universal of high probability, or what is called a "probability universal."

THE MAINTENANCE OF PRIMARY AND FAMILY RELATIONSHIPS

The reasons for maintaining primary relationships are as numerous and varied as the reasons for originally beginning such relationships. Some of the more popular and frequently cited reasons will be mentioned here.

The most obvious reason is that the individuals love each other and want to preserve their relationship. They wish to maintain what they have because alternative couplings do not seem as inviting or as potentially enjoyable—the individuals' needs are being satisfied and so the relationship is continued. In some cases these needs are predominantly love and mutual caring, but in other cases the needs that are being met may not be quite so positive. For example, one individual may maintain a relationship because it provides a means of exercising control over another person, which may seem very important. Another might continue the relationship because it provides ego gratification or some form of humiliation, each according to his or her specific need.

Often the relationship neither involves great love nor great need satisfaction but is maintained because it is relatively convenient. Perhaps both partners work together—they may jointly own a business or a house—or have certain mutual friends that are important to them. In these cases it may be more convenient to stay together than to break up and go through the difficulties involved in finding another person to live with or another business partner or perhaps another social escort. At times both feel the same way about the relationship and here there is seldom any difficulty; no one is "fooling" anyone. At other times, the relationship is one of great love for one partner and one of convenience for the other.

Relationships are often kept together because of the children involved. Children are often (fortunately or unfortunately) brought into the world to save a relationship. In some cases they do; or at least the union is preserved. The parents stay together because they honestly feel, rightly or wrongly, that it is in the best interests of the children to preserve the relationship. In other cases, "the children" are just a socially acceptable excuse for the fear of being alone, for convenience, for financial advantage, and so on.

Fear motivates many to stay together. The individuals may fear the outside world; they may be fearful of being alone and of facing others as "singles." They may remember the horrors of the singles bars, the "one night stands," and the loneliness of the weekends and may elect to preserve their current relationship as the better alternative. Sometimes the fear may be of social criticism: "What will our friends say? They always thought we were such a great couple. They'll think I'm a failure because I can't hold on to another person." Sometimes the fear stems from the consequences of violating some religious or parental tenet.

Financial advantages—especially today—may motivate many couples to stick it out. Divorces are expensive both emotionally and financially. And now since the Michele Marvin and Billie Jean King cases, "palimony" and "galimony" are as much feared as alimony so people with considerable amounts of money are fearful of breaking up because they fear losing half of their wealth or even more. Also, depending on where the individuals live and their preferred life-style, being single can be expensive. The cost of living in New York, Philadelphia, Houston, Chicago, San Francisco, Los Angeles, and many other cities is almost prohibitive for single people and so many may stay together rather than face additional economic problems.

Still another reason is inertia—perhaps a major reason for the preservation of many relationships. Many people just "go along with the program" and it hardly occurs to them to consider changing their status—to change seems to be too much trouble. Inertia—the tendency for a body at rest to remain at rest and a body in motion to remain in motion—is greatly encouraged by the media. It is easier for many individuals to remain in their present relationship and to seek vicarious satisfactions from situation comedies, dramas, and especially soap operas wherein the heroes and heroines do all the things the viewer would do if he or she were not so lazy and resistant to change.

Few relationships stay together for one single reason. Rather, there are usually a multiplicity of reasons that vary in terms of intensity and from one relationship to another. Obviously, the more intense the reasons, the more likely the relationship will be preserved. But because so many of the reasons for relational preservation are subconscious, it is difficult if not impossible to discover why a particular couple stays together or breaks up or to predict which relationships will last and which ones will not.

COMMUNICATION PATTERNS IN PRIMARY RELATIONSHIPS AND FAMILIES

Each primary relationship functions with a unique set of communication patterns. No two relationships will evidence exactly the same interpersonal communication structures. But amid this diversity and uniqueness, there seem general patterns that can be identified and that may serve as general classifications or types. Each interpersonal relationship may then be viewed as a variation on one of these basic types. To this end, four major patterns are identified.

The Equality Pattern

The equality pattern probably exists more in theory than in reality, but it is a good starting point for examining communication in primary relationships. In the *equality pattern* each party shares in the communication transactions equally; the roles played by each are equal. Thus, each party is accorded a similar degree of credibility by the other; each is equally open to the ideas, opinions, and beliefs of the other; each engages in self-disclosure on a more or less equal basis. Here there is no leader or follower, teacher or student, opinion-giver or opinion-seeker; rather they both play these roles equally for each other. Because of this basic equality the communication exchanges themselves—over a substantial period of time—are equal. For example, the number of questions asked, the depth and frequency of self-disclosures, the nonverbal behavior of touching and eye gaze would all be about equal.

Both parties share equally in the decision-making processes—the insignificant ones about which movie to attend as well as the significant ones about where to send the child to school, what church to attend, what house to buy, and so on. Conflicts in equality relationships may occur with some frequency but they are not seen as threatening to the individuals or to the relationship itself. They are seen, rather, as exchanges of ideas, opinions, and values. Even when these individuals disagree they disagree agreeably. The disagreement is not seen as due to one being stupid and the other being smart but to the inevitable clash of ideas and the differences in values and perceptions that are a part of long-term relationships. Put in terms of the content relationship postulate discussed in Unit 2, these conflicts are content rather than relational in nature. This couple has few power struggles within the relationship domain.

If a communication model of this relationship were drawn in which arrows were used to signify individual messages, there would be an equal number of arrows emanating from each person. Further, if the arrows were classified into different types, the types would likewise be similar. A representation of this is given in Figure 26.1A.

The Balanced Split Pattern

In the *balanced split* communication pattern the equality of the previous type of relationship is maintained but here each person is in control or in authority over different domains. Each person, for example, is seen as an expert but each is an expert in different areas. For example, in the traditional nuclear family the husband maintains high credibility in business matters and, say, in politics. The wife, on the other hand, maintains high credibility with such matters as child care and cooking. Although this is changing, these patterns can still be seen clearly in numerous traditional families. There are also areas of overlap where both parties have some expertise but neither one has a great deal more than the other. For example, both parties may know the same amount about religion, health, or art, in which case neither would be perceived as more credible than the other.

Conflict with these individuals is generally nonthreatening since each has specified areas of expertise and so the win-lose patterns are more or less predetermined before the conflict begins. To take our traditional example again, if the conflict is over business the husband wins; if the conflict is over child care the wife wins—neither party is terribly hurt by the conflict. This balanced split pattern is diagrammed in Figure 26.1B.

The Unbalanced Split Pattern

In the *unbalanced split* relationship, as the name implies, one person dominates; one person is seen as an expert on more than half of the areas of mutual communication. This pattern is diagrammed in Figure 26.1C. In many unions this expertise takes the form of control. Thus, in the unbalanced split one person is more or less regularly in control of the relationship. In some cases this person is the more intelligent or more knowledgeable but in many unions it is the one who is more physically attractive. In this latter case the less attractive one compensates by giving in to the other person, allowing the other person to win the arguments, for example, or have his or her way in decision making.

The person in control makes more assertions, tells the other person what should be and what will be done, gives opinions freely, and seldom asks for opinions in return except perhaps to secure some kind of ego gratification from confirmation or from convincing the other person of the logical sophistication of the argument. The noncontrolling person, conversely, asks questions, seeks opinions, and looks to the other person for decision-making leadership.

The Monopoly Pattern

In a *monopoly* relationship, one person is seen as the authority. This person lectures rather than communicates, pontificates rather than talks with another person. Rarely if ever does this person ask questions to seek advice and

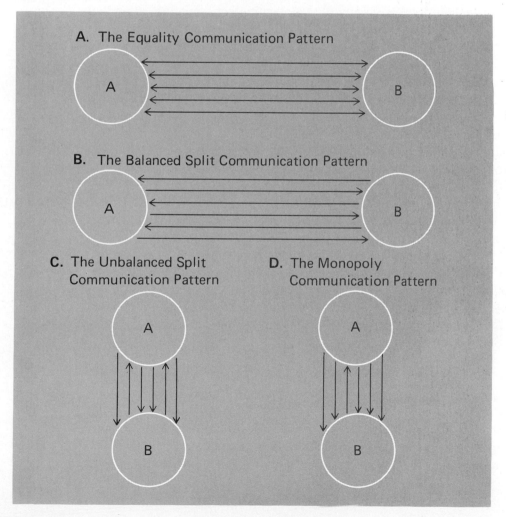

FIGURE 26.1
Communication
Patterns in
Primary
Relationships.

reserves the right to have the final say. In this type of union the arguments are few because both individuals already know who is boss and who will win the argument should one arise. When the authority is challenged, perhaps from outside instigation—"Don't let him walk all over you," "Be a man, stand up to her"—there are arguments and bitter conflicts. One reason the conflicts are so bitter here is that these individuals have had no rehearsal for adequate conflict resolution. They do not know how to argue or how to disagree agreeably, so their arguments frequently take the form of hurting the other person.

The controlling person tells the partner what is and what is not to be. The noncontrolling person looks to the other for permission, for opinion leadership, for decisions to be made, almost as would a child to an all-knowing, all-powerful parent. In many cases these unions are more like child-parent relationships. One individual (the "parent") gains gratification from playing the parental role, from ordering, guiding, and caring for the other person while the "child" gains gratification from having his or her needs met and for not having to make decisions and suffering any of the negative consequences attendant upon wrong or inadequate decisions. This pattern is diagrammed in Figure 26. 1D.

In thinking about these four types of communication patterns, it is easy to identify with the equality or balanced split pattern and surely most of us would consciously wish to be a part of these unions rather than either of the others. But many of our decisions are based on subconscious factors and our motivations are not always "logical" and "mature." Further, many people clearly opt for the unbalanced split and the monopoly patterns, some viewing themselves as the controlling agents but others viewing themselves as the controlled. What makes for happiness, satisfaction, and productivity in a relationship varies with the individuals. An equality pattern that might produce satisfaction in one relationship may lead to dissatisfaction among individuals who need either to control another person or to be controlled. The pattern that makes you happy might make your father and mother or your son and daughter grossly unhappy. A clear recognition of this relativity seems an essential prerequisite to understanding relationships that exist among others and the role that communication plays in the maintenance of those relationships.

CONFLICTS IN PRIMARY RELATIONSHIPS
AND FAMILIES

Conflict is an inevitable part of all relationships and especially primary relationships. Some of the reasons for conflicts in primary interpersonal relationships and some of the strategies employed to resolve them are considered here.

Conflict Development

Each conflict in a primary relationship or family is unique in its origin, its development, and in its eventual resolution (should there be one). Notwithstanding this uniqueness, some reasons are noted more frequently and stand out as more significant than do others—these are examined here.

Intimacy Claims

At times intimacy claims may create conflicts (or at least be at the base of some primary relationship conflicts). In most primary relationships—especially those of considerable intensity—the members make extensive intimacy claims on one another. Such claims may include, for example, expectations that the partner will sympathize and empathize, attend to self-disclosures with total absorption, or share the other's preferences with equal intensity. These intimacy claims often restrict personal freedom and often take the form of possessiveness when one member of the relationship becomes defined (functionally as well as verbally) as a part of the other person—"my woman," "my husband," "my child," and in terms that are not so neutral or favorable. When parties involved in such a relationship enter into a conflict, it is often exaggerated because these intimacies are threatened. Any attempt to take away the few intimacies that our society allows us is fiercely resisted. Intense intimacy claims often put pressure on people which some find difficult to live with on a day-to-day basis. To be always responsive, always sympathetic, always loving, always attentive, is more than many people can manage.

Intimacies Outside the Primary Relationship or Family

Often resented and frequently the cause of conflict are intimacies which occur outside the primary relationship. Largely because of the need that each person has for the other, such intimacies are seen as potential threats. Such extraprimary intimacies are resented at a number of different levels—by the spouse whose partner is involved in such an intimacy and by the parent when the child becomes interested in another person. When the child establishes an intimacy beyond the family, it is saying, in effect, "I can get along without you" and this is often resented and resisted with considerable energy by many parents.

Usually we think of these intimacies as behavioral; the husband or wife takes a lover or has an affair. But frequently these extraprimary intimacies occur in thought or in speech and not in external behaviors. The husband who sits in front of the television and moans over *Charlie's Angels* may not behaviorally engage in any extraprimary intimacy but an extra intimacy has been created. In the mind of the wife (and probably the husband too), their own intimate relationship has been invaded by the thoughts of and the desire for this other intimacy.

Undefined Expectations

At times conflicts center on relatively "trivial" issues such as who will do the dishes and the wash, who will cook, who will iron, or who will use the new car and who will use the old one. To an outsider these are "trivial" issues, but we need to recall that in these conflicts the content (the who will wash or who will iron, for example) is often not the essential focus of the conflict. Often such conflicts center on relational dimensions. The fact that there are frequent conflicts over who will do the dishes may mean that the individuals have problems that go beyond the "trivial" dishes and perhaps center on more significant issues such as who is the boss or whose time is less valuable and should therefore be devoted to the trivial. Often conflicts over such "trivial" issues are masking resentment and hostility concerning some general dissatisfaction or unhappiness. At times these conflicts are generated because some other more significant conflict has not been adequately resolved and the ill feeling one person feels toward the other has not yet been dissipated.

Male-female communication patterns and role expectations are changing drastically making it difficult for both sexes to know what is and what is not appropriate.

At times the expectations each person has of the other may be unrealistic and when reality enters the relationship, conflict may ensue. This type of situation often occurs early in a relationship where, for example, the individuals think that they will want to spend all their time together. When it is discovered that neither one does, each resents this "lessening" of feeling in the other. Unrealistic sexual expectations are also a frequent source of conflict. In our culture the man is supposed to be always ready and always in a sexually aggressive mood. Many women believe this stereotype and are soon rudely instructed in the reality of the male sex drive. On the other hand, those who perceive women basically as sexual gratifiers rather than uniquely motivated, feeling people, will accuse them of withholding love when the women do not constantly exhibit a Lolita mentality. The resolution of such conflicts lies not so much in meeting these expectations but in demonstrating that the original ones were indeed unrealistic and in substituting satisfying and attainable expectations.

Sexual Problems and Differences

Few primary relationships are free of sexual problems and differences that cannot easily be resolved and that often generate conflicts of considerable magnitude. In fact, sexual problems rank among the top three problems in almost all studies of newlyweds. When these same couples are surveyed later in their relationship, the sexual problems have not gone away, they are just talked about less; apparently the individuals resign themselves to living with the problems. In one survey, for example, 80 percent of the respondents identified their marriages as either "very happy" or "happy" but some 90 percent of these said that they had sexual problems.

One of the consequences of sexual problems and differences is that they lead the individuals to seek sexual satisfaction outside of the primary relationship. At times the individual does not seek sexual satisfaction outside the relationship but instead comes to resent (consciously or subconsciously) the other person, blaming the partner for his or her own sexually unfulfilling life.

Financial Difficulties

In surveys of problems among couples, financial difficulties are invariably mentioned. Especially today, few families are free of financial problems. This is particulary true when the family is large; when the children are small, expensive, and non-contributing; and when only one spouse can work. Financial difficulties are not localized in their effect but rather create numerous other problems as well. For example, financial difficulties often create sexual problems. Men who earn little or who worry about not being good providers often avoid sex during paydays, when their perceived inadequacy is particularly salient. This avoidance feeds back and causes sexual difficulties especially because the man is not aware of why he is avoiding sexual intimacy. Often partners will perceive this decreased drive as an indication that they are no longer interest-ing to their mates or that they have found someone outside of the relationship.

One member of the relationship may come to resent the other for not earn-ing enough money because this may mean that he or she will not be able to do the things that peers are doing—not driving the right car, not going to Europe on vacation, not having the children in private school, and so on.

These are actually just a few of the potential sources of primary relation-ship conflicts. A few others may be briefly hinted at here. (1) Intrapersonal con-flicts—conflicts within the self—often carry over into the interpersonal realm. An individual's insecurity or aggressiveness or "workaholism" will frequently influence any interpersonal interaction and cause conflicts. (2) The privateness of a primary relationship often leads to conflicts because it is here that hostile and often violent expression is given free reign. Verbal abuses that might best be left unspoken or verbalized in a more "polite" manner frequently receive their most excessive expression is private. At a more extreme level of conflict we know that physical abuse and beatings occur with much greater frequency in private than they do in public. (3) Change, or rather the inability to deal with change, frequently causes problems. The parents who cannot deal with their child's becoming a fully functioning sexual being, or the child who cannot deal with changes in the parents' relationship, as in, say, separation or divorce, are obvious potential sources of conflict. (4) Different standards and role expenta-tions often create problems as when, for example, the traditional husband finds himself married to an untraditional wife.

Conflict Strategies

Earlier, in Unit 23, some of the strategies employed in interpersonal con-flicts were identified. These were general conflict strategies applicable to all types of relationships. Here some of the conflict strategies used in primary rela-tionship conflicts are considered. I here follow the insightful analysis of Mary Anne Fitzpatrick and Jeff Winke (1979) who identify five main conflict strate-gies: manipulation, nonnegotiation, emotional appeal, personal rejection, and empathic understanding.

In *manipulation* there is an avoidance of open conflict. Here the individ-ual attempts to divert the conflict by being especially charming (disarming, actually) and getting the other individual into a receptive and noncombative frame of mind before disagreeing. That is, the conflict situation and the other individual are manipulated so that the manipulating individual may eventually win the battle, argument, or disagreement.

Nonnegotiation is a type of conflict avoidance in which the individual refuses to discuss the conflict or disagreement and even refuses to listen to the other person's argument or point of view. Actually, of course, one cannot really avoid a conflict since avoidance is in itself a way of dealing with the conflict, much like not responding to another's request is itself a response. At times this nonnegotiation takes the form of hammering away at one's own point of view until the other person gives in, a technique that has been called "steamrolling."

The *emotional appeal* strategy involves crying, sulking, pouting, demonstrating anger, and in fact any means that will succeed in arousing the emotions of the other person. The individual may, for example, appeal to the other person's love and affection—"How could you do this and say you still love me?"— or may promise to behave in the future or to be more loving or more caring.

In *personal rejection* the individual withholds love and affection and seeks to win the argument by getting the other person to break down under this withdrawal. Here the individual acts cold and uncaring, attempting to demoralize the other person. In withdrawing affection, the individual hopes to make the other person question his or her own self-worth. Once the mate is demoralized and feels less than worthy, it is relatively easy to get one's own way by simply making the restitution of love and affection contingent upon resolving the conflict in the individual's favor.

In *empathic understanding* we have the one strategy of conflict resolution that would be called "adult" and "mature" by most individuals. Here there is an emphasis on cooperating and understanding the other person's point of view. Each person attempts to state their own position calmly, with reason, with a degree of tentativeness, and with a willingness to change and bend. The emphasis here is not on winning a war but on achieving a mutually satisfying peace.

In preliminary research based on reported usage of these conflict strategies, a number of differences have been identified depending on the sex of the individual and on the type of relationship involved. In Table 26.1 the conflict

For Opposite-Sex Relationship Conflicts
1. manipulation
2. nonnegotiation
3. emotional appeal
4. personal rejection
5. empathic understanding

For Same-Sex Relationship Conflicts
1. nonnegotiation
2. personal rejection
3. manipulation
4. empathic understanding
5. emotional appeal

Source: From Mary Anne Fitzpatrick and Jeff Winke, "You Always Hurt the One You Love: Strategies and Tactics in Interpersonal Conflict," *Communication Quarterly* 27 (winter 1979): 3–11.

TABLE 26.1
Rank Order
of Frequently
Used Conflict
Strategies

strategies are given for opposite-sex and for same-sex relationships in order of frequency of usage. In opposite-sex relationships we attempt to manipulate more and to use emotional appeal more than in same-sex relationships. Perhaps the most interesting fact about the usage of these strategies is the relative infrequency of empathic understanding for both opposite-sex and same-sex relationships. Men, it has been found, generally favor nonnegotiation as a strategy whereas women seem to favor personal rejection, empathic understanding, and emotional appeal, all of which require considerable understanding of the other individual to employ successfully. In casual relationships manipulation and nonnegotiation are used a great deal whereas emotional appeal and empathic understanding are used very little. With marrieds, emotional appeals and personal rejections are used a great deal but unfortunately empathic understanding is used little.

How can we explain these results? We might attempt to explain each one individually by noting, for example, that marrieds may feel they know each other a great deal better and hence do not have to enter a conflict ready to

Without an openness to communication, meaningful family interaction becomes impossible.

understand the other's point of view; rather, they already know it and disagree with it. A generalization that might account for all these results is that we use what works; the strategies that work are the ones that are used with greatest frequency with no apparent concern for their ultimate effect on the relationship. Thus, for example, marrieds who know each other well and who have a great deal invested in their relationships can effectively hurt the other person with emotional appeals and personal rejection, and hence "win the argument" with these strategies. Empathic understanding will not allow us to win as many conflicts as we would like and so we use it little. Further, because marrieds know each other well they can effectively manipulate the emotions and perceived self-worth of the other person, they are in a powerful position and most likely to win their battles with these particular strategies. In casual relationships we do not know enough about the other individual to manipulate him or her and consequently cannot use emotional appeal very effectively. Furthermore, we usually do not care a great deal about the casual relationship and so we employ the strategies that will simply enable us to win the battle or get out of the conflict situation, namely manipulation and nonnegotiation.

Clearly we would need a great deal more research before we would be able to say with any degree of confidence that the strategies we employ are not the result of our intelligence, our education, and our concern for the other person but rather the result of our desire to win the battle, to have our way, and to remain in control. Nevertheless, it does appear from the little research and evidence that is available that we select the strategies that will best enable us to win.

IMPROVING COMMUNICATION WITHIN PRIMARY RELATIONSHIPS AND FAMILIES

Communication is improved in primary interpersonal relationships by the application of the same principles that improve communication in any other context. Yet, to be most effective, these principles need to be adapted to the uniqueness of the primary relationship context. The purpose of this section, then, is to suggest how the general principles of effective communication may be best applied to primary interpersonal relationships.

Empathic Understanding

One of the five conflict strategies previously noted was empathic understanding. We noted that although it was the most mature response, it was not used very much in close-knit relationships. Nevertheless, if meaningful communication is to be established, then we must learn to see the world from the other person's point of view, to feel that person's pain and insecurity, to experience the other person's love and fear. Empathy is an essential ingredient if a primary relationship or a family is to survive as a meaningful and productive union. It is essential, for example, that the individuals be allowed—and in fact encouraged—to explain how and why they see the world, their relationship, and their problems as they do.

Self-Disclosures

The importance of self-disclosure in the development and maintenance of a meaningful interpersonal relationship has been noted throughout. The research on self-disclosure, however, suggests that total self-disclosure may not be rewarding and effective. In fact, research indicates that at times it may be expedient to omit, for example, past indiscretions, certain fears, and perceived personal inadequacies since these disclosures may lead to negative perceptions and perhaps damage the relationship in some way. In any decision as to whether or not to self-disclose, the possible effects on the relationship should be considered. But it is also necessary, it seems to me, to consider the ethical issues involved, specifically the right of the other person to know about those behaviors and thoughts that may influence the choices she or he makes. Certainly, these decisions are not easy to make and yet they have to be faced by all individuals involved in such intimate relationships.

If we survey the relationships around us, we would probably find too little self-disclosure as well as too little acceptance of the disclosures once they are made by others. Carefully reversing this process would seem effective; most relationships would profit from increased self-disclosures and from a greater acceptance of disclosures in general. The type of self-disclosures I am advocating are disclosures of present feelings rather than the detailing of one's past sexual experiences or past psychological problems. The sharing of present feelings will also help a great deal in enabling each person to better empathize with the other; each will come to understand better the other's point of view if these self-disclosures are made. It has been found, for example, that the length of time a couple spends together is not related to the amount of understanding they have of each other, indicating that self-disclosure is not a normal and accepted part of daily interaction in most relationships.

When self-disclosures are made it is particularly important that clear and unmistakable support for the person be demonstrated—nonverbally and verbally. This does not mean that you have to agree with the disclosure itself, only that you should support the act of disclosing and the person as a whole.

Openness to Change

If there is one general quality that seems essential to effective interpersonal relationships, I think it is one's openness to change, to experimentation. Throughout any significant relationship there will be numerous and significant changes in each of the individuals and in the relationship as a whole. The person who is open to these changes—who accepts them as a normal and natural part of life—will be better able to adjust to and control the changes as they occur. Again, I am not suggesting that we should willingly accept the results of any specific change but rather that we accept the process of change and realize that change is normal and that nonchange is the exception.

Fighting Fair

Conflict, as already noted, is inevitable; it is an essential part of every meaningful interpersonal relationship. The goal should not be to have a relationship free of conflict but rather to manage conflict effectively and productively. And perhaps the most general rule to follow is to FIGHT FAIR. Winning at all costs, beating down the other person, getting one's own way, and the like are appropriate (perhaps) in business, politics, and the boxing ring but they have little use in a primary relationship or family. Instead, cooperation, compromise, and mutual understanding need to be substituted. If we enter a conflict with a person we love with the idea that we want to win and we want the other person to lose, then the conflict has to have the effect of hurting at least one partner, though very often both get hurt in the process. In such "go-for-broke" situations the loser gets hurt and in response frequently retaliates to hurt the winner, with the effect that no one wins in any meaningful sense. On the other hand, if we enter a conflict with the idea of resolving the conflict and of reaching some kind of mutual understanding, neither party need be hurt and in fact both parties may benefit from the clash of ideas or desires and from the airing of differences. In too many relationships, the most important part of a conflict is not the relationship or the other person but rather the "I," the "me," and winning the battle—the object of the battle being to subjugate and beat down the other individual. If we keep in mind the primacy of the relationship and the importance of the other person, we will be less likely to use the boxing ring model to resolve interpersonal conflict.

Acceptance of Less than Perfection

When we look at other people's relationships we often see only the surface and on the surface most relationships look pretty good. We do not see the day-to-day hassles over money, the snoring during the night, the disagreements. Instead we are presented with a picture of near harmony. Few couples or families, for example, openly fight in front of others; in most primary relationships fighting takes place in private. We do, however, see these day-to-day problems in our own relationships—usually we see them all too vividly.

Consequently, other relationships often appear to be a great deal better than our own, but in actual fact, they are probably much like our own. The major difference it seems is in our perception of the two relationships. If we look upon our own relationship as unsatisfying (regardless of how good or bad it may appear to others), then this may become a self-fulfilling prophecy and we *will* be unhappy in it. If, on the other hand, we realize that no relationship is perfect, it may help us to stay in touch with reality and not be disappointed so easily when problems are encountered. No mate—however beautiful or handsome, wise, urbane, sexy, and charming—is perfect. To aim for or expect perfection can only result in disappointment.

Again, to be accepting of less than perfection does not mean that we should not try to improve ourselves and our relationships or that we should be content to have relationships filled with problems. Rather, it is to emphasize that any meaningful relationship *will* have problems and that it is best to deal with these problems—to correct or to alleviate them in some way—rather than to long for that utopian relationship that does not really exist.

SOURCES

A great deal of research and theory is being directed at understanding family communication. Useful popular sources include Sven Wahlroos, *Family Communication* (New York: New American Library, 1974), Jane Howard, *Families* (New York: Berkley Books, 1978), and Harvey White, *Your Family Is Good for You* (New York: Berkley Books, 1980). Perhaps the best overview of the area is presented by Kathleen M. Galvin and Bernard J. Brommel, *Family Communication* (Glenview, Ill.: Scott, Foresman, 1982). The discussion of conflicts in the family owes much to Robert O. Blood, Jr., "Resolving Family Conflicts," in Fred E. Jandt, ed., *Conflict Resolution through Communication* (New York: Harper & Row, 1973), pp. 221–239. An interesting analysis of family communication and the strategies on lessening problems is presented in Edwin J. Thomas, *Marital Communication and Decision Making: Analysis, Assessment, and Change* (New York: Free Press, 1977). The study of conflict strategies was conducted by Mary Anne Fitzpatrick and Jeff Winke, "You Always Hurt the One You Love: Strategies and Tactics in Interpersonal Conflict," *Communication Quarterly* 27 (Winter, 1979):3–11. The relationship between the time a couple spends together and their mutual understanding is covered in J. Richard Udry, Harold A. Nelson, and Ruth O. Nelson, "An Empirical Investigation of Some Widely Held Beliefs About Marital Satisfaction," *Marriage and Family Living* 23 (1961):338–390. A useful summary of this and related studies may be found in Edgar W. Butler, *Traditional Marriage and Emerging Alternatives* (New York: Harper & Row, 1979). For an interesting discussion of the different types of families, see Mary Anne Fitzpatrick and Julie Indvik, "The Instrumental and Expressive Domains of Marital Communication," *Human Communication Research* 8 (Spring 1982):195–213.

26.1 ANALYZING A FAMILY TRANSACTION

Carefully read the accompanying transaction, paying particular attention to the following communication issues:

1. the communication problems facing this family;
2. the strategies that this family uses in communicating and in dealing with its problems;
3. the effectiveness-ineffectiveness of their strategies; and
4. the alternative strategies that might prove more effective in dealing with these problems—that is, if you were called in by this family to analyze their communication patterns and make suggestions for their improvement, what would you say?

Small groups may be formed in which each student pools his or her insights and recommendations concerning the interaction. Each small group may then report to the entire class concerning the problems identified and the recommendations they would make for the improvement of the family's communications. An alternative procedure is to have a general class discussion in which the class as a whole seeks to identify the major communication problems and to offer solutions for the improvement of the interpersonal communication process within this particular family.

In either case some attention should be directed to the formulation of general principles that might be advanced for effectively communicating within families. That is, what general rules should members of a family follow in order to make their communications more effective?

AN INTERPERSONAL TRANSACTION

Participants:

Margaret:	mother, housewife, junior high-school history teacher; 41 years old
Fred:	father, gas station attendant; 46 years old
Diane:	daughter, receptionist in an art gallery; 22 years old
Stephen:	son, college freshman; 18 years old

Communication Context:

*Margaret is in the kitchen finishing preparing dinner—lamb chops,
Fred's favorite though she does not care much for them. Diane is going
through some records. Stephen is reading one of his textbooks. Fred
comes in from work and throws his jacket over the couch but it falls to the
floor.*

Fred *(bored but angry, looking at Stephen):* **What the hell did you do
with the car last night; it stunk like hell. And you left all your damn
school papers all over the back seat.**
Stephen *(as if expecting the angry remarks):* **What did I do now?**
Fred: *You stunk up the car with your damn pot or whatever you kids
smoke, and you left the car looking like hell. Can't you hear?*
Stephen *(says nothing; goes back to looking at his book but without
really reading).*
Margaret: *O.K. Dinner's almost ready. Come on. Wash up and sit down.*
(at dinner)
Diane: *Mom, I'm going to go to the shore for the weekend with some
friends from work.*
Margaret: *O.K. When will you be leaving?*
Diane: *Friday afternoon, right after work.*
Fred: *Like hell you're going. No more going to the shore with* **that** *group.*
Margaret: *Fred, they're nice people. Why shouldn't she go?*
Fred: *Because I said so, O.K? Finished. Closed.*
Diane *(Mumbling):* *I'm 22 years old and he gives me problems. You make
me feel like a kid, like some stupid little kid.*
Fred: *Get married and then you can tell your husband what to do.*
Diane: *I wish I could.*
Stephen: *But nobody'll ask her.*
Margaret: *Why should she get married? She's got a good life—good job,
nice friends, good home. Listen, I was talking with Elizabeth and Cara
this morning and they both feel they've just wasted their lives. They raised
a family and what have they got? They got* **nothing!** *(To Diane):* *And
don't think sex is so great either; it isn't, believe me.*
Fred: *Well, they're idiots.*
Margaret: **They're idiots?** *(Snidely)* *Yeah, I guess they are.*
Diane: *Joanne's getting married.*
Margaret: *Who's Joanne?*
Stephen: *That creature who lives with that guy Michael.*
Fred: *Watch your mouth, wise-ass. Don't be disrespectful to your mother
or I'll teach you how to act right.*
Margaret: *Well, how do you like the dinner?*
(prolonged silence)
Diane: *Do you think I should be in the wedding party if Joanne asks me?
I think she will; we always said we'd be in each other's wedding.*
Margaret: *Sure, why not. It'll be nice.*
Fred: *I'm not going to no wedding; no matter who's in it.*

Stephen: *Me neither.*

Diane: *I hope you'll both feel that way when I get married.*

Stephen: *By then I'll be too old to remember I got a sister.*

Margaret: *How's school?*

Stephen: *I hate it. It's so big. Nobody knows anyone. You sit in these big lecture halls and listen to some creep talk. I really feel lonely and isolated, like nobody knows I'm alive.*

Fred: *Listen to that college talk bullshit. Get yourself a woman and you won't feel lonely, instead of hanging out with those pothead faggots.*

Diane (looking to Margaret, giving a sigh as if, here we go again)

Margaret (to Diane, in whisper): *I know.*

Diane: *Mom? Do you think I'm getting fat?*

Stephen: *Yes.*

Fred: *Just don't get fat in the stomach or you'll get thrown out of here.*

Margaret: *No, I don't notice it.*

Diane: *Well, I just thought I might be.*

Stephen (pushing his plate away): *I'm finished; I'm going out.*

Fred: *Sit down and finish your damn supper. You think I work all day for you to throw the food away? You wanna go smoke your dope?*

Stephen: *No. I just want to get away from you—forever.*

Margaret: *You mean we both work all day; it's just that I earn a lot more than you do.*

Fred: *No, I mean I work and you babysit.*

Margaret: *Teaching junior high-school history isn't baby sitting.*

Fred: *What the hell is it then—you don't teach them anything.*

Margaret (to Diane): *You see. You're better off single. I should've stayed single. Instead . . . Oh, well. I was young and stupid. It was my own fault for getting involved with a loser. Just don't you make the same mistake.*

Fred (to Stephen): *Go ahead. Leave the table. Leave the house. Who cares what you do?*

26.2 PRIMARY RELATIONSHIP COMMUNICATION

This exercise is designed to encourage you to examine more closely the communication patterns operative in your own primary relationship(s). The exercise is divided into a number of related phases:

1. Select the primary relationship on which you wish to focus for this experience. The primary relationship may be within your immediate family, you and your closest intimate, you and your husband or wife, your extended family, or any other primary relationship. Before progressing any further, it will help if you record all the names of the individuals in this relationship and their relationship to you.

2. For each of the 15 communication characteristics listed in the "Primary Relationship Communication Questionnaire," indicate the member of the

primary relationship to whom this characteristic applies most closely. Do this for all 15 characteristics before reading any further.

PRIMARY RELATIONSHIP COMMUNICATION QUESTIONNAIRE

For each characteristic, indicate the name of the member of the primary relationship to whom it most closely applies.

1. Has the greatest general credibility: ————————————
2. Self-discloses the most: ————————————
3. Self-discloses the least: ————————————
4. Most open-minded: ————————————
5. Most closed-minded: ————————————
6. Has the final say in making the important decisions: ————
7. The most authoritarian: ————————————
8. Most apt to avoid conflict rather than confront it: ————
9. Most apt to become emotional and to use an emotional strategy in conflict situations: ————————————
10. Tries hardest to achieve empathic understanding in conflict situations:

————————————

11. Most apt to use manipulation as a conflict strategy: ————
12. Most apt to use personal rejection as a conflict strategy: ————
13. Has the greatest commitment to the preservation of the relationship: ——
14. Has changed the most since the relationship began: ————
15. Has the most intrapersonal conflicts: ————————————

3. After all 15 statements have been answered, write down one or more implications of your answers for the relationship as a whole or for the other members of the relationship as individuals. For example, let us assume that you are concentrating on your immediate family (you, your mother, and your father). For "has the highest general credibility" you might note that this applies foremost to your father. This attribution of credibility to your father has various implications. One implication might be that your father is the one who is looked to for information or advice and he is the one expected to make most of the decisions. Another implication might be that you resent this unchallenged credibility which your mother attributes to him and this in turn causes you to purposely avoid asking his advice.

4. After each person has completed the "Primary Relationship Communication Questionnaire" and has indicated one or more implications for each characteristic, discuss your responses in groups of five or six. In discussing your responses, try to develop hypotheses that might be applicable to primary relationship communication in general. Such hypotheses would be based on reasonable assumptions as to the general principles operating in

primary relationship communication. From our previous example, we might formulate the hypothesis that, "In a nuclear family it is the father who has the greatest credibility." Another hypothesis might be, "The most credible person is resented the most by the second most credible person, or by the person who is growing intellectually at the most rapid rate." Each group should keep a list of their hypotheses.

5. After all groups have discussed the characteristics and have developed a set of hypotheses, share these with the entire class and consider, for example:

a. Which hypotheses seem most reasonable? Which seem to be agreed upon by most groups?

b. How might you go about testing the validity of the various hypotheses? That is, how might you go about discovering if these hypotheses are true or false?

26.3 THE TELEVISION RELATIONSHIP

This exercise is designed to enable you to effectively review the concepts discussed in this unit and to gain some insight and experience in the difficult task of analyzing family communication. The class should be divided into several small groups each of which should select a different television program that centers on a family. Suitable examples are "The Jeffersons," "Happy Days," "Diff'rent Strokes," "Little House: A New Beginning," "Dallas," "Dynasty," "One Day at a Time," "Knots Landing," and "Falcon Crest."

Each member should watch the assigned television show and respond to the accompanying questions. After viewing the show and completing the questions, members should meet in their small groups and discuss their responses, working toward consensus in their answers. After recording the group's responses (noting any significant differences of opinion), each small group should report to the entire class the results of its discussions. A general class discussion should then follow and might concentrate on the implications of the responses to question 8.

1. Who constitutes the "family"? List the members of the "family" or "primary relationship" and identify their major roles within the family structure. Are there some persons on the show whose status in the family is not quite clear? That is, is there doubt as to whether some persons are or are not members of the family? Identify these and explain the reasons for the lack of a clear status.

2. In this unit we identified several characteristics that all primary relationships or families had in common: relatively clear definition of roles, commitment to the preservation of the relationship, a recognition of responsibilities to each other, a shared history and future, and a shared living

space. Are these characteristics evidenced in the family portrayed in the program you viewed? Are there other characteristics that might be offered to define their relationships? Are there characteristics included in the unit that are not evidenced in the program?

3. Aside from good ratings, what seems to keep this family together? What factors might you point to that seem to account for the maintenance of the family relationship? Identify specific elements of plot or dialogue that demonstrate these factors.

4. What type of communication pattern best seems to describe this particular family? You may find it convenient to begin by singling out selected dyads within the family and identifying the type of communication pattern that best describes their interactions. You may then expand the dyad to include more and more people until the entire family is included. Diagram the communication pattern(s). Can you identify specific elements of dialogue that led to your conclusions? Do the communication patterns used most frequently in the show cause any difficulties? Explain.

5. In this unit a number of reasons were cited as potential causes of conflict development in primary or family relationships: intimacy claims; intimacies outside the primary relationship or family; undefined expectations; sexual problems and differences; and financial difficulties. Others, briefly noted, were intrapersonal conflicts, privateness, change, and different standards and role expectations. Were the causes of conflict noted here operative in the conflicts in the episode viewed or more generally in the entire program's history? What other causes might be noted? Are there causes noted here that do not seem to operate in television shows? Why?

6. Identify the conflict strategies utilized most often by the central characters in this show: manipulation? nonnegotiation? emotional appeal? personal rejection? empathic understanding? Are these strategies effective as used?

7. If the characters on this television show constituted a real family and wished to improve their family communication, what suggestions would you make? It is particularly important here that you fit the suggestions to the specific individual and to the specific family situation. For this question draw not only on the suggestions noted in this unit (empathic understanding, self-disclosure, openness to change, fighting fair, and the acceptance of less than perfection), but on those discussed throughout the text.

8. It is often difficult to see what these shows teach us about families and primary relationships and about the communication that goes on within them because it is difficult for us to separate what we gain from television from that gained through other means. Further, we probably internalize a great deal from watching television that we fail to recognize consciously as having its origin in television. And so, it may prove helpful to fantasize a bit and imagine a Martian coming to earth, trying to discover something about what a family is and how it

operates. For the purposes of this exercise, assume that this Martian has no information other than that gained from this television series. What would our Martian conclude about earth families and primary relationships? State this information in the form of principles or statements about what constitutes a "family" and about what takes place in a family or primary relationship. Cover the major areas discussed in this unit: the characteristics that all families have in common, the factors that keep the family together, the communication pattern that best describes the family's interactions, the sources of conflict, the conflict strategies used, and the application of the principles of effective interpersonal interaction.

DETERIORATION OF INTERPERSONAL RELATIONSHIPS

Upon completion of this unit, you should be able to:
1. explain the nature of the deterioration of relationships
2. explain how psychological, behavioral, and contextual changes might account for the deterioration of relationships
3. explain how relationship changes may alter the relationship between two persons
4. explain the role of communication in the deterioration of relationships
5. identify the characteristics that figure into managing the deterioration of relationships

Just as a relationship may grow and progress, becoming stronger and more meaningful, it can also wane and regress, becoming weaker and less meaningful. Some of the dimensions of what might be called relational deterioration are considered here. Specifically, I consider the nature of deterioration, the role of communication in the deterioration of relationships, the general causes of relationship deterioration, and some aspects of what we might call relational deterioration management.

THE NATURE OF RELATIONAL DETERIORATION

Relational deterioration refers to the weakening of the bonds holding people together. At times the relationship may be weakened only mildly and may appear normal to outsiders; to the participants, however, it is clear that the relationship has weakened significantly. The obvious extreme of relational deterioration is the complete termination of the relationship. In between these two extremes are an infinite number of variations. Relational deterioration exists on a continuum from just a little bit less than intimate to total separation and total dissolution.

The Process of Deterioration

The process of deterioration may be gradual or sudden. Murray Davis, in *Intimate Relations*, uses the terms "passing away" to designate gradual deteri-   **436** oration and "sudden death" to designate immediate or sudden deterioration. An example of "passing away" is when one of the parties in a relationship develops close ties with a new intimate and this new relationship gradually pushes out the old intimate. An example of "sudden death" is when one or both of the parties break a rule that was essential to the relationship (for example, the rule of complete fidelity), and both realize that since the rule has been broken, the relationship cannot be sustained and, in fact, must be terminated immediately.

The Responsibility for the Deterioration

The deterioration or termination of a relationship may be the primary responsibility of both parties, one of the parties, or neither party—a possibility that we often fail to consider. In the first case, both parties may wish to go their separate ways, perhaps each with a new intimate or perhaps alone. In either case they both agree that separation is the best choice. In the second case, one of the parties wants to leave while the other party wants to remain in the relationship. These are the types of relationships movies and romantic novels are made of—the struggle to hold together a family, a marriage, or a friendship. In the third case, neither party wants the relationship to deteriorate, but perhaps one of the parties says something that is so detrimental to the other person and to the relationship, to use Murray Davis's example, that it becomes apparent that the relationship cannot survive.

All relationships are different; what pulls one relationship apart may well hold another together. The death of a child, for example, will at times function to destroy a marriage and at other times will solidify it. Outside threats usually strengthen a relationship, though at times they have the effect of tearing it apart.

The Negatives and the Positives

Not all relationships should be retained as they are or even retained at all. Not all breakups are bad, and few, if any, bad breakups are all bad. While in the midst of a breakup this may be difficult to appreciate, but in retrospect it seems almost always to be true.

At times relationships are unproductive for one or both parties, and a breakup is often the best alternative. Such a termination may provide a period for the individuals to regain their independence and to again become self-reliant. Some relationships are so absorbing that there is little time available for reflection on oneself, on others, and on the relationship itself. Sometimes distance helps.

One of the major problems with some relationships is that they prevent one or both parties from developing new relationships, from becoming involved with new intimates, from developing new friends and associations. A termination of such a relationship provides the individuals with opportunities to develop these new associations and to explore different types of relationships with different types of people.

These are obviously not the only redeeming characteristics of terminating a relationship that might be mentioned; each relationship is different, and each individual is different. What one finds a benefit, one may find a burden. The freedom to explore new relationships may be viewed by one person as a challenging and exciting opportunity; to another person it may be threatening and frightening. And so it would be foolhardy to specify with any degree of authority what the specific benefits may be to specific people in specific relationships. The only point I want to make here is that relational deterioration does not have to have only negative consequences. For the most part, it is up to the individual to draw out of any decaying relationship some positive and productive characteristics, a lesson learned that can be used later on.

SOME CAUSES OF RELATIONAL DETERIORATION

In all interpersonal interactions, the causes of relational deterioration are as numerous as the individuals involved, and so it is with considerable modesty that I even attempt to identify some of them. In reviewing these it is important to recognize that each relationship follows a different pattern and each responds differently to different influences. Having offered this qualification, perhaps the best place to start is to look at some of the reasons why relationships are developed and see how changes in these factors may lead to deterioration.

Reasons for Establishing the Relationship Have Diminished

In Unit 21 I noted some factors that are important in establishing relationships. When these are no longer operative or when they are changed drastically, it may be a cause of relational deterioration. One of the major reasons why people seek relationships is to alleviate loneliness. When loneliness is no longer lessened by the relationship, when one or both of the individuals experience loneliness for prolonged or frequent periods, the relationship may well be on the road to decay. If relationships are established and maintained in part because they are stimulating to the individuals, then relationships will decay when that stimulation is removed or significantly lessened. This is often seen in marriages. Before marriage they said "I love you," held each other's hands, hugged each other tight, and otherwise demonstrated their affection for each other. After some years of marriage that emotional and physical stimulation often fades. Such shows of affection were among the important reasons why the relationship was established and maintained; to allow them to become just memories jeopardizes the relationship.

We are extremely complex creatures, and regardless of how long we live we will probably never fully understand ourselves. We need constantly to learn more about ourselves and we often establish a relationship to this end. When we cease to gain self-knowledge, the relationship is not fulfilling one of its major functions and may soon show signs of decay.

The reason most often mentioned for relational deterioration is that the initial attractiveness that brought the individuals together is gone—the pot belly, the baldness, the sagging buttocks, the lines in the face, the extra weight, and so on all contribute to the loss of the attractiveness. Similarly, in long-term relationships people have a tendency to ignore or drop the social niceties they once thought essential when the relationship was in its formative stages. The common courtesies—the phone call to say "I'll be late," the card on a birthday or anniversary, the flowers for no reason at all—are often dropped, forgotten, or somehow considered unimportant but these also contribute to the loss of attractiveness. Those who assume that physical and personality attractiveness are no longer important after 5, 10, or 20 years of a relationship are probably fooling themselves. They seem to be attempting to find an excuse for sloppiness, for not exercising, for not keeping on a diet. Or perhaps they are trying to con-

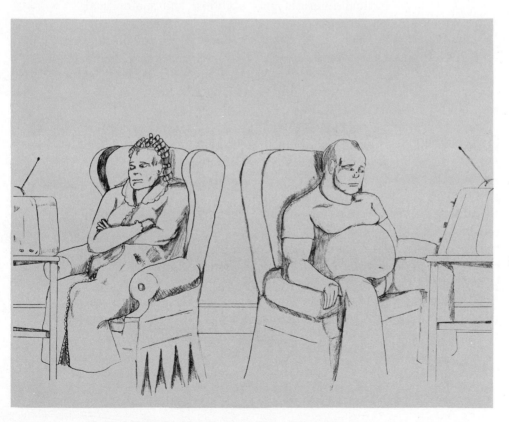

Interpersonal relationships—like anything else—deteriorate when not actively nourished and cultivated.

vince themselves that they are still desired despite the weight, the sagging, and the wrinkles. And perhaps they are right. I suspect, however, that even if they are still desired, it could be more so.

Relationships are also established and maintained because in such a relationship one's pleasures are maximized and one's pains are minimized. When that ceases to be the case, the relationship stands little chance of survival. The reason, I think, is obvious. These needs are so great that when they are not met within the existing relationship, their satisfaction and fulfillment will be sought elsewhere. When a new relationship better serves these needs, the old relationship may deteriorate.

Relational Changes

In addition to those factors that in one form help to establish a relationship and in another form help to dissolve it, there are a number of other factors that might be mentioned as causes of relational deterioration. *Psychological change* in one or both parties may contribute to relational deterioration. Prominent among psychological changes would be the development of incompatible attitudes, vastly different intellectual interests and abilities, and major goal changes. To the extent that these are incompatible with those of the other individual, the relationship will be shaky. This does not mean that one person cannot be a Democrat and the other a Republican. It does mean, however, that a staunch atheist and a devout Fundamentalist are going to have some problems. When one party in a marriage believes in open marriage and the other does not, they are probably heading for difficulties.

Behavioral change, like psychological change, is also significant. For example, the individual who once devoted much time to the other person and to the development of the relationship and who then becomes totally absorbed in business or in school and devotes all free time to business activities or studying is going to find significant repercussions from this change. The individual who becomes addicted to drugs or alcohol will likewise present the relationship with a serious problem.

Contextual change may also exert considerable influence on the relationship. Some relationships cannot survive separation by long distances as when, for example, one of the parties is forced to move far away. When I moved to Illinois from New York to pursue graduate work, my primary relationship survived two years of long-distance separation because it was particularly strong and because it continued to serve many of the needs already mentioned. But I witnessed many other relationships decay and terminate because the individuals were not able to surmount the physical distance barriers. This is a particularly difficult problem for people in the military. The physical separation is too stressful for many people so many such relationships deteriorate, as stereotyped in the "Dear John" letters of war years. Long incarceration in prison or long hospital confinement are also context changes that may lead to severe trouble.

When there is a significant *status change* between two people or between one member and a third party, the relationship may undergo considerable change and possibly deteriorate. This type of situation is seen, for instance, when students and teachers develop a romantic relationship. The relationship develops as a student-teacher relationship and is maintained for some time as that. But as the student matures and perhaps becomes a teacher too or otherwise assumes a position equal to or superior in status to that of the teacher, their relationship undergoes considerable change; frequently, this results in some kind of deterioration. In F. Scott Fitzgerald's *Tender Is the Night* we see the same kind of situation, though here it is between a young psychiatrist, Dick Diver, and a wealthy and beautiful patient, Nicole Warren. While Nicole is mentally ill and in need of Dick's care, the relationship flourishes for both; each apparently well serves the needs of the other. But as Nicole gets stronger, Dick gets weaker; the relationship changes drastically and ultimately deteriorates. In the *Blue Angel*—the famous German movie with Marlene Dietrich and Emil Jannings—we see a similar relationship between a sophisticated and well-respected schoolteacher, Professor Immanuel Rath, and a low-class cabaret entertainer, Lola Frohlich. Their relationship prospers as long as she is able to look up to him and respect him. When their relationship changes and he becomes her servant, a willing victim of Lola's humiliation and abuse, their relationship becomes a mockery and dies.

Third Party Relationship

Sometimes the relationship changes because of the development of another relationship with some third party. At times this may be a romantic interest; at other times it may be a parent; frequently it is a child. When an individual's needs for affection or attention were once supplied by the other party in the primary relationship and are now supplied by a friend or a child, the primary relationship is in for considerable alteration and sometimes deterioration.

A Note on Commitment

An important factor influencing the course of deterioration is the degree of commitment the individuals have toward each other and toward the relationship itself. All of our relationships are held together in part by our degree of commitment. And the strength of the relationship, including its resistance to possible deterioration, is often directly related to the degree of commitment of the individuals. When relationships show signs of deterioration and yet there is still a strong commitment to the relationship—a strong desire to keep the relationship together—the individuals may well surmount the obstacles and reverse the process of deterioration. When their commitment is weak and the individuals doubt that there are good reasons for staying together, relational deterioration seems to come faster and stronger.

Sometimes "commitment" is conceived in terms of material considerations; people may feel committed because they have invested all their money together or because they have established a business or own real estate together. At other times the commitment is based on time considerations. People may feel that since they have lived together for these past 10 or 15 years, there is so much time that would be lost if the relationship were terminated. College students who have dated the same person for three or four years often feel that the time investment has been so great that they might as well continue the relationship, and often allow and encourage it to progress to a permanent relationship or perhaps marriage. Although much could be said for this attitude, it seems to me that time is never wasted if something is learned from it *or*, more importantly, if we have lived in the present and enjoyed the relationship for its day-to-day value rather than for what it will mean 10 or 20 years from now. It is far better to terminate a 4-year-old relationship that is unsatisfactory than to continue it for the rest of one's life. Unfortunately, only to those who are not now or who have never been in such a relationship will this seem obvious. Sometimes the commitment is based on emotional investment; so much emotional energy may have been spent on the relationship that the individuals find it difficult even to consider dissolving it. Or people may feel committed because they care for each other and for the relationship and feel that for all its problems and difficulties, the relationship is more good than bad, more productive than destructive, more pleasurable than painful. And this, it seems to me, is the kind of commitment that will function to stem and perhaps reverse relational deterioration. Other bases for commitment (for example, materialism, time, and emotional investments) may function to preserve the surface features of the relationship but will probably have little influence on preserving its meaning and intimacy.

All of these "causes" of relational deterioration are also the effects of relational deterioration. For example, just as the contextual changes may influence the deterioration of a relationship, they may also be an effect of the deterioration. Thus, when things start to go sour, the individuals may remove themselves physically from one another in response to the deterioration. This physical separation in turn functions as a cause of further deterioration by driving the individuals further apart emotionally and psychologically. Similarly, the degree of commitment that the individuals have for each other may lessen as other signs of deterioration manifest themselves. In turn, the lack of commitment may also function as a cause of deterioration in, for example, lessening the need the individuals may feel to resolve conflicts or to leave the channels of communication open.

COMMUNICATION IN RELATIONAL DETERIORATION

Like relational development, relational deterioration involves unique and specialized communication patterns, and I will describe and analyze some of the communication patterns employed during relational deterioration. These patterns are in part a response to the deterioration; we communicate the way we do because of the way we feel our relationship is deteriorating. These patterns are also causative, however, in the sense that our deteriorating relationship is itself influenced by our communication patterns. In fact, it would be impossible to determine which communication pattern is cause and which is effect.

Withdrawal

Perhaps the easiest communication pattern to see is that of a general withdrawal. Nonverbally, this withdrawal is seen in the greater space each person seems to require and the ease with which tempers and other signs of disturbance are aroused when that space is encroached upon. When people are close emotionally they can occupy close physical quarters. But when they are growing apart they need a wider space. Other nonverbal signs would include the failure to engage in direct eye contact, the failure to look at each other generally, and the lessening of touching behavior. All these changes seem to be a part of the desire to withdraw physically from the emotional pairing. Verbally, withdrawal is seen in a number of different ways. Where once there was a great desire to talk and to listen, there is now less desire and perhaps none. At times phatic communication (Unit 21) will also be severely limited since the individuals do not want any of its regular functions served. At other times, however, phatic communication (or what would appear to be phatic communication) is engaged in as an end in itself. Whereas phatic talk is usually a preliminary to serious conversation, here phatic communication is used as an alternative or to forestall serious talk. And so people in the throes of dissolution may talk a great deal about insignificant events—the weather, a movie on television, or a neighbor down the hall. The topics are not important. What is important is that by focusing on these topics, the individuals are able to avoid confronting the serious issues that might be raised if the silence were to become too unpleasant.

Self-Disclosure

Self-disclosing communications decline significantly. Self-disclosure may not be thought worth the effort if the relationship is dying. We only wish to self-disclose to people we feel close to, and when a relationship is deteriorating we feel all but close to the other person and so we naturally have no desire to self-disclose. We also limit our self-disclosures because we feel that the other person may not be accepting of our disclosures—an essential assumption if disclosures are to be made in the first place.

In our discussion of self-disclosure in Unit 7, I noted that self-disclosure generally leads to increased trust, which in turn leads to increased self-disclosure, and so on. The result is a spiral with ever-increasing self-disclosure and trust. In relational deterioration trust decreases although the reason is not always clear, and certainly it is not always the same from one relationship to another. Yet it seems almost universal that in relationships that are experiencing difficulty, one of the first changes is a marked decrease in trust. In marital relationships in which divorce proceedings are often fought so bitterly and in which the parties battle over every asset, it is easy to see why trust is withdrawn at the first signs of relational deterioration. We may fear that the trust we put in the other person will soon be used against us.

Supportiveness

Where once supportiveness characterized the relationship, defensiveness is now the more prevalent characteristic. In many relationships that are deteriorating one party blames the other; no one wants to assume the blame for the failure of a relationship, and it seems difficult to believe that no one really caused the breakup. Instead, it is easier to blame the other person. The primary method available for dealing with accusations of blame is defensiveness. We want to protect our egos; we want to continue believing that we are not to blame, that it is not our fault. And perhaps we want especially to believe that we are not the cause of another person's and our own pain.

Deception

Deception also increases as relationships break down. Sometimes this takes the form of clear-cut lies which may be used to avoid getting into added arguments over the reasons for staying out all night or for not calling or for being seen in the wrong place with the wrong person. At other times the lies may be used because of some feeling of shame; we do not want the other person to think less of us even though we fully realize that the relationship is deteriorating. Perhaps we want to save the relationship, and so we do not want to add an additional obstacle. At other times, although we may wish to see the relationship terminated, we do not want to appear to be the cause of the problem. And so we lie. Sometimes the deception takes the form of avoidance—the lie of omission. We talk about everything we did last night except what is really important and what is the crux of the difficulty. Whether by omission or commission, deception runs high in relationships that are deteriorating. One of the problems with this is that deception has a way of escalating. And although we may tell ourselves that we lied to protect the other person or to avoid some greater problem (both of which may be true), we have at the same time created a climate, in our own minds and ultimately in the mind of the other person, of distrust, disbelief, and falsity rather than truthfulness.

Evaluative Responses

One of the most obvious communication changes is the increase in negative evaluation and the decrease in positive evaluation. Where once we praised the other's behaviors or talents or ideas, we now criticize them. Often the behaviors have not changed significantly; what has changed is our way of looking at them. What was once a cute habit now becomes annoying and perhaps repulsive. What was once "different" now becomes eccentric or inconsiderate. What was once friendliness now becomes a sign of promiscuity. When we like someone we seem able to tolerate almost anything. When we begin to dislike someone and want to terminate the relationship, we seem able to tolerate very little. This negative evaluation frequently leads to outright fighting and conflict, and although conflict is not necessarily bad, it often happens that in relationships that are deteriorating the conflict is not resolved. Neither party may care enough to go through the effort of resolving the conflict, and so it either surfaces the next day or perhaps escalates into an all-out battle. Seldom does it go away. One of the characteristics of such conflicts is that a great deal of time is needed for them to be resolved, and there is a marked increase in the cooling-off period, and in a way, there is a need for increased space.

RELATIONAL DETERIORATION MANAGEMENT

One recent book in interpersonal communication devotes the entire chapter on "The Deterioration of Interpersonal Relationships" to "behaviors that you and your relational partners can employ to thwart deterioration." I think this is a very narrow view to take. The issue is not how to keep all relationships intact but rather how to manage them to mutual satisfaction so that each person is better able to grow and develop. I think relational partners may be taught with equal effect how to terminate a relationship as how to thwart termination. To keep a relationship intact may be foolish if the relationship is destructive to one or both parties.

When relationships go bad, there are three basic alternatives: (1) to keep it as it is, and make no change, (2) to dissolve the relationship, and (3) to change one or more of the elements, that is, to attempt to make the relationship different and better. Of these three possibilities, I reject only the first one as illogical; the second and third are both candidates for serious consideration. I, therefore, offer suggestions not for keeping a relationship intact but rather for managing deterioration, whether that entails an attempt to save the relationship or an attempt to terminate it as quickly as possible.

Flexibility

Perhaps flexibility, a willingness to bend and to change, is the major quality in successful relational management, whether we are talking about the development or the deterioration of a relationship. If one or both of the parties lose flexibility, the problems confronting the individuals stand little chance of being dealt with effectively. This flexibility includes a willingness to be open to the other person's feelings, to recognize one's own subjectivity in viewing the situation, and to listen openly to alternative points of view and always with a willingness to change if the situation calls for it.

Tentativeness

One of the characteristics of language noted in Unit 9 is that it is a great deal easier to change when extreme positions are avoided. When positions are stated as absolutes, it is psychologically difficult for an individual to retract what has been said. "I could never love you again," "I can't bear to touch you," or "I always hated your mother" are statements that will prove at best difficult. Similarly, it should be recognized that decisions are not necessarily absolute or final or permanent; they can be changed and should be changed if the situation seems to warrant it. To assume that decisions are permanent and unalterable prevents one from exploring other possible decisions and from recognizing that a mistake may have been made and that now a better decision might be instituted.

Openness to Communication

One of the major failures in communication is closing the channels of communication so that any attempt to resolve differences becomes impossible. There must always be a willingness to communicate because the only way relational deterioration is going to be dealt with is through communication. This is not to say that the parties should continue to communicate at all costs. At times it may be necessary, even helpful, to separate, to be with one's own thoughts and to cool off by oneself or with another person. The willingness to continue communication at a later time, however, must always be there.

Selfishness and Honesty

We need to recognize that in all aspects of relationships, but especially in relational deterioration, we have an obligation not only to our partner but also to ourselves, as well as to perhaps various other people. I think we forget that we owe ourselves something, too. A good example of this is the individual who stays in a relationship, even though it is unproductive and causes only grief, for fear of hurting the other person. But this only causes this person to hurt herself or himself instead. This is a foolish kind of deception. While the other person may be content to live with this kind of relationship, often it would be better to terminate it. I would venture to say that if one party is unhappy in a relationship, then the other party is probably unhappy as well.

Closely related to the obligation to self is honesty. Some people are so desirous of saving a relationship that they never express their dissatisfactions, fears, and unfulfilled ambitions. They rest content with the surface satisfactions of a relationship. When a relationship is deteriorating we need to be honest enough with ourselves and with the other person to confront the sources of the difficulty—to look honestly at ourselves, at the other person, and at the relationship itself and to analyze what has gone wrong and what will have to be changed if the relationship is to survive. And, more importantly, we need to ask ourselves if the survival of the relationship is in the best interests of the parties involved. It may be—or it may not be. Both possibilities need to be considered.

That there are tremendous difficulties in breaking up should not blind us to the very real difficulties that may be faced in staying together.

SOURCES

On relational deterioration, see Murray S. Davis, *Intimate Relations* (New York: Free Press, 1973), Kenneth L. Villard and Leland J. Whipple, *Beginnings in Relational Communication* (New York: Wiley, 1976), Michael D. Scott and William G. Powers, *Interpersonal Communication: A Question of Needs* (Boston: Houghton Mifflin, 1978), and Mark L. Knapp, *Social Intercourse: From Greeting to Goodbye* (Boston: Allyn & Bacon, 1978). Albert Ellis and Robert Harper, *A Guide to Successful Marriage* (No. Hollywood, Calif.: Wilshire Book Co., 1973), contribute some interesting insights to the problem of relational deterioration. Also see J. S. Wallerstein and J. B. Kelley, *Surviving the Breakup: How Children and Parents Cope With Divorce* (New York: Basic Books, 1980). Relational deterioration within a family context is well-covered in Kathleen M. Galvin and Bernard J. Brommel, *Family Communication: Cohesion and Change* (Glenview, Ill.: Scott, Foresman, 1982). Michael J. Cody has presented an interesting five-stage model of relationship breakdown; see his "A Typology of Disengagement Strategies and an Examination of the Role Intimacy, Reactions to Inequity and Relational Problems Play in Strategy Selection," *Communication Monographs* 49 (September 1982):148–170.

27.1 SELF-CONCEPT: PART II

Below is a set of semantic differential scales identical to the ones you filled out in Experiential Vehicle 5.1. Fill in these scales now.

Happy								Sad
Positive								Negative
Healthy								Sick
Strong								Weak
Beautiful								Ugly
Honest								Dishonest
Good								Bad
Self-confident								Not self-confident
Active								Passive
Interesting								Boring
Graceful								Awkward
Pleasant								Unpleasant
Powerful								Powerless
Fast								Slow
Successful								Unsuccessful
Sociable								Unsociable
Realistic								Unrealistic
Optimistic								Pessimistic
Brave								Cowardly
Organized								Disorganized

The scales you completed at the beginning of the term should now be recovered and compared with the scales you have just completed. Examine carefully all the differences. Differences of two or three scale positions are generally significant and bear special attention.

It is important to recognize that changes do not just happen. Rather, they happen because of something, and this something is what we should attempt to discover. Therefore, for each change you feel is significant and real, attempt to determine the causes. Jot down any notes you wish, and in groups of five or six discuss these changes. Feedback from other group members concerning these changes should be free and honest and should be welcomed by each member. Again, it is wise to recall the five characteristics of effective interpersonal communication: openness, empathy, supportiveness, positiveness, and equality. **448**

1. What is the nature of the change?
2. Why is it assumed that this change is real?
3. How is this change manifested? Do you act differently as a result of the change?
4. Do other people notice the change in you? Here feedback from the group members is especially important. (Of course, it is possible that real changes cannot be seen by this group.)
5. What were the causes of these changes? (*Note:* Look for causes, not a single cause. All behavior and all changes have multiple causes.)
6. What role do you feel this course and your experiences in it played in these changes? Be as specific as possible.

27.2 MALE AND FEMALE

This exercise is designed to increase your awareness of those matters that may prevent meaningful interpersonal communication between the sexes. It is also designed to encourage meaningful dialogue among class members.

The women and the men are separated; one group goes into another classroom and one group stays in the room. The task of each group is to write on the blackboard all the things that they dislike having the other sex think, believe, do, or say about them in general. The women should write on the board all the things that men think, believe, say, or do in reference to women that they dislike and that prevent meaningful interpersonal communication from taking place. The men should do likewise.

After this is done, the groups should change rooms. The men go into the room in which the women have written their dislikes and the women go into the room in which the men have written their dislikes. The men discuss what the women have written and the women discuss what the men have written. After satisfactory discussion has taken place, the groups should get together in the original room. Discussion might center on the following:

1. Were there any surprises?
2. Were there any disagreements? That is, did the men (or women) write anything that the women (or men) argued they do not believe, think, do, or say?
3. How do you suppose the ideas about the other sex got started?
4. Is there any reliable evidence in support of the beliefs of the men about the women or the women about the men?
5. What is the basis for the things that are disliked? Put differently, why was each statement written on the blackboard?
6. What kind of education or training program (if any) do you feel is needed to eliminate these problems?
7. Specifically, in what ways do these beliefs, thoughts, actions, and statements prevent meaningful interpersonal communication?
8. How do you feel now that these matters have been discussed?

27.3 RESEARCH FINDINGS AND THEORIES ON INTERPERSONAL RELATIONSHIPS: REVIEW QUIZ VI

Following are 12 statements dealing with interpersonal relationships that have been discussed in the preceding units. Some are supported by research findings and well-conceived theories; others are contradicted by the research findings and theories. Which are TRUE? Which are FALSE? For those that are FALSE, indicate why they are FALSE and rewrite them so that they are TRUE.

1. In most instances, when a relationship deteriorates there is a process of depenetration in which the breadth and the depth of the relationship become more narrow and shallow, more closely resembling relationships in their beginning stages.

2. Although attractive people will be given preference by uneducated individuals, both attractive and unattractive persons are treated in the same way by educated individuals.

3. Children younger than, say, 6 or 7 do not have preferences based on physical attractiveness.

4. The qualities that men and women judge as important in a partner are, for the most part, the same.

5. On the basis of the gain-loss theory we would hypothesize that increases in rewards will have less impact than will constant invariant rewards. That is, we will like a person more if that person has always liked us and less if that person's liking for us increases over time.

6. On the basis of the matching hypothesis we would predict that when people are given the opportunity to ask a person for a date they will select the most attractive person to ask first, the second most attractive person to ask next, and so on until a "yes" response is obtained.

7. Generally, there is more research evidence supporting similarity than complementarity in attraction.

8. Jealousy is a reliable measure of the extent to which one person cares about another.

9. According to the two-factor theory of love, we would expect physiological arousal from running or fighting to increase the likelihood of love occurring.

10. Although men and women seem to experience love to a similar degree, men indicate greater love for their same-sex friends than do women.

11. Research on conflict resolution in primary relationships supports the conclusion that men and women are today using the same strategies for resolving such conflicts.

12. Manipulation is the most frequently employed conflict strategy in opposite-sex relationships, outranking nonnegotiation, emotional appeal, personal rejection, and empathic understanding.

GLOSSARY OF TERMS

Listed here are definitions of the technical terms of interpersonal communication—the words that are peculiar or unique to this discipline. These definitions should make new or difficult terms a bit easier to understand. For the most part the words included here are used in this text. Also included, however, are terms that although not used here may be used in the conduct of a course in interpersonal communication. All italicized terms within definitions also appear as entries in the glossary.

Abstraction.   A general concept derived from a class of objects; a part representation of some whole.

Abstraction process.   The process by which a general concept is derived from specifics; the process by which some (never all) characteristics of an object, person, or event are perceived by the senses or included in some term, phrase, or sentence.

Accent.   The stress or emphasis that is placed on a syllable when pronounced.

Accommodation.   A state of cold-war conflict; a condition in which the parties, although still in conflict, agree not to battle; a state in which the conflicting individuals have adjusted to each other's position and in which interpersonal communication may take place although real cooperation is absent.

Action language.   Movements of the body, for example, the way in which one walks, runs, or sits.

Adaptors.   Nonverbal behaviors that, when emitted in private or in public without being seen, serve some kind of need and occur in their entirety, for example, scratching one's head until the itch is eliminated.

Adjustment, principle of.   The principle of verbal interaction that claims that communication may take place only to the extent that the parties communicating share the same system of signals.

Affect displays.   Movements of the facial area that convey emotional meaning, for example, anger, fear, and surprise.

Allness.   The assumption that all can be known or is known about a given person, issue, object, or event.

Alter adaptors.   Nonverbal movements (see *adaptors*) learned in the manipulation of material things, for example, changing a tire.

Ambiguity.   The condition in which a word or phrase may be interpreted as having more than one meaning.

Analogic communication.   Communication consisting of continuous rather than discrete signals; nonverbal communication systems are in most instances analogic. See *digital communication*.

451

Arbitrariness. The feature of human language that refers to the fact that there is no real or inherent relationship between the form of a word and its meaning. If we do not know anything of a particular language, we could not examine the form of a word and thereby discover its meaning.

Argot. A kind of *sublanguage*; cant and jargon of a particular class, generally an underworld or criminal class, which is difficult and sometimes impossible for outsiders to understand.

Attention. The process of responding to a stimulus or stimuli; usually some consciousness of responding is implied.

Attitude. A predisposition to respond for or against an object, person, or position.

Attraction. The state or process by which one individual is drawn to another, by having a highly positive evaluation of that other person.

Attribution theory. A theory concerned with the processes involved in attributing causation to a person's behavior.

Balance. A state of psychological comfort in which all the attitude objects in our minds are related as we would want them to be or as we would psychologically expect them to be.

Batons. Bodily movements that accent or emphasize a specific word or phrase.

Belief. Confidence in the existence or truth of something; conviction.

Blindering. A misevaluation in which a label prevents us from seeing as much of the object as we might see; a process of concentrating on the verbal level while neglecting the nonverbal levels; a form of *intensional orientation*.

Body language. A form of nonverbal communication in which messages are communicated by gesture, posture, spatial relations, and so forth; a popular term covering all aspects of nonverbal communication.

Breadth. The number of topics about which individuals in a relationship communicate.

By-passing. A misevaluation caused when the same word is used but each of the individuals gives it a different meaning.

Cant. A kind of *sublanguage*; the conversational language of a special group which is generally understood only by members of the subculture.

Censorship. Legal restrictions imposed on one's right to produce, distribute, or receive various communications.

Certainty. An attitude of closed-mindedness which creates a defensiveness among communication participants; opposed to *provisionalism*.

Channel. The vehicle or medium through which signals are sent.

Channel capacity. The maximum amount of information that a communication channel can handle at any given time.

Chemistry-binders. A class of life characterized by the ability to combine chemicals in order to grow and survive; plants are chemistry-binders.

Cliché. An expression that is overused and calls attention to itself; "tall, dark, and handsome" as a description of a man would be considered a cliché.

Closed-mindedness. An unwillingness to receive certain communication messages.

Code. A set of symbols used to translate a message from one form to another.

Codifiability. The ease with which certain concepts may be expressed in a given language.

Cognitive complexity. The state of having numerous different concepts for describing people.

Cohesiveness. The property of togetherness. As applied to group communication situations it refers to the mutual attractiveness among members; a measure of the extent to which individual members of a group work together as a group.

COIK. Acronym for "clear only if known," referring to messages that are unintelligible for anyone who does not already know what the messages refer to.

Communication gap. The inability to communicate on a meaningful level because of some difference between the parties, for example, age, sex, political orientation, or religion.

Communication network. The pathways of messages; the organizational structure through which messages are sent and received.

Competence. Language competence refers to a speaker's ability to use the language; a knowledge of the elements and rules of the language. Communication competence refers to the rules of the more social or interpersonal dimensions of communication and is often used to refer to those qualities that make for effectiveness in interpersonal communication. See *performance.*

Competition. An interpersonal process in which persons strive to attain something and at the same time to prevent others from attaining it.

Complementary relationship. A relationship between two or more persons in which one person's behavior serves as a stimulus for a different type of behavior from the other person(s). Examples of complementary relationships would be those between the dominant and the submissive, the talker and the listener, the lover and the loved, the parent and the child, the employer and the employee. See *symmetrical relationships.*

Conditioning. An approach to the control of behavior in which the learning or unlearning of behaviors is dependent on their consequences.

Conflict. An extreme form of competition in which a person attempts to bring his or her rival to surrender; a situation in which one person's behaviors are directed at preventing or interfering with or harming another individual; interpersonal disagreement.

Connotation. The feeling or emotional aspect of meaning, generally viewed as consisting of the evaluative (for example, good-bad), potency (strong-weak), and activity (fast-slow) dimensions; the associations of a term. See *denotation.*

Context of communication. The physical, psychological, social, and temporal environment in which communication takes place.

Correspondent inferences. Inferences concerning the causes of another's behavior based on behaviors that have only one motivation and which are uncommon and about which we have considerable confidence.

Credibility. The degree to which a receiver perceives the speaker to be believable. See *ethos.*

Credibility gap. A tendency between or among people to disbelieve each other and to doubt the honesty and integrity of each other; the difference between the image a person tries to convey (highly positive) and the image a receiver perceives (usually less positive), which is often taken as a measure of the extent to which the public image is disbelieved.

Date. An *extensional device* used to emphasize the notion of constant change and symbolized by a subscript: for example, John Smith$_{1973}$ is not John Smith$_{1983}$.

Decoder. Something that takes a message in one form (for example, sound waves) and translates it into another form (for example, nerve impulses), from which meaning can be formulated (for example, in vocal-auditory communication). In human communication the decoder is the auditory mechanism; in electronic communication the decoder is, for example, the telephone earpiece. See *encoder.*

Decoding. The process of extracting a message from a code, for example, translating speech sounds into nerve impulses. See *encoding.*

Defensiveness. An attitude of an individual or an atmosphere in a group characterized by threats, fear, and domination; messages evidencing evaluation, control, strategy, neutrality, superiority, and certainty are assumed to lead to defensiveness. Opposed to *supportiveness.*

Deictic movements. Bodily movements that point to an object, place, or event.

Delayed reactions. Reactions that are consciously delayed while the situation is analyzed.

Denotation. Referential meaning; the objective or descriptive meaning of a word. See *connotation.*

Depth. The degree to which the inner personality—the inner core of an individual— is penetrated in interpersonal interaction.

Derived credibility. See *intrinsic credibility.*

Determinism, principle of. The principle of verbal interaction that holds that all verbalizations are to some extent purposeful, that there is a reason for every verbalization.

Dialect. A specific variant of a language used by persons from a specific area or social class; dialects may differ from the "standard" language in phonology, semantics, or syntax, but they are intelligible to other speakers of the language.

Digital communication. Communication signals that are discrete rather than continuous; opposed to *analogic communication.*

Directive function of communication. Communication intended to persuade; communication that serves to direct the receiver's thoughts or behaviors.

Disconfirmation. The process by which one ignores or denies the right of the individual even to define himself or herself.

Displaced speech. Speech used to refer to that which is not present or in the immediate perceptual field.

Dogmatism. Closed-mindedness in dealing with communications.

Dyadic communication. Two-person communication.

Dyadic consciousness. An awareness of an interpersonal relationship or pairing of two individuals; distinguished from situations in which two individuals are together but do not perceive themselves as being a unit or twosome.

Ectomorphy. The skinny dimension of body build.

Elementalism. The process of dividing verbally what cannot be divided nonverbally, for example, speaking of body and mind as separate and distinct entities.

Emblematic movements. *Elements* used to illustrate a verbal statement, either repeating or substituting for a word or phrase.

Emblems. Nonverbal behaviors that directly translate words or phrases, for example, the signs for O.K. and peace.

Emotive function of communication. Communication that tells us something about the speaker as opposed to the external world or serves some personal need of the speaker.

Empathy. The feeling of another person's feeling; feeling or perceiving something as does another person.

Encoder. Something that takes a message in one form (for example, nerve impulses) and translates it into another form (for example, sound waves). In human communication the encoder is the speaking mechanism; in electronic communication the encoder is, for example, the telephone mouthpiece. See *decoder.*

Encoding. The process of putting a message into a code, for example, translating nerve impulses into speech sounds. See *decoding.*

Endomorphy. The fatty dimension of body build.

Entropy. A measure of the extent of disorganization or randomness in a system. Entropy is a measure of the degree of uncertainty that a destination has about the messages to be communicated by a source. Entropy is high if the number of possible messages is high and low if the number of possible messages is low.

E-Prime. A form of the language that omits the verb "to be" except when used as an auxiliary or in statements of existence. Designed to eliminate the tendency toward *projection,* or assuming that characteristics that one attributes to a person (for example, "Pat is brave") are actually in that person instead of in the observer's perception of that person.

Equality. An attitude that recognizes that each individual in a communication interaction is equal, that no one is superior to any other; encourages *supportiveness;* opposed to *superiority.*

Etc. An *extensional device* used to emphasize the notion of infinite complexity; since one can never know all about anything, any statement about the world or an event must end with an explicit or implicit *etc.*

Ethics. The branch of philosophy that deals with the rightness or wrongness of actions; the study of moral values.

Ethos. The aspect of persuasiveness that depends on the audience's perception of the character of the speaker; to Aristotle *ethos,* or ethical proof, depended upon the speaker's perceived goodwill, knowledge, and moral character. More commonly referred to as speaker *credibility.*

Euphemism. Polite words and phrases designed to replace taboo expressions.

Evaluation. A process whereby a value is placed on some person, object, or event.

Experiential limitation. The limit of an individual's ability to communicate, as set by the nature and extent of his or her experiences.

Extensional devices. Linguistic devices proposed by Alfred Korzybski for making language a more accurate means for talking about the world. The extensional devices include the working devices *etc., date,* and *index* and the safety devices *hyphen* and *quotes.*

Extensional orientation. A point of view in which primary consideration is given to the world of experience and only secondary consideration is given to the labels. See *intensional orientation.*

Fact-inference confusion. A misevaluation in which one makes an inference, regards it as a fact, and acts upon it as if it were a fact.

Factual statement. A statement made by the observer after observation and limited to what has been observed. See *inferential statement.*

Fear appeal. The appeal to fear to persuade an individual or group of individuals to believe or to act in a certain way.

Feedback. Information that is fed back to the source. Feedback may come from the source's own messages (as when we hear what we are saying) or from the receiver in the form of applause, yawning, puzzled looks, questions, lettters to the editor, increased or decreased subscriptions to a magazine, and so forth.

Field of experience. The sum total of an individual's experiences which influences his or her ability to communicate. In some views of communication, two people can communicate only to the extent that their fields of experience overlap.

Forms of address. The different modes of addressing people: the titles or names used to address people.

Frozen evaluation. See *static evaluation.*

Gain-loss theory. A theory hypothesizing that increases in rewards will have greater impact than will constant invariant rewards.

Game. A simulation of some situation with rules governing the behaviors of the participants and with some payoff for winning; in *transactional analysis, game* refers to a series of ulterior transactions which lead to a payoff; in TA, *game* also refers to a basically dishonest kind of transaction where participants hide their true feelings.

General semantics. The study of the relationships among language, thought, and behavior.

Ghostwriting. The procedure by which one writes or prepares messages for someone else and the identity of the real author is kept hidden.

Grammar. The set of rules of *syntax, semantics,* and *phonology.*

Heterophily. The degree of difference between individuals. See *homophily.*

Homophily. The degree of similarity between individuals. See *heterophily.*

Honorific. Expressing high regard or respect. In some languages certain pronouns of address are honorific and are used to address those of high status. In English such expressions as "Dr.," "Professor," and "the Honorable" are honorific.

Hyphen. An *extensional device* used to illustrate that what may be separated verbally may not be separable on the event or nonverbal level; although one may talk about body and mind as if they were separable, in reality they are better referred to as body-mind.

Iconic signals. Signals that bear real or nonarbitrary relationships to their referents; opposed to *arbitrariness.*

Identification. In general semantics, a misevaluation whereby two or more items are considered as identical; according to Kenneth Burke, a process of becoming similar to another individual; a process of aligning one's interests to those of another. Burke sees identification as a necessary process for persuasion.

Ideographs. Bodily movements that sketch the path or direction of a thought.

Idiolect. An individual's personalized variation of the language.

Illustrators. Nonverbal behaviors that accompany and literally illustrate the verbal messages, for example, upward movements that accompany the verbalization "It's up there."

Immanent reference, principle of. The principle of verbal interaction that holds that all verbalizations make some reference to the present, to the specific context, to the speaker, and to the receivers.

Index. An *extensional device* used to emphasize the notion of nonidentity (that no two things are the same) and symbolized by a subscript, for example, politician$_1$ is not politician$_2$.

Indiscrimination. A misevaluation caused by categorizing people or events or objects into a particular class and responding to specific members only as they are members of that class; a misevaluation caused by failing to recognize that each individual is an individual and is unique; a failure to apply the *index.*

Inferential statement. A statement that can be made by anyone, is not limited to the observed, and can be made at any time. See *factual statement.*

Information. That which reduces uncertainty; that which is new.

Intensional orientation. A point of view in which primary consideration is given to the way in which things are labeled and only secondary consideration (if any) to the world of experience. See *extensional orientation.*

Interchangeability. The feature of language that makes possible the reversal of roles between senders and receivers of messages. Because of interchangeability all adult members of a speech community may serve as both senders and receivers; persons may produce any linguistic message they can understand.

Interpersonal communication. Communication between persons, generally distinguished from mass communication and public communication. Often used as a general term to include intrapersonal communication, dyadic communication, and small-group communication. At times the term is used to designate communication that is personal and intimate rather than impersonal.

Interpersonal conflict. A conflict between two persons; a conflict within an individual caused by his or her relationships with other people.

Intimate distance. The closest proxemic distance, ranging from touching to 6 to 18 inches.

Intrapersonal communication. Communication with oneself.

Jargon. A kind of *sublanguage;* the language of any special group, often a professional class, which is unintelligible to individuals not belonging to the group; "shop talk."

Kine.   An individually produced bodily movement.

Kineme.   The range of bodily movements that are functionally important or that communicate different meanings.

Kinesics.   The study of the communicative dimension of facial and bodily movements.

Kinetographs.   Nonverbal movements that depict a bodily action or some nonhuman physical action.

Language.   The rules of *syntax, semantics,* and *phonology*; a potentially self-reflexive structured system of symbols that catalogue the objects, events, and relations in the world. *A Language* refers to the infinite set of grammatical sentences generated by the grammar of any language, for example, English, Italian, Bantu, Chinese.

Learnability.   The feature of language that refers to the fact that any normal human being is capable of learning any language as a first language. Learnability is dependent upon and follows from language being traditionally or culturally transmitted.

Level of abstraction.   The relative distance of a term or statement from the actual perception; a low-order abstraction would be a description of the perception, whereas a high-order abstraction would consist of inferences about inferences about descriptions of a perception.

Life positions.   The sets of directions or scripts by which people live their lives; in transactional analysis four such scripts are defined, each of which describes how one views oneself and how one views others: I'm O.K., You're O.K.; I'm O.K., You're not O.K.; I'm not O.K., You're O.K.; I'm not O.K., You're not O.K.

Linguistic relativity.   A theory that holds that the language we speak influences what we perceive and think, Since different languages catalogue the world differently, speakers of different languages will see the world differently.

Linguistics.   The study of language; the study of the system of rules by which meanings are paired with sounds.

Listening.   An active process of receiving aural stimuli.

Loving.   An interpersonal process in which one feels a closeness, a caring, a warmth, and an excitement for another person.

Machiavellianism.   The techniques or tactics by which control is exerted by one person over another.

Macroscopic approach to communication.   The focus on broad and general aspects of communication.

Mass communication.   Communication mediated by some medium, for example, television, newspapers, billboards, or movies.

Matching hypothesis.   An assumption that we date and mate people who are similar to ourselves—those who match us—in physical attractiveness.

Meaningfulness.   A principle of perception that refers to the fact that we assume that the behavior of people is sensible and stems from some logical antecedent and that it is consequently meaningful rather than meaningless.

Mere exposure hypothesis.   The theory that holds that repeated or prolonged exposure to a stimulus may result in attitude change toward the stimulus object, generally in the direction of increased positiveness.

Mesomorphy.   The muscular dimension of body build.

Message.   Any signal or combination of signals that serve as a *stimulus* for a receiver.

Metacommunication.   Communication about communication.

Metalanguage.   Language used to talk about language.

Microkinesics.   The area of *kinesics* concerned with bodily movements that communicate different meanings.

Microscopic approach to communication.   The focus on minute and specific aspects of communication.

Model.   A representation of an object or process.

Multiordinality.   In general semantics, a condition whereby a term may exist on different levels of abstraction.

Multivalued orientation.   A point of view that emphasizes that there are many sides (rather than only one or two sides) to any issue.

Negative feedback.   Feedback that serves a corrective function by informing the source that his or her message is not being received in the way intended. Negative feedback serves to redirect the source's behavior. Looks of boredom, shouts of disagreement, letters critical of newspaper policy, and the teacher's instructions on how to better approach a problem would be examples of negative feedback.

Negative reinforcement.   The strengthening of a particular response by removing an aversive stimulus. See *positive reinforcement*.

Neutrality.   A response pattern lacking in personal involvement; encourages *defensiveness*; opposed to *empathy*.

Noise.   Anything that distorts the message intended by the source. Noise may be viewed as anything that interferes with the receiver's receiving the message as the source intended the message to be received. Noise is present in a communication system to the extent that the message received is not the message sent. Noise may originate in any of the components of the communication act, for example, in the source as a lisp, in the channel as static, in the receiver as a hearing loss, in written communication as blurred type. Noise is always present in any communication system, and its effects may be reduced (but never eliminated completely) by increasing the strength of the signal or the amount of redundancy, for example.

Nonallness.   An attitude or point of view in which it is recognized that one can never know all about anything and that what we know or say or hear is only a part of what there is to know or say or hear.

Object adaptors.   Nonverbal behaviors (see *adaptors*) that make use of some kind of prop which itself does not serve any instrumental function, for example, scratching your head with a pencil or chewing on your necklace.

Object language.   Language used to communicate about objects, events, and relations in the world; the structure of the object language is described in a *metalanguage*; the display of physical objects, for example, flower arranging and the colors of the clothes we wear.

Obstinate audience.   A view of the audience, particularly the public and mass communication audience, as critical, selective, and active.

Olfactory communication.   Communication by smell.

Openness.   See *productivity*.

Opinion.   A tentative conclusion concerning some object, person, or event.

Paralanguage.   The vocal (but nonverbal) aspect of speech. Paralanguage consists of voice qualities (for example, pitch range, resonance, tempo), vocal characterizers (for example, laughing or crying, yelling or whispering), vocal qualifiers (for example, intensity, pitch height), and vocal segregates (for example, *uh-uh*, meaning "no," or *sh*, meaning "silence").

Perception.   The process of becoming aware of objects and events from the senses.

Performance.   The actual utterances that a speaker speaks and a hearer hears. See *competence*.

Personal distance.   The second-closest proxemic distance, ranging from 1.5 feet to 4 feet.

Persuasion.   The process of influencing attitudes and behavior.

Phatic communion.   Communication that is primarily social; communication designed to open the channels of communication rather than to communicate something about the external world; "Hello," and "How are you?" in everyday interaction are common examples.

Phonology. The study of the sounds of language.

Pictics. The study of the pictorial code of communication.

Pictographs. Bodily movements that draw pictures in the air of the general shape of the thing being talked about.

Pitch. The highness or lowness of the vocal tone.

Polarization. A form of fallacious reasoning by which only the two extremes are considered; also referred to as "black-or-white" and "either-or" thinking.

Positive feedback. *Feedback* that supports or reinforces behavior along the lines it is already proceeding in, for example, applause during a speech.

Positive reinforcement. The strengthening of a particular response by making a reward contingent upon it. The process may be visualized in three stages: (1) a response is emitted, for example, a child says "daddy"; (2) a reward is given, for example, a smile or candy or touching; (3) the response, "daddy," is strengthened, that is, it is more likely to occur under similar circumstances. See *negative reinforcement*.

Prekinesics. The area of *kinesics* that is concerned with the physiological aspects of bodily movements.

Prevarication. The feature of human language that makes lying possible.

Primacy effect. The condition by which what comes first exerts greater influence than what follows. See *recency effect*.

Problem orientation. A focus on a problem and its possible solutions rather than on controlling the group processes; encourages *supportiveness*; opposed to *control*.

Process. Ongoing activity; nonstatic; communication is referred to as a process to emphasize that it is always changing, always in motion.

Productivity. The feature of language that makes possible the creation and understanding of novel utterances. With human language we can talk about matters that have never been talked about before, and similarly we can understand utterances that we have never heard before. Also referred to as *openness*.

Projection. A psychological process whereby we attribute characteristics or feelings of our own to others; often used to refer to the process whereby we attribute our own faults to others.

Provisionalism. An attitude of open-mindedness that leads to the creation of *supportiveness*; opposed to *certainty*.

Proxemics. The study of the communicative function of space; the study of how people unconsciously structure their space—the distance between people in their interactions, the organization of space in homes and offices and even the design of cities.

Public communication. Communication in which the source is one person and the receiver is an audience of many persons.

Public distance. The farthest proxemic distance, ranging from 12 to over 25 feet.

Punctuation of communication. The breaking up of continuous communication sequences into short sequences with identifiable beginnings and endings or stimuli and responses.

Punishment. Noxious or aversive stimulation.

Pygmalion effect. The condition in which one makes a prediction and then proceeds to fulfill it; a type of self-fulfilling prophecy but one that refers to others and to our evaluation of others rather than to ourselves.

Quotes. An *extensional device* used to emphasize that a word or phrase is being used in a special sense and should therefore be given special attention.

Rapid fading. The evanescent or nonpermanent quality of speech signals.

Rate. The speed with which we speak, generally measured in words per minute.

Receiver. Any person or thing that takes in messages. Receivers may be individuals listening to or reading a message, a group of persons hearing a speech, a scattered television audience, or a machine that stores information.

Recency effect.   The condition in which what comes last (that is, most recently) exerts greater influence than what comes first. See *primacy effect*.

Recurrence, principle of.   The principle of verbal interaction that holds that individuals will repeat many times and in many different ways who they are, how they see themselves, and, in general, what they think is important and significant.

Redundancy.   The quality of a message that makes it totally predictable and therefore lacking in information. A message of zero redundancy would be completely unpredictable; a message of 100 percent redundancy would be completely predictable. All human languages contain some degree of redundancy built into them, generally estimated to be about 50 percent.

Reflexiveness.   The feature of language that refers to the fact that human language can be used to refer to itself; that is, we can talk about our talk and create a *metalanguage*, a language for talking about language. See *self-reflexiveness*.

Regulators.   Nonverbal behaviors that regulate, monitor, or control the communications of another person.

Reinforcement.   The strengthening of a particular response. See *positive reinforcement, negative reinforcement*.

Reinforcement/Packaging, Principle of.   The principle of verbal interaction that holds that in most interactions, messages are transmitted simultaneously through a number of different channels which normally reinforce each other; messages come in packages.

Rejection.   A response to an individual which rejects or denies the validity of an individual's self view.

Reliability.   The degree of agreement that can be obtained from a number of different observers; the degree to which an instrument or observers will yield the same results on repeated observations.

Response.   Any bit of overt or covert behavior.

Rhythmic movements.   Bodily movements that depict or visually imitate the rhythm or pacing of an event.

Role.   The part an individual plays in a group; an individual's function or expected behavior.

Self-acceptance.   Being satisfied with ourselves, with our virtues and vices, abilities and limitations.

Self-adaptors.   Nonverbal behaviors (see *adaptors*) that serve some personal need, for example, autoerotic activity.

Self-concept.   An individual's self-evaluation; an individual's self-appraisal.

Self-disclosure.   The process of revealing something significant about ourselves to another individual or to a group, which would not normally be known by them.

Self-fulfilling prophecy.   The situation in which we make a prediction or prophecy and fulfill it ourselves, for example, expecting a class to be boring and then fulfilling this expectation by perceiving it as boring.

Self-reflexive abstracting.   A form or type of abstracting in which the abstraction is of itself, as when, for example, we think about our thinking, love our love, or fear our fear.

Self-reflexiveness.   The property of being able to refer back to itself; for example, language is self-reflexive because it can be used to refer to itself. See *reflexiveness*.

Semantic differential.   A device for measuring connotative meaning consisting of 7-point, bi-polar scales; generally three dimensions of meaning are measured: evaluation, potency, and activity.

Semantic reaction.   A total reaction; a reaction of the organism-as-a-whole; a reaction that is determined by what the whole situation means to an individual.

Semanticity.   The feature of human language that refers to the fact that some words have denotations in the objective world. All human languages possess semanticity, but not all words have denotations (for example, *of, the,* and *is* do not have objective referents in the real world).

Semantics. The area of language study concerned with meaning.

Semantogenic. Caused by semantics or labels; used most widely in reference to a problem or disorder whose origin may be found in the labels, For example, stuttering has been labeled semantogenic because some particular behavior was labeled "stuttering," according to the semantogenic theory.

Sequential communication. Communication in which messages are passed from A to B, B to C, C to D, and so on; linear communication.

Shyness. The condition of discomfort and uneasiness in interpersonal situations.

Sign. Something that stands for something else and that bears a natural, nonarbitrary relationship to it, for example, dark clouds as a sign of rain. See *symbol.*

Sign language. Gesture language that is highly codified, for example, a hitchhiker's gesture.

Signal and noise, relativity of. The principle of verbal interaction that holds that what is signal (meaningful) and what is noise (interference) is relative to the communication analyst, the communication participants, and the communication context.

Signal reaction. A conditioned response to a signal; a response to some signal that is immediate rather than delayed. See *symbol reaction.*

Silence. The absence of vocal communication; often misunderstood to refer to the absence of any and all communication.

Slang. The language used by special groups which is not considered proper by the general society; the language made up of the *argot, cant,* and *jargon* of various subcultures which is known by the general public.

Social distance. The third proxemic distance, ranging from 4 to 12 feet; the distance at which business is usually conducted.

Social exchange theory. A theory hypothesizing that we develop relationships in which our rewards or profits will be greater than our costs, and that we avoid or terminate relationships in which the costs exceed the rewards.

Social kinesics. The area of *kinesics* concerned with the role and meanings of different bodily movements.

Social penetration theory. A theory concerned with relationship development from the superficial to the intimate levels and from few to many areas of interpersonal interaction.

Somatotype. Body type measured in terms of the degree to which one is fat, muscular, and skinny.

Source. Any person or thing that creates messages. A source may be an individual speaking or writing or gesturing or a group of persons formulating an advertising policy or a computer solving a problem.

Space-binders. A class of life that maintains itself by moving about in space and combining materials from various different places; animals.

Spatial movements. Bodily movements that depict spatial movements, for example, rapid hand motions to depict the passing of a speeding car.

Specialization. The feature of human language that refers to the characteristic of human language serving no purpose other than that of communication. Human language (unlike a dog's panting, for example) does not serve any biological function; it is a specialized system.

Speech. Messages utilizing a vocal-auditory channel.

Speech community. A group of persons using the same language.

Spontaneity. The communication pattern in which one verbalizes what one is thinking without attempting to develop strategies for control; encourages *supportiveness;* opposed to *strategy.*

Stability.   The principle of perception that refers to the fact that our perceptions of things and people are relatively consistent with previous conceptions.

Static evaluation.   An orientation that fails to recognize that the world is characterized by constant change; an attitude that sees people and events as fixed rather than as constantly changing.

Status.   The relative level one occupies in a hierarchy; status always involves a comparison, and thus one's status is only relative to the status of another. In our culture occupation, financial position, age, and educational level are significant determinants of status.

Stereotype.   In communication, refers to a fixed impression of a group of people through which we then perceive specific individuals; stereotypes are most often negative (Martians are stupid, uneducated, and dirty) but may also be positive (Venusians are scientific, industrious, and helpful).

Stimulus.   Any external or internal change that impinges upon or arouses an organism.

Stimulus-response models of communication.   Models of communication that assume that the process of communication is a linear one, beginning with a stimulus that then leads to a response.

Strategy.   The use of some plan for control of other members of a communication interaction which guides one's own communications; encourages *defensiveness*; opposed to *spontaneity*.

Subjectivity.   The principle of perception that refers to the fact that one's perceptions are not objective but rather are influenced by one's wants and needs and one's expectations and predictions of the perceiver.

Sublanguage.   A variation from the general language used by a particular subculture; *argot, cant,* and *jargon* are particular kinds of sublanguages.

Superiority.   A point of view or attitude that assumes that others are not equal to oneself; encourages *defensiveness*; opposed to *equality*.

Supportiveness.   An attitude of an individual or an atmosphere in a group that is characterized by openness, the absence of fear, and a genuine feeling of equality; messages evidencing *description, problem orientation, spontaneity, empathy, equality,* and *provisionalism* are assumed to lead to supportiveness. See *defensiveness*.

Symbol.   Something that stands for something else but that bears no natural relationship to it, for example, purple as a symbol of mourning. Words are symbols in that they bear no natural relationship to the meaning they symbolize. See *sign*.

Symbol reaction.   A reaction that is made with some delay. See *signal reaction*.

Symmetrical relationship.   A relation between two or more persons in which one person's behavior serves as a stimulus for the same type of behavior in the other person(s). Examples of such relationships include situations in which anger in one person encourages or serves as a stimulus for anger in another person or in which a critical comment by one person leads the other person to respond in like manner. See *complementary relationship*.

Syntax.   The area of language study concerned with the rules for combining words into sentences.

Taboo.   Forbidden; culturally censored. Taboo language is that which is frowned upon by "polite society." Themes and specific words may be considered taboo, for example, death, sex, certain forms of illness, and various words denoting sexual activities and excretory functions.

Tactile communication.   Communication by touch; communication received by the skin.

Territoriality.   A possessive or ownershiplike reaction to an area of space or to particular objects.

Theory. A general statement or principle applicable to a number of related phenomena.

Time-binders. A class of life that survives by passing information on from one generation to another, thus making knowledge cumulative; human beings.

Total feedback. The quality of speech that refers to one's ability to receive all the communications that one sends.

Traditional transmission. The feature of language that refers to the fact that human languages (at least in their outer surface form) are learned. Unlike various forms of animal language, which are innate, human languages are transmitted traditionally or culturally. This feature of language does not deny the possibility that certain aspects of language may be innate.

Transactional. The relationship among elements in which each influences and is influenced by each other element; communication is a transactional process since no element is independent of any other element.

Transactions. The patterns of interaction between people.

Two-valued orientation. A point of view in which events are seen or issues are evaluated in terms of two values, for example, right or wrong, good or bad. Often referred to as the fallacy of black-or-white and *polarization*.

Undelayed reaction. A reaction that is immediate; a signal response; a reaction made without any conscious deliberation.

Universal of interpersonal communication. A feature of interpersonal communication that is common to all interpersonal communication acts.

Universal of language. A feature of language that is common to all known languages.

Validity. The degree to which an observation or instrument measures what it is supposed to measure.

Value. The relative worth of an object; a quality that makes something desirable or undesirable; an ideal or custom about which we have emotional responses, whether positive or negative.

Variable. A quantity that can increase or decrease; something that can have different values.

Vocal qualifiers. Aspects of *paralanguage*, specifically, intensity, pitch height, and extent of vocalizations.

Vocal segregates. Aspects of *paralanguage*, specifically, such vocalizations as "uh-uh," "uh-huh," "sh," and pauses.

Voice qualities. Aspects of *paralanguage*, specifically, pitch range, vocal lip control, glottis control, pitch control, articulation control, rhythm control, resonance, and tempo.

Volume. The relative loudness of the voice.

Word association. A method for measuring connotative meaning; a way of measuring the meaningfulness of words; a projective technique in which associations to stimulus words are analyzed in terms of their psychological significance.

NAME INDEX

83 84 85 9 8 7 6 5 4 3 2 1